Regional
Power Rivalries
IN THE
New Eurasia

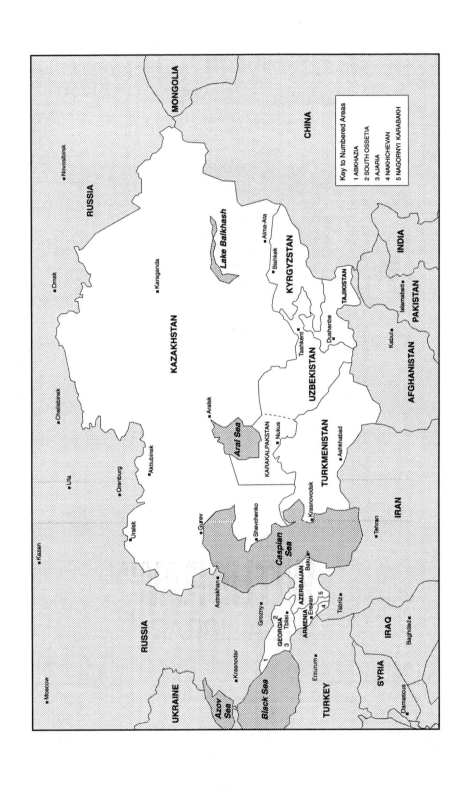

Regional Power Rivalries
IN THE
New Eurasia

Russia, Turkey, and Iran

EDITED BY

Alvin Z. Rubinstein
AND
Oles M. Smolansky

M.E. Sharpe
Armonk, New York
London, England

Library of Congress Cataloging-in-Publication Data

Regional power rivalries in the new Eurasia : Russia, Turkey, and Iran /
edited by Alvin Z. Rubinstein and Oles M. Smolansky
p. cm.
Includes bibliographical references and index.
ISBN 1-56324-622-8 (alk. paper).—ISBN 1-56324-623-6 (pbk. : alk. paper)
1. Former Soviet republics—Relations—Iran.
2. Iran—Relations—Former Soviet republics.
3. Former Soviet republics—Relations—Turkey.
4. Turkey—Relations—Former Soviet republics.
5. Former Soviet republics—Foreign relations.
6. Iran—Foreign relations—1979– .
7. Turkey—Foreign relations—1980– .
I. Rubinstein, Alvin Z.
II. Smolansky, Oles M.
DK68.7.I7R44   1995
303.48′247055—dc20
95-6805
CIP

Printed in the United States of America

The paper used in this publication meets the minimum requirements of
American National Standard for Information Sciences—
Permanence of Paper for Printed Library Materials,
ANSI Z 39.48-1984.

BM (c)   10   9   8   7   6   5   4   3   2   1
BM (p)   10   9   8   7   6   5   4   3   2   1

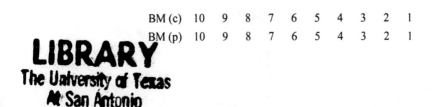

Contents

About the Editors and Contributors

Alvin Z. Rubinstein is professor of political science at the University of Pennsylvania, and senior fellow of the Foreign Policy Research Institute. His published works include *Soviet Foreign Policy since World War II* (4th ed., 1992), *Red Star on the Nile*, and *Soviet Policy toward Turkey, Iran, and Afghanistan.* His book *Moscow's Third World Strategy* was awarded the Marshall Shulman Prize of the American Association for the Advancement of Slavic Studies.

Oles M. Smolansky, university professor of international relations at Lehigh University, is a native of Ukraine. His published works include *The Soviet Union and the Arab East under Khrushchev, The USSR and Iraq: The Soviet Quest for Influence*, and numerous book chapters and articles in professional journals. His book *The USSR and Iraq* was awarded the Marshall Shulman Prize of the American Association for the Advancement of Slavic Studies.

Henri J. Barkey is associate professor of international relations at Lehigh University. His published works include *The State and the Industrialization Crisis in Turkey*, an edited volume, *The Politics of Economic Reform in the Middle East*, as well as articles in *Survival, Comparative Political Studies,* and *Orient.*

Patricia M. Carley is program officer for the former Soviet Union and Turkey at the United States Institute of Peace, where she also works on broader issues such as the Organization for Security and Cooperation in Europe (OSCE) and Western relations with the Islamic world. Her dissertation work at the London School of Economics focused on Turkic and Islamic identity in Soviet Central Asia and Turkey. Before joining USIP, Patricia Carley was a staff adviser at the Commission on Security and

Cooperation in Europe (the Congressional Helsinki Commission), where she authored numerous reports on the former Soviet republics, including the Central Asia section of *Human Rights and Democratization in the Newly Independent States* (1993). She has also worked as a consultant on Central Asian affairs to various government agencies, as well as the World Bank and the Rand Corporation.

Sergei Gretsky, a native of Belarus, received his Ph.D. in Medieval Islam from the Academy of Sciences of Tajikistan. From 1991 to 1993, he taught at Dushanbe Pedagogical University in Dushanbe, Tajikistan. He is also a coinvestigator in a project on "Central Asia and Conflict" with the Center for Post-Soviet Studies, Washington, DC. Among his publications are articles on Islam and on the Tajik civil war. At present, he is a contract researcher for the U.S. Information Agency.

George S. Harris is director of analysis for the Near East and South Asia in the Bureau of Intelligence and Research, Department of State, Washington, D.C. He has been a lecturer at Johns Hopkins University. Among his published works are *The Origins of Communism in Turkey; Troubled Alliance: Turkish-American Problems in Historical Perspective, 1945–1974*; and *Turkey: Coping with Crisis*.

Mohiaddin Mesbahi is associate professor of international relations at Florida International University. In 1993–94 he was a visiting fellow at St. Antony's College, Oxford University. He is author of numerous articles and book chapters on Soviet-Iranian relations and security issues in Central Asia. He is editor of *Russia and the Third World in the Post-Soviet Era* (1993) and *Central Asia and the Caucasus after the Soviet Union: Domestic and International Dynamics* (1994). He is the author of the forthcoming *Russia and Iran: From Islamic Revolution to the Collapse of Communism* (London: MacMillan; New York: St. Martin's Press).

Gareth M. Winrow is associate professor of political science and international relations at Bogazici University, Istanbul, Turkey. His recent publications include *Where East Meets West: Turkey and the Balkans* (1993), and articles on Turkish foreign policy in the Caucasus and Central Asia, regional security issues, and NATO in the journals *Central Asian Survey, Oxford International Review, Il Politico, European Security*, and *Journal of South Asian and Middle Eastern Studies*. He is also author of *The Foreign Policy of the GDR in Africa*.

Preface

The breakup of the Soviet Union in December 1991 came with dramatic suddenness and profoundly changed the geopolitics of the Eurasian land mass. Losing about a quarter of its territory and almost 40 percent of its population, Russia accepted the independence of the other fourteen union republics that, with it, had comprised the USSR. Of these, six predominantly Muslim entities—Azerbaijan, Kazakhstan, Kyrgyzstan, Tajikistan, Turkmenistan, and Uzbekistan—had been created by Stalin in the 1920s and 1930s as tactical nation-states. As Vernon Aspaturian has argued, their creation was intended "to play a pivotal role not in Soviet diplomacy but in world communism—to generate discontent in European colonial dependencies as a prelude to their communization"; but in the end, because of dysfunctional internal policies and the absence of external opportunities, they played a negligible role both in Moscow's conventional and unconventional diplomacy.[1] However, Stalin had several other tangible, interrelated purposes in mind for these republics: to strengthen the administration of a weak polyglot imperial system; to give form (but not substance) to the Bolshevik espousal of the principle of national self-determination; and to enable Moscow to carry out a policy of divide and rule by separating ethnolinguistic groups across two or more union republics, and in particular by weakening the separatist-minded Uzbeks by building up the Kazakhs, Turkmens, Kyrgyz, and Tajiks.

The USSR's collapse and the emergence of the independent republics along the southern frontier of the Russian Federation also eliminated the common border separating the Russian/Soviet empire from its long-term historical antagonists, the Turks and the Iranians. In fact, the Soviet collapse established a huge buffer zone in Central Asia and Transcaucasia between the Russian Federation on the one hand and Turkey and Iran on the other. However, the demise of the USSR also transformed this buffer zone into an area of competition between these immediate and highly interested outsiders.

A greatly altered environment necessitates reassessment of long-held assumptions about the aims and behavior of Russia, as well as of Iran and Turkey. It also requires an analysis of the goals pursued by the local elites in Transcaucasia and Central Asia, some of whom (particularly in the Caucasus) are torn between determination to consolidate their power and a desire to alter the territorial boundaries that Stalin capriciously cobbled for service in another epoch. In the meantime, however, the freedom of action of all of the newly independent republics remains severely circumscribed by the realization that they remain heavily dependent on Russia economically, technically, and even militarily; and they have very limited access to the outside world. Such vulnerability need not in and of itself contravene the nation-building process or the institutionalization of political power and national assertiveness. Much will depend on the extent to which the personal ambitions and national goals of the leaders are consonant with fostering domestic development, accommodation with old adversaries, and regional stability. Equally important will be the role of Russia. Will it remain satisfied with accepting the post-Soviet reality or will it insist on reestablishing its military, economic, and political influence, if not direct control, over the former parts of the empire?

In exploring the relations of some of the newly independent former Soviet republics of Transcaucasia and Central Asia with Russia, Iran, or Turkey, it may be useful to draw upon the experiences of other Third World countries with the Soviet Union and the United States during the heyday of the Cold War. Two lessons, in particular, seem relevant. First, in the past, many Third World governments elicited military and economic support, often far beyond their needs, from Washington or Moscow. In the thrall of their mutual fascination, the superpowers often underestimated the extent to which they were, in turn, being used by their clients. In their quest for strategic advantage vis-à-vis one another, the United States and the Soviet Union took on whichever clients were available, subsidizing them lavishly in the process. But the Cold War is over and, as a consequence, local leaderships must look to their security and developmental needs without the luxury of a reliable patron-protector.

Second, the former Soviet republics need to tailor ambitions to capabilities. Excessive reliance on a great power can warp a leadership's priorities, encouraging a militarization of politics and foreign policy and a preoccupation with staying in power at the expense of democratization and the development of an economically viable political system. Too often in the past, Third World elites proclaimed their commitment to economic development, but then proceeded to act in a very different manner. They may have wanted to modernize, but when confronted with a choice of policy options, they gravitated toward the one that promised more power.

The record of Third World governments in Africa and the Middle East is a doleful one: mismanaged affairs, squandered resources and opportunities, and grandiose economic plans whose consequences were swollen bureaucracies and declining efficiency and production. As the new nations of Transcaucasia and Central Asia seek to adapt to their status as independent nations, they bear the additional burdens of the Soviet legacy: artificial boundaries that divide ethnic groups; distorted economic development that makes self-sufficiency, even in basic foodstuffs, almost an impossible dream; institutions that depended on Moscow for money, direction, and expertise; and a reckless ecological degradation that cannot be ignored.

These new nations, no less than Russia, face a time of troubles. The chapters that follow examine the relationships between Russia, Turkey, or Iran and one or more of the countries of Transcaucasia or Central Asia, as well as the emerging bilateral relationships between Russia and Ukraine, on the one hand, and Turkey or Iran, on the other. How were these relationships affected by the collapse of the USSR? How does Yeltsin's policy differ from Gorbachev's? In the evolving relationships between Turkey, Iran, and the newly independent republics of the Commonwealth of Independent States (CIS), what considerations have prompted the parties involved to seek rapprochement and cooperation? What are the problems or key issues dominating the relationship? How do the relations between Turkey or Iran on the one hand and CIS republics on the other affect regional security and stability in Transcaucasia or Central Asia? What light do they shed on Russia's emerging involvement in these regions? Finally, are there any generalizations that can be made about the implications of these diverse regional developments for U.S. foreign policy?

Many questions. These essays represent a tentative beginning in exploring them and assessing their implications for the region's future. Eight of the essays were originally prepared for panels at the annual meeting of the American Association for the Advancement of Slavic Studies in November 1994. Chapter eight was written specifically for this volume, and grateful acknowledgment is made to the Foreign Policy Research Institute for its permission to include chapter ten, which was published in the Fall 1994 issue of *Orbis*, a quarterly journal of world affairs.

Finally, we would like to thank Patricia Kolb, Ana Erlić, Elizabeth

Granda, and the staff of M. E. Sharpe for the skill and professionalism with which they worked with us in a spirit of genuine collaboration to bring this endeavor to completion.

Alvin Z. Rubinstein
Oles M. Smolansky

Note

1. Vernon V. Aspaturian, *Process and Power in Soviet Foreign Policy* (Boston: Little, Brown and Company, 1971), p. 480.

Part I

Old Rivals, New Relationships

1

The Russian Federation and Turkey

George S. Harris

Geography has predisposed Russia and Turkey to a history of conflict. Thus, although both underwent revolutions in the first quarter of the twentieth century, wiping the slate clean to become allies of convenience, their cooperation was never free of suspicion. Without a strong anchor of mutual interest once both regimes had gained general international acceptance, they reverted to hostility during the Second World War. By the start of the Cold War, Stalin's designs on Turkish independence had brought Ankara and Moscow close to armed conflict. The patterns formed at this time continued to hamper relations long after the threat of actual hostilities had waned.

Despite this reserve, Stalin's demise paved the way for gradual warming between Turkey and the USSR, visible principally in the economic field. By the mid-1960s, the Turks began to receive occasional Soviet project aid and eventually became one of the largest recipients. Then, by the 1980s, Ankara started extending hard-currency credit to its northern neighbor as a way to facilitate trade.

In this way, by the Gorbachev era, a number of earlier irritants had been softened or eliminated. Though the Turks were concerned to the end not to antagonize what they saw as the colossus to the north, Ankara—especially in the post-Brezhnev period—began to reach out to some of the Turkic peoples who had been cut off from Turkish influence since the consolidation of the Soviet state.

Under Yeltsin, Turkish ties with the Russian Federation grew more complex than in the last days of Gorbachev. Opportunities for investment and business in Russia, as well as Turkey's interest in buying weapons that could be used against insurgents at home, offered new scope for cooperation. Parallel interests in not humiliating Iraq also fostered a coincidence of views that might not have been possible during the Cold War.

On the other hand, the breakup of the Soviet Union reawakened some old problems, especially in the Caucasus. Although Ankara's effort to play the Turkic card was faltering and uncertain, it conflicted with Russian ambitions to dominate the Near Abroad. The disintegration of Yugoslavia also fed Turkish-Russian rivalries in the Balkans. And Russia's interest in a relationship with NATO raised the specter for the Turks that Russia might gain political acceptance by Europe ahead of Turkey. All this feeds mutual suspicions, limiting the speed with which these two ancient foes have been able to move toward genuine warmth in their relations.

Yet the overall direction has been positive. Leaders on both sides seem committed to improving relations, even if other political contenders are not. As long as these hard-line elements do not come to power in either country, the chances seem good that Russia and Turkey will eventually work out the problems that difficult geography and troubled history have inflicted on their relationship.

The Formative Years

Turkey's revolutionary leader, Mustafa Kemal Ataturk, was intensely political in his approach. He readily understood the value of ties with the newly emergent Soviet regime both to protect his rear and as a source of financial and material support in the conflict with the Western powers at the end of the First World War. His inclination to do business with Moscow was shown by his dispatch of a mission to explore relations immediately after forming a revolutionary government in Ankara in 1920.

But Ataturk and his successors feared the internationalist pull of communist dogma on the Turkish people. He thus first set up his own domestic Turkish Communist Party, run by figures loyal to him. When the Soviet leaders refused to admit this creation into the Comintern in 1921, he turned next to a policy of suppressing communism in Turkey. Shortly after expelling the Western invaders and establishing the Turkish Republic in 1923, Ataturk branded the Communist Party illegal. Continuing efforts by its leaders to organize an underground party or to carry on propaganda from outside Turkey were irritants in relations between Ankara and Moscow right up until the collapse of the Soviet Union. Yet particularly until the revolutionary Turkish state was admitted to the League of Nations in 1932, close ties with Moscow seemed essential to Ataturk.[1]

For the Soviet leadership, revolutionary Turkey offered the prospect of distracting the West during the final struggle with Wrangel and his White Russian forces. In addition, Ataturk's regime became a partner in the destruction of the fledgling Caucasus republics. Mutual antipathy for Dashnak Armenia led the Turkish eastern army to move in tandem with the advancing Red Army, which installed Soviet republics in place of the independent Caucasian entities. Turkey's Treaty of Moscow with revolutionary Russia in March 1921 and its Treaty of Kars with the fledgling Soviet Caucasian republics in October 1921 somewhat assuaged Moscow's fears that Ataturk's brand of nationalism would threaten Soviet dominance of the Turkic republics. But especially with Stalin's poisoned gift to Azerbaijan of Nagorno-Karabakh, with its Armenian majority, the ground was laid for the reemergence of this issue after the breakup of the Soviet Union.[2]

Ataturk's concerns were exclusively political. He harbored no antipathy toward the economic doctrines associated with communism. Indeed, by the end of the 1920s he permitted a group of ex-communists, who had broken politically with Moscow, to develop a state-directed economic policy for Turkey, built on five-year plans and supported by economic assistance from the USSR. While he adopted many of this group's economic recipes, he kept close watch over these former communists and eventually ended their activity when conservative business elements launched a vociferous campaign accusing them of sedition.[3]

For their part, the Soviet leaders never abandoned their desire to expand their influence inside Turkey. Moscow used Soviet commercial agencies, principally the Arkos branch in Turkey, to give jobs to its sympathizers and dangle attractive deals before important Turkish officials until the Turks had these agencies closed at the end of the 1920s, labeling them fonts of subversion. The expectations of the Soviet embassy in Ankara that War Minister Voroshilov's visit to Turkey in 1933 would open access to Turkey's military leadership, heretofore completely off limits for Soviet diplomats, illustrated the continuing ambition to gain purchase over Turkey even in the years of outward harmony.[4]

Ataturk's determination to revise the Lausanne Treaty to eliminate restrictions on Turkish sovereignty over the Black Sea Straits contributed to the erosion of trust between the two countries. Although the Montreux Convention of 1936 put the states of the Black Sea littoral in a special, favored category, Moscow's retrospective assessment of this convention found it wanting. The secret Ribbentrop-Molotov Accord to divide eastern Europe in 1940, giving the Soviets a free hand in the Straits, demonstrated that Turkish suspicions of the Kremlin were well founded. And Ankara's insistence on its sovereign right to decide how to apply international regulations on passage through the Straits has remained a sore point in relations, outlasting even the Cold War.[5]

Return to Hostility

The death of Ataturk in 1938 and the advent of the reputedly pro-German Numan Menemencioglu as Turkish foreign minister only added to friction with the Soviet Union. Accordingly, Turkish reluctance to antagonize Nazi Germany (though Turkey remained formally neutral) led to a sharp deterioration in relations with the Soviet Union after the war. The wartime upsurge of pan-Turanist activity, heretofore sternly repressed in Turkey, was an added irritant to Moscow, which was sensitive about the possibilities of dissidence among the Turkic peoples inside the Soviet Union. The specter of Soviet ire soon ended this flirtation with pan-Turanism; although that doctrine calling for the unity of the Turkic peoples was not to reemerge until the latter years of the Soviet state, the Kremlin leaders were not mollified.

From Stalin's point of view, the lesson of the Second World War was clear: security demanded the creation of a buffer zone of satellites on the USSR's borders. The Soviets championed the Kurdish Republic of Mahabad in 1945–46, ringing alarm bells in Ankara. Moscow also moved directly to test Turkish resolve. In an act defining the Cold War, the Kremlin in 1945 demanded both the return of Turkey's Kars and Ardahan provinces and a base on the Straits and joint control of that waterway. These demands were expanded by Georgian scholars, who called for large areas along the Black Sea coast to be ceded to Soviet Georgia. Perhaps Stalin counted on the emerging communist movement in Turkey to soften up the Turks. Whatever the Soviet calculation, Ankara's stiff resistance blunted this campaign to subjugate Turkey even before the United States came forth with the Truman Doctrine to underwrite Turkish independence in 1947.[6]

Turkey's entry into NATO in 1952 provided reassurance against the Soviet military threat. More than that, the alliance used Turkish territory as an "unsinkable aircraft carrier" as part of its plan to respond to attacks on any NATO member by carrying a future war into Soviet heartland. This raised Turkey's strategic profile in Moscow's calculus, a status reinforced by the emplacement of liquid-fueled medium-range Jupiter missiles on Turkish soil at the end of the 1950s.

Nonetheless, following the death of Stalin in 1953, the Soviets gradually softened their attacks on Turkey. Officially dropping the territorial claims that had ruined relations with Ankara, the new leaders in the Kremlin moved toward a doctrine of coexistence. It was not until Khrushchev's era, however, that Soviet spokesmen began to maintain that it would be possible to normalize relations without Turkey's having to leave NATO.[7]

As Moscow continued to harp on "Turkey's militarization," it took time for the Turks to believe the new assurances. In part, that was also because Khrushchev orchestrated a Soviet leap over Turkey's Northern Tier alliance with Iran, Iraq, and Pakistan. What especially concerned Turkish leaders was that, after establishing an arms supply arrangement with Egypt in 1955, the Soviets seemed to be making deep inroads into Syria. By 1957, the Menderes government in Turkey reacted by ordering a troop mobilization on the border with Syria. At that point, the Egyptians intervened to proclaim unity with Syria, forming the United Arab Republic and sending troops to take charge. Thereupon the crisis evaporated with great suddenness, suggesting that Turkish concern over Syria's becoming a Soviet satellite had been artificially inflated. By the end of his decade in power, Prime Minister Menderes had accepted an invitation to visit Moscow.[8]

This visit was aborted by the 1960 military coup which overthrew Menderes in Turkey. Not until the Cuban missile crisis in 1962, which propelled the Turks into the vortex of the closest brush with a nuclear exchange of the Cold War, did Ankara seriously consider reappraising relations with the USSR. At this time, the Great Power focus on Turkish missiles aroused fears among the Turkish elite that NATO membership could carry dangerous costs. Moreover, the willingness of Washington and Moscow, in their haste to escape war, to trade off missiles in Turkey and Cuba without even consulting Ankara added further uncertainty.

Moves toward Détente

The removal of the Jupiter missiles reduced Turkey's strategic value at a stroke, clearing the way for fitful normalization of relations with the Soviet Union. Khrushchev, however, did not fully comprehend the sea change that had occurred. He failed to seize the opportunity presented by the sudden, sharp downturn in Turkey's relations with the United States over President Johnson's blunt warning to Turkey not to send its troops to intervene in Cyprus in June 1964. Despite Turkish public outcry against the United States aroused by this missive, it was only after Khrushchev's ouster that fall that the new Soviet leaders began to capitalize on Turkey's estrangement from its allies.[9]

In this new era of détente, a measure of cooperation between Ankara and Moscow became possible. Turkey even scaled back American operations from Turkish soil after a U.S. reconnaissance plane crashed in the Black Sea in 1965. At the same time, Russia and Turkey began exchanges of high-level visits to mark the course toward normalizing relations. With the wheels thus greased, in the 1970s Moscow provided several hundred million dollars' worth of economic projects, committing to Turkey a significant proportion of its world aid budget as the base for a gradually expanding commercial relationship.[10]

While the warmth that had characterized Turkey's ties with the West was absent from the growing relationship with the Soviet Union, the two made an effort to improve the political atmosphere as well. In April 1972 they signed a Declaration of Principles of Good Neighborliness in Ankara. At the same time, they addressed the thorny Cyprus problem, agreeing that a solution should be based on the interests of the two communities on the island and should reject "enosis" (union with Greece). That agreement glossed over continuing differences over Turkey's role in Cyprus, which dogged this issue all during the Soviet era. But the commitment to expand relations was further elaborated in the Political Document on the Principles of Good Neighborly and Friendly Cooperation concluded in June 1978.[11]

Negotiation of these documents provided the context for Turkish prime minister Ecevit to declare on May 15, 1978, that the Soviet Union was not a threat to Turkey. As evidence of good faith, Turkey let the Moskva, Kiev, and Minsk warships pass through the Straits classified as cruisers. Had the Turkish government heeded those of its allies who argued that these ships were aircraft carriers because they had flight decks and carried fixed-wing aircraft, it would have had to prohibit their passage under the Montreux Convention.[12]

But this détente could not overcome all suspicions. Ecevit's tenure as prime minister was episodic. In any event, he represented those who were inclined to give the Soviet Union the benefit of the doubt. Many others still saw the USSR as distinctly threatening. They recalled the discovery that Soviet arms were being channeled to the Greek Cypriots in 1966 and the Soviet invasion of Czechoslovakia in 1968. Soviet attempts to justify the intervention in Czechoslovakia in theoretical terms through the Brezhnev doctrine, insisting that no communist regime could be allowed to be overthrown, was unsettling to many in Turkey. Furthermore, some observers suspected that the USSR was fostering the wave of terrorism that shook Turkey at the end of the 1960s and in the 1970s. The refusal of the Kremlin to rein in the clandestine radios broadcasting from Eastern Europe in the name of the Turkish Communist Party, even after Moscow radio had somewhat softened its tone toward Turkey, fed these suspicions.[13]

On the Soviet side, the leadership seemed unable to suppress its underlying concern about the edge Turkey seemed to give NATO in the larger context of East–West relations, especially arms control issues in the Strategic Arms Reduction Talks (SALT) and the Intermediate-range Nuclear

Forces (INF) Negotiations. Hence, for all the professions of coexistence between differing social systems, continuing criticism by senior Soviet officials of Turkish military outlays and modernization plans suggested that Moscow did not regard Turkey's military force as truly legitimate. And continuing Soviet criticism of American facilities in Turkey only reinforced this impression. In 1978, the Soviets campaigned, though in vain, for Ankara to prohibit U.S. facilities in Sinop and Diyarbakir from reopening after Washington finally dropped its arms embargo imposed in the wake of Turkey's 1974 intervention in Cyprus. And in 1980, Soviet propaganda against allowing the United States to fly U-2s over Turkish territory to verify Soviet engagements in SALT II reinforced the impression that Moscow had still not truly come to terms with Turkey's military alliance.[14]

Another aspect of Turkish policy that raised potential difficulties for the USSR was the gradual revival of Turkish interest in establishing contact with the Turkic world of the Soviet Union. Exploratory travel to Central Asia and the Caucasus by Turkish journalists, academicians, and members of parliament in the early months of 1967 was followed by the visit of Turkish prime minister Demirel to Uzbekistan and Azerbaijan during his trip to the USSR in September of that year. These were closely controlled encounters, but nonetheless were reflective of a desire among Turkish conservative circles to reinvigorate sentimental bonds with the rest of the Turkic world, which these Turks believed would—if free of Moscow's inhibitions—look to Ankara for inspiration.

For Turks, several issues in the period just before Gorbachev took power were especially corrosive of mutual trust. One was a new demonstration that the Brezhnev doctrine was still alive by the Soviet invasion of Afghanistan in December 1979. Turkey had long felt a special kinship with the Afghans, who were the first to establish diplomatic relations with Ataturk's nationalist movement. Not surprisingly, therefore, the Turks joined their NATO allies in roundly condemning the invasion.

This reminder that détente had not made the Soviet Union harmless was sharpened by the media attacks launched by the USSR after the military regime took over in Turkey in 1980. Soviet charges of bowing to U.S. pressure and of persecuting the left did not go down well with the generals then at the helm in Turkey. Although state-to-state relations were not interrupted, there was a noticeable coolness between the two.[15]

Another concern for the Turks was that, as Mutual and Balanced Force Reduction talks got under way to consider the disengagement of forces in Central Europe, Soviet ground forces would be withdrawn to locations inside the USSR where they would increase the threat to Turkey. But Ankara was not successful in eliciting from Moscow a guarantee that any withdrawals would not pose a danger to Turkey. That concern put Turkey in an uncomfortable position with its allies, as the principle of reducing offensive threat in the central front held obvious appeal to NATO in general.

Finally, the perennial Cyprus chestnut continued to divide Turkey and the Soviets. The move in 1983 to create an independent "Republic of Northern Cyprus" met universal international rejection, in Moscow no less than elsewhere in the world. But the Soviets continued to insist that only through an international conference under the UN (in which they would inevitably play a major role) could an acceptable solution be found, a recipe the Turks found particularly distasteful. And the Kremlin continually criticized the Turks for intending to bring the divided island into NATO. Although Turkey's main antagonist over Cyprus remained Greece, this Soviet diplomacy formed a background irritant, dimming the chances for real harmony and serving to enhance friction between Greece and Turkey.[16]

Gorbachev and Perestroika

Return to a civilian regime in Turkey in 1983 did not by itself do much to rewarm relations with the USSR. Until well after Gorbachev came to power in 1985, Moscow's skepticism over the nature of the Turkish regime continued. The overall appraisal of Soviet media thus was that "the Ozal cabinet does not intend to introduce any substantial changes" from those policies followed by the military rulers. Commentators even claimed that Turkey would be used by American forces as a staging ground for cruise missiles and to carry out new adventures in the Middle East. Against that background, Moscow's vocal defense of human rights activists being prosecuted by the Ankara government on nebulous charges did nothing to endear it to the Turkish regime.[17]

This negative appraisal of Turkey's civilian government, however, did not prevent a significant step forward in economic relations. In preparation for the visit of Soviet premier Nikolai Tikhonov in December 1984, Turkey signed an accord for Soviet natural gas in return for Turkish goods and services and/or foreign exchange, a key step in permitting expansion of trade. Once the necessary pipeline through Bulgaria to western Turkey had been completed in 1987, it would be possible to go well beyond the previous clearing arrangements, under which the Turks racked up a sizable, but largely unusable, credit balance, as Turkish importers preferred Western to Soviet goods. It would take time to overcome the problems of the past, however, and the economic agreement Tikhonov concluded for commercial relations, envisaging an increase of trade to $6 billion over five years, proved overly optimistic.[18]

The advent of Gorbachev soon brought a visible change in the environment for political cooperation. The Turks watched with fascination as he laid the ground for domestic reform with his call for restructuring and openness. And they were heartened by his willingness to question the Brezhnev doctrine in Afghanistan and rethink the Soviet foreign agenda. Soviet sniping at Prime Minister Ozal ended amid a rash of invitations for high-level visits.

That changed atmosphere led Ozal in 1986 to take the opportunity to travel to the Soviet Union, the first Turkish prime minister to do so in over a decade. But with his strategic vision of the centrality of NATO in Turkey's foreign relations, he was not ready to abandon Cold War rhetoric. He thus took care to explain to his domestic and international audience that, while the trip provided new economic opportunities, "we are members of different camps [and] Turkey is very careful towards Russia in general political terms." That elicited from *Pravda* a reminder that "membership in different military alliances did not prevent positive and constant development of relations." Yet at the same time, the Soviet leaders could not pass up the opportunity to encourage the Turks not to let NATO station additional tactical nuclear weapons in Turkey, a project that Moscow suggested was Western "nuclear blackmail" to keep Turkey and the Soviet Union apart.[19]

In conjunction with Ozal's visit, Moscow agreed to open a new land crossing point with Turkey at Sarp on the Black Sea border, with visas issued in Ankara and Moscow pending the opening of a Soviet consulate in Hopa or Trabzon in Turkey. At the same time, Turkish and Soviet delegations met to discuss cooperation in fishing in the Black Sea, "based on equality and good neighborliness." But the Turks were reluctant to bring these talks to conclusion on the basis of the Soviet draft agreement. Hence these "constructive and frank" talks broke up with a mandate merely to collect scientific data. It would be some two years before an accord could be reached.[20]

If trade had begun to blossom, other matters were slower to change. In particular, the Cyprus issue cut in so many different ways that it would prove one of the most difficult to be affected by Gorbachev's restructuring. While Moscow sought to block Turkey's efforts to gain international recognition of the "Turkish Republic of Northern Cyprus," activity on this front also reflected a larger Soviet strategy aimed at removing regional conflict from the Soviet agenda with Washington. Such considerations led *Pravda* on January 22, 1986, to publicize an urgent proposal to resolve the festering dispute on the island.

This Soviet recipe conflicted with Turkish positions on all major points. Moscow called for a solution worked out by the Cypriots themselves; for demilitarization to reflect a nonaligned status for the island; for the removal of all foreign troops, bases, and facilities; and for the abolition of treaties (viz., the Treaty of Guarantee, giving the Turks security rights on the island) that encroached on the sovereignty of the Cyprus Republic. To accomplish this design, Moscow proposed an international conference under UN auspices to be attended by the Republic of Cyprus (an institution the Turks considered representative solely of the Greek community) and all UN Security Council members, thereby assuring the USSR a role. Although both the Turkish and Greek Cypriot communities would be invited along with Greece and Turkey, this internationalization of the negotiations had long since been specifically rejected by the Ankara government.[21]

Of even greater import for the future was the resurrection of a long-buried issue: increasingly bitter conflict between Armenians and Azeris just across Turkey's borders. As central authority weakened in the Soviet Union, and as restructuring and openness eroded the strict controls of the past, the various national groups began openly jockeying for position. After Soviet Armenia and Azerbaijan began to spar over the fate of Nagorno-Karabakh in 1988, however, Turkey's traditional hands-off policy toward the Turkic peoples of the USSR came into conflict with growing pressures in Turkey to come to the aid of the Azeris.

The bloody repression of Azeri nationalists in Baku in January 1990 brought these contradictions of Turkish policy into sharp focus. Out of concern not to arouse Soviet anger, the Turkish government echoed Gorbachev's self-serving description of these events as a reflection of Armenian-Azerbaijani ethnic friction. By condemning "foreign elements" for causing the trouble between the Armenians and Azeris, Turkish officials downplayed the resistance to Soviet rule which the disturbances also exemplified.[22]

Turgut Ozal, now president of Turkey, was in the United States at the time, and made what some in Turkey considered a major gaffe in his zeal to avoid upsetting relations with Moscow over these incidents. Dismissing Turkey's interest in the events, he explained that the Azeris, unlike the Turks of Turkey, were Shiite Muslims and thus were oriented toward Iran. No doubt with parallels to his own Kurdish problem in mind, Ozal stressed that Turkey would not provide any assistance to the Azeris without Soviet consent.

Meanwhile in Turkey, the foreign minister tried to square the circle. While explaining that the Turks considered the Baku repression an "internal affair" of the Soviet Union, he warned that this stand should not be taken as lack of concern over what was happening. At the same time, he enunciated the pious hope that the Azeris would "be helpful concerning the just moves which we believe the Soviet government will undertake."[23]

Not surprisingly, the Turkish government suffered sharp attacks from its parliamentary opposition for not adequately defending the interests of fellow Turks. The then Turkish opposition leader Suleyman Demirel complained that "the slaughter of so many people contradicts the Soviet policy of glasnost." He noted that "one cannot remain just an observer." This domestic reaction was only heightened by criticism coming from the opposition Azerbaijani Popular Front, which asked Turkey to extend military aid under the 1921 Kars Treaty. This strong criticism assured that in the future no Turkish leader would attempt to defend Moscow on nationality issues.[24]

Gorbachev and his colleagues also tried to walk the narrow line between branding Turkish interest as interference and being appreciative of Ankara's reluctance to criticize Soviet heavy-handedness. Soviet officials indicated that they were pleased by "the declared position" of the Turkish president and government. The Soviet ambassador in Ankara maintained that his country regarded the "desire of the Turks in the Soviet Union to establish closer ties with Turkey and to cooperate in the economic, cultural, and social fields as natural." But he warned that it would be dangerous if this cooperation fostered independence or the expectation of independence by Turkey. TASS in Moscow was critical of the Turkish opposition and warned against sending "military equipment" to Nakhichevan. At the same time, the Soviet government rejected Turkey's proposal to extend humanitarian aid, saying that it could not accept aid "with political aims."[25]

Such difficulties with the Soviet Union merely played up the uncertainties of the era of "new thinking." On the one hand, Soviet leaders talked grandly of force reductions and withdrawals from the central front. On the other, Soviet propagandists continued their efforts to disrupt Turkey's cooperation with the United States and made overtures to Greece. This assured that defense officials would be among the last in Turkey to advocate letting down their guard. The Turkish Defense Ministry thus urged NATO that despite the INF agreement and signs of détente in Soviet policies, "Turkey's conventional forces should be strengthened." "As a country sharing a border with the Soviet Union . . . it is important . . . to prevent situations that may lead to less security for us."[26]

In this frame of mind, the Turks reacted with greater caution than their NATO allies to Gorbachev's dramatic offer at the UN at the end of 1988 to trim conventional forces by 500,000 over two years. An official organ of the Turkish government characterized the Soviet move as bringing "many uncertainties since the nature of the personnel and kind of arms are not stated," and expressed concern that the forces might be redeployed closer to Turkey. The Turks were further dismayed when in April 1990 Moscow and Damascus reached an agreement on the modernization and training of the

Syrian army. That Syria was not a party to the European conventional arms reduction talks suggested to Ankara a double standard.[27]

Yet as perestroika and glasnost picked up in intensity, several nagging irritants were removed. In June 1989 Bizim Radyo, the clandestine Turkish Communist Party organ, ended thirty-one years of radio broadcasts. In Ankara that was taken as a Soviet gesture, for Turkish leaders had long maintained that such a station could operate only with Moscow's support. Ankara reciprocated the following year by releasing two jailed top leaders of the Turkish United Communist Party after an intense campaign in the Soviet media.[28]

Also important in promoting greater confidence was the Soviet withdrawal from Afghanistan. Moreover, Soviet diplomats now came forward, attempting to mediate an end to the mass expulsion of ethnic Turks from Bulgaria that had begun in the mid-1980s. In Turkey, it was accepted without question that Moscow had the levers to make the Bulgarian regime comply. Although Moscow's efforts were largely unavailing until Zhivkov's fall in November 1989 ushered in a more enlightened Bulgarian regime, the minor concessions the Soviets won from Bulgaria elicited some appreciation in Turkey.[29]

This period also saw exchanges of naval visits, which emphasized a gradual relaxation of military tensions. Yet as late as June 1989 *Krasnaia zvezda*, which represented harder-line elements in the Soviet military, was still complaining that the modernization of American early warning radar in Turkey was "clearly out of step with the times."[30]

The crisis over the Iraqi invasion of Kuwait in August 1990 tested the political relationship evolved during the Gorbachev era. Turkey was a potential front-line state in this conflict as its NATO partner, the United States, prepared to prevent further Iraqi military advances in the Middle East and then to roll back the invasion of Kuwait. From Turkey's point of view, the ability of Washington to enlist Soviet cooperation in this venture was of major importance. The world had never before seen Soviet approval of joint action with the United States against an erstwhile client. Thus the Turkish authorities in Ankara wasted no time in summoning the Soviet ambassador for an official reading of the Soviet position on the Iraqi move.[31]

While Gorbachev privately assured the White House that Soviet policy would be consistent with Washington's, the public posture of senior Soviet officials was different. They evinced considerable reluctance to countenance the use of force against Iraq. Accordingly, Moscow called Turkey "consistent [and] balanced" for favoring an economic embargo to compel Iraqi compliance with UN resolutions. Soviet commentators made clear, however, that American use of Turkish bases should be permitted only in the event of an attack on Turkey. And Soviet officials criticized the U.S.-led military buildup in the region, saying that Moscow did not support a complete blockade of Iraq because that would be a step "toward a very dangerous war."[32]

Despite these reservations, the Soviets joined with the West in the Security Council to vote for a series of resolutions calling the Iraqi government to end its occupation of Kuwait and imposing sanctions to force compliance. To the end, however, Gorbachev sought to find a diplomatic route for a solution. Even after the air bombardment commenced and as late as the day before Desert Storm's ground operations began, he was holding highly publicized negotiations with the Iraqi foreign minister, trying to arrange for Iraqi withdrawal.

Gorbachev's efforts met a positive response from major Turkish opposition figures. Former prime minister Demirel called the Soviet withdrawal plan a "beautiful opportunity" for "responsible" leaders. But he added that if war came, the "Soviet Union bears an ethical responsibility" because it provided weapons to Iraq. Beyond opposition politicians, press commentary indicated that a significant part of the Turkish elite opposed military operations against Iraq.[33]

In consonance with his strategic vision of Turkey as a vital asset for the West, President Ozal took a different tack. He dismissed Gorbachev's peace plan as an effort to prevent the United States from winning a decisive military victory in the Gulf. Foreign Minister Alptemocin made clear that Turkey rejected the conditionality of the Soviet plan for Iraqi withdrawal from Kuwait. And over clear Soviet displeasure about operations from NATO bases in Turkey, the Turkish parliament voted to permit the air war to be mounted from facilities on Turkish soil.[34]

While the Ankara regime, like its Western allies, was willing to cut Moscow considerable slack in concerting policy, that tolerance was tested by some intemperate Soviet media attacks on political and military "hotheads" in Turkey, who were accused of wanting to take advantage of the situation to annex the Mosul and Kirkuk oil fields. Of more significance, the Soviet Foreign Ministry voiced its unhappiness at NATO's dominance of the military alliance in the conflict, a theme that foreshadowed continuing concern on the part of Moscow that in the "New World Order" it would be left out of the planning for international peacekeeping operations. And Soviet troop reinforcements in the Caucasus raised concern among the Turks.[35]

These differences, however, did not destroy growing confidence in Ankara that Gorbachev's "new thinking" had set the Soviet Union on a basically more pacific course. In keeping with a desire to encourage this benign trend, President Ozal traveled to Moscow in March 1991, just after the war's end, on a previously scheduled visit. Not only was he able to warm up relations once there, as a harbinger of things to come he included two significant republics on his itinerary: Kazakhstan and Azerbaijan. As a result of Ozal's trip, Russia agreed to allow Turkey to reopen its consulate general in Baku, which had been closed for half a century.

Because Turkish leaders saw Gorbachev's personality as largely responsible for the relaxation of East–West tension, they were initially anxious when word arrived of the conservative coup ousting him from the presidency in August 1991. While officially they expressed hope that whatever was happening in Moscow would not interrupt the reform effort, it was clear that they were deeply concerned about the effect on relations with Turkey. Their relief at Gorbachev's return was heartfelt and palpable, though they gave Boris Yeltsin much of the credit for the favorable outcome.[36]

The CIS Era

As the transition accelerated from the Soviet Union to the Commonwealth of Independent States in the latter half of 1991, the Turks focused their attention more and more on the individual Turkic components of the USSR. Yet to the end, the Ankara government took extreme care not to appear to be working around Moscow, but rather appealed for understanding by the Soviet leadership that popular pressure in Turkey gave no option but to emphasize direct ties.

Ankara thus reacted cautiously to the initial declarations of independence of the republics, alleging that such status did not necessarily mean breaking away from the "Union." As late as November 5, 1991, the Turkish government said "it would do everything possible to boost relations with the Soviet Union, but called on Moscow to show understanding for Ankara's decision to recognize the recently declared independence of Azerbaijan."[37] Yet by the end of the year, Turkey had formally recognized the various Turkic states and was proposing early establishment of diplomatic relations. It refused, however, to exchange ambassadors with Armenia until the latter specifically renounced claims on Turkish territory.

The new Turkish coalition government formed under Prime Minister Suleyman Demirel in November 1991 took note of the change in Russia, but Demirel dwelt more on the difficulties of ongoing Cyprus negotiations than on relations with the disappearing Soviet world in his initial foreign policy statement. It would be some months before the government enunciated a clear policy of working with the new Turkic republics to consolidate their independent status. Behind that policy lay the unspoken premise that Turkey did not want the Russians to recreate the Soviet Union by dominating the Near Abroad. But conscious of Russia's military might, the Ankara leadership sought to avoid generating controversy with its northern neighbor.[38]

One of the first tests of the new relationship was the sputtering conflict between Armenia and Azerbaijan. The newly independent states joined the Conference on Security and Cooperation in Europe (CSCE); and that body immediately agreed to send experts to report on the Nagorno-Karabakh conflict. Despite the affirmation by this mission that Karabakh belonged to Azerbaijan, by early May 1992 Armenian forces completed the conquest of Azeri strongholds in Nagorno-Karabakh and began shelling the Azerbaijani enclave of Nakhichevan, ignoring a cease-fire that Iran had tried to arrange.

This brought Turkey into the conflict in a way that raised the specter of a major confrontation with Russia. When Turkey's foreign minister condemned Armenian "aggression" with vague references to possible military action, CIS commander-in-chief Marshal Shaposhnikov warned that Russia could not "remain indifferent" to such action. *Izvestiia* ominously predicted that "Turkish intervention" could lead to a Third World War because if Turkey sent forces into Nakhichevan, that would be considered a "NATO attack on the CIS." Turkey quickly backed away from threats of war in this instance, although the following year new prime minister Tansu Ciller pledged to react if Armenian forces entered Nakhichevan.[39]

Azerbaijani defeats on the ground also led to a series of government shifts in Baku that brought Turkey's preferred candidate, Abulfaz Elchibey, to power in June in place of predecessors more closely tied to Moscow. With Turkish backing, Elchibey, during his year in office, attempted to speed the departure of Russian troops, blocked Azerbaijani ratification of the treaty on membership in the CIS that had been signed by his predecessors, and generally rejected independent Russian mediation of the dispute with Armenia.[40]

Recognizing the potential for friction, Moscow and Ankara moderated their rhetoric. After consultations during Prime Minister Demirel's visit to Moscow at the end of May 1992, both sides acknowledged the need to coordinate their policies toward regional disputes. Yeltsin and Demirel also agreed to denounce Armenian bellicosity.

While that reduced tension in the relationship, it did not eliminate differences. Turkey and Russia, along with other interested parties, participated in the so-called "Minsk group," which attempted to bring hostilities to an end under the broad mandate of CSCE. But this effort did not produce an early cease-fire, and continuing Azerbaijani military defeats discredited Elchibey, leading in June 1993 to his replacement by Haidar Aliev, a former

Soviet Politburo member who reputedly was pro-Russian. Turkey temporarily stopped arms shipments to Azerbaijan as a sign of its dissatisfaction. Aliev, however, in fact sought to work with Turkey and generally maintained his independence from Moscow. Nevertheless, he did take Azerbaijan into the CIS, while refusing to accept the return of Russian border guards on Azeri territory.[41]

In this new situation, Moscow became increasingly interested in pursuing its own mediation. In 1993 Yeltsin dispatched Vladimir Kazimirov as a special envoy to develop a peace plan calling for Russian troops to separate the combatants, an endeavor that caused uneasiness in Ankara. Prime Minister Tansu Ciller, who took that post after Ozal died in April 1993 and was replaced as president by Demirel, made clear that Turkey would want to send its forces as peacekeepers if Russian troops were to be used in that capacity. This remains a sticking point with Moscow.

Another cause of tension grew out of the disintegration of Yugoslavia and the Serbian attacks against the Muslims in Bosnia. Public opinion in Turkey had long been suspicious that religious considerations governed European attitudes toward Muslims and accounted for the difficulties Turkey faced in gaining membership in the EC. When Europeans then failed effectively to come to the defense of the Bosnian Muslims, great frustration was apparent in Turkey. Ankara pushed for Turkish forces to be included in all military and peacekeeping operations to help their coreligionists. In the meantime, to equalize the contest the Turks called for the partial lifting of the arms embargo imposed by the UN on the warring parties to allow military supplies to reach the Bosnians.[42]

Russia, on the other hand, appeared sympathetic to the Serbs, who were the party mainly responsible for pushing the Muslims into small separate enclaves, where resupply of food and medicine as well as all military equipment was either restricted or cut off entirely. By February 1994, when the international outcry against the slaughter of Muslim civilians finally energized outside peacekeepers to make limited interventions to improve access to these beleaguered communities, Moscow dispatched its own forces to take part in the peacekeeping process.

That Russian move, which was widely seen as favorable to the Serbs, gave the Turks an argument to overcome the reserve with which Turkish forces had previously been regarded by the international community. Turkish aircraft had been reluctantly accepted as part of the force to impose a no-fly zone on the conflict area in Bosnia. In June 1994 Turkish ground forces were also allowed to take part in the peacekeeping operations. But Turkish insistence that the embargo be lifted for the Bosnians was still rejected by much of the international community, including the Russians.

And clearly Ankara remains suspicious that the Russians will protect rather than press the Serbs.[43]

Even larger defense issues still find Russia and Turkey at odds in the Yeltsin period. Turkish leaders have never been entirely sanguine about the stability of the regime in Russia. They have had some confidence in the aims and intentions of Boris Yeltsin, but they have been uneasy about repeated challenges to his power. The shakeup in October 1993, when Yeltsin defeated one more attempt to curb his powers, reinforced that concern in Ankara.

This anxiety was also inflamed by a letter from Yeltsin in September 1993 requesting that Russia be granted an exception to the Treaty on Conventional Armed Forces in Europe (CFE) to permit it to augment its forces in the north Caucasus because of instability in the region. Ankara reacted in shock, regarding this demand as a device "to increase Russia's pressure on countries in the south Caucasus region." Although there was relief in Ankara when its NATO allies stood firm in rejecting such a change, Turkish observers worried that "Russia's military presence in the Caucasus will significantly exceed CFE limits if the present trend is allowed to continue."[44]

Turkey's mistrust of Russian military aims was heightened still further by the enunciation of a new military doctrine by Moscow in November 1993. This doctrine, implying a possible first use of nuclear weapons if attacked or threatened by a country allied to countries possessing nuclear weapons, was seen in Turkey as a "restatement of the Brezhnev Doctrine in a different form."[45]

Against this background, in May 1994 General Gures, chief of the Turkish General Staff, issued a statement criticizing Russia for continuing to pursue an imperial policy in the region and thus posing a considerable threat to Turkey. While Turkey's president and prime minister distanced themselves from this position, the Russian government made clear that Gures's statement "went far beyond the limits of the admissible." This did not settle the matter; another sharp speech by Turkey's defense minister followed, detailing the worrisome nature of Russia's military doctrine and Russian efforts to "pressure" Azerbaijan to "establish a military base" just as in Armenia. To be sure, some of this concern was directed at NATO as justification for continuing military aid to Turkey. But the sharpness of the rhetoric made clear that Ankara saw a present danger from Russia, which it feared might be seeking to revive domination of the area around Turkey.[46]

Other CIS issues also caused friction. Russia was uneasy at Turkey's willingness to speak out for the Turkish-speaking Gagauz minority in Moldova. In addition, Turkey's efforts to establish closer relations with Ukraine even beyond the bounds of the Black Sea Economic Cooperation project put it somewhat at odds with Russia, which viewed the Kiev regime as the backbone of resistance to its influence in the Near Abroad. Closer to home for the Turks, their emotional support for Georgian independence conflicted with Moscow's designs to regain influence by manipulating warring factions in order to keep Russian border guards on Turkey's border with Georgia.

These differences also colored the increasingly strident controversy over use of the Black Sea Straits. Congestion in this waterway led the Turks to consider additional regulations for piloting ships in its narrow confines. Russia objected to the idea of such restrictions on the grounds that they violated the Montreux Convention, a charge the Turks strongly denied. But behind the Russian position lay concern that Turkish regulations would impede Russia's efforts to keep its hand in Azerbaijani and Turkmen oil production. Russian interest in using Novorossiisk as an oil transshipment point for tankers through the Straits led Turkey to warn that such an increase in tanker traffic would tie up the Straits for other commerce and would present an unacceptable level of danger to Istanbul.[47]

Turkey had a clear commercial interest in collecting transit fees for pipelines to be built from Baku and Turkmenistan. Yet its focus on safety did reflect undeniable reality. In March 1994 a large tanker collided with another ship and burned in the Bosporus in sight of Istanbul. Foreign Minister Cetin took the occasion to point out that safety required that oil be shipped by pipeline. Turkey announced that new regulations for passage through the Straits would be imposed in July 1994. The Russians strongly objected and publicly refused to accept the legitimacy of the changes, marking still another unsettled controversy.[48]

Russian policy toward the Kurds, a matter that had remained dormant for some years, came to the fore again without warning in early 1994. During the increasingly bitter domestic struggle in Turkey against Kurdish insurgents at the end of the 1980s, the Russians had not taken a stand on this delicate issue. But in the spring of 1994, a conference of the insurgent Workers' Party of Kurdistan (PKK) was publicly convened in Moscow, much to the consternation of the Turks. While the Russian Foreign Ministry attempted to distance itself from the gathering, which it called "unofficial," claiming that it would not permit similar gatherings in the future, its spokesmen obliquely warned that Turkey, too, should not play with dissidents in Russia. Indeed, some Turkish commentators saw the conference as a move to retaliate for Turkish involvement with the Chechens, including the "unofficial" reception of Chechen leader Dudaev the previous year. But this did not end the question. A confederation of CIS Kurdish Organizations was created in Moscow at the end of October 1994 in part to "give assistance to our fellow Kurds who are waging a struggle against the Turkish regime." That aroused great unhappiness in Turkish political circles, which also worried that Russia might use the new body to press concessions from Ankara on regional policy disputes.[49]

Finally, Ankara's sponsorship of Turkic solidarity, convening occasional summits of Turkic-language states in Turkey, drew complaints from the Russian Foreign Ministry. It divined a "tendency toward isolation of Turkic-language states . . . which objectively opposes them to the neighboring states." And on this basis, the ministry found Turkey guilty of "stirring up conflicts, including those on territory of the Commonwealth."[50]

This panoply of disputes by no means represented the totality of the Turkish-Russian relationship. The end of the Cold War also opened the way for new areas of cooperation. One was the possibility of Russia's providing military items that Turkey could not acquire from its Western allies. The Turkish authorities sought to deal with the sharpening domestic conflict with Kurdish insurgents at the end of the 1980s by increasingly extensive military operations. This created a need for armor and helicopters free of NATO restrictions; the Russians offered an attractive alternative when the Germans cut off supplies to Turkey because of growing objections at home in October 1992. As German supplies phased out, Russia agreed to sell helicopters and armored personnel carriers. After some haggling, the two settled on a mutually acceptable payment arrangement of part cash and part charged against the unused Turkish credit in the bilateral clearing account.[51]

The Black Sea Economic Cooperation project initiated by Ankara offered another avenue for cooperation. Originally conceived in 1990, this initiative sought to encourage economic links among the Black Sea regional states, and broadened to include all the Caucasus countries after the demise of the Soviet Union. The effort to harmonize economic policies still has a long way to go before major trade barriers are removed. But all parties seem pleased at the existence of this forum.[52]

Even in regional issues there was at times a parallelism in approach that put Russia and Turkey in the same camp. As time went on, this came to be true in policy toward Iraq. Both Russia and Turkey felt the need to be part of the general international consensus on dealing with Saddam Hussein's regime. Each had special reasons for wanting to see the economic embargo on Iraq lifted. Ankara felt the impact of losing the lucrative oil transit fees from the pipeline through Turkey from the northern Iraqi fields; Moscow hoped that permitting Iraqi oil sales would provide Baghdad with foreign exchange to repay extensive debts to Russia for military equipment supplied in an earlier era. Thus Turkey from its vantage point inside the alliance with the United States and Russia as a permanent member of the UN

Security Council both pressed for easing of international restrictions on Iraq. Both took care to do so within the parameters of their relationship with the United States, which remained strongly opposed to diminishing pressure on Saddam Hussein's regime.[53]

Prospects

Russia and Turkey have strong vested interests in keeping their differences under control and promoting general amity. Yet it is clear that they have their work cut out for them in managing their complex relationship. Russia is by no means ready to abandon its sphere of influence in the Caucasus. It has a strong interest in seeing that ethnic conflicts in this troubled part of the world do not bring the newly independent republics on its periphery into conflict with each other. And it is especially intent on preventing ethnic conflict from spilling over into Russia proper.

These considerations will lead the Yeltsin regime to pursue its own mediation in the Azerbaijan conflict with Armenia, despite willingness to blend that into the CSCE and UN negotiating processes. Indeed, Yeltsin's regime seems to believe that it must be seen to be active in order to head off domestic opponents who support far more extreme measures toward restoring the Soviet empire.

Ethnic conflict in the Caucasus offers Russia manifold opportunities to regain influence in that region. Its alternation between support of Abkhaz separatists and the Shevardnadze regime secured Georgian adherence to the CIS. Similar tactics of first opposing the Turkish-oriented Elchibey and then supporting Aliev assured Azerbaijani participation in the CIS, even though a return of Russian troops to that state seems unlikely.

Turkish policy toward the CIS is based on a feeling of identity with the Turkic republics and a desire to make sure that Moscow does not gain undue influence over them or reincorporate them into a new imperial state. This means accommodating whatever indigenous leadership comes to power in these states, even if former Soviet officials occupy the top spots. In addition, these considerations will push Turkey to reinforce cultural and educational links as well as encourage business deals with these newly independent states. Turkish interest in oil, which occupies a central place in this strategy, will require careful management. Efforts to promote pipelines from Central Asia and Azerbaijan will continue to clash with Russian interest in dominating oil production and/or transportation in and from these areas.

Although these problems are manageable, and are likely to be handled without serious conflict, they will serve to keep the Turkish-Russian relationship far from warm. And if Boris Yeltsin should be forced out of power by his opponents, his successors would be unlikely to inspire similar confidence among the Turks. That would be translated into even greater Turkish concern over Russian military intentions and perplexity about how far to go in supporting the independence of the CIS republics.

Notes

1. See George S. Harris, *The Origins of Communism in Turkey* (Stanford, CA: Hoover Institution Press, 1967), passim.

2. The Kars Treaty set the boundaries with Turkey in the Transcaucasus. While the parties agreed that the Nakhichevan oblast "formed an autonomous territory under the protection of Azerbaijan," the treaty did not specify, as was sometimes later alleged, that Turkey was in any way a guarantor of this status. The treaty did not refer to Nagorno-Karabakh at all.

3. Harris, *Origins*, epilogue, especially pp. 146–47.

4. For Arkos, see *SSSR i Turtsiia, 1917–1979*, ed. M.A. Gasratian and P.P. Moiseev (Moscow: Izdatel'stvo "Nauka," Glavnaia redaktsiia vostochnoi literatury, 1981), p. 79; and Dr. Fethi Tevetoglu, *Turkiye'de Sosyalist ve Komunist Faaliyetleri (1910–1960)* (Ankara: Ayyildiz Matbaasi, 1967), pp. 402, 936. On Voroshilov, see USSR, Ministerstvo inostrannykh del SSSR, *Dokumenty vneshnei politiki SSSR*, vol. 16 (Moscow: Izdatel'stvo politicheskoi literatury, 1970), pp. 623–27.

5. George S. Harris, "The Soviet Union and Turkey," in *The Soviet Union and the Middle East: The Post–World War II Era*, ed. Ivo J. Lederer and Wayne S. Vucinich (Stanford, CA: Hoover Institution Press, 1974), p. 25.

6. George S. Harris, "Cross-Alliance Politics: Turkey and the Soviet Union," in *The Turkish Yearbook of International Relations: 1972* (Ankara: Ankara Universitesi Basimevi, 1974), pp. 6–10.

7. Ibid., pp. 14–15.

8. Harris, "The Soviet Union and Turkey," pp. 39–41.

9. Soviet commentators at first called Johnson's letter "a smokescreen, an attempt to give the United States an alibi just in case Cyprus is attacked." Harris, "Cross-Alliance Politics," p. 24.

10. George S. Harris, *Troubled Alliance: Turkish-American Problems in Historical Perspective, 1945–1971* (Washington, DC: American Enterprise Institute, 1972), chapter 7, especially pp. 165–66.

11. "Deklaratsiia o printsipakh dobrososedskikh otnoshenii mezhdu Soiuzom Sovetskikh Sotsialisticheskikh Respublik i Turetskoi Respublikoi," *Izvestiia*, April 18, 1972; "Politicheskii dokument o printsipakh dobrososedskogo i druzhestvennogo sotrudnichestva mezhdu Soiuzom Sovetskikh Sotsialisticheskikh Respublik i Turetskoi Respublikoi," *Izvestiia*, June 24, 1978.

12. *Milliyet*, May 16, 1978.

13. Yilmaz Altug, "The State of International Détente and Turkish Foreign Policy," *The Turkish Yearbook of International Relations: 1975* (Ankara: Ankara Universitesi Basimevi, 1977), pp. 25–36; Moscow Radio, October 19, 1984, in Foreign Broadcast Information Service, *Daily Report* (hereafter FBIS), III (Soviet Union), October 23, 1984, pp. 6–8; *Milliyet*, December 27, 1984.

14. Duygu Bazoglu Sezer, *Turkey's Security Policies* (London: International Institute for Strategic Studies, Adelphi Paper 164, 1981), pp. 34–35.

15. Moscow Radio, February 16, 1981, in FBIS, III, February 17, 1981, p. G 1; *Pravda*, July 2, 1981, p. 4, in FBIS, III, July 8, 1981, pp. G 4–6.

16. TASS, November 17, 1983, in FBIS, III, November 22, 1983, p. G 11; *Milliyet*, November 23, 1983, in FBIS, VII (Western Europe), November 29, 1983, p. T 7.

17. Vitaly Alexandrov, "Turkey: Though the Government Is a Civilian One . . . ," *New Times*, January 1984, no. 4, pp. 14–15; *Krasnaya Zvezda*, March 2, 1984, p. 3, in FBIS, III, March 6, 1984, pp. G 12–13.

18. *Hurriyet*, December 27, 1984; on the failure to publish a joint communiqué, see *Cumhuriyet*, December 28, 1984, in FBIS, VII, January 2, 1985, pp. T 1–3.

19. "Premier Ozal on His Visit to the Soviet Union," *NewSpot*, August 8, 1986, no. 86/32, p. 7.

20. "Turco-Soviet Cooperation in Fishery," *NewSpot*, October 21, 1988, no. 88/43, p. 5.

21. *Pravda*, January 22, 1986, p. 4.

22. Ankara Radio, January 16, 1990, in FBIS-WEU-90-010, January 16, 1990, p. 12.

23. Ankara Television, January 18, 1990, in FBIS-WEU-90-013, January 19, 1990, p. 28.

24. *Hurriyet*, January 21, 1990, in FBIS-WEU-90-018, January 26, 1990, p. 30; Anatolia, January 20, 1990, in FBIS-WEU-90-014, January 22, 1990, p. 11. See note 2 above.

25. Ankara Television, January 22, 1990, in FBIS-WEU-90-015, January 23, 1990, p. 25; TASS, January 24, 1990, in FBIS-SOV-017, January 25, 1990, p. 29; *Hurriyet*, January 26, 1990, in FBIS-WEU-90-021, January 31, 1990, p. 27; Ankara Television, January 27, 1990, in FBIS-WEU-90-019, January 29, 1990, p. 26.

26. *Pravda*, March 30, 1987; "NATO Nuclear Planning Group Meeting," *NewSpot*, November 4, 1988, no. 88/45, p. 3.

27. "Viewpoint: Gorbachev's Prospects," *NewSpot*, December 16, 1988, no. 88/51, pp. 1, 7; *Hurriyet*, May 4, 1990, in FBIS-WEU-90-088, May 7, 1990, p. 26.

28. *Hurriyet*, June 9, 1990; *Sovetskaia Rossiia*, May 2, 1990, in FBIS-SOV-90-087, May 4, 1990, p. 33; *Pravda*, April 12, 1990, in FBIS-SOV-90-075, April 18, 1990, p. 34.

29. For example, Anakara Radio, June 27, 1989, in FBIS-WEU-8-122, June 27, 1989, p. 42.

30. TASS, June 24, 1989, in FBIS-SOV-89-125, June 30, 1989, p. 29; *Krasnaia zvezda*, June 22, 1989, in FBIS-SOV-89-131, July 11, 1989, pp. 13–14.

31. Anatolia, August 3, 1990, in FBIS-WEU-90-151, August 6, 1990, p. 28.

32. Anatolia, August 11, 1990, in FBIS-WEU-90-156, August 13, 1990, p. 28; Anatolia, August 24, 1990, in FBIS-WEU-90-165, August 24, 1990, p. 50.

33. Ankara Radio, February 22, 1991, in FBIS-WEU-91-037, February 25, 1991, p. 43.

34. Ankara Television, February 19, 1991, in FBIS-WEU-91-034, February 20, 1991; Anatolia, February 23, 1991, in FBIS-WEU-91-037, February 25, 1991, p. 38.

35. *Sovetskaia Rossiia*, February 16, 1991, in FBIS-SOV-91-0035, February 21, 1991, p. 26; *Pravda*, January 3, 1991, pp. 1, 4, in FBIS-SOV-91-002, p. 12.

36. Anatolia, September 11, 1991, in FBIS-WEU-91-176, September 11, 1991, p. 12.

37. Anatolia, November 6, 1991, in FBIS-WEU-91-216, November 7, 1991, p. 24; Ambassador Bilal N. Simsir, "Turkey's Relations with Central Asian Turkic Republics (1989–92)," *Turkish Digest*, vol. 6, no. 28 (Summer 1992), pp. 13–15.

38. *Turkish Daily News*, December 14, 1991, in FBIS-WEU-91-242, December 17, 1991, p. 53.

39. *Izvestiia*, May 23, 1992, in FBIS-SOV-92-103, May 28, 1992, p. 5.

40. *Sabah*, May 20, 1992, in FBIS-WEU-92-100, May 22, 1992, p. 43.

41. *Hurriyet*, December 23, 1993, in FBIS-WEU-93-249, December 30, 1993, p. 28.

42. Anatolia, August 28, 1992, in FBIS-WEU-92-172, September 3, 1993, p. 30; Agence France Press, February 2, 1994, in FBIS-EEU-94-023, February 3, 1994, p. 24.

43. *NewSpot*, June 24, 1994, no. 13-1994-11, p. 1.

44. *Wehrtechnik*, July 1992, in FBIS-WEU-92-172, September 3, 1992, pp. 33–37; *Sabah*, September 25, 1993, in FBIS-WEU-93-186, September 28, 1993, p. 54; *Milliyet*, April 14, 1994, in FBIS-WEU-94-073, April 15, 1994, p. 53.

45. *Sabah*, November 11, 1993, p. 13, in FBIS-WEU-93-219, November 16, 1993, p. 86.

46. Interfax, June 8, 1994, in FBIS-SOV-94-111, June 9, 1994, p. 17; *Turkish Daily News*, July 27, 1994, p. A 2, in FBIS-WEU-94-147, August 1, 1994, p. 54.

47. Anatolia, September 3, 1992, in FBIS-WEU-92-173, September 4, 1992, p. 34.

48. Interfax, April 15, 1994, in FBIS-SOV-94-074, April 18, 1994, p. 24.

49. *Ozgur Ulke*, July 18, 1994, in FBIS-WEU-94-143, July 26, 1994, p. 50; *Nezavisimaya Gazeta,* November 2, 1994, in FBIS-SOV-94-213, November 3, 1994. p. 1.

50. ITAR-TASS, October 18, 1994, in FBIS-SOV-94-202, October 19, 1994, p. 11.

51. *Milliyet*, August 13, 1992, in FBIS-WEU-92-164, August 24, 1992, pp. 39–40; *Turkish Daily News*, May 25, 1993, p. 11, in FBIS-WEU-93-110, June 10, 1993, p. 68.

52. Graham E. Fuller and Ian O. Lesser, *Turkey's New Geopolitics: From the Balkans to Western China* (Boulder, CO: Westview Press, 1993), pp. 103–4.

53. *Hurriyet*, September 10, 1993, p. 20, in FBIS-WEU-93-180, September 20, 1993, p. 57.

2

Moscow and Tehran
The Wary Accommodation

Alvin Z. Rubinstein

The fall of the Soviet Union transformed relations between Moscow and Iran to something neither country had ever known in their more than four centuries of imperial interaction. Coming with breathtaking suddenness, the Soviet demise was an unprecedented historical event: no other empire in history had collapsed and disappeared so quickly, without so much as a nudge from a foreign war or a civil war. The Soviet Union was not weakened by starvation; its population was not polarized, rebellious, or particularly alienated; on the contrary, during the final years of the Soviet Union, most of the population was enjoying a standard of living higher than any in their living memory. The ultimate irony was destruction by a leadership committed to extensive reform.

The emergence of former Soviet union-republics to the status of independent nation-states in the Caucasus (Armenia, Azerbaijan, and Georgia) and in Central Asia (Kazakhstan, Kyrgyzstan, Tajikistan, Turkmenistan, and Uzbekistan) has drastically altered the geopolitics of Central Asia and the Middle East overnight. Iran (along with Turkey and Afghanistan), which had been forced to adapt to the omnipresence of Russian military power and expansionist ambitions throughout the nineteenth and twentieth centuries, now finds itself without Russia situated along its northern border and with hitherto unimaginable opportunities and options.

For the first time in several centuries, Russia and Iran are separated by a geographically significant ethnolinguistic strategic buffer zone, in which the nascent nationalism of long-subjugated peoples is destined to affect the aims and policies of these two historic empires and imperial adversaries. Both Russia and Iran must come to terms with new regional actors and sociopolitical and religious forces over which they have limited influence. Their capacity to shape events has been weakened by economic and socio-political strains: in Russia's case, by the flawed consequences of Gorbachev's perestroika and glasnost and by Yeltsin's pallid reforms; in Iran's case, by the costly aftermath of eight years of war with Iraq. Neither has found a formula for sustained growth or societal cohesion. Thus, their prospects in the Caucasus and Central Asia are still changing, and as heav-ily dependent on what they accomplish at home as on the effectiveness with which they succeed in making the most of opportunities in the region.

In Moscow, one school of thought wonders whether the former non-Rus-sian areas can in some way be reincorporated under Russia's hegemony; in Tehran, foreign policy analysts wonder whether the new states can remain independent. Much will depend on the ability of the newly independent countries to develop viable political systems and avoid the mistakes of Third World countries whose impoverishment can be attributed mainly to the flawed policies of megalomaniacal leaderships. If, for example, the new republics of the former Soviet Union use scarce resources to acquire arms for the furthering of nationalist ambitions, their independence will soon be in jeopardy.

The Gorbachev Interregnum

During Mikhail Gorbachev's period in power, relations between Moscow and Tehran moved from bad to good. The hostility and tension that existed in 1985 were reminiscent of the latter years of the Stalin period. However, by the time of Gorbachev's downfall (and that of the Soviet Union), the two countries were resuming the extensive and mutually advantageous relation-ship that they had enjoyed during most of the Brezhnev era.

Recall that notwithstanding Stalin's attempt to wrest control of Iran's Kurdish and Azerbaijani provinces away from Tehran, and the intense sus-picion rooted deeply in history and incompatible ideological outlooks, self-interest had proved a facilitator of political accommodation. Despite concluding a defense agreement with the United States in March 1959, the Iranian government acted almost immediately to allay Soviet security con-cerns over its implications. In September 1962, the shah announced that no foreign country would be permitted to have missile forces on Iranian soil, and that Iran would not become a party to "aggression" against the Soviet Union. These assurances, coupled with the fact that Iran did not maintain a large military force along the Soviet-Iranian border, opened the way to a

Soviet-Iranian rapprochement. In early 1966, an economic agreement was signed for the construction of a major steel complex, which was finished in 1973, as well as for the Trans-Iranian Gas Pipeline, which started pumping natural gas to Soviet and European markets in October 1970.[1] A fifteen-year treaty of economic and technical cooperation, signed in 1972, established the framework for an expanding trade and technological relationship. Government-to-government relations improved to the point that each even returned the other's defectors.

The overthrow of the shah in January 1979 and the establishment the following month of an Islamic republic took Moscow by surprise; still the Brezhnev leadership saw no reason that the previous mutually advantageous relationship should not continue. But the Soviet government's failure to denounce Iraq's attack on Iran in September 1980; its own invasion of Afghanistan in December 1979; and its insistence on reaffirming, despite Tehran's repeated repudiations, the validity of Articles 5 and 6 of the 1921 Soviet-Iranian treaty, which gave Soviet forces the right to intervene in Iranian affairs if a third party threatened to attack the USSR from Iranian territory or if Moscow considered its border threatened, quickly soured relations between Moscow and Tehran. When Moscow tilted openly toward Iraq in 1982, after Iran had succeeded in driving Iraqi forces from most Iranian territory, Tehran's hostility led to a crackdown on the Iranian Communist (Tudeh) Party. In 1985, Gorbachev embarked Moscow on a more active policy in the Persian Gulf; this included the introduction of a Soviet naval presence in October 1986 and the reflagging and protection of some Kuwaiti tankers—interpreted by Tehran as further evidence of Moscow's pro-Baghdad policy.

At the same time, Moscow responded to Tehran's hints of a desire for better relations: In February 1986, amidst fierce fighting on the Iran–Iraq front, First Deputy Foreign Minister Georgii Kornienko was sent to Tehran, making him the highest-ranking Soviet official to visit Iran since Ayatollah Khomeini's 1979 revolution. In December 1986, the Iranian-Soviet Standing Commission for Economic Cooperation met in Tehran for the first time in six years. And in August 1987 the two countries agreed to expanded economic cooperation, including greatly increased natural gas deliveries by the early 1990s; construction of power plants and oil refineries; and the return of Soviet technicians, removed in 1985 because of Iraqi air attacks. Even though the Soviet Union supported the UN Security Council's call for an immediate cease-fire between Iran and Iraq and its warning that sanctions would be imposed unless compliance was forthcoming, Iran edged toward normalization of relations with Moscow.

When the Iran–Iraq War ended with a cease-fire on August 20, 1988,

Moscow was well positioned for good relations with Iran. Gorbachev, like his predecessors since Khrushchev, wanted to improve relations with, as well as between, Iran and Iraq. However, in pursuit of its objectives, Moscow was not prepared to back just any action of a client. For example, in March 1973, when Iraq sent troops into Kuwait to strong-arm it into relinquishing the islands of Bubiyan and Warbah, which would have enhanced the defenses of the port of Umm Qasr, the USSR joined with the Arab League in condemning the action, and Iraq quickly withdrew. During the early stages of the Iran–Iraq War, Moscow's dissatisfaction with Saddam Hussein's unwillingness to stop the fighting and to seek a political solution was expressed by refusal "to provide Baghdad with badly needed military equipment" as long as Iraqi forces were on the offensive.[2]

The level and character of Soviet involvement in the Middle East was determined by the mutuality of interest that was dominant in the relationship with a client or potential client at any given time. Thus, in 1986 and 1987, uneasy over the growing U.S. military presence in the Gulf, Moscow blocked efforts in the UN Security Council to impose sanctions on Iran, even when the Iranian forces were threatening to achieve a breakthrough toward Basra. Moscow tried to balance its global objective of limiting U.S. influence with its regional interest in maintaining relations, however difficult, with Iraq and Iran. By the end of the Iran–Iraq War, Moscow's shared concern with Tehran over the resurgent American position in the Gulf prompted the two to reexamine their relationship.

The Soviet leadership sought a rapprochement that could be effected without jeopardizing ties with Iraq, though Gorbachev realized, as had Brezhnev, that Iran was strategically the more important power. Friendly relations with Iran offered an attractive combination of stable, secure borders, strategic denial of military facilities to the United States, economic complementarity, an expanding market for arms sales, and a diplomatic wedge for improving relations with the Arab states of the Gulf.

On the Iranian side, the crucial impetus came from Ayatollah Khomeini. In an extraordinary letter sent to Gorbachev in early January 1989, there was a "clear acknowledgement of the supreme role that reforms in the Soviet Union and especially Gorbachev's revisionism had played in changing the Iranian perception and more significantly Khomeini's perception of the Soviet Union."[3] Khomeini congratulated Gorbachev for his revisions of Soviet ideology, noting that these "seem likely to disrupt and revolutionize the dominant balance of interests around the world."[4] He noted that Marxism could not provide answers to the moral crisis that apparently afflicted Soviet society "as it is based on doing away with God and religion which has certainly dealt the heaviest and biggest blow to the Soviet Union":

> Today Marxism and (Marxist) economic and social method have reached
> a dead end. . . . It is clear to all that, from now on, Communism should be
> sought in the museums of world political history. Marxism has no answer to
> any of the real problems of human beings.[5]

Khomeini's letter was "conciliatory, not combative or politicized," and it
left no doubt "that Iran now considered a new opening with the Soviet
Union a worthy objective."[6]

In late February, Soviet foreign minister Eduard Shevardnadze personally delivered Gorbachev's reply to Khomeini. A month later, Iranian foreign minister Ali Akbar Velayati went to Moscow to make arrangements
for a visit in June by the Speaker of the Iranian parliament, Hojatolislam Ali
Akbar Hashemi Rafsanjani.

The importance of Rafsanjani's visit, coming as it did two and a half
weeks after Ayatollah Khomeini's death and before the forty-day period of
mourning had passed, cannot be overestimated. Gorbachev looked forward
to comprehensive cooperation in all fields. The joint communiqué referred
to "a long-term program for economic, commercial, scientific, and technical
cooperation until the year 2000," an agreement for "the construction of the
Mashhad-Serakhs-Tedzhen railway line," and agreements in the realms of
culture, religion, and "other areas of mutual interest."[7] Gorbachev expressed a readiness to cooperate with Iran to strengthen its defense capability and allowed Rafsanjani to conclude his trip with a speech at a mosque in
Baku, the center of Shiite Islam in the republic of Azerbaijan. Before the
year was over, Shevardnadze again visited Iran, rail service was resumed
between the two countries, and agreements were signed for pumping Iranian natural gas to the USSR after a ten-year hiatus (operations began in May
1990). Gorbachev anticipated a take-off in Soviet-Iranian relations and
hoped to do as much with Soviet-Iraqi relations.

But his attempt to restore a businesslike relationship with both Baghdad
and Tehran was short-circuited by Iraq's invasion and occupation of Kuwait
on August 2, 1990. In this crisis, the first of the post–Cold War era, the
USSR found itself openly aligned with the United States and the overwhelming majority of the international community against Iraq. Though
unhappy at alienating a client of long standing, the détente with Washington
took precedence. Moscow voted for UN Security Council resolutions calling for withdrawal of Iraqi troops, the imposition of an economic and
military embargo, condemnation and invalidation of Iraq's annexation of
Kuwait, and, on November 29, 1990, it joined with the United States in
passing a resolution that sanctioned the use of "all necessary means to
uphold and implement" all relevant resolutions to restore international
peace and stability to the region. But all the while Moscow was doing its

best to persuade Saddam Hussein to back off from a confrontation with the United States–led international coalition that was poising for attack in Saudi Arabia. These efforts failed, and the result was Iraq's defeat.

One consequence of the Gulf War was to bring Moscow and Tehran even closer together. Both supported UN Security Council resolutions and the actions taken against Iraq; both maintained diplomatic relations with Baghdad all through the crisis and postcrisis period; and neither participated in military operations against Iraq. During and after the Gulf crisis, the two consulted regularly—in part to ensure that the United States did not take undue advantage of the fluid situation. For example, in early March 1991, USSR deputy foreign minister Aleksandr Belonogov met in Tehran with Iranian foreign minister Velayati to ensure that the cease-fire agreement was made permanent, that no moves were made by the United States to overthrow Saddam Hussein by force, and that a reliable system of regional security was based on an approach that took into consideration all realities—that is, Soviet and Iranian interests.[8]

Although the August 1991 attempt to depose Gorbachev failed—another instance of pathetic incompetence among the men with whom Gorbachev had surrounded himself—it seriously undermined the waning vestiges of Communist legitimacy. In a matter of four months the Soviet era was to come to a dramatic end, more rapidly than most foreign observers expected. Yet in the months immediately following Gorbachev's restoration to office, the affairs of state continued, almost as if nothing untoward had happened; after all, the Soviet Union was still a superpower and a powerful patron– protector of many Third World states.

One month after the coup attempt, in a gesture intended to reaffirm the importance of the new Moscow–Tehran connection, Gorbachev sent a personal envoy, Academician Evgenii Primakov, with a message for President Rafsanjani, informing him of recent domestic events and emphasizing the Soviet Union's continued active engagement in world affairs and its commitment to full cooperation with Iran "both through specific republics and the union as a whole."[9] In addition, according to an Arab journalist citing "informed diplomatic sources in Tehran," Primakov discussed Moscow's economic difficulties and requested that Soviet payments for the purchase of natural gas be deferred for the time being and that deliveries of gas be continued through the winter months.[10] Judging by Primakov's upbeat comments at the end of his visit, the Iranians agreed to the postponement. Primakov also noted that Middle East leaders with whom he had met, "while welcoming the processes of strengthening self-determination and sovereignty of the republics, consider it necessary that a united economic and military-strategic area of the USSR be preserved." They "want a USSR presence in the Near and Middle East, because this would preserve the balance of power. Nobody wants some power to maintain a monopoly position there. These states understand that our country creates an area of stability in this region with its new policy of non-confrontation with anyone, a policy oriented toward searching for ways of making interests coincide with those of other countries."[11]

When Velayati visited Moscow at the end of November 1991, he not only met with Eduard Shevardnadze (who had been reappointed foreign minister on November 19 after having been forced to resign the previous December over political differences with Gorbachev), but also signed a memorandum on the principles of political, economic, and cultural cooperation with Egor Gaidar, the deputy chairman of the Russian government, headed by Boris Yeltsin; and during unprecedented visits by an Iranian foreign minister to Kazakhstan, Kyrgyzstan, Tajikistan, Turkmenistan, Uzbekistan, and Azerbaijan, he concluded a variety of agreements that foreshadowed the formal establishment of diplomatic ties with these soon-to-be-sovereign republics a month later.[12]

Events quickly overshadowed Primakov's confident words. By the end of December, the Soviet Union was relegated to the realm of history.

Transformed Policy Determinants under Yeltsin

The sudden emergence of fifteen sovereign states from the chrysalis of the former Soviet Union raised completely new security considerations for Russia and Iran. As it adapted aims to capabilities and constraints, Moscow had to reassess the relative importance of long-established policy determinants. The following determinants affecting policy toward Iran during the Gorbachev and Yeltsin eras underwent extensive revision: geographic; strategic; ethnic; Islamic; economic; domestic (policymaking); international (constraints).

Geographic Determinants

Of all the altered facts and calculations in the relationship between Moscow and Tehran, none is more important than the end of a shared 1,200-mile border. After centuries of contiguity and conflict between the declining Iranian empire and the expanding Russian/Soviet empire, Russia is no longer a direct threat to Iran: a buffer zone of eight countries separates the two. Although shorn of 25 percent of its territory, Russia's land boundaries are actually slightly larger than during the Soviet period. The longest boundary is with Kazakhstan; it is also the most undelineated and ethnically parlous. Russian acceptance of the territorial status quo in Transcaucasia and Central Asia, at least for the foreseeable future, depends in great measure on the fate of the Russians living in this part of the Near Abroad (a term Russia has used since early 1992 to denote Russians residing in former Soviet republics). For Iran, the key to consolidation of the strategic buffer that keeps Russia at a distance is to foster nation-building in the new republics of the region.

Strategic Determinants

With the end of the Soviet Union, Russia's strategic situation changed overnight. Although still a formidable nuclear power, Russia's reduced size, population, resources, and equally vulnerable borders mean that Yeltsin's security concerns are quite different from Gorbachev's. First, they are primarily regional, more akin to those of the czarist era than the late Soviet era. In his magisterial work, William C. Fuller examines strategies that were successful in Russia's past and those that led to disaster. He notes that though expansion brought a measure of defensive cushioning against attack, it also resulted in the absorption of large numbers of non-Russian peoples, requiring maintenance in the borderlands of heavily garrisoned forces because, "if war came, there was the very real risk that Russia would find itself squaring off against a foreign aggressor while simultaneously combating an internal insurrection."[13] Imperial strategy was at its best during the seventeenth and eighteenth centuries, when Russia pursued its ambitions "patiently, rationally, and consistently" against its principal adversaries— Sweden, Poland, and the Ottoman Empire. By contrast, from the mid-nineteenth century on, its manifestly imperialist aims contravened the best interests of the empire's security: "Aggrandizement in Central Asia provoked a spiral of conflict with Great Britain . . . and expansion into Manchuria both impaired the empire's western defenses and brought about a calamitous war with Japan."[14] In the 1960s and 1970s, Moscow's neo-imperial overextension under Khrushchev and Brezhnev also gravely weakened the center, although this did not become clear until much too late in the Soviet period. Decision making lacked coherence "owing to the structure of autocratic politics" in which considerations of prestige often contradicted the needs of security of the state.[15] During the final decades of both the czarist and communist regimes, there was a mismatch between ambitions and capabilities, and a failure to apportion resources prudently or overcome Russia's economic and technological inferiority vis-à-vis major competitors. Russian strategists might benefit from a look back in order to prepare for the future. The parallels between past and present are useful and highly suggestive. Whether the postcommunist Russian leadership learns from them in restructuring the economy and society and in adapting defenses to realistic threats instead of remembered grandeur remains to be seen.

Second, Yeltsin's strategic relationship with the United States is also quite different from Gorbachev's. Whereas in the latter's case there was a grudging respect due from one superpower to another and a desire to reduce global tensions, in the former's case there is a superficial reconciliation based on a professed commitment to democratization and a market-oriented economy, and a gnawing sense of unease on both sides, as policy differences crystallize for which there are no obvious solutions.

Iran is one important area where Russian and American interests are adversarial rather than accommodative. Iran and Russia are both rethinking their strategic objectives, not just toward one another but also toward Transcaucasia and Central Asia where they are once again, as in the eighteenth and early nineteenth centuries, rivals. Russia is better informed on these regions, having ruled them for so long, but Iran may be better able to exploit certain linguistic, religious, and cultural affinities. Their competition will remain political and economic, not military, absent any Russian recourse to force in order to reincorporate former Muslim republics into its security sphere.

Ethnic Determinants

In the past, ethnic particularism and religion were suppressed or kept subordinated; seldom did they affect foreign policy decisions. But they will in the future. Although it has relinquished the non-Russian republics of the former Soviet Union, Russia is still in a quandary: should it develop as a Russian nation-state or as a pared-down revived imperial system? Russia's population today is about 160 million, of whom approximately 80 percent are Russians; the Soviet Union's population was about 293 million, of which the Russians constituted just a bit more than 50 percent. The fate of Russians living in Kazakhstan and Ukraine, in particular, will significantly affect Russia's policy toward these two countries.

In the absence of any military threats, currently unforeseen, Russia's security is not in jeopardy from any of the former Soviet republics. However, Russian secessionist movements—for example, in Ukraine's Crimean region or in northern Kazakhstan where Russians predominate—could quickly become priority issues on Moscow's foreign policy agenda. Political considerations, not the quest for resources or markets, make ethnicity a volatile force.

What happens in Turkmenistan, Uzbekistan, and Tajikistan will also have important consequences for Russian-Iranian relations. These nations contain sizable non-Russian ethnic minorities, the result of Stalin's deliberate policy of creating tactical union republics with borders that divided ethnolinguistic groups, the better to prevent the birth of nationalism. Having unexpectedly had independence thrust on them, the Muslim elites in the Central Asian republics are growing accustomed to ruling in their own nation-state. Their attachment to sovereignty over their own domain may transcend irredentist claims against their neighbors, thus giving less excuse for any manipulative Russian intrusiveness. The appeal of nationhood is a potent force. It may well serve to keep both Russia and Iran at bay, and in that way coincidentally foster pragmatic policies toward the other in both Moscow and Tehran.

Islamic Determinants

Islam is not unknown to Russia. There have been centuries of interaction between the two—first across porous borderlands, then through imperial expansion, conflict, and diverse attempts at absorption and co-existence, and finally the emergence in the late Soviet period of an Islamic renaissance "connected with the growth of nationalism and a slowly growing awareness among the intelligentsia that was reflected in the rebirth of Islamic traditions. This was most apparent in Central Asia."[16] What form Islam takes in the republics of the former Soviet Union will depend primarily on internal developments there that are largely beyond Russia's control. These, in turn, will be affected by the way Islam's multidimensionality coheres in different republics. Islam is at once a religious faith, a political identity, a code of ethics, and a cultural system, but this multidimensionality is rife with fault lines that produce different kinds of political systems and foreign policies. The challenge for Russian policymakers will be to deal with the Islamic nations and movements in their vicinity in ways that foster Russia's national interests.

The Islamic factor affects Russian foreign policy in three ways; Russia must contend with: the political demands and aspirations of the millions of Muslims living in the Russian Federation, some of whom seek virtual independence (Tatarstan and Chechnya, among others); the fate of Russians living under Muslim rule in the Near Abroad; and the intrusive efforts of Islamic states, primarily Turkey and Iran, but also Pakistan and Saudi Arabia, to influence developments in Central Asia and the Caucasus.

Economic Determinants

During the Soviet period, economic considerations accounted for little of what generated Moscow's policy toward the Middle East. Trade was desired—and relations with Iran in the late 1960s and 1970s were particularly fruitful in this regard—but primarily to promote diplomatic objectives. In 1955 Khrushchev had epitomized this thinking with his comment, "We value trade least for economic reasons and most for political purposes." Nonetheless, Moscow drove a hard bargain when it clearly had the upper hand; in the 1970s, Iran and Afghanistan sold their natural gas to the USSR at prices well below the going international rate because their alternative would have been no buyer at all. Still, it was strategic considerations, not economics, shaping Moscow's approach.

The post-Soviet Russian leadership has made the development of profitable economic relationships a top priority. It needs markets and reliable sources of hard-currency earnings. In this respect, no country looms more importantly than Iran, which covets what Russia can provide, namely, arms, an outlet for Iranian natural gas, and access to industrial equipment and advanced technology.

Domestic Considerations

Foreign policy is no longer the exclusive preserve of a small clique of top leaders. Its formulation in the post-Soviet period is susceptible to varied inputs, especially from parliament and the media. Although the constitution adopted in December 1993 vests exclusive authority over the conduct of foreign policy in the hands of the president, parliament can, nonetheless, exercise considerable influence if it can mobilize a clear consensus among the deputies. For example, through its strong statements it pushed the Ministry of Foreign Affairs (MFA) to become actively engaged in a search for a solution to the Bosnian crisis; it has also limited the government's flexibility in negotiating with Japan over the contested Kurile islands; and it has repeatedly drawn attention to the economic importance of good relations with the Arab states. In Russia's slowly evolving pluralistic political system, the president can no longer ignore the wishes of a parliament that is itself trying to establish a role in shaping the country's foreign policy—a policy that will "be the product of the conflicts and compromises that are an integral part of parliamentary government. In sum, foreign policy will be an unpredictable melange depending upon who gains the upper hand at different times and over different issues."[17]

International Constraints

Russia's leaders have yet to grasp fully the implications of the changes in the geopolitical structure of the Caucasus and Central Asia wrought by the breakup of the Soviet empire. Most of the new republics' trade is still with the Russian Federation, and military ties remain close, in large measure because republic leaderships want a Russian military connection as protection against internal challenges to their rule; but there is little to substantiate the thesis, increasingly heard in Western commentaries, that the empire is striking back, at least insofar as Central Asia is concerned. True, extremist voices like that of Vladimir Zhirinovsky proclaim their intention of restoring the empire, albeit peacefully, once the new republics succumb to their irreconcilable internal divisions and political ineptness.[18] But the Russian government, mindful of its need for international support and of the republics' membership in the United Nations and universal recognition as sovereign states, has been far more prudent in its policy pronouncements.

On January 25, 1993, the Ministry of Foreign Affairs issued a document entitled "Concept of Foreign Policy of the Russian Federation," which set forth in general terms the country's foreign policy agenda. With respect to Central Asia, the document recognizes an urgent need for protecting "the external borders of the Commonwealth" (CIS), and Russia's responsibility "for ensuring stability and human rights and freedoms in the space of the former USSR" and for negotiating treaties and agreements that provide human rights guarantees for Russians living outside the Russian Federation.[19] It can be interpreted as a kind of Russian "Monroe Doctrine," in which Moscow's aims are a combination of security, traditional great power manipulation of weaker neighbors, and strategic denial. The absence of a coherent neo-imperial ideology, the absorption with reform and transformation at home, the need for the West's good will in order to integrate Russia into the world economy and give it access to international credits and markets, the quest for stability on its southern tier, and the reluctance to use the military to impose political domination make it unlikely that there will be a repetition of the Bolshevik success in mounting an imperial comeback in the post-1917 period.[20]

Interestingly, in promulgating Russian aims in the Middle East, the MFA concept document has paragraphs on the importance of the Arab world, the Persian Gulf, Afghanistan, and Turkey, but virtually nothing of a direct nature on Iran. This notwithstanding, however, the reality of Russian-Iranian relations in the post-Soviet period is a full agenda that encompasses unrest in the Caucasus and Tajikistan, the civil war in Afghanistan, Gulf security, arms, and trade. Indeed, Russia's interaction with Iran is every bit as complex and intense as with the United States and the European powers.

Convergence

An ailing Russia and a pariah Iran are now brought together by much more than the overriding strategic considerations that underlay their accommoda-

tion in the past. Their relationship, complex and increasingly comprehensive, is driven by necessity and pragmatism, devoid of illusions or any of the
affinities—cultural, ideological, religious—that so often shape alignments
in periods when the danger of war is not a serious determinant of foreign
policy. The cooperation is prompted by calculations of mutual economic
advantage; by an interest in stability on their borders; and by a desire to
limit U.S. influence in the region. These convergent aims, noticeable particularly in the 1960s and 1970s, but then overshadowed by other considerations during the period of the Iran–Iraq War and Moscow's military
adventure in Afghanistan, again emerged at the end of the Gorbachev period, and have taken on new significance in the post-Soviet era. This time
the convergence portends a lengthy period of high-profile political accommodation. No lingering resentments threaten the process of Russo-Iranian
reconciliation, a striking contrast to the situation besetting U.S.-Iranian efforts to improve relations, which must first overcome persisting disagreements over the 1979–80 hostage crisis, Iran-supported terrorism in
Lebanon, Egypt, and elsewhere in the Middle East, Iranian assets frozen in
the United States, and an intense anti-Americanism that permeates influential Iranian clerics who accept Russia, the lesser Satan because of Ayatollah
Khomeini's 1989 letter to Gorbachev.

The Quest for Mutual Economic Benefit

The economies of both Russia and Iran are in trouble. Yet neither sees a
better prospect for commercial complementarity. Moreover, as Tehran as-
sesses the situation, tensions with the United States heighten the importance
of the Russian connection.[21]

The benefits that each foresees derive, first and foremost, from the exchange of Russian arms for Iranian oil and natural gas; second, from Russian industrial equipment and technology for oil and other goods; and
finally, from the development of infrastructure—railroads, bridges, natural
gas pipelines—that would expand trade between them and with the republics of Azerbaijan, Turkmenistan, Uzbekistan, Tajikistan, and Kazakhstan.

To Iran, Russia's key commodity is arms. The only great power that is
able and willing to provide Iran with the wherewithal it seeks to overcome
its military weakness highlighted during the war with Iraq, Russia has entered agreements for arms sales that go beyond those concluded in 1988
under Gorbachev. For the most part, Russian commentators defend the
sales, arguing that they will not destabilize the Gulf, and that U.S. criticisms
reflect more an interest in edging a competitor out of the lucrative Gulf
arms bazaar than in deterring the development of Iran's military potential.

Russia is selling a wide range of weapons. According to one think-tank, it is providing "multi-role combat aircraft, with the MiG-29 and 31 (the latter not yet supplied outside of Russia)" and Su-24 fighter-bombers, which are designed to make the Iranian Air Force "one of the strongest in the Gulf theater" by the late 1990s; air defense missile batteries and advanced radars; large quantities of T-72 main battle tanks and armored personnel carriers; surface-to-surface missiles; and three Kilo-class diesel submarines, "the most advanced non-nuclear submarine available." Moreover, all acquisition programs are planned with the embargo on arms sales to Iran during the Iran–Iraq War in mind to ensure "an unequivocal requirement that every transaction involve the transfer of self-production capabilities to Iran."[22]

The sale of the Kilo-class submarines, in particular, provoked strong U.S. objections. Apparently, it was arranged during President Rafsanjani's visit to the Soviet Union in June 1989 when, on a trip to Leningrad, "he was shown samples of Baltic Fleet naval armaments. These apparently impressed the president's advisers, leading to a long-term agreement on $6 billion worth of arms supplies."[23] The first Kilo was delivered to the Iranians in October 1992, the second in late 1993; the third, however, has not, as of early 1995, been delivered, in part out of a desire to accommodate to U.S. criticisms, but primarily because Iran has fallen behind in its payments. Moreover, Washington's allegations should be kept in military perspective, because the Kilo's primary threat is as a minelayer. Each Kilo "can carry 36 mines, which can be sown without surfacing."[24] True, such a capability, when linked to the acquisition of new aircraft and antiship missiles, enhances the Iranians' "ability to interdict naval shipping going through the Straits of Hormuz."[25] But minelaying is primarily a defensive tactic; certainly interrupting shipping in the Gulf would affect Iran as well as other states.

Indeed, Iranian sources maintain that their arms purchases are defensive and appropriate to Iran's situation. Regarding the purchase of the submarines, Mohammad Hasan Mohazeb, editor of the Tehran daily Abrar, observed:

> You seem to forget that we're not only a Persian Gulf power but that we also have a large window on the Indian Ocean. All countries bordering the Indian Ocean have full fledged navies. Why can't we have ours? Under the imperial regime [of the late Shah Mohammad Reza Pahlavi] the U.S. had convinced the Iranian Ministry of Defense to buy six U.S.-made submarines. The deal was canceled only days before the downfall of the shah.[26]

Moreover, Mohazeb noted, Iran spent far less on defense than countries such as Saudi Arabia and Iraq.

However, a year later, in March 1994, the Iranian parliament increased defense spending from 1.5 percent of the GNP to 2.5 percent, a rise that can be attributed to a combination of factors—inflation, the growing costs of military modernization, and higher prices for high-tech weapons. The increase is significant but consistent with a posture that is defensive in character.

A different and potentially more threatening aspect of Iran's military-related buildup is its development of a nuclear infrastructure capable of producing nuclear weapons. Iran has signed contracts with Russia and China to build major nuclear power plants. During a visit to Tehran in March 1993, Foreign Minister Kozyrev said Russia's assistance is predicated on Iran's continued acceptance of safeguards by the International Atomic Energy Agency (IAEA) and adherence to the nonproliferation treaty (NPT). During a seven-day inspection tour in June 1992, IAEA officials failed to uncover any evidence of diversions of fissionable material or of hidden industrial sites; in November 1993 it inspected previously unchecked sites without turning up any evidence of a secret nuclear weapons program.

Nonetheless, Western concerns persist. Iran's heavy investment in the acquisition of nuclear technology and its hiring of specialists from Russia, North Korea, Western Europe, and elsewhere conjures up Iraq's success in pursuing a clandestine nuclear weapons program, even while it permitted IAEA inspections of its established facilities. As was acknowledged by the deputy director of Russia's Kurchatov Atomic Energy Institute, which is involved in the building of an atomic power plant in Iran, specialists with classified information on nuclear weapons could easily slip across the border between Azerbaijan and Iran to work on military-related research.[27] Iran is, after China, Russia's most important customer for arms and the name of the game is hard currency. As such, its military buildup seems more likely to depend on the price of oil than on second thoughts in Moscow. Although it has signed multi-billion-dollar arms agreements, the actual deliveries appear to be spaced out over a period of years. Growing domestic difficulties require attention that may serve to discourage any sudden large-scale increases in military expenditures. In addition, other factors limit the scope and effectiveness of Iran's arms acquisition buildup:

> divisions within Iran's military; the lack of trained technicians, pilots, and other skilled personnel; the variety of equipment, complicating maintenance; uncertainty regarding supplies; the attempt to switch sources and types of equipment; the absence of significant domestic production capability despite frequent claims; and the attempt to rebuild and modernize across the board, which puts great strain on resources, both human and financial.[28]

Hence, even with Russia's extensive sales, Iran will need time to upgrade its military capability to the level it attained relative to its regional adversaries on the eve of the Iran–Iraq War.

Economically augmenting the benefits that Russia derives from arms sales to Iran is an extensive cooperation, as yet in its infancy, at the heart of which is the exchange of Iranian energy for Russian equipment and technology. The flow of energy, whether oil, natural gas, nuclear power, or water, fosters a conflict-containment attitude and a propensity toward joint projects. A case in point is natural gas. One result of the rapprochement between the Soviet Union and Iran in the mid-1960s was the construction of the Iranian Gas Trunkline (IGAT-1) from Khuzistan in southwestern Iran to the Soviet border at Astara, on the western coast of the Caspian Sea, where it connected with Soviet pipelines. Completed in 1970, IGAT-1 enabled Iran to sell its natural gas to the Soviet Union, and through it to Western Europe. Broken off during the Khomeini period, in large measure because of disagreement over pricing, commercial operations resumed at the end of the 1980s. But this was short-lived. With the collapse of the Soviet Union and the eruption of ethnic conflicts and internal struggles for power in Azerbaijan, Armenia, and Georgia, the flow of natural gas dropped. In time it will pick up. In June 1994, Iran seemed on the verge of contracting with Moscow to complete the construction of the nuclear power station near the southern Iranian town of Bushehr that had been started in the 1970s by two German firms but never finished because of the Iran–Iraq War. Fearing that its construction might acquire a military dimension, Germany decided not to resume the project. This opened the way for Russia to offer itself as contractor to complete the nuclear plant and, in the process, to expand Iranian-Russian relations in the field of power engineering.

Russia and Iran have a vested interest in seeing that regional political instability does not disrupt their bilateral cooperation. According to one member of Kozyrev's delegation to Tehran in March 1993, Moscow assured Tehran that it wanted to establish "a strategic partnership . . . aimed at securing stability in Central Asia and the Transcaucasus."[29] Iran's ability to pay for its imports from Russia depends on an improved system of transportation and unimpeded access to the natural gas pipelines.

With its enormous reserves of natural gas, Iran has ambitious plans for gas liquefaction plants and export terminals. To enhance the attractiveness of such proposals to international investors, it hopes to draw Turkmenistan, Azerbaijan, Armenia, Kazakhstan, and Uzbekistan into arrangements greatly expanding the existing network of pipelines without Russia, or reducing projected levels of Iranian-Russian economic cooperation. Iranian analysts emphasize that such pipelines will be environmentally user-friendly and accord with international pressures to use cleaner fuel and preserve the forests: "Another advantage of this proposal is the fact that its implementation and success require a high level of regional cooperation and dialogue."[30] In April 1992, Iran signed an agreement with Turkmenistan to pump gas to Mashhad whence a pipeline would eventually be built westward to link with IGAT-1 and IGAT-2 near Rasht; other lines could, the Iranians suggest, be constructed to Kerman and Bandar Abbas on the Persian Gulf, providing access to South Asia.[31] Tehran has emerged as "Armenia's only promising partner, given the 5-year economic blockade imposed by Azerbaijan, Turkey's hostile attitude and continuing chaos in Georgia," and it is receptive to the construction of a 166-kilometer gas pipeline from Tabriz to Mekhri.[32] It has also explored possibilities of providing Kazakhstan with an outlet to the sea for its oil, gas, and other commodities. Predating the end of the Soviet Union, Iran's courtship pressed for "the establishment of air travel between the capitals of the two countries, transit of goods between the two as well as exploitation of ports and shipping facilities at the Caspian Sea."[33] Since Kazakhstan became independent, Iran has intensified its efforts. During a visit to Almaty in October 1993, President Rafsanjani signed agreements for joint cooperation "in the fields of transportation, communication, agriculture, energy, marine matters, trade and industry, banking, customs and consular affairs."[34] Notable for their absence were cultural accords. President Nursultan Nazarbaev of Kazakhstan fears Islamic fundamentalism and prefers not to permit Iran to open book shops, which would be free to distribute speeches of Ayatollah Khomeini.[35] All the Iranian plans have been slow to materialize, requiring as they do considerable international investment, which has not been forthcoming, in part because of the U.S. government's opposition. With respect to Kazakhstan, China has been making far more rapid and impressive inroads than Iran.

An important adjunct of the expansion of Russian-Iranian economic ties is building the necessary infrastructure. Since the two countries no longer share a common border, the flow of their trade depends on the cooperation of the intervening republics of Turkmenistan, Kazakhstan, Uzbekistan, and Azerbaijan. In September 1993, a bridge connecting Turkmenistan and Iran across the Tedzhen (or Tajan) River was opened. It provides ready access between both the Serakhs (there is one town on each side of the border), and has two crossings, one for rail traffic, and one for vehicles and pedestrians. The railway line is a symbol of Irano-Turkmen cooperation. Turkmenistan is extending its railway line to the border; once the Iranians, who are still at the planning stage, construct a line from Sarakhs to Mashhad, linking the Turkmen and Iranian railways, "the world nations can draw upon a railroad starting from the port of Shanghai in the Pacific, and extending through northern China, Kazakhstan, Kirghizia, Tajikistan, Uzbekistan, and Turkmenistan republics. It will be subsequently connected through Iran and Turkey to the European continent and the Atlantic."[36] When completed, the rail lines across Eurasia would be the modern counterpart of the Old Silk Route of a thousand years ago. For its part, Russia has been supportive of efforts to develop the region's railways, but its current interest lies more in plans to expand the network of natural gas pipelines.[37]

Interest in Stability

Moscow and Tehran recognize that for trade to flourish, there must be stability in the region between them. Whatever their differences, which do exist (see below), they are for the time being secondary to the task of pushing economic relations. Thus, for example, during Rafsanjani's tour of Central Asia in October 1993, Radio Moscow opined that Iran had apparently given up on exporting Islamic fundamentalism, and was instead seeking mutually beneficial commercial ties with all the countries in the region.[38]

In the Caucasus, the two countries are working to negotiate a settlement between Armenia and Azerbaijan. Whatever agreement they can reach will probably leave Moscow in a stronger position than at any time since the collapse of the Soviet Union; but as long as Russia's military presence is kept limited, Iran may be satisfied. Russian peacekeeping forces did enter Azerbaijan (and Georgia), but only by invitation, and to date they have acted as if Moscow had in mind to play the role in Transcaucasia of a great power balancer rather than of resurgent neo-imperial state. Iran is apparently not beset by forebodings of Russian expansion.

Russia has maintained close military relations with Tajikistan, Uzbekistan, Turkmenistan, and Kyrgyzstan, in large measure because of requests from the pro-Moscow leaders of these republics, who desire a residual Russian military presence as defense more against domestic challenges than external threats; none of them fears a return of Russia's rule. All the treaties that Russia has signed with the four Muslim Central Asian republics reaffirm the inviolability of existing borders, which is somewhat reassuring to Iran: for Moscow to contravene them would be to incur strong international reactions. Still, the presence of Russian troops in Turkmenistan and Tajikistan along their borders with Iran cannot help but keep Tehran wary. (Kazakhstan's situation is different, bordering as it does on Russia and containing a sizable Russian/Slavic population that predominates in the northern half of the country.)

Meanwhile, Moscow supports Iran's attempts to foster regional economic cooperation—quite possibly because Tehran is not in a position to challenge Russia's special bilateral connections with the Central Asian republics. For example, the Organization for Cooperation of Caspian Sea Littoral States, Iran's Caspian Sea initiative advanced in October 1992, calls for collaboration by the littoral states—Russia, Kazakhstan, Turkmenistan, Azerbaijan, and Iran. It seeks ways to stimulate oil and gas extraction, environmental protection, and modernization of key ports. But the initiative may be premature. Judging by the successes and failures of other attempts at regionalism, the Iranian variant lacks the necessary preconditions for success—a community of market-oriented economies, decreasing control by the central government, a free-trade zone to attract investors, low tariffs, efficient customs operations, and so on.[39] Indeed, according to the Iranian ambassador to Russia, Nematollah Izadi, the breakup of the Soviet Union is still a strong factor adversely affecting Russian-Iranian economic relations. Direct rail service between Tehran and Moscow has been stopped, and air routes are dangerous. Izadi asserts,

> It is necessary to reequip the ports of the two countries on the Caspian Sea in order to create the possibility of service by sea, but railways linking the two countries must also exist. It is necessary to restore the railway link through Dzhulfa. It would be desirable for the problem of communications between the countries, which have a direct bearing on the daily life of the peoples, to be solved regardless of the conflicts and political disagreements.[40]

The institutions and infrastructure essential for regional cooperation are weak. Still, there is serious interest in closer economic ties, and this entails a commitment to political stability in the region.

The convergent Russian and Iranian interest in keeping their disparate long-term aims in the region from undermining their relationship can be seen in the policy each has followed toward the Azeri-Armenian war over Nagorno-Karabakh in the Caucasus and toward the civil war in Tajikistan. These two conflicts have been the most violent and most costly to erupt so far on the territory of the former Soviet Union.

Throughout the Soviet period, Armenia chaffed at the arbitrary administrative shift in the 1920s of the predominantly Armenian area of Nagorno-Karabakh to Azerbaijan. In 1988, emboldened by perestroika and Gorbachev's indecisiveness, it began agitating for the return of the enclave. Four years later, the Soviet Union having passed into history, "communal violence and escalating national passions" erupted "into an exhausting war of attrition that also helped bring down Azerbaijan's first democratically elected president, Abulfaz Elchibey."[41] Elchibey's setbacks at the hands of the Armenians on the battlefield and his systematic alienation of Russia undermined his position. Irate at his pro-Turkish orientation and his grant of extensive oil concessions to Western companies to the detriment of

Russia's economic interests, Moscow exploited Azerbaijan's growing instability by meddling in its political affairs. In late June 1993, a military coup with probable Russian support toppled Elchibey and Azerbaijan's ex–Communist Party boss, Haidar Aliev, returned to power as president along with Suret Huseinov, a free-booter and mysterious deal-maker with close ties to the Russian military, as prime minister. Soon afterward, Aliev joined the Commonwealth of Independent States (CIS) and canceled Elchibey's agreements with Western oil companies. A pleased Moscow's hand was evident in "the evisceration of the anti-Russian, nationalist" Elchibey government, and Moscow took part as well in the announcement of "the legal suspension of activities of a group called Sadval," a Moscow-based Azeri separatist group, and the halt to the anti-Azerbaijan propaganda of Russian newscasters, who switched to the phrase "Nagorno-Karabakh" instead of the "Republic of Nagorno-Karabakh."[42] The underlying objective for Moscow seems to be to nudge Azerbaijan, Armenia, and Georgia back into the Russian fold.

Iran has had a very limited role in the power play in the Caucasus.[43] The interest is there, the leverage is not. Sharing borders with Armenia and Azerbaijan, Iran has the immediate problem of dealing with the influx of thousands of Azeri refugees fleeing the fighting. It has been active from the very beginning in attempts to arrange a cease-fire in Nagorno-Karabakh and broker a settlement. Over the years, Russian foreign minister Andrei Kozyrev and Iranian deputy foreign minister Mahmud Va'ezi have met frequently in generally friendly circumstances. Early on, Va'ezi noted that Russia was affected by "the situation in Nagorno-Karabakh . . . more than anybody else."[44] Iran's helpful role has frequently been acknowledged by Russian officials. Stability demands peaceful borders. In an interview in Moscow, Iran's ambassador stressed this point:

> Neither man, nor government, functions for a single reason only. We do not want a war to continue near our border, and we are doing what we can for its cessation. The sides themselves ask for our impartiality, and we try not to disappoint their hopes.[45]

Iran also has good reason to fear destabilizing consequences of continued fighting. An adherent of Shiite Islam like Azerbaijan, it worries that its 15 million Azeris (twice the population of Azerbaijan) could become politicized and polarized along ethnic lines. The longer the war goes on, the more dangerous the unpredictable political fallout. Moreover, with Moscow wielding the strongest sword and ultranationalists in the Duma pressing for greater assertiveness in defense of national interests, Russia's military presence is becoming increasingly intrusive; and Moscow keeps trying to obtain the UN's imprimatur for its arrogation of the role of peacekeeper in the

Caucasus. For the moment, neither Azerbaijan nor Armenia is keen on "the return of Russian troops on a permanent basis."[46] In such a volatile environment, Tehran is intent on avoiding any confrontation. In late summer and early fall of 1993, an Armenian offensive close to the border prompted Tehran "to order its armed units to cross into Azerbaijan. The move elicited a strong reaction from Moscow," with Kozyrev declaring that "no matter what . . . [Iran's] motives are, [the move] cannot meet with our understanding or support," and the Iranians immediately withdrew their forces.[47] Between Russia's desire to reestablish a preeminent position and assume the role of arbiter in Transcaucasia and Iran's aim of encouraging the independence and peaceful coexistence of the region's new states in order to constrain Russia's neo-imperial impulses, there still exists considerable room for diplomatic maneuver under conditions that allow for continued good Russian-Iranian relations and regional stability.

In Tajikistan, the Russian-Iranian convergence is more difficult to sustain, because each favors different groups and holds a contrary view of what the solution should entail. Still, notwithstanding Russia's partnership and extensive military presence, on the one hand, and Iran's support of Islamist groups, including Afghan-based Tajiks mounting cross-border attacks, on the other, Russia and Iran are feinting rather than fighting. One explanation is the absence of a common border between Iran and Tajikistan; the other, the importance of the Russian-Iranian relationship.

The civil war that has been raging since independence is a product of the Soviet era, when clans from the districts of Khujand and Kulob monopolized the power they continue to try to retain. According to Olivier Roy, "Russia has followed no clear-cut strategy with regard to Tajikistan," and its military involvement on behalf of the government dominated by pro-Moscow ex-communists is a combination of concern over the possible spread of Islamic fundamentalism, the protection of the Russian minority, and the threat to Tajikistan from militants in Afghanistan.[48] One Western-based Tajik scholar, however, dismisses fears of a "fundamentalist threat":

> The political use of the word "fundamentalism" in Tajikistan originated when the Communist Party, rejuvenated after a short setback during the aftermath of August 1991 coup, began advertising itself as the savior of the people of Tajikistan against "Islamic fundamentalism." The word "fundamentalism" appeared in government newspapers and nationalist demands were described as subversive acts carried out by Islamists interested in creating an Islamic state.[49]

"Localism," not "Islamism," is, according to most observers, the principal divisive force. Iran did "make inroads in Tajikistan" because of historic linguistic (Tajiks speak a Persian dialect) and cultural affinities and of Tajikistan's need to find a "godfather" among foreign countries, especially at a time when Moscow, Ankara, and the West were courting the Uzbeks.[50] Uzbekistan's President Islam Karimov, who played an important part in persuading Moscow of the supposed "Islamic fundamentalist" threat in Tajikistan, is intent on his own long-term irredentist ambitions, because 25 percent of Tajikistan's population is Uzbek, and he may envisage a breakup of Tajikistan from which Uzbekistan could benefit.

Moscow has little cause for dissatisfaction over Iran's policy in Tajikistan. According to Shahrbanou Tadjbakhsh,

> Shiite Iran is much too cautious and too preoccupied with its own internal socio-economic problems to play a decisive role in the events of Sunni Tajikistan. . . . In fact, apart from verbal condemnation of the massacre of Muslims in Tajikistan [in January 1993], Iran did not openly support the opposition. . . .[51]

Since June 1994, talks have been held in Tehran between the Tajik government of President Imomali Rahmonov and the various opposition groups, with Iran and Russia working together to promote an inter-Tajik dialogue and an end to the fighting.[52]

Limit U.S. Influence in the Region

A final convergence of objectives between Moscow and Tehran, impossible to document with much precision but open to a compelling case on historical, geopolitical, and domestic grounds, is the desire to limit the influence of the United States in the Persian Gulf and, especially by Russia, in Central Asia.

Increasingly evident in the writings of influential Russian analysts is the theme that Russia's foreign policy priority is not the United States, Western Europe, or the World Bank, but relations with the republics of the former Soviet Union. According to Aleksei G. Arbatov, director of the Center for Geopolitical and Military Forecasts in Moscow, the uncritically pro-West orientation of the Yeltsin government came to an end "with the aborted presidential visit to Japan in August 1992. . . . The cancellation of the summit at the very last moment, and the incomprehensible official explanations of this erratic step, were the first time that Boris Yeltsin yielded so obviously to the nationalists' massive political campaign. The conservative offensive against the government's foreign policy has gained momentum ever since."[53] One harsh critique of Kozyrev's early stewardship even came from Andranik Migranian, a member of Yeltsin's Presidential Council:

Kozyrev and other Russian leaders substituted for one ideological purpose, Marxist-Leninist, in accordance with which it was essential to expand the Soviet model all over the world and counteract the policy of the United States and the West on all azimuths, another ideological purpose, in accordance with which there has since the liquidation of the CPSU and Marxist-Leninist ideology been a complete unity of goals and values between the United States and the West and Russia. Russia, according to this logic, automatically became a part of the civilized world community, and for this reason the need for the formulation of specific national-state interests of Russia in respect to the far abroad was no longer an issue. And as far as the Near Abroad is concerned, it was assumed that the former Union republics and the socialist countries of East Europe had immediately become wholly detached and independent and in respect to which Russia has no specific interests and that in respect to all current or newly emergent problems in these regions Russia would act with the United States and other Western countries, sharing with them joint responsibility for political and economic stability in these regions.[54]

Ranging far and wide in condemning what he considered to be unwarranted unilateral concessions to the West, Migranian cited, among other things, the "total absence" of a "positive" policy on the Gulf. Thus, at the time of the Gulf crisis, the Soviet Union, "on whose position the fate of the UN mandate for the realization of military intervention depended to a decisive extent," pursued a "romantic" foreign policy of support for the United States and the Western countries in the Security Council, based on "utopian and philanthropic considerations" for which it received nothing in exchange.[55]

The Russian government increasingly sees its national interest as lying in the assertion of a greater independence from the United States in its dealings with Iraq. Ever since early 1993, it has been reconsidering its position. For example,

[A]fter the U.S. air attacks on Iraq in January 1993, Russia expressed its concern over the scale of the attacks and gave warning that such attacks might require a new mandate from the Security Council. At about the same time, Sergei Glazev, the Minister for Foreign Economic Relations, stated that Russia had lost $2.5 bn in arms sales and had suffered other economic losses as the result of the UN embargo on Iraq.[56]

Clearly looking forward to Iraq's resumption of debt payments once the embargo on oil sales is lifted, Moscow has been conducting talks with Iraqi officials on trade and economic cooperation.[57] In the process, it hopes to mollify the ultraconservative groups who charge Russia with kowtowing to the United States and its ideologically driven anti-Saddam policy toward Iraq.

According to Viktor Posuvaliuk, Yeltsin's special representative in the Near East and the head of the North Africa and Near East Department of the

Ministry of Foreign Affairs, "Baghdad has already gone a considerable way toward compliance with UN Security Council Resolution 687," which requires Iraq to permit extensive disarmament and inspection procedures that ensure the destruction, removal, or rendering harmless, under international supervision, of (a) all ballistic missiles with a range of greater than 150 kilometers; (b) all nuclear weapons and nuclear weapons–related material and manufacturing facilities; and (c) all chemical and biological weapons.[58] Russia is obviously expecting that sanctions will be lifted in the not too distant future, and wants to be prepared for full-scale resumption of economic cooperation.

Moscow would like to see a diminished U.S. role in the Gulf. It shares Iran's position that whatever the faults of the Iraqi regime, "the United States has not been empowered to solve the problems in the region."[59] But unlike Iran, Russia has chosen not to make an issue of the matter. It accepts U.S.—and great-power—involvement in Gulf affairs. For the moment, it is in no position, nor does it have any reason, to engage the United States on questions of security in the Gulf. In contrast to Iran, Russia did not raise any objections to the defense cooperation agreement concluded between the United States and Kuwait in September 1991; indeed, in late November 1993, it signed one of its own with Kuwait, to Iran's displeasure. Still, there is a shared underlying interest by Russia and Iran in limiting U.S. influence so as to give them a greater opportunity to exercise some of their own. Moreover, from Moscow's perspective, there is fear of a reconciliation between the United States and Iran, leaving Russia, again, the odd country out in the Gulf. Remembering the Reagan administration's clumsily handled attempt to open a dialogue with Iranian "moderates," Russia was quick to interpret Clinton's postinaugural comments on Iraq and Iran as presaging an effort to improve relations with Iran.[60]

Divergences

In the post-Soviet period, important differences have emerged between Russia and Iran. Although none is likely to jeopardize their businesslike reconciliation, each perceptual and policy difference is potentially significant, and together, they are a constant reminder to the two countries of how much separates them. The divergences may be examined under three headings: strategic-military, cultural-political, and regional.

Strategic-Military Divergences

With the end of the Soviet Union, the tone for Yeltsin's foreign policy was set early on by Foreign Minister Kozyrev, who stated that "joining the civilized world" is in Russia's interest, and that national security would be fostered by reducing arsenals and strengthening relations with neighbors. The preliminary report on foreign policy drafted by the Russian Ministry of Foreign Affairs in early 1992 emphasized the importance of developing "ties of alliance with the United States and other Western countries, with NATO, and with the West European Union, as well as the maximum use of multilateral agreements for creating both a global security system and its regional analogues. Russia acts on the assumption that no country is its enemy; thus, it does not intend to use force other than for the purpose of repelling aggression."[61]

This strategic blueprint, associated with Kozyrev, was quickly challenged by Sergei Stankevich, another Yeltsin adviser. Stankevich conceded that the emphasis on the United States and Germany was "rational, pragmatic and natural: That is where the credits are, that is where the aid is, that is where the advanced technology is." But a Western orientation, he argued, ignores the unique historical-cultural alloy of Slavic and Turkic, Orthodox and Muslim, elements that ought to constitute an integral part of any Russian foreign policy. Geopolitically, Russia must work closely not only with countries that are situated to the south of the former Soviet republics, but also with those far afield such as Mexico and Brazil in Latin America, South Africa, India, and Southeast Asia.[62] Stankevich's exposition remains more of a countervailing concept to Kozyrev's Western orientation than a clearly developed "Eastern" complement or alternative, but it is symptomatic of the continuing flux in Russia's perceptions of its strategic interests.

With respect to the Gulf, most Russian analysts would agree with Victor Posuvaliuk's comment to an Arab journalist:

> Russia reserves for itself the right to be represented in the general surroundings [of the Middle East], including the regions adjacent to our southern borders. I find the questions concerning our presence in the Gulf, for example, surprising. Russia is a superpower and a permanent member of the Security Council, and it possesses one of the world's biggest fleets. It is natural that we would be present everywhere to ensure our interests, without competing with anybody.[63]

Such an all-encompassing approach to the Arab countries of the Gulf Cooperation Council was rooted in Gorbachev's policy of normalizing relations with all countries instead of relying primarily on radical, anti-American states, such as Iraq and the People's Democratic Republic of Yemen (PDRY). As a consequence, noted one Russian journalist, Moscow discarded its former "inflexible policy principle that, 'a friend is always right'—a policy that untied the hands of its ideological clients, so that they felt free to engage in all sorts of adventures, including military escapades, with full confidence that Moscow would support them. . . . The recent history of Iraq serves as an eloquent example of it."[64] Instead, Moscow's interest is "to achieve political stability as a vital precondition of economic renewal," and it is pursuing this in the Gulf in cooperation with the moderate Arab countries. Economic possibilities have whetted Russia's strategic interest. To help open broader channels for its commerce, Moscow is receptive to defense cooperation agreements with GCC countries nervous over Iran's growing regional assertiveness and eager for protective great powers.

Iran would prefer that no great power maintain a military presence in the Gulf. Soon after becoming president in June 1989, Rafsanjani told a Tehran audience that the time for outside powers' being invited in to police the Gulf was past. Iran, he said, is opposed "to the existing policy which entails seeking protection from foreigners and guaranteeing security through a foreign naval presence. We find this absolutely unacceptable"; the Gulf does not need a policeman, he said, nor does Iran want "to become the policeman":

> An excuse they [Western powers] frequently put forth is that the proximity of the Soviets to the Persian Gulf necessitates their presence here. I believe this is no longer the case. In the Gorbachev era, the Soviets have assumed a correct posture. For now and the foreseeable future, a Soviet threat in the Persian Gulf is nonexistent, especially when you take into consideration the friendly and constructive relations between the Islamic Republic and the Soviet Union. We believe that we have insured the security of this region from the northern flank and we will continue to coexist in peace and tranquility. There is no reason for their presence in the south. It serves no purpose for them to remain. The only reason is to provoke us so we will fight one another. Hence, if there are any points of contention among us, we should resolve them ourselves. Although we are the largest country in the region, although we have the longest coastline, and although we are one of the oldest nations in the region, we are willing to cooperate with the smaller nations in the region—even if others are reluctant to do so.[65]

As long as Russia aspires to involvement in the Gulf and elsewhere in the Middle East, tensions between Moscow and Tehran arising out of differing strategic perceptions and agendas are inevitable.[66] Russia's growing ties to the United States and Israel, Iran's oft-identified "most dangerous" enemies, cannot help but make Iran uneasy and fearful of some kind of American-Russian collusion.[67]

Cultural-Political Divergences

Since the late Soviet period, decision makers in Moscow have been increasingly concerned about Islam for domestic as well as external reasons.

Khomeini's Islamic revolution and the war Moscow waged in Afghanistan had intensified an interest in ethnicity and religion among the Soviet Union's 60 million Muslims. By Gorbachev's time, under glasnost, national movements such as *Birlik* (Unity) in Uzbekistan and *Rastokhez* (Resurrection) in Tajikistan were becoming politicized and broadening their base.[68] Broadcasts and literature originating in Iran found receptive audiences among some intellectual and traditionalist Muslims in the countryside. However, the undercurrents of restiveness did not threaten Soviet rule.

In the post-Soviet period, Moscow has more cause for continual monitoring of Iran's Islamist impact and militant Islam, because what happens in Central Asia and Azerbaijan impinges on Russia's security. By contrast, what happens in the Arab world is of marginal interest to Moscow, which considers that to be the West's problem. Russian assessments (like those of their Western counterparts) differ greatly. Viacheslav Ushakov, a leading journalist, is not disturbed by the desire of Ayatollah Ali Khameni, Khomeini's successor as Iran's foremost militant cleric, to spread the Iranian revolution:

> The policy of exporting the Iranian revolution to other countries, including the new Central Asian states ... [centers on] dispatching thousands of Muslim preachers and mullahs to propagandize "all-conquering" Islam, and Tehran is giving active financial assistance with building mosques abroad, training officiants, and distributing the Koran and other religious literature. The Central Asian republics are now the target of radio propaganda—mainly religious in content—from Tehran, Qom, and Mashhad, which, as a rule, is conducted in the local languages and dialects. Iran is ... urging ... their people to follow the Islamic path of development and presenting itself as a model and an example of true progress.[69]

But Ushakov concludes that cultural programs and propaganda are not enough to establish Iran's influence in the region. What the new republics, which are "experiencing great economic difficulties," need is financial, economic, and technical aid, and Iran, which has its own socioeconomic problems, is in no condition to provide these. Even when a country embraces its Islamist vision and theocratic approach to rule, one Western journalist observed, Iran does not show itself a generous patron-proselytizer, as in the case of Sudan where it refused to provide desperately needed petroleum until payment in cash had been forthcoming.[70]

Aleksei Vasil'ev, director of the Russian Academy of Sciences' Africa Institute, fears that Russia is being pressed to take a position in the confrontation between the West and Islam and, in the process, may unnecessarily incur high costs. He sees three basic threats to Russia associated with its coming to terms with Islam.[71] First, there is the problem of its dealings with countries of the Muslim world outside of the former Soviet Union: "Following the twists and turns of Western political behavior, Russia may get into confrontation with countries with which it has no contradictions," for example, with Iran and Libya, "which have taken no anti-Russian actions on the governmental level ... if continued, such behavior will inevitably further weaken the already greatly deteriorated position of Russia in the Moslem world." A second and even greater threat may eventuate if Russia fails "to launch a dialogue and cooperation with the Moslem nations of the Near Abroad." The issue is not just one of economic dislocation or "difficulties along thousands of miles of common borders," but "the fate of Russian-speaking populations in the former Soviet republics. The ghost of Bosnia and Herzegovina is stalking Central Asia and Transcaucasia." Finally, the character of Russia itself is threatened; Russia must come to terms with Islam for its own health, not just its security:

> A special feature of Russia's historic development and geostrategic position is that it has not just lived next to the Moslem world; Russia has been as it were within that world, it was a border situation not only in the geographical sense. The confrontation between the two civilizations has been going on for a thousand years, but there has also been an intermingling and interaction of the cultural, sociopolitical and anthropological aspects.

Though for different reasons, Vasil'ev argues, like Ushakov, that Islamic fundamentalism is no real threat to Russia. Admitting that "applying historical parallels to fundamentalists may be risky," he nonetheless emphasizes that, thus far, militant Islam has gained virtually no foothold among Moslems in Russia. This could change, however, if ignorance and misconceptions between non-Muslims and Muslims are exploited rather than dissipated and if the "interethnic crisis continues to deepen."[72]

D. Malysheva, a researcher at the Russian Institute of World Economics and International Relations, emphasizes the complexity of the political-religious situation in Central Asia and of the challenge confronting Russia.[73] A rebirth of ethnic nationalism and religious commitment is occurring, but it is too early to determine whether the net result will be stabilizing or destabilizing. The threat comes not from Islam, but from "political Islam or Islamism." For the time being, political Islam is not able to play "a major mobilizing role in the region":

> There are no influential and well-organized Muslim parties and movements in the region with traditions of political struggle, and there are no charismatic leaders capable of compensating for the lack of political organizations and rallying the other Muslims. Islamism is opposed by the still monolithic and rigid regime in the region.[74]

Although the waning of Russia's influence in Central Asia "could kindle the political ambitions of neighboring states and intensify the struggle for spheres of influence," Malysheva feels the present situation, which is characterized by the dominance of "moderate Muslim currents" that want to maintain historic ties to Russia, is promising enough to warrant a guarded optimism about the future.

The above sampling of current Russian assessments is fairly typical. Emerging from all of them are three political judgments about the cultural ideological challenge of Islam. First, Russia's Islamic problem is quite different from the West's. Second, the specter of militant Islam, which for the moment is evident in significant fashion only in Tajikistan, may owe more to the fractious aftermath of the Soviet withdrawal from Afghanistan and the lobbying of Uzbek president Karimov for a Russian military presence in Tajikistan than to Iranian intriguing. Third, Iran's state-to-state relations with Russia have been pragmatic and proper. Notwithstanding the militancy of the Khomeini-minded clerics, Rafsanjani's policy has been one of restraint. Iran's foreign policy bears a resemblance to China's during the "revolutionary" years of Mao's "Great Proletarian Cultural Revolution" (1966–70): toward countries on its border, Beijing was moderate and even conciliatory; toward those in noncontiguous, far-off areas, it was stridently ideological and "revolutionary." Iran's role, intensely debated in the West, in shaping the policy of the Lebanese fundamentalist Shiite movement— Hezbollah ("Party of God"), with which it is intimately associated—is important but far from absolute. According to a leading specialist on the movement, although Iran is Hezbollah's main backer, "Khomeini did not issue direct orders to Hezbollah in the operative sphere. Hezbollah faced the dilemma of interpreting not only God's silence, but Khomeini's."[75] Attributing instability in Central Asia or Transcaucasia to Iranian behavior is even more problematic, given the traditional cultural-political divide between Shiite Iranians and Sunni Turkic peoples.

Regional Issues

A region in which there have been divergent interests is Tajikistan. For a time before and after the civil war that broke out in May 1992, the Iranians proceeded on their own, believing that "their close linguistic and cultural ties with the Tajiks" afforded them special access. But they soon learned that the struggle was not one of "the Muslims against the infidels," but was clan-driven.[76] This prompted Tehran to suggest to Moscow that the two act together.[77] Their efforts have yet to bear fruit, but Iran has been Russia's most helpful partner in trying to find a political solution. Each, however, may still try to buttress the position of its preferred client(s).

Any consideration of Russian and Iranian interests and involvement in Tajikistan's civil war must also bring in the Uzbek and Afghan factors. Tehran knows that Uzbekistan, which is close to Moscow and suspicious of Iran, would like to keep its traditional enemy Tajikistan weak, and that it continually pushes for a strong Russian military intervention as the way to prevent a spread of Islamic fundamentalism. Afghanistan is quite a different situation. In the course of the Tajik civil war, Tajik oppositionists fled to neighboring Afghanistan. As a condition for a political settlement, they want a guarantee of safety for refugees wishing to return from Afghanistan. Tajikistan's President Imomali Rahmonov has countered with a demand for a cessation of cross-border attacks by Tajik oppositionists aided by fundamentalist and anti-Russian Tajiks living in the area of northeast Afghanistan controlled by Ahmed Shah Massoud, the noted mujahiddin ("freedom-fighters") commander. Himself a Tajik, Massoud is not known to be pro-Iranian, and in the region under his control he has promoted a moderate Islam.

After Moscow invaded Afghanistan in December 1979, Iran funneled assistance mostly to the eight pro-Khomeini Afghan Shiite parties that it helped organize. In the words of author Graham Fuller, "Tehran has sought to promote the Afghan Shi'a as Iran's primary means of influencing Afghan politics. . . ."[78] But with the withdrawal and subsequent collapse of the Soviet Union, the different mujahiddin groups began forming tactical alliances in an attempt to seize power. The main fighting has taken place around Kabul and in the predominant Pushtun-speaking areas where the seven Sunni groups, who were based in Peshawar (Pakistan) during the Soviet occupation of Afghanistan, operate. Of the thirty provinces of Afghanistan, only Bamiyan, located in the center of the country with a large Hazara population, is controlled by a coalition of pro-Iran Shiite parties. Bamiyan, together with Herat, Farah, and Nimroz, which border Iran, has been quiet and friendly with Tehran. Elsewhere in Afghanistan, Iran's influence appears to be limited. It has little leverage over the Tajik nationalist groups in northeastern Afghanistan who are intent on toppling the Rahmonov regime in Dushanbe, Tajikistan.

A second region of possibly divergent interests is the Persian Gulf. Border disputes plague all the countries in the Gulf, but when Iran is involved, the Arabs close ranks, polarizing the environment. Russia's courtship of the Arab-constituted Gulf Cooperation Council (GCC), which mistrusts Iran's territorial, political, and ideological aims, might lead it to uphold Arab claims against Tehran.

When Britain withdrew from the Gulf in November 1971, Iran and the newly established United Arab Emirates (UAE) agreed that Lesser Tunb

and Greater Tunb—two uninhabited islands in the Strait of Hormuz—
would go to Iran, and that the nearby island of Abu Musa was "to be
managed by a kind of *de facto* condominium in which Iran" and the UAE
maintained their claims to sovereignty, even while "each cooperated with
the other in an arrangement which could be characterized as an 'agreement
to disagree.' "[79] Iran's forces occupied part of the island for security purposes, and the UAE (formerly called Sharjah) administered and maintained
jurisdiction over the other part. Iran ended this arrangement in April 1992
when it seized control of the entire island, alleging national security considerations.[80] The GCC states condemned the Iranian action, but by mid-1993
the furor subsided, in part because Iran claimed that the disagreement was
due to a misunderstanding, but mainly because the GCC was not able to
generate support in the UN Security Council for a major showdown with
Iran. Throughout, Russia maintained a strict neutrality, in contrast to the
Western powers, which criticized Tehran's policy. Another ongoing Iranian-
Arab dispute is between Iran and Iraq over the Shatt-al-Arab estuary, and it
awaits negotiation of all the issues associated with their recent eight-year war.

Bosnia is another potential area of divergence. There have been reports
of Iranian arms shipments to the Bosnian Muslim government in Sarajevo,
in contravention of the UN embargo of arms to all parties to the conflict.[81]
Should the level of fighting intensify as a consequence of an influx not only
of arms but also of "volunteers," Moscow's pro-Serb outlook could prompt
a strong reaction that would adversely affect Russian-Iranian relations.

All of this, of course, is speculation. The reality is that for the time being
common concerns transcend competitive ambitions. As long as the governments in Moscow and Tehran remain committed to their present priorities
in Central Asia and Transcaucasia, their relationship is solidly grounded in
congruent interests.

Regional Implications

In its approach to regional politics in the past, Moscow reacted to, rather
than initiated, events; it proved adept at exploiting opportunities provided
by developments over which it had little control. Relations with Iran serve
as a case in point. During the Soviet period, overtures from the shah ushered in a period of Soviet-Iranian accommodation. Relations deteriorated
during the Iran–Iraq War, but afterward, with Khomeini's encouragement,
they again improved. In the post-Soviet era, Rafsanjani's conciliatory and
pragmatic course has suited Moscow's needs and outlook. But Moscow
could compromise its own purposes if it once again tries, as it did in the
Soviet period, to establish equally close and beneficial relations with all

parties in the Gulf region. This could lead to its being manipulated by one side or the other in a regional dispute—Iran or Iraq, Iran or Saudi Arabia, Iraq or Kuwait—with the result that it must alienate Iran or a key Arab state; or if it equivocates, it could end up with attenuated ties to all parties. Either way, the net effect would be to heighten the importance of a U.S. connection for one or more parties in the region.

In the post-Soviet period, Russia and the United States have generally cooperated in the Middle East in pursuing the commonality of goals that crystallized in the late Gorbachev period—to oppose aggression, foster peaceful resolution of regional conflicts, counter terrorism, and prevent proliferation of nuclear and unconventional (chemical and biological) weapons. A similar complementarity of interests and outlook does not extend to the Near Abroad regions of former Soviet republics in Central Asia and Transcaucasia, but there has been no case that has yet turned critical enough to force either side to take a stand that would test the limits of their accommodation.

Moreover, looming as a problem in U.S.-Russian relations is Iran, the regional power of the future in the Gulf. To the extent that Moscow builds it up militarily, Russia must incur the resentment of the GCC states and the hostility of the United States. The GCC states' fear of Iran is rooted in history, the fragility of their status as nation-states and of their political legitimacy, and the military potential of Iran, whose population is three times that of the GCC states and larger than that of all the Arab populations of the Gulf-Arabian Peninsula region combined. Russian arms sales to Iran will result in intensified GCC efforts to obtain U.S. security guarantees, and will thereby ensure Washington's active involvement and military presence in the region—a situation both Moscow and Tehran oppose.

For the moment, political and economic expediency prevail. Strategic myopia keeps each political actor riveted to a narrow national agenda in which domestic considerations are increasingly controlling. Looking ahead, the "guesstimate" here is that as long as Iran does not challenge Russia's position in the Near Abroad areas of Central Asia and Transcaucasia, Moscow and Tehran are embarked on a long-term cooperation that will be limited primarily by what Russia can deliver and by the degree of stability in the new republics—the land bridges between them.

Notes

1. Rouhollah K. Ramazani, *Iran's Foreign Policy 1941–1973* (Charlottesville: University of Virginia Press, 1975), pp. 333–38.

2. Oles M. Smolansky and Bettie M. Smolansky, *The USSR and Iraq: The Soviet Quest for Influence* (Durham, NC: Duke University Press, 1991), pp. 233, 258–79.

3. Mohiaddin Mesbahi, "Gorbachev's 'New Thinking' and Islamic Iran: From Con-

tainment to Reconciliation," in *Reconstruction and Regional Diplomacy in the Persian Gulf*, ed. A.H. Entessar (New York: Routledge, 1992), p. 269.

4. As quoted in Mesbahi, ibid.

5. Ibid., pp. 269–70.

6. Ibid.

7. FBIS-SOV, June 26, 1989, p. 19.

8. FBIS-SOV, March 7, 1991, pp. 20–21.

9. FBIS-SOV, September 19, 1991, p. 9.

10. Safa Ha'iri, "Primakov Reaches Deal With Hashemi-Rafsanjani," Al-Hayah (London) in Arabic, September 19, 1991, as translated in Foreign Broadcast Information Service, *Daily Report, Soviet Union* (hereafter FBIS-SOV), September 23, 1991, p. 10.

11. FBIS-SOV, September 23, 1991, p. 11.

12. FBIS-SOV, November 29, 1991, p. 42; and FBIS-SOV, December 3, 1991, p. 22.

13. William C. Fuller, Jr., *Strategy and Power in Russia 1600–1914* (New York: The Free Press, 1992), p. 452.

14. Ibid., p. 457.

15. Ibid., p. 458.

16. Alexei V. Malashenko, "Islam versus Communism: The Experience of Coexistence," in *Russia's Muslim Frontiers*, ed. Dale F. Eickelman (Bloomington: Indiana University Press, 1993), p. 67.

17. Jan S. Adams, "Who Will Make Russia's Foreign Policy in 1994?" RFE/RL Research Report, vol. 3, no. 6 (February 11, 1994), p. 40.

18. For example, Aleksandr Prokhanov's interview with Vladimir Zhirinovsky in *Zavtra*, no. 6 (February 1994), pp. 1–2, as translated in FBIS-USR/Russia, March 9, 1994, pp. 4–10. See also the interview with Dmitrii Rogozin, who is chairman of the irredentist-oriented Congress of Russian Communities in *Moscow News* (May 13–19, 1994), p. 2.

19. FBIS Report: Central Eurasia: Foreign Policy Concept of the Russian Federation, March 25, 1993, pp. 4–5.

20. Mohiaddin Mesbahi, "Russian Foreign Policy and Security in Central Asia and the Caucasus," *Central Asian Survey*, vol. 12, no. 2 (1993), pp. 210–12.

21. FBIS/Russia International Affairs, June 17, 1993, pp. 15–16.

22. *The Middle East Military Balance 1992–1993* (Tel-Aviv: Jaffee Center for Strategic Studies, 1993), pp. 144–48. See also, Shahram Chubin, "Iran's Strategic Aims and Constraints" (pp. 72–74), and Michael Eisenstadt, "Déja Vu All Over Again?: An Assessment of Iran's Military Buildup" (pp. 99–117) in *Iran's Strategic Intentions and Capabilities*, ed. Patrick Clawson (Washington, DC: National Defense University, April 1994).

23. FBIS-SOV, April 7, 1992, p. 13. That an agreement to sell the submarines was signed during the Gorbachev period was confirmed by then Speaker of the Russian Supreme Soviet, Ruslan Khasbulatov, during a trip to Saudi Arabia. *Komsomol'skaia pravda*, June 10, 1992, p. 1.

24. "Iran Goes Shopping for a Navy," *Navy News and Undersea Technology*, April 11, 1994.

25. Philip Finnegan, "Iran Navy Buildup Stirs U.S.-Arab Response," *Defense News*, December 6–12, 1993, p. 1.

26. As quoted in Claude van England, "Iranian Military Renewal: Keeping Up with the Gulf," *Christian Science Monitor*, March 4, 1993.

27. Kirill Belianov, *Literaturnaia gazeta*, January 20, 1993, as cited in *Commonwealth of Independent States and the Middle East* (hereafter referred to as CIS/ME), vol. 18, no. 1 (1993), p. 23.

28. Shahram Chubin, *Iran's National Security Policy: Capabilities, Intentions and Impact* (Washington, DC: The Carnegie Endowment for International Peace, 1994), pp. 38, 40.

29. CIS/ME, vol. 18, no. 4 (1993), p. 5.

30. Narsi Ghorban and Mohammad Sarir, "Oil and Gas: An Outlook for Future Cooperation among the Persian Gulf States," *The Iranian Journal of International Affairs*, vol. 5, nos. 3–4 (Fall/Winter 1993/94), pp. 749–50.

31. Ibid.

32. FBIS-USR/Caucasus, December 15, 1993.

33. FBIS-SOV, November 29, 1991, p. 56.

34. FBIS-SOV/Central Asia, October 26, 1993, p. 64.

35. Nazarbaev's juggling act includes attempts to court as well as balance Russia and China, and the United States and Iran. For example, he received President Rafsanjani and Secretary of State Warren Christopher both on October 24, 1993.

36. Abbas Maleki, "Iran's North Eastern Border: From Sarakhs to Khazar (The Caspian)," *The Iranian Journal of International Affairs*, vol. 4, nos. 3–4 (Fall/Winter 1992), p. 626.

37. FBIS-SOV/Russia International Affairs, April 8, 1994, p. 10.

38. Radio Moscow in Persian, October 19, 1993, 1600 GMT. See also, Dmitry Volsky, "Iran—Central Asia: Export of Commodities, and Not of Ideological Merchandise," *New Times International* (October 1993), pp. 57–65.

39. Robert D. Hormats, "Making Regionalism Safe," *Foreign Affairs*, vol. 73, no. 2 (March/April 1994), p. 102.

40. Interview with Leonid Mironov, "On the Foundation of Islamic Values," in *Aziia i Afrika Segodnia*, no. 7 (July 1993), pp. 13–16, as translated in FBIS-USR/Russia, September 22, 1993, p. 50.

41. Karen Dawisha and Bruce Parrott, *Russia and the New States of Eurasia* (New York: Cambridge University Press, 1994), p. 87.

42. Thomas Goltz, "Letter from Eurasia: The Hidden Russian Hand," *Foreign Policy*, no. 92 (Fall 1993), pp. 115–16.

43. Goltz's article, for example, makes no mention of Iranian intriguing in Azerbaijan or Armenia. Ibid.

44. FBIS-SOV/Russia, March 31, 1992, p. 14.

45. Vladimir Abarinov, "The Third Way," *Nezavisimaia gazeta*, February 9, 1993, p. 4.

46. Elizabeth Fuller, "Russia, Turkey, Iran, and the Karabakh Mediation Process," *RFE/RL Research Report*, vol. 3, no. 8 (February 25, 1994), p. 33.

47. See Oles M. Smolansky, "Russia and the Transcaucasus: The Case of Nagorno-Karabakh," chapter 8 in this volume.

48. For an informative assessment of the Tajik situation, see Olivier Roy, *The Civil War in Tajikistan: Causes and Implications* (Washington, DC: United States Institute of Peace, December 1993).

49. Shahrbanou Tadjbakhsh, "The Bloody Path of Change: The Case of Post-Soviet Tajikistan," The Harriman Institute *Forum*, vol. 6, no. 11 (July 1993), p. 5.

50. Roy, *Civil War in Tajikistan*, p. 24.

51. Tadjbakhsh, "The Bloody Path of Change," p. 5.

52. FBIS-SOV/Russia International Affairs, September 20, 1994, pp. 4–5; and FBIS-SOV/Russia International Affairs, October 12, 1994, p. 9.

53. Alexei G. Arbatov, "Russia's Foreign Policy Alternatives," *International Security*, vol. 18, no. 2 (Fall 1993), p. 24. See also Suzanne Crow, "Why Has Russian Foreign Policy Changed?" *RFE/RL Research Report*, vol. 3, no. 18 (May 6, 1994), pp. 1–6.

54. Andranik Migranyan, "Russia and the Near Abroad: Formulation of a New Foreign Policy Course of the Russian Federation," *Nezavisimaia gazeta*, January 12, 1994, pp. 1, 4, in FBIS-USR/Interstate Affairs, February 14, 1994, p. 14.

55. Ibid.

56. Roland Dannreuther, "Russia, Central Asia and the Persian Gulf," *Survival,* vol. 35, no. 4 (Winter 1993), p. 108.

57. Moscow ITAR-TASS, April 7, 1994, in FBIS-SOV/Russia International Affairs, April 8, 1994, p. 15.

58. Ivan Menshikov, "Moscow Is Active: And Gives Notice of Its Special Role in the Region," *Segodnia*, March 12, 1994, p. 5, in FBIS-SOV/Russia International Affairs, March 30, 1994.

59. Vladimir Abarinov, "The Third Way."

60. Vladimir Abarinov, "Intrigue with an Unexpected Outcome," *Nezavisimaia gazeta*, January 28, 1993, p. 4.

61. As quoted in FBIS-SOV, March 3, 1992, p. 32.

62. *Nezavisimaia gazeta*, March 28, 1992, p. 4.

63. *Al-Hayah* in Arabic, September 17, 1992, p. 5, in FBIS-USR/Russia, October 2, 1992, p. 50.

64. A. Shumilin, "Tell Me Who Your Friend Is in the Middle East: The Interests of Russia Require Its Presence in the Area of the Persian Gulf," *Komsomol'skaia pravda*, February 4, 1993, p. 3, in FBIS-USR/Russia, March 6, 1993, p. 58.

65. Address by Ali Akbar Hashemi Rafsanjani, president of the Islamic Republic of Iran (translated by Jubin Goodarzi), *Middle East Journal*, vol. 44, no. 3 (1990), pp. 463–65, excerpts.

66. See Viacheslav Ushakov, "What Is Impeding Cooperation?" *Pravda*, July 24, 1993, 3 in FBIS-USR/Russia, August 18, 1993, p. 66.

67. Iran's nervousness at a perceived move by the United States to establish a military presence in the area was evident when one of its admirals charged—erroneously, as matters turned out—that Kazakhstan had invited U.S. naval forces to operate in the Caspian Sea. Moscow INTERFAX in English, February 24, 1994, in FBIS-SOV/Central Asia, February 25, 1994, p. 4; and "Kazakhstan Accused of Inviting U.S. Forces," *Washington Times*, February 28, 1994, p. 7.

One Western scholar maintains that "what deeply concerns Iran is the exclusionist approach of both the United States and the GCC states to the future security of the Persian Gulf, largely because of their continuing suspicion of Iran's intentions." R.K. Ramazani, "Iran's Foreign Policy: Both North and South," *Middle East Journal*, vol. 46, no. 3 (Summer 1992), p. 403.

68. Yaacov Ro'i, "The Islamic Influence on Nationalism in South Central Asia," *Problems of Communism,* vol. 39, no. 4 (July/August 1990), pp. 57–59.

69. Viacheslav Ushakov, "Iran's Islamic Card—Will It Be Played in Central Asia?" *Pravda*, March 3, 1993, p. 3, in FBIS-SOV/International Affairs, March 10, 1993, p. 5.

70. Charles Richards, "Tehran's Minaret Casts Thin Shadow over Middle East," *The Independent* (London), June 19, 1993.

71. Aleksei Vasil'ev, "Difficulties Can Be Overcome. Is Islamic Fundamentalism Such a Threat to Russia?" *Nezavisimaia gazeta*, March 11, 1994, p. 5, in FBIS-USR/Russia, April 6, 1994, pp. 97–100.

72. Ibid., p. 98.

73. D. Malysheva, "Central Asia—Muslim Challenge to Russia?" *Mirovaia ekonomika i mezhdunarodnye otnosheniia*, no. 12 (December 1993), pp. 10–14, in FBIS-USR/Interstate Affairs, February 14, 1994, pp. 38–40.

74. Ibid., p. 39.

75. Martin Kramer, *Hezbollah's Vision of the West* (Washington, DC: The Washington Institute for Near East Policy, 1989), p. 12.

76. Sergei Tsekhmistrenko, "Adamishin Prods Tajik Opposition toward Compromise," *Kommersant-Daily* in Russian, March 6, 1994, p. 4, in FBIS-SOV/International Affairs, March 8, 1994, p. 1.

77. This is a far cry from June 1992, when President Rafsanjani greeted the then president of Tajikistan, Rahmon Nabiev, on his first official visit, with an offer of "all-round assistance," and the seeming invitation to a special relationship. (Nabiev was deposed in September 1992 and died in April 1993).

78. Graham E. Fuller, *Islamic Fundamentalism in Afghanistan: Its Character and Prospects* (Santa Monica, CA: RAND, 1991), p. 15.

79. Shahram Chubin, "The Persian Gulf: After Desert Storm and Before the New World Order," *Middle East Monitor*, vol. 2, no. 1 (March 1993), pp. 27–28.

80. For details, see Richard Schofield, "Disputed Territory, the [Persian] Gulf Cooperation Council and Iran," *Iranian Journal of International Affairs*, vol. 5, nos. 3 and 4 (Fall/Winter 1993/1994), pp. 626–30. Schofield observes that the GCC condemnation of Iran contrasted, "of course, with its traditional reticence to comment publicly on rifts between member states themselves, whether or not these involved territorial disputes, and also disputes with Arab neighbors of the GCC."

81. John Pomfret, "Iran Ships Material for Arms to Bosnians," *Washington Post*, May 13, 1994, p. 1.

Part II

CIS and Iran

3

Ukraine and Iran

Oles M. Smolansky

Ukraine proclaimed its independence in December 1991. Soon afterward, Kyiv embarked upon an active policy of establishing relations with the countries of the Middle East, paying special attention to the Islamic Republic of Iran. In retrospect, it is obvious that Ukraine's decision to pursue an active policy in the Middle East had been prompted by economic as well as political considerations. Of these, as soon became apparent, the former was a more important factor than the latter. Nevertheless, both had an impact on the Ukrainian decision makers and were deeply rooted in the socioeconomic and political situation that had developed in Eurasia after the dissolution of the USSR.

Specifically, to appreciate the magnitude of the economic problems that Kyiv was facing in the early 1990s, it is important to keep in mind that, before the collapse of the Soviet Union, Ukraine was consuming approximately 65 million tons of petroleum a year. The bulk of that amount (some 55 million tons) was imported from Russia while the rest was produced in Ukraine itself. The situation regarding natural gas was also bleak—only 15 to 20 percent of the country's requirements were met from domestic production. The rest was being supplied by Russia and Turkmenistan. (The latter satisfied 28 percent of Ukraine's needs.) The shortage of fuel made itself felt in 1992 and has grown progressively worse since. The problems, as Kyiv saw them, were twofold: On the one hand, Ukraine's own production of oil and gas continued to decline, creating increased reliance on imports from its traditional suppliers. On the other hand, the latter were facing economic crises of their own, making it more difficult for them to meet Kyiv's demands. It might be noted in passing that the decrease in fuel extraction had not been caused by the demise of the USSR. Although the latter remained the world's largest petroleum producer well into the 1980s, extraction began to decline due to the exhaustion of the old wells and the lack of advanced technology, to mention but two prominent problems. At the same time, the breakdown of the old order obviously did not help matters and, in the early 1990s, the general economic malaise affected the energy sector as well.

In any event, the export of oil and gas to independent Ukraine became a hostage to economic restraints (the size of the quotas and the price of the fuel) as well as to political manipulation. Specifically, as differences between Ukraine and Russia began to mount, revolving around such issues as nuclear weapons, the Black Sea Fleet, and the Crimea, economic pressure in the form of withholding supplies and of raising prices was used in an attempt to wrest political concessions from Ukraine. From Kyiv's perspective, this was an unacceptable state of affairs. As one official put it in early 1992, if not attended to early and effectively, "an energy shortage may strangle Ukrainian independence."[1]

Not surprisingly, Kyiv began searching for ways to escape its predicament. Some officials believed that Ukraine had no choice but to continue cooperating with Russia and Turkmenistan, while others felt that Ukraine would be well advised to find new suppliers of fuel. In this connection, the oil-rich Persian Gulf region of the Middle East suggested itself as a logical source of petroleum and, possibly, of natural gas. Iran, in particular, was mentioned as a partner with whom Ukraine should enter into close economic cooperation. It was recognized that such a relationship entailed serious logistical, technical, and financial problems. The Persian Gulf oil would have to be shipped to Ukraine at a time when it possessed neither a tanker fleet nor adequate terminals to receive large amounts of fuel. In addition, Ukraine had no refineries capable of processing much more than 3 million tons of Iranian oil, characterized by a high sulphur content. (Most of the west Siberian "light," refined in Ukraine, does not fall into this category.) Finally, and most importantly, according to the experts at the Ukrainian Ministry of Economics, Kyiv would need to pay $6 to $8 billion a year (in retrospect, an inordinately large estimate) for Iranian petroleum and gas while in 1991 exports had netted Ukraine only 6 billion rubles (approximately $55 million).[2] Nevertheless, by early 1992, it appeared that Kyiv had decided to seek a solution to its fuel problems by means of cooperation with Iran.

Ukraine's interest in the Islamic Republic can be attributed to several factors. Exhausted by the long war against Iraq, Iran found itself in a difficult economic position in the late 1980s and early 1990s, prompting Tehran to look for new commercial opportunities. More developed industrially than its Arab neighbors (with the exception of the oil and petrochemical sectors), much of Iran's infrastructure had been created with Soviet assistance. It now required new machinery as well as spare parts and maintenance expertise, which Ukraine was in a position to provide. In addition, Iran was hoping to expand its petroleum and gas production, and fuel-hungry Ukraine looked like a potentially promising partner. It also represented a vital link in ambitious gas and oil pipeline projects, designed to transport Iranian fuel to the markets of Western Europe. All of these considerations combined to create an image of a mutually attractive economic environment and a base upon which bilateral relations could be built. Moreover, the bulk of Iran's armed forces had been equipped with Soviet-made weapons. Ukraine, which had inherited large quantities of them, was thus in a position to provide replacements, spare parts, and training. Finally, Tehran welcomed the breakup of the USSR because the emergence of independent states in Transcaucasia and Central Asia not only weakened its ancient enemy but also created a buffer zone between Iran and Russia. The leaders of the Islamic Republic were well aware that in Eurasia, Ukraine had the potential to emerge as an important counterweight to Russia and its possible future urge to reestablish the empire. For all of these reasons, Iran recognized Ukraine's independence earlier than most other states and then proceeded to establish close cooperation with it.

Rapprochement

As subsequently disclosed by First Deputy Premier Kostiantyn Masyk, one of the chief architects of the Kyiv–Tehran rapprochement, five days after Ukraine's independence had been approved by a national referendum, held on December 1, 1991, an Ukrainian government delegation flew to Baku (Azerbaijan) and met with a group of Iranian and Azeri officials. Negotiations between them yielded the initial tripartite "protocol of intent . . . on cooperation in the field of the oil and gas industry."[3] In January 1992, a high-level Iranian delegation, which included members of parliament, financiers, and economists and was led by Foreign Minister Ali Akbar Velayati, arrived in Kyiv and was warmly received by top Ukrainian officials. President Leonid Kravchuk, in particular, stated that Ukraine wished "to establish profound, good relations with Iran." Diplomatic relations between the two states were established during the visit and a "memorandum of understanding," which provided for economic cooperation, was signed. Also raised by Foreign Minister Anatolii Zlenko was the question of some eighty Ukrainian POWs, held by the Afghan mujahiddin. Velayati promised Tehran's assistance in seeking their release.[4]

Fuel must have figured prominently in the talks between Velayati and the Ukrainian officials, as attested to by the arrival in Kyiv a short while later of Oil Minister Gholam Reza Aqazadeh-Kho'i. Kyiv Radio explained that the government's interest in negotiating "possible deliveries of [Iranian] oil" had been aroused by Russia's use of its "monopoly right," as evidenced by its decision to raise the price of petroleum. Moscow's resolve "forced [Kyiv] to look for more profitable partners" in the Middle East and in the Commonwealth of Independent States (CIS). (The broadcast referred to the visit to Ukraine by Prime Minister Hasan Hasanov of Azerbaijan, whose arrival coincided with that of Aqazadeh.)[5]

On January 29, 1992, Kyiv and Tehran concluded an agreement that provided for the delivery to Ukraine of 4 million tons of petroleum and of 3 billion cubic meters of gas a year. In return, Ukraine undertook to supply Iran with petroleum products, chemicals, building materials, machinery, and machine tools.[6] Aqazadeh announced that Iran would purchase from Ukraine "300,000 tons of billets and the same amount of scrap iron and other goods," while Moscow Radio added that Kyiv also intended to supply Iran with raw materials (including manganese ore), "industrial installations," foodstuffs, as well as arms. Not only did Kyiv inherit large quantities of weapons from the former USSR (three Soviet military districts had been located in Ukrainian territory), but its defense industry was also suffering huge losses due to vastly reduced demand.[7] The supposition that arms had been a part of the deal appeared to have been borne out by public pronouncements of some Ukrainian functionaries. Masyk, for one, said that Kyiv was in a position to supply Tehran with weapons as part of the concluded four-year deal. In any event, on paper it looked like the "contract of the century," as *Izvestiia* put it, and an elated Masyk spoke of eventual Iranian deliveries to Ukraine of 75 billion cubic meters of gas and 50 to 70 million tons of oil a year.[8] These were enormous figures; even much lesser amounts would have effectively broken Russia's stranglehold on the Ukrainian economy.

Another grandiose agreement, signed by Ukraine, Iran, and Azerbaijan, provided for the construction of three pipelines, intended to transport natural gas from Iran's southern fields to Europe via Azerbaijan and Ukraine. According to Aqazadeh, the construction was to start in 1992, with the first pipeline becoming operational in 1996. The initial annual capacity of 25 billion cubic meters would eventually be increased to 75 billion.[9] As subsequently noted in *Keyhan* newspaper (London), Ukraine and Iran undertook jointly to "provide the equipment and tools necessary to build the pipeline." Its construction and operation would be managed by a company for which Azerbaijan would provide 10 percent of the capital, and Ukraine and Iran

45 percent each. *Izvestiia* estimated the building cost at some $7 billion.[10] Finally, Aqazadeh revealed that the two countries were also negotiating a deal to construct an oil pipeline. With an annual capacity of 50 to 70 million tons, it would become operational in 1996 and would carry Iranian petroleum to Ukraine and Central and Western Europe.[11]

Although Kyiv's and Tehran's motives were understandable, it was obvious even in early 1992 that, in their public pronouncements, the two governments chose to overlook the major difficulties their extravagant plans were bound to face. For example, some experts from the Russian Ministry of Fuel and Energy were wondering why Ukraine, Azerbaijan, and Iran had chosen to disregard Russia, which offered the "optimal route" for the projected pipeline. In fact, Moscow had been neither consulted nor asked to participate in the undertaking, leaving unanswered the question of how the Iranian gas was going to be transported from Azerbaijan to Ukraine. Specifically, if Russia was to be bypassed, the pipeline would have to cross Armenia and/or Georgia, ending in a terminal on the east coast of the Black Sea. From there, it would have to be shipped to Ukraine by sea—a cumbersome and impractical arrangement. Moreover, the political situation in Transcaucasia—with conflicts in Nagorno-Karabakh and, later, Abkhazia—did not lend itself to sustaining an enterprise of such magnitude.

The Russian specialists noted also that their country could supply gas to Ukraine if Iran undertook to satisfy the requirements of southern Russia. The existing pipeline network could be used for such purposes, making it unnecessary to build new pipelines. In retrospect, it seems obvious that Russia was being excluded deliberately—at least for the time being—but Kyiv's and Tehran's understandable desire to go it alone was bound to run into the Russian obstacle. In any event, the Ministry of Fuel and Energy pointed out that the Iranian gas was likely to compete with the Russian exports, which were then meeting approximately 30 percent of Europe's requirements. For all of these reasons, Moscow made it clear that it would oppose the construction of a new gas pipeline on its territory.[12]

Transit rights aside, and given the enormous cost of the undertaking, it was not clear who was going to provide the capital necessary to finance this ambitious project. What should have been obvious was that neither of the three signatories, nor all of them combined, possessed the means to proceed with the pipeline construction. The same conclusion applied to the projected oil pipeline. In addition to the construction costs, Kyiv had to be concerned about its ability to pay for the 4 million tons of petroleum a year, which Iran undertook to deliver in 1992 and beyond. At the cost of some $120 per ton, the transaction carried a price tag that no Ukrainian government could realistically expect to meet. Even with the projected barter of Ukrainian raw materials, goods, and foodstuffs, the financial burden was likely to become unbearable. Under these circumstances, the sale or barter of military equipment would have to become an integral part of the deal. Nor was it by any means certain that Iran would be able to absorb all the goods that Ukraine seemed anxious to offer. Over and beyond all this, there were also logistical problems. As alluded to above, the transportation, storage, and refining of even 4 million tons of Iranian oil presented Kyiv with serious difficulties. But even if they could be overcome, this amount would not have solved Ukraine's petroleum problems.

Nevertheless, undeterred by these uncertainties, Kyiv and Tehran pushed ahead. In early February 1992, they signed a memorandum on developing economic relations and set up a permanent commission on transportation.[13] Later in the month, Masyk visited Tehran and met with Aqazadeh and Minister of Mines and Metals Hussein Mahlujchi. According to the Iranian account, Masyk and Aqazadeh discussed the ways of implementing the January accords. However, even at this early juncture, it was becoming apparent that the sweeping agreements would not be easy to implement. For example, Aqazadeh reiterated Iran's willingness to sell oil to Ukraine. However, since the latter had no hard currency, it would have to sell some of its products to Iran. To work out the details, he expected, would require time. The same applied to the problems connected with the construction of the pipelines: they could be solved only by conducting "thorough studies by Iranian and Ukrainian experts." Finally, with respect to the delivery of 3 billion cubic meters of Iranian gas to Ukraine, Aqazadeh agreed in principle to go through with the deal but cautioned that "the price and the time of delivery" had to be negotiated first. In other words, Kyiv was given to understand that no early solution to its energy problems could be expected from Iran. Masyk's negotiations with Mahlujchi, in contrast, appear to have been more successful. The Iranian minister stated that, in 1992, his country would purchase from Ukraine iron ore, rolled steel, and spare parts for the Soviet-made equipment at the Isfahan steel mill. Tehran was also interested in purchasing Ukrainian coal.[14]

Although the subject had not come up in public statements issued during these negotiations, the Russian media again suggested that Kyiv was interested in selling arms to Tehran. Moscow Radio, broadcasting in Farsi, said that Iran had made its petroleum available for "some extremely attractive goods or advanced technology" and that Ukraine could offer it some of the latest weapons. One of the few instances when the topic was discussed publicly occurred during a press conference held at the Ukrainian Ministry of Foreign Affairs soon after Masyk's return from Tehran. When asked about Ukrainian arms sales to Iran, a spokesman replied that Kyiv was "not engaged in this business." But he also made it clear that the issue was of vital interest to Ukraine because it did manufacture weapons and because it was "necessary . . . to do something with them." It was also essential to convert military-related industries to civilian production, a task that required considerable resources.[15] Otherwise, in March 1992, the Iranian minister of transportation visited Kyiv and signed a letter of understanding that provided for cooperation in establishing "air, sea, road and railway connections" between the two states. It was agreed that the pertinent ministries would conduct "feasibility studies on the transit of Iranian goods to Europe."[16]

The above-mentioned problems in Ukrainian-Iranian relations notwithstanding, the two governments pursued their rapprochement in late spring 1992. While Tehran continued to see in Ukraine a potentially attractive political and economic partner, Kyiv was driven by its frustration with Russia's economic and political policies as well as with the perceived intransigence of Turkmenistan, which kept raising the price of gas to levels that Ukraine found unacceptable. The high point of the interaction occurred in April, when President Kravchuk paid an official visit to Iran.

Judging by the official accounts, the presidential visit was very successful. Before departing, Kravchuk stated that the two countries had "laid the foundations of close [bilateral] cooperation" of a "peaceful character," and that this represented no threat to third countries (meaning Russia) but was designed to allow Ukraine and Iran "to influence the political situation in Europe and the Middle East." (He did not elaborate.) Five documents, including the fifteen-year Treaty of Interstate Relations between Iran and Ukraine, were signed during the visit, dealing with technological, economic, commercial, and political cooperation between the two states. According to *Izvestiia*, the sale of military equipment was also discussed, but the negotiating sessions were reportedly dominated by the issue of Iranian economic aid to Ukraine. In this connection, Aqazadeh reiterated that, in 1992, Ukraine would receive between 4 and 5 million tons of Iranian oil. He also provided additional details on the tripartite gas pipeline project. The first fifty-six-inch-diameter pipeline was scheduled to be built within a three-year period and would be financed, in part, by the not otherwise identified "international financial sources."[17] The construction of two additional pipelines, each with an annual capacity of 25 billion cubic meters of natural gas, would begin in 1996.[18]

Otherwise, Kravchuk expressed an interest in expanding "political, economic and cultural cooperation" between Ukraine and Iran. Iranian President Ali Akbar Hashemi Rafsanjani echoed these sentiments but added that

Tehran and Kyiv "can jointly work toward establishment of world peace, security and regional stability." He did not elaborate, but during the meeting between the foreign ministers, Velayati went on record welcoming Ukrainian-Iranian cooperation "in the Black Sea and the Persian Gulf region"—a curious formulation since Iran is not a Black Sea power and Ukraine is not a Persian Gulf power. Given these facts, it would appear that Tehran was interested in using its Ukrainian connection to counterbalance Turkey in the Black Sea area. (It will be recalled that the two Middle Eastern neighbors were engaged in a fierce competition in Transcaucasia and in Central Asia, regions where Ukraine did exert some influence.) Conversely, reference to the Persian Gulf constituted a thinly veiled attempt to secure Kyiv's diplomatic and political support in Iran's latent and open conflicts with some of its Arab neighbors, notably the United Arab Emirates and Saudi Arabia. However, the Ukrainian officials appeared determined to steer clear of these unnecessary entanglements. Foreign Minister Zlenko diplomatically acknowledged "the role [played] by Iran in the sensitive Middle East region"—a formulation so general as to be innocuous—and referred to Tehran's and Kyiv's efforts to help resolve the conflict in Nagorno-Karabakh.[19]

On the political plane, Tehran attempted to boost Kyiv's position in the ongoing competition with Moscow while seeking Ukraine's backing in its rivalry with Turkey and the United States. Thus, while Rafsanjani praised Kravchuk's "crucial role" in the establishment of the CIS (that is to say, in the dissolution of the USSR), the *Tehran Times* noted that "one of the primary tasks which Ukraine has been and is still preoccupied with will be to act as a counterpoise to the power of Russia." In this pursuit, Ukraine and the other former Soviet republics enjoyed Iran's full support. The *Tehran Times* also warned them to "stay clear of reliance on other [i.e., Western] powers that may have ulterior motives even as they come to . . . [the newly independent republics'] aid."[20] In any event, the effort to drive a wedge between Ukraine and Turkey, and Ukraine and the Western powers, proved futile. Nor did Kyiv, as noted, subscribe to the Iranian position in the Persian Gulf.

In the ensuing months, Ukraine and Iran continued their efforts to broaden economic cooperation. In mid-May 1992, they signed a letter of intent on cooperation in the extraction and processing of coal and, in late July, an Iranian industrial exhibition opened in Kyiv. Nevertheless, according to the Ukrainian media, oil was expected to remain Iran's main export item to Ukraine. In return, Tehran would receive "the most sophisticated measuring instruments, farming machinery, and metallurgical raw materials." In September, the list was broadened to include "metal and mining equipment."[21] But the main event of the summer was the official signing in

Baku, in July 1992, of the tripartite agreement to proceed with the construction of the gas pipelines. According to Moscow Television, the cost of the
project had, in the meantime, risen to $12 billion, of which Ukraine and Iran
were to contribute $5.5 billion each. How they (and Kyiv in particular) were
to come up with that amount was left unexplained. It might be noted parenthetically that, at the same time, Tehran also engaged a French company to
conduct "the necessary technical studies . . . concerning the possibility of
exporting Iranian gas via Turkey."[22]

Gradual Cooling of Relations

Nevertheless, in the fall and winter of 1992–93, it had become obvious that
the urgency of the earlier contacts no longer marked Iranian-Ukrainian
relations. To be sure, in December 1992, President Abulfaz Elchibey of
Azerbaijan—the third party to the pipelines accords—visited Kyiv and
signed a treaty of friendship and cooperation between Azerbaijan and
Ukraine. His discussions with Kravchuk covered a number of subjects,
ranging from Ukrainian mediation in the Nagorno-Karabakh conflict to the
future of the CIS, which neither president, at that time, had much use for.
With regard to the fuel problem, the leaders said merely that an agreement
providing for the delivery of the Azeri oil would be signed in due course
and that its volume would depend on Ukraine's ability to supply Azerbaijan
with food products.[23]

Nor was much progress being achieved in Kyiv's relations with Tehran.
One indication was provided in February 1993, when it was announced that
the cabinet of ministers had "allocated $1.8 million to state corporation
'Ukrgaz' to form the Ukrainian part of the statutory fund in the joint Iranian-Azeri-Ukrainian company," charged with the construction of the gas
pipelines between Iran and Ukraine.[24] Considering that a whole year had
elapsed before any action on the project was taken—a year marked by
severe fuel shortages in Ukraine and by Kyiv's frantic efforts to secure
additional supplies from its traditional sources (Russia and Turkmenistan)—it was obvious that the Ukrainian government was not taking the
idea seriously. If Kyiv had not totally given up on the plan, it had at least
come to the realization that implementing it would prove much more difficult than originally thought. Timing aside, the allocation of less than $2
million to the statutory fund provided another illustration of the above
contention.

This certainly appears to have been the impression evoked in Tehran,
which, for reasons of its own, had remained committed to the project. Iran's
interest was not difficult to understand. Hard-pressed domestically and con-

fronted with Washington's determination to isolate Tehran politically and economically, the Islamic Republic was looking for both political reassurances and, even more importantly, for new outlets for its exports, above all oil and natural gas. As already noted, the Iranian government believed that Western Europe in particular was interested in purchasing sizable quantities of Iranian gas. Tehran also found in Azerbaijan and Ukraine two states that had expressed an interest in the pipeline projects. Russia remained a major problem, since Iranian gas would compete with Russian gas for the Western European markets. Nevertheless, it was apparently felt in Tehran (though, perhaps, not in Kyiv) that, given sufficient incentives, Moscow would eventually be brought around to accept the proposed pipeline network.

In any event, the extent of Iran's annoyance with Ukraine's footdragging was revealed during Aqazadeh's second visit to Kyiv, which took place in February 1993. As reported by Moscow Radio, during his meeting with Supreme Council Speaker Ivan Pliushch, the oil minister expressed hope that this visit would prove more productive than the first and called upon the Ukrainian government to "hasten up the implementation of . . . [bilateral] agreements on cooperation." Aqazadeh reminded Pliushch that an agreement on the supply of 4 million tons of Iranian oil had been signed a year ago and that the term of the contract was about to expire. Lack of progress, he added, was "due to Ukrainian procrastinations." The same was true of the gas pipeline agreement: "Ukraine [had] failed to make its contribution to the venture." The minister went on to say that "Iran was selling oil on the world market for hard currency, but could deliver it to Ukraine, as an exception, on a barter basis." In return, Tehran would accept not only industrial and agricultural products but also weapons, needed to modernize the Iranian armed forces. In this connection, Aqazadeh disclosed that Russia had previously agreed to supply Iran with all the military equipment it needed. "However," he added, "Iran could have a similar agreement with Ukraine."[25] It might be noted in passing that requests for arms are not usually made in public. Therefore, Aqazadeh's use of a public forum provided but another illustration of the degree of Tehran's annoyance with Kyiv's failure to live up to the agreements negotiated in early 1992.

Pliushch's remarks were also interesting. According to Moscow Radio, the Speaker "expressed anxiety over the dragged-out solution of [the] cooperation problems" and blamed Kyiv for the failure to "adopt a decision on the payment of Ukrainian contribution to the joint gas supply venture." Given the frequently strained relations between the government and the parliament, blaming the executive branch came easily to the Speaker of the Supreme Council. Nevertheless, leveling such accusations in the presence of foreign dignitaries is a practice not ordinarily sanctioned by diplomatic protocol. Equally unusual was Pliushch's statement that Ukraine would not sell (or barter) weapons to Iran.[26] As noted, similar sentiments had been expressed previously by some members of the government. Hence, the Speaker's emphatic rejection of the possibility was probably intended to rebuff those officials who wished to engage in the lucrative arms trade. Otherwise, Pliushch spoke in favor of promoting Tehran–Kyiv relations and of implementing the 1992 accords. This meant, in part, "the starting of the Iran–Europe gas pipeline project which is to transit Ukrainian territory." Finally, Pliushch promised to instruct "the appropriate commission of the Ukrainian parliament to see to it that the oil deal would be honored."[27]

On the executive side, Aqazadeh met with First Deputy Prime Minister Ihor Iukhnovs'kyi. According to an Iranian account, the talks dealt mainly with "economic, commercial, scientific, industrial and technical" cooperation between the two states, including the construction of the gas pipeline. In this connection, Aqazadeh noted that "several European countries . . . [had] already shown interest . . . [in] purchas[ing] Iranian gas." For his part, Iukhnovs'kyi "expressed Ukraine's willingness to purchase oil from Iran and [to] provide cereals, industrial goods and mineral[s] . . . in return." He also invited Tehran to invest in Ukraine's aircraft industry.[28]

The major achievement of Aqazadeh's visit was the signing, on February 12, 1993, of an economic cooperation agreement. It specified that, in 1993, Iran would supply Ukraine with 4 million tons of petroleum, the same amount that should have been (but was not) delivered in 1992. In return, Iran would receive unspecified amounts of sugar and wheat. Should Kyiv prove unable to deliver these commodities, it would have to reimburse Tehran in cash. Since Ukraine has no tanker fleet of its own, the oil would be delivered in Iranian vessels. The countries also refined their gas pipeline agreement. According to Aqazadeh, it would pass through Azerbaijan, Russia, and Ukraine, initially delivering 25 billion cubic meters of gas to Western Europe, mainly Germany. "On the basis of this agreement, Iran and Ukraine will each receive 45 per cent of the income from gas transport and Azerbaijan will get the remaining 10 per cent."[29] What Russia would get out of this and why it should agree to cooperate was once again left unexplained. It is noteworthy, however, that Iran did not consider itself as Russia's competitor in the context of the fuel exports to Ukraine. Rather, as Aqazadeh put it, Tehran was merely acting "in the framework of international rules of free trade." Be that as it may, the agreement specified that Ukraine would contribute a "major part of the equipment needed for [the construction of] the pipeline." Its cost would "be deducted from earnings generated by exports." As an inducement, Aqazadeh promised that once the pipeline was completed Ukraine would "have all the gas she needs."[30]

Once the dust raised by Aqazadeh's visit had settled, however, Ukrainian-Iranian relations once again reverted to their previous unhurried pace. This was demonstrated during the March 1993 visit to Kyiv of an Iranian government delegation headed by Deputy Foreign Minister Mahmud Va'ezi. Judging by public accounts of his sojourn in the Ukrainian capital, Va'ezi had been dispatched to speed up the implementation of the existing agreements. Equally obvious was Kyiv's determination verbally to support Tehran's initiatives but not to commit itself to any concrete course of action.

Thus, in a meeting with Iukhnovs'kyi, who, in addition to his job as first deputy premier, was also chairman of the joint Iranian-Ukrainian Economic Commission, the officials discussed "the delivery of oil products from Iran to Ukraine, and . . . the technical method of mutual settlements." As Va'ezi put it, "the main thing now is to define the priority directions of delivery of oil and oil products, and to agree on prices." He emphasized that Iran was prepared to "begin delivering oil now" but added that "Ukraine ought to pay $30 million for this." Iukhnovs'kyi saw no problem with the "method of mutual settlements" and called on Tehran "to outline the range of goods" that it would accept as payment for petroleum. Cash and hard currency, he implied, were not available for such purposes. Otherwise, the officials reached an understanding "in various fields including oil, gas, mines and banking affairs" and agreed to hold the first meeting of the joint commission in April. In a meeting with Pliushch, Va'ezi declared that his government was "sincerely interested in the stabilization of Ukraine's economy" and assured Kyiv that it "could have trust in Iran as a reliable trade partner." The Speaker responded by saying that "[t]he Ukrainian nation and government . . . consider Iran as a powerful friend in the region and are keen on expansion of bilateral relations."[31]

During a press conference, Va'ezi elaborated on some of the points made earlier during his stay. For example, he held that the economies of the two states were "mutually complementary." Ukraine possessed "highly developed coal and metallurgical industries" and could assist Iran in developing its own. In return, Tehran could render aid with respect to the fuel supply. It could also exchange "citrus plants, tea, and fruit" for sugar and wheat. Moreover, both states were interested "in developing cooperation in the sphere of air and sea transport, construction, and other spheres." Va'ezi noted also that, to facilitate the purchase of Iranian oil, Tehran was prepared to extend to Kyiv a credit line of $50 million. Nevertheless, the Iranian official displayed annoyance with Ukraine's footdragging. Asked when Iranian oil would begin arriving in Ukraine, Va'ezi asserted rather bluntly that this depended entirely upon Kyiv: "There are no 'ifs' on our part. As soon as Ukraine is ready to receive the cargo, the deliveries will start."[32]

In May 1993, a Ukrainian parliamentary delegation, headed by Pliushch, visited Iran and was received by President Rafsanjani. The Speaker used the opportunity "to confirm the agreements between the two countries" and announced that, "in view of the many common grounds for cooperation between . . . [them], Ukraine is eager to expand [bilateral] relations." The president, in turn, praised what he described as the two governments' "firm political will for strengthening all-round ties," and expressed hope that "more practical and effective steps will be taken toward the implementation of . . . [previously reached] agreements, in particular in the field of energy and the transfer of gas."[33]

The comments by Hasan Ruhani, secretary of Iran's Supreme National Security Council, were more pointed. He spoke of "the obligations assumed by Ukraine concerning the transit of Iranian natural gas to Europe. This agreement, achieved between Tehran, Kiev, and Baku," Ruhani insisted, "must be implemented." Pliushch, as already noted, "confirmed Ukraine's loyalty" to the existing agreements and reiterated its willingness to expand relations with Iran. He noted that Ukraine remained "ready to send its specialists to Iran with the aim of developing technical cooperation"—a clear indication that the widely heralded relationship between Kyiv and Tehran had produced few tangible results.[34]

The strongly worded Iranian complaints were not lost on the Ukrainian delegation. Upon his return to Kyiv, Pliushch stated bluntly that his meeting with Rafsanjani (and presumably with other officials) had been "intense" and "quite difficult." The president insisted on being told "why contractual obligations . . . [were] not being implemented." While chiding the Supreme Council for some of the problems that had marred Iranian-Ukrainian relations, Pliushch left no doubt that, in his opinion, the executive branch of the government deserved most of the blame for the existing state of affairs. The main conclusion he drew from the trip was the following: "If we continue to work in this way for international links, especially for mutually advantageous interstate economic relations, then we will not add to our authority, but unfortunately we will lose it." According to Pliushch, his Iranian hosts had pleaded with him to "somehow influence the persons responsible . . . so that contractual obligations are implemented." He, in turn, attempted to persuade them that Ukraine was "a young state" whose representatives sometimes refused to take the responsibility for the implementation of the concluded agreements. But Pliushch left no doubt about what he thought of the irresponsible behavior of the members of the executive branch: "[Ukraine] lose[s] from this . . . and lose[s] more than the Iranian side."[35] Even allowing for political differences between the two branches of government, this was a strong indictment of Ukrainian officials engaged in formulating and implementing their country's policy toward Iran.

In spite of the existing strains, the two sides endeavored to improve and broaden their relations. In June 1993, the Iranian minister of heavy industry arrived in Kyiv and announced that Tehran was "fully ready to promote industrial cooperation with Ukraine." But he, too, took the opportunity to remind the Ukrainian officials of the agreements negotiated in the past and expressed hope that "obstacles in the way of expansion of bilateral cooperation will be removed."[36] In July, the ministers of transportation signed "a memorandum of understanding" on cooperation in the sphere of transportation as well as "three separate agreements on air, road and sea transport." The land accord provided for the opening of "a new route . . . for the transit of goods between Iran and Europe, using roads . . . [in] Azerbaijan, Russia and Ukraine." According to Radio Tehran, this arrangement made it unnecessary for Iran to rely upon the road networks of Turkey, Bulgaria, and Yugoslavia. The air agreement established direct weekly service between the two capitals, while the maritime accord provided for mutual use of ports for the import, export, and transit of goods. It might be noted in passing that in September, Iran and Russia also signed a letter of understanding on road, sea, and air transportation between them. Though not as comprehensive as the Tehran-Kyiv accord, it did provide for Iran's use of the Russian transportation infrastructure.[37]

In the meantime, responding to Washington's pressure (discussed later in this chapter), some Ukrainian commentators, reflecting the official government line, continued to extol the advantages of the Kyiv–Tehran relations. To begin with, they criticized American and British calls for isolating Iran and pointed to Japan and Germany, both engaged in far-flung economic relations with the Islamic Republic. In fact, as Serhii Danylenko pointed out, "over the last three years, [even] U.S. exports to Iran rose fivefold and reached $780 million." Moreover, contrary to some Western charges, "the internal stability of the Iranian regime" rested on a solid foundation, as attested to by the steady return of Iranian immigrants and "the re-election of the pragmatic . . . Rafsanjani."

Turning to bilateral relations, Danylenko described them as "a success of Ukrainian diplomacy that has far surpassed [the efforts of] its CIS neighbors." These relations were "advantageous to both sides . . . [because they] offered each other those goods that are in demand on their respective markets." Iran, in particular, could supply Ukraine with "light industry products, . . . some foodstuffs," and oil. (The latter, Danylenko noted, would now have to be delivered by means of a pipeline, due to the Turkish government's decision to close the Straits to increased petroleum traffic—

an issue explored below.) In turn, Ukraine offered Iran "oil-extraction equipment, turbines, generators, and other equipment for hydroelectric power plants." Danylenko concluded by calling for more pragmatism in Ukrainian foreign policy. "In specifying our priorities in external economic ties," he argued, "we must not 'worship' the West alone. We have simply no right to assign a minor role to the Middle East—a region that is rich in energy sources and goods that Ukraine badly needs, a region where the output of Ukrainian enterprises will be in demand." In this scheme of things, Iran occupied a special place: it should become Ukraine's bridge to the Middle East.[38]

It is noteworthy that Danylenko's article appeared after it had become evident that the Kyiv–Tehran accord on the supply of oil had run into some serious—and previously unforeseen—difficulties. In July 1993, Azerbaijan, the "junior partner" in the tripartite gas and oil pipeline consortium, implicitly expressed doubts about the viability of the project. On July 6, its deputy premier announced that Azerbaijan's own oil pipeline would go through the province of Nakhichevan and Iran to the Turkish Mediterranean terminal at Yumurtalik.[39]

New Problems

Ukraine's ability to receive Iranian oil was negatively affected by two other developments—one domestic, the other regional. Specifically, in the summer of 1993, the Odesa Oblast Council, whose approval was required, refused to sanction Kyiv's decision to begin the construction of a new oil storage terminal at Ilichevs'k with an annual capacity of up to 40 million tons. The first phase of the project (12 million tons) was scheduled to be completed in late 1994. Eventually, Ukraine's own tanker fleet would be built to carry Persian Gulf petroleum to the Odesa facility. As noted by Ruslan Bodelan, chairman of the Odesa Oblast Council, "a specially created public commission" examined the issue and concluded that the new oil terminal "will be . . . the last huge nail in the coffin of the virtually moribund Black Sea, where industrial pollution already exceeds all permissible norms many times over." Given these circumstances, Bodelan continued, the Oblast Council refused to give its formal sanction to the government's request. It is noteworthy that Bodelan's statement appeared in *Pravda*, which continues to present the views of the Russian Communist Party. It is equally interesting that, on the issue of the new Odesa terminal, unusual harmony prevailed across Russia's political spectrum. According to Ukrainian sources, the "unofficial" Russian reaction to the project was decidedly negative. Moreover, Moscow "warned that if Ukraine is going to purchase oil in Iran for hard currency (there are no other variants), then Russian oil will also be sold only for hard currency and at world prices."[40]

While tempers were flying high in Kyiv and Odesa, however, it became apparent that the problem of the new oil terminal may not have been the real issue after all. Taking its clue from the Ukrainian ecologists, Ankara, apprehensive about a major ecological disaster, let it be known that it would not permit the passage through the narrow Turkish Straits of additional tens of millions tons of oil.[41] Turkey's attitude may well have delivered the *coup de grâce* to the Iranian-Azeri-Ukrainian oil pipeline project and, conceivably, to the petroleum deal itself.

Moreover, in March 1994, presidents Leonid Kravchuk and Suleyman Demirel of Turkey approved a joint pipeline project designed to transport Iraqi oil to markets in Central and Western Europe. (Turkey was said to have concluded an agreement with Baghdad to that effect.) Eventually, the presidents hoped, other Persian Gulf producers, and "primarily Iran," would avail themselves of the opportunity to export their oil by means of the proposed Turkish-Ukrainian network. Described as being at an early stage, the scheme raised, but did not address, some important questions. As in the case of the Iranian-Azeri-Ukrainian pipeline, it was not clear as to who would finance the project. (Certainly, Ukraine and Turkey were in no position to assume such a burden.) Nor was the issue of the various routes addressed publicly. The news report said merely that oil would be shipped from the terminal at the Turkish end of the Iraqi pipeline on the Mediterranean via Turkey's pipeline (part of which was yet to be built) to a Black Sea port. Tankers would then carry petroleum between Odesa and the European markets.[42] Nor did anybody bother to explain how Iranian or any other Gulf oil (other than Iraq's) was going to get to Turkey. Barring yet another pipeline project, it would have to be shipped in tankers. However, since this required a sea voyage to the Mediterranean, it was not clear why the tankers should not simply proceed to their traditional West European destinations.

If these and other problems could be resolved, the benefits accruing to both sides would be substantial. Turkey would emerge as a vital link in the Persian Gulf–Europe petroleum pipeline network. It would also resolve to its satisfaction the issue of the supertanker use of the Straits; oil would presumably be shipped to Odesa by tankers, loading at a Turkish Black Sea port other than Istanbul. Ukraine would benefit by totally bypassing Russia, thus lowering its dependence on Moscow. It could also hope to earn some badly needed hard currency for the use of its pipelines and to receive some Middle Eastern oil as well. As for Iran—it was bound to be very upset at this turn of events and showed its utter displeasure during Zlenko's ensuing visit to Tehran.

But in the meantime, in late 1993–early 1994, Ukraine and Iran attempted to maintain a facade of normalcy in their bilateral relations. In October 1993, Acting Prime Minister Iukhym Zviahil's'kyi received the Iranian ambassador and reiterated his government's "willingness to expand diplomatic and economic relations with Iran." He noted in particular Kyiv's interest in purchasing Iranian oil. The officials discussed some of the issues of "industrial, economic and political cooperation" between the two states. The expansion of relations as well as unspecified international issues were also discussed between Deputy Foreign Minister Va'ezi and the visiting chairman of the Supreme Council's Foreign Policy Committee.[43]

In April 1994, Foreign Minister Zlenko, heading "a high ranking politico-economic delegation," arrived in Tehran on a three-day official visit. During his meetings with Velayati and Rafsanjani, Zlenko emphasized Ukraine's willingness and readiness to cooperate with the Islamic Republic "in all fields of mutual interest." He felt that the two countries had lagged in their efforts to strengthen cooperation and said that Kyiv was prepared to do its share to improve bilateral relations. Similar sentiments were also expressed by Zlenko's Iranian hosts. In addition to the president and the foreign minister, the Ukrainian official also met with Oil Minister Aqazadeh. They decided to "form a joint economic and trade cooperation commission . . . [which] will review existing problems in the implementation of agreements which have already been signed . . . [by] the two countries." Zlenko reiterated Kyiv's readiness "to cooperate with . . . Iran in the fields of oil, energy, metals, transportation, and tourism."[44]

In a joint statement, the sides agreed to consult and cooperate with each other in efforts "to resolve regional problems and restore peace and security . . . in the former Soviet republics." They also "voiced satisfaction with the existing economic relations" and promised to work together to "remove [the existing] difficulties." It was announced that the first meeting of the joint economic commission would "be held in Tehran in the near future." Publicly, the sides seemed to be content with the visit and its results. Nevertheless, Radio Tehran quoted Zlenko as saying that "the present level" of bilateral relations was "not compatible with the needs of the day." For this reason, both political and economic cooperation between the two countries "should . . . be increased to higher and desirable levels." Tehran agreed, describing Iran and Ukraine, aware "of their common interests, . . . [as] moving ahead in consolidating the foundations of bilateral ties."[45]

One of the positive results—and even that was confined to paper only—was a "preliminary agreement" that provided for the delivery to Ukraine of an additional 3 billion cubic meters of gas a year. Since the construction of the Iranian-Azeri-Ukrainian pipeline had not yet gotten off the ground due mainly to Kyiv's inability "to supply the pipes and other building materials," Tehran agreed to pump the above amount of gas to Azerbaijan. (A gas pipeline between Iran and Transcaucasia had been built during the Soviet period.) This arrangement would enable Turkmenistan, which supplied gas to both Baku and Kyiv, to increase its Ukrainian quota by 3 billion cubic meters a year. Moscow Radio, which disclosed this information citing sources in the Ukrainian embassy in Tehran, pointed out, however, that Azerbaijan had been contacted about this arrangement (and presumably approved of it) but that Turkmenistan had not been told. This obviously begged the question of whether it would agree, especially since, in February, Ashgabat "stopped direct gas deliveries to Ukraine when the Ukrainian debt rose to $700 million."[46]

The situation concerning the shipment of petroleum was even bleaker: "The contracts on deliveries of Iranian oil to Kiev are recognized as dead and buried." The tripartite pipeline, as noted, did not materialize and the sea delivery of large quantities of petroleum via the Turkish Straits was torpedoed by Ankara. Hence, the Moscow newspaper *Kommersant-Daily* concluded that Kyiv's hopes for fuel independence from Russia had ended in a failure or, as Zlenko put it, in "a stalemate." Nevertheless, *Kommersant-Daily* insisted, the Ukrainian and Iranian officials had concocted "a new deal." According to this information, Tehran "intends to buy from Kiev military hardware manufactured in Ukraine, in particular Antonov-type military transport planes and spares for them. Since there are no diplomatic constraints for such . . . [transactions]," it was concluded, "this understanding appears rather realistic."[47]

Arms

As mentioned earlier, rumors of Ukrainian arms sales to Iran, originating mostly in Moscow, had been circulating since early 1992. Because of their persistence, the subject deserves a closer look. In March 1993, one of Kravchuk's advisers was quoted by an Israeli publication to the effect that Kyiv had refused to sell arms to countries like Libya, Iraq, Iran, and Syria "on moral grounds, although they promised a higher payment than the market prices." The only item that Ukraine had agreed to deliver to Iran was spare parts. In May 1993, during Pliushch's visit to Tehran, Cairo's *al-Ahram*, "citing British and U.S. intelligence" sources, asserted that "Ukraine has delivered eight cruise missiles to Iran that can be targeted at any ship in the Strait of Hormuz from the Iranian coast." The story was picked up by Moscow Radio, which insisted that Ukraine and Iran had concluded a secret "military-technical cooperation agreement" designed to modernize Tehran's armed forces. The understanding was said to provide for the delivery of MiG-29 fighter planes, T-72 tanks, air defense equipment, and cruise missiles to Iran. Moscow Radio described the missile sale as irresponsible, in that "one-fifth of the oil used by the world passes through the Strait" of Hormuz, and explained that Kyiv was very much interested in peddling arms because they were "among the few competitive items that Ukraine can offer." Generally speaking, Moscow did not find weapons sales abroad objectionable. After all, it, too, was hard at work trying to sell arms. Russia also happened to be one of Iran's main suppliers. What Moscow claimed to disapprove of was the alleged sale of missiles that "the international community" had strenuously opposed.[48] Moscow Radio failed to mention that "the international community" had also strongly objected to the sale of Russian submarines to Iran. (Consummated late in the Gorbachev period, the deal provided for the sale to Iran of three diesel-powered submarines. Two of them were delivered in 1993.)

The subject of foreign arms sales was raised again, this time by the Ukrainian press later in 1993 in connection with the projected sale of tanks to Pakistan. It seems that in the fall, Kyiv and Islamabad had signed a contract providing for the delivery of a new "100 percent Ukrainian T-84 tank." In October, the Ukrainian government, then headed by Zviahil's'kyi, had to decide whether or not to honor the contract. Those in favor of the deal argued that the sale would become the "financial foundation" for manufacturing tanks in Ukraine. This argument was supported by the claim that, in order to obtain Arab oil, Ukraine must support "the leading Muslim countries." The opponents insisted that the tanks were being sold to a country that was a "party to the civil war in Tajikistan" and the transaction would drag Ukraine into that Central Asian conflict. Finally, the deal would force Kyiv to side with Pakistan in its confrontation with India, a course of action that was not necessarily in Ukraine's interest.

While Kyiv was debating these issues, some commentators insisted that, in its dealings with foreign countries, Ukraine be guided by determination to secure its "material and political advantages." In this connection, it was argued that Masyk's earlier efforts to establish close relations with Iran had backfired precisely because they did not pay sufficient attention to Ukrainian interests. Thus, Kyiv could not hope to compete with Moscow, which had traditionally supplied Tehran with modern weapons and was building an atomic electric power plant in Iran. Moreover, Russia had used Ukraine's close cooperation with the Islamic Republic "to undermine Ukraine's relations with Turkey" and, the analyst might have added, with the United States. In any event, by late 1993, some Ukrainian commentators began to suggest that Kyiv's Iranian policy may have been ill advised, if not outright counterproductive.[49]

Some of this soul-searching was no doubt influenced by the attitude adopted by the United States. It will be recalled that Washington's relations with Tehran had been strained for a long time and that, throughout most of the 1980s and 1990s, both the Republican and Democratic administrations endeavored to isolate Iran politically and economically. With this in mind, the United States had tried, with varying success, to persuade other countries to limit their cooperation with the Islamic Republic. In 1993, such pressure was also exerted on Ukraine. Thus, after the cruise missile story broke, Kyiv was specifically requested to curtail the delivery of all types of military equipment to Iran.[50] Since at that time Ukrainian-American relations were marred by other problems—disposal of nuclear weapons, lack of progress in political and economic reforms that the West was urging the Kravchuk administration to undertake—it made no sense to aggravate them further by acknowledging the charges that appeared in *al-Ahram* or were regularly advanced by Moscow. Little wonder, therefore, that in 1993 all allegations of arms sales to Iran were denied by the Ukrainian officials. For example, upon his return from Tehran, Pliushch was asked about the reported cruise missile sale. The Speaker stated, "unequivocally . . . we are not delivering any . . . missiles and we are not going to deliver any."[51]

However, as rumors of Ukrainian arms sales to Iran persisted, Washington remained concerned. In December 1993, the U.S. Department of State reportedly "urged . . . [Kyiv] to show restraint in trading weapons . . . [to] countries whose policies give [the United States] cause for concern." *Izvestiia*, which broke the story, reminded its readers that, in the spring, Washington had complained to Moscow about the sale of three diesel-powered submarines to Iran. Now, American concern was aroused by Kyiv's reported agreement to provide Tehran with the antiship cruise missiles. Interestingly, *Izvestiia* found Ukraine's desire to move into the profitable international arms market understandable. It had inherited an arms industry and large quantities of weapons from the USSR. It also had to import fuel. Hence, it was only natural for Kyiv to want to barter arms for petroleum and natural gas.[52]

According to London's *al-Sharq al-Awsat*, in December 1993, the United States convinced President Yeltsin to cancel the sale to Iran of a third submarine (the first two had already been delivered) and of two nuclear-power stations. Tehran reacted by accusing Moscow of "submitting to Washington's pressures." Recognizing an opportunity, Ukraine reportedly stepped in. Foreign Minister Zlenko announced that Kyiv "decided to supply Iran with spare parts for the Soviet-made weapons in the Iranian arsenal." He added that Ukraine was "determined to strengthen its relations" with Tehran and regarded Washington's pressure as "improper." Borys Tarasiuk, a senior Ukrainian disarmament expert, added that Iran was not "one of the states to which Ukrainian exports are banned." Only Serbia, Libya, Cuba, North Korea, and South Africa were included in this category. (In contrast, Kyiv Radio, in a report on Tarasiuk's comments, mentioned only Yugoslavia, South Africa, and Iraq as being banned.) In any event, Tarasiuk acknowledged that "certain types of arms" either have been or might be sold to Iran. In doing so, he said, "Ukraine is pursuing its own economic interests and observes security principles." He did not elaborate.[53]

The tension aroused by these charges and countercharges continued. In early February 1994, *Sovetskaia Rossiia* reported that Ukraine had offered "a substantial part of its share of the former Soviet navy," including missile and torpedo boats, destroyers, and minelayers, to the Persian Gulf countries. Less sensational—but clearly overblown—proved to be a story which appeared in *al-Sharq al-Awsat*. Quoting "high-level diplomatic sources," it reported that Washington had "finally succeeded in 'persuading' Ukraine to withdraw a [November 1993] offer to sell Iran $1.2 billion worth of modern weapons." The credit for the breakthrough belonged to President Clinton, who reportedly had lobbied Kravchuk during his recent visit to Kyiv.[54]

There can be no doubt that relations between Ukraine and the United States improved significantly after Kravchuk's commitment to abide by the nuclear nonproliferation treaty and to rid Ukraine of the nuclear-armed ICBMs. This was evidenced, in part, by Zlenko's comments on Kravchuk's March 1994 visit to Washington. The foreign minister said that the Clinton administration had recently "reinterpreted its policy with regard to Ukraine." As demonstrated by the deliberations between the two presidents, "the United States [now] assigns an important part in its policy for our state." However, to ascribe the relative insignificance of Kyiv's weapons trade with Tehran to American pressure is to miss an important point. According to "official sources," Ukraine's *total* arms sales in 1993 amounted to $29 million. "Unofficial government sources" cited the figure of $100 million. Whatever the correct amount, and given the fact that approximately two million workers were employed in Ukraine's defense-related industries, these were rather paltry sums.[55] Whatever Washington's preferences may have been, the major share of the blame for Kyiv's lack of initiative rested with the Ukrainian government itself.

Conclusion

In light of this record of Iranian-Ukrainian relations, one may well wonder why the intensive interaction, which included high-level visits, negotiations, and agreements, produced so few concrete results. In retrospect, it would appear that the initial outburst of enthusiasm, which both Kyiv and Tehran exhibited in establishing bilateral relations, was genuine. Put differently, in late 1991–early 1992, both states, for reasons of their own, felt a need to establish and expand cooperation. Ukraine, determined to wrest from Russia political as well as economic independence, needed to import large quantities of fuel and saw in Iran a major potential supplier of petroleum as well as of natural gas. At that juncture, even the appearance of ability to diversify by importing oil from other sources provided Kyiv with important leverage in its invariably tortuous negotiations with Moscow. Tehran, coping with pressing economic problems of its own, detected the possibility of entering the West European natural gas market by utilizing the pipeline system already in place in Ukraine. (Reference is made here to the Soviet gas pipeline network, used in part to export natural gas to Western Europe.) Nor was it much of a secret that Ukraine was a major producer of pipes and compressor stations that would be required for the construction of the missing pipeline links in Azerbaijan and Russia. Hence, Tehran set out to establish close relations with Kyiv in the hope that, jointly and in cooperation with Baku, they might prove able to complete this ambitious project. Economic considerations were reinforced by political interests. Both Ukraine and Iran distrusted Russia and were determined to weaken its influence, particularly in the outlying republics of the former USSR. In short, in 1992 it appeared that Kyiv and Tehran were pursuing at least some complementary objectives and that cooperation between them would benefit them both.

Nevertheless, as noted, even at this early stage it was by no means certain that the most important single Iranian-Ukrainian project—the gas pipeline (or pipelines)—was practical or even feasible. For example, it was not too far-fetched to suspect that Iran might find it difficult to allocate 25 billion cubic meters of gas for export to Ukraine and Western Europe. And if that was the case, what about 75 billion cubic meters that Tehran had promised it would pump upon the completion of the three-pipelines complex? For its part, Ukraine was assured that, after the pipelines became operational, all of its gas needs would be met. But this left unanswered the question of payments, since there is a limit to how much sugar, wheat, minerals, fertilizer, and spare parts Iran can consume. Nor was there much hope that Ukrainian hard-currency reserves would grow significantly in the years ahead.

Some in Kyiv argued that modern weaponry, of which Ukraine had inherited vast arsenals, should be used to pay for Iranian fuel. Someone once said that one destroyer would buy at least one year's supply of petroleum. Since Ukraine expected to receive a part of the Black Sea Fleet, the bartering of a few aging naval vessels might indeed have appeared as a

profitable business proposition. Regardless of the merits of the case, however, it should be borne in mind that Iran's naval needs are rather limited. In
the early 1990s, the Iranian navy was already stronger than its counterparts
in the other Persian Gulf states. At the same time, even with additional
acquisitions from Russia or Ukraine, Tehran could not hope to challenge the
U.S. Navy either in the Persian Gulf or in the Indian Ocean. In short, the
potential Iranian naval market was limited and could not provide any long-
term relief for the fuel-starved Ukrainian economy. The opportunities in the
other military sectors were better, but they, too, were circumscribed by such
factors as (1) competition with Russia, which over the past decade had
emerged as Iran's major arms supplier; (2) Tehran's growing economic
problems and declining oil revenues; and (3) Kyiv's own unwillingness to
sell Iran some of the weapons systems it was seeking, among them the
cruise missiles.

Getting back to the main theme, however, and assuming for the sake of
argument that both Tehran and Kyiv had originally believed in the viability
and mutual benefit of their cooperation, in retrospect it seems obvious that
later in 1992 and beyond, at least one of the parties, namely Ukraine, began
to have second thoughts about the practicality of some of the planned projects. Kyiv's attitude manifested itself, in part, in assuring the Iranians of its
good will and determination to cooperate on the pipeline and other projects,
but in reality doing little about them.

The delay in implementing the bilateral accords can be ascribed to a
number of factors. In addition to simple bureaucratic bungling and occasionally concerted Russian and American pressure, the financial resources
required to fund the pipeline project or the outright purchase of Iranian oil
were simply not available, due in part to the steady decline of the Ukrainian
economy. The logistical problems, too, were highly complex. As indicated
above, Ukraine had no tanker fleet and the Odesa refinery had a limited
capacity which, even under optimal circumstances, could satisfy only a
fraction of the country's petroleum needs. In addition, Premier Kuchma's
plan to build a new terminal near Odesa had initially run into determined
local opposition, while Turkey refused to permit increased supertanker traffic in the Straits. Finally, and most importantly, even if all these problems
could be solved and the money, by some miracle, did become available,
how much Iranian oil could Ukraine be expected to receive and to absorb?
As argued earlier, surely not much more than 4 million tons, the amount
that was used in the Kyiv–Tehran discussions and that constituted some 15
percent of Ukraine's petroleum requirements. What all, of this meant, of
course, was that the old sources of fuel (above all, Russia and, to a lesser
extent, Turkmenistan) had to remain available to keep the Ukrainian econ-

omy afloat. It is inconceivable that the Kyiv officials were unaware of these rather uncomplicated facts.

How, then, from Ukraine's point of view, did Iran fit into this grim picture? In the short run, rapprochement with Tehran was no doubt seen as a political ploy intended to strengthen Kyiv's hand in its difficult negotiations with Moscow. At the very least, it created the impression of the possibility of acquiring new sources of fuel. Ukraine's dealings with the Central Asian republics and Kuchma's spring 1993 trip to the Arab Persian Gulf capitals, too, fall into this category. In the longer run, if the complex of problems surrounding it were resolved and the gas pipeline were built, Ukraine would benefit considerably by receiving Iranian natural gas and collecting hard-currency revenues for its passage through Ukrainian territory on the way to Western Europe. Hence, it was in Kyiv's interest to stay on friendly terms with Tehran even though Iran was not in the position to solve Ukraine's energy problems. Unfortunately for Kyiv, however, Tehran did not see it that way. Though not accusing Ukrainian officials of negotiating in bad faith, the Iranians publicly berated their unwillingness to live up to agreements that had been negotiated and signed by President Kravchuk and the members of the Ukrainian government. As a result, some of the top Ukrainian officials were made to look like rank amateurs, incapable of conducting a coherent foreign policy. It may be safely assumed that the Iranian gambit did not enhance Kyiv's reputation as a solid player in international affairs.

In sum, Iran did not turn out to be the answer either to Ukraine's fuel problems or to its vitally important relations with Russia. Although, for reasons of its own, the Islamic Republic was genuinely interested in supporting Kyiv economically and politically, Tehran's ability to "deliver the goods" was circumscribed not only by its own economic weaknesses but also by the ineptitude of the Ukrainian functionaries who guided Kyiv's Iran policy. Not only did they overestimate their country's ability to live up to the terms of the agreements they had negotiated, but they also seemed oblivious to the fact that close identification with Iran did not earn Ukraine any kudos with Turkey or with the Arab states of the Persian Gulf, where Tehran's regional ambitions are viewed with suspicion and concern. Danylenko was correct in arguing that Kyiv had "no right to assign a minor role to the Middle East."[56] But to think that the oil-rich region could provide Ukraine with the fuel it needed in exchange for what Ukraine had to offer, or that Iran was Ukraine's "bridge" to the Middle East, was to err seriously on both counts. By mid-1994, the consequences of these mistaken notions were there for all to see.

Given American determination to keep Iran isolated politically and economically, Kyiv's early attempts to consolidate and expand relations with Tehran provoked a negative reaction in Washington. It bears pointing out, however, that even in 1992–93 Ukraine's efforts to befriend the Islamic Republic paled in comparison with the issue of nuclear disarmament that the United States was pursuing consistently and resolutely. Nevertheless, the rapprochement between Ukraine and Iran was an irritation. The Kravchuk administration, as noted, had defended itself by arguing that the Western powers were themselves divided on the issue of cooperation with Tehran, and that Kyiv should, therefore, be left alone to pursue its own interests. In the end, the entire episode proved to be but a tempest in a teapot. On the one hand, the Ukrainian government itself was split on the wisdom of too close an association with Iran and eventually opted to lower significantly the level of intensity that had marked the early stages of its relations with Tehran. On the other hand, given Ukraine's critical economic situation and the magnitude of its problems with Russia, it made no sense to antagonize the United States for the sake of grandiose but ultimately unrealistic schemes.

In the end, Kyiv opted to maintain modest commercial contacts with Iran but refrained from any activity that would significantly damage Ukraine's standing in Washington. Considering the magnitude of the political and economic problems the country has faced since 1992, problems the West could help alleviate, this was a sensible course to follow.

Notes

1. *Uriadovyi kur'er* (Kyiv), no. 8 (February 1992), p. 5.
2. Serhii Hutsalo, ibid., no. 11 (March 1992), p. 7.
3. Interview with *Pravda Ukrainy* (Kyiv), 23 May 1992, as quoted in Foreign Broadcast Information Service (hereafter FBIS-USR), June 19, 1992, p. 86.
4. Moscow Radio, January 23, 1992, as quoted in Foreign Broadcast Information Service, Central Eurasia (formerly Soviet Union) (hereafter FBIS-SOV), January 24, 1992, p. 82; and *Uriadovyi kur'er*, no. 4 (January 1992), p. 2, respectively. Subsequently, the problem of the POWs was raised regularly during the meetings of Ukrainian and Iranian officials. Tehran's efforts, if any, have not been successful.
5. Kyiv Radio, January 28, 1992, as quoted in FBIS-SOV, January 29, 1992, p. 57.
6. S. Tsikora, *Izvestiia* (Moscow), February 4, 1992.
7. See Tehran Radio, February 6, 1992, as quoted in FBIS-Near East and South Asia (hereafter FBIS-NES), February 7, 1992, pp. 19–20; and Moscow Radio, January 23, 1992, as quoted in FBIS-SOV, January 24, 1992, p. 82, respectively.
8. V. Mikheev, *Izvestiia*, February 12, 1992; and O. Musafirova, *Komsomol'skaia pravda*, February 4, 1992, respectively.
9. Aqazadeh's press conference of February 6, 1992. Tehran Radio, February 6, 1992, as quoted in FBIS-NES, February 7, 1992, pp. 19–20.
10. See *Keyhan*, June 25, 1992, as quoted in FBIS-NES, July 9, 1992, p. 50; and S. Tsikora, *Izvestiia*, February 4, 1992, respectively.

11. See note 9.

12. The above two paragraphs are based on the Moscow Radio broadcast of February 8, 1992, as quoted in FBIS-SOV, February 10, 1992, p. 65.

13. Moscow Radio, February 7, 1992, as quoted in FBIS-SOV, February 7, 1992, p. 77.

14. Tehran Radio, February 24, 1992, as quoted in FBIS-NES, February 24, 1992. pp. 70–71.

15. Moscow Radio, February 25, 1992, as quoted in FBIS-SOV, February 27, 1992, p. 55; and Kyiv Radio, March 4, 1992, as quoted in FBIS-SOV, March 6, 1992, p. 42, respectively.

16. Tehran Radio, March 10, 1992, as quoted in FBIS-NES, March 10, 1992, p. 39.

17. V. Volodin, *Izvestiia*, April 27, 1992; and Tehran Radio, April 25, 1992, as quoted in FBIS-NES, April 27, 1992, p. 53.

18. Tehran Radio, April 26, 1992, as quoted in FBIS-NES, May 5, 1992, pp. 52–53.

19. Tehran Radio, April 25 and 26, 1992, as quoted in FBIS-NES, April 27, 1992, pp. 52 and 53, respectively. The subject of the Nagorno-Karabakh conflict, which Iran attempted to mediate, came up regularly during high-level Kyiv–Tehran and Kyiv–Baku negotiations. Kravchuk usually insisted on impartiality but, during Elchibey's presidency, gently leaned in Azerbaijan's favor. See, for example, Moscow Radio and Kyiv Radio of December 10, 1992. Both quoted in FBIS-SOV, December 11, 1992, p. 25.

20. *Tehran Times*, April 30, 1992, as quoted in FBIS-NES, May 12, 1992, p. 46.

21. Kyiv Radio, May 19, 1992, as quoted in FBIS-SOV, May 20, 1992, p. 43; July 24, 1992, as quoted in FBIS-SOV, July 27, 1992, p. 45; and Kyiv Television, September 26, 1992, as quoted in FBIS-SOV, September 29, 1992, p. 30, respectively.

22. Moscow Television, July 11, 1992, as quoted in FBIS-SOV, July 14, 1992, p. 21; and *Keyhan*, June 25, 1992, as quoted in FBIS-NES, July 9, 1992, p. 51, respectively.

23. Kyiv Radio, December 10, 1992, as quoted in FBIS-SOV, December 11, 1992, p. 25.

24. Moscow Radio, February 2, 1993, as quoted in FBIS-SOV, February 3, 1993, p. 34.

25. Moscow Radio, February 11, 1993, as quoted in FBIS-SOV, February 12, 1993, p. 45. It is noteworthy that Aqazadeh subsequently described reports on Ukrainian arms supplies to Iran as "an invention" (Moscow Radio, February 12, 1993, as quoted in FBIS-SOV, February 17, 1993, p. 49). Nevertheless, First Deputy Defense Minister General Mir Miran accompanied Aqazadeh and held discussions with his Ukrainian counterpart, General Ivan Bizhan. Moscow Radio, February 11, 1993, as quoted in FBIS-SOV, February 12, 1993, p. 45.

26. Moscow Radio, as quoted in FBIS-SOV.

27. Tehran Radio, February 12, 1993, as quoted in FBIS-SOV, February 17, 1993, p. 48; and Moscow Radio, February 11, 1993, as quoted in FBIS-SOV, February 12, 1993, p. 45.

28. Tehran Radio, February 13 and 12, 1993, as quoted in FBIS-NES, February 17, 1993, p. 56; and FBIS-SOV, February 17, 1993, p. 48, respectively.

29. As quoted by Tehran Radio, February 13, 1993, as quoted in FBIS-NES, February 17, 1993, pp. 55–56.

30. Ibid., p. 56; and Moscow Radio, February 12, 1993, as quoted in FBIS-SOV, February 17, 1993, p. 49.

31. Kyiv Television, March 16, 1993, and Tehran Radio of the same day, as quoted in FBIS-SOV, March 17, 1993, p. 45. The joint commission "to coordinate the movement of energy sources to . . . [Ukraine] and of agricultural products from Ukraine" was

founded earlier in March. See *Molod' Ukrainy* (Kyiv), March 10, 1993, as quoted in FBIS-SOV, March 16, 1993, p. 42.

32. Kyiv Radio, March 17, 1993; and *Holos Ukrainy* (Kyiv), March 18, 1993, as quoted in FBIS-SOV, March 18, 1993, p. 48, and March 23, 1993, p. 32, respectively. It would appear that the figure of $50 million in Iranian credit, quoted by Kyiv Radio, was incorrect. *Holos Ukrainy* cited the correct figure of $30 million.

33. Tehran Radio, May 12, 1993, as quoted in FBIS-NES, May 13, 1993, p. 50; and Kyiv Radio, May 12, 1993, as quoted in FBIS-SOV, May 13, 1993, p. 41.

34. Kyiv Radio, May 11, 1993, as quoted in FBIS-SOV, May 12, 1993, pp. 20–21; and *Holos Ukrainy*, May 12, 1993, as quoted in FBIS-NES, May 13, 1993, p. 50.

35. Kyiv Radio, May 13, 1993, as quoted in FBIS-SOV, May 17, 1993, p. 60.

36. Tehran Radio, June 16, 1993, as quoted in FBIS-SOV, June 18, 1993, p. 44.

37. Tehran Radio, July 9 and September 8, 1993, as quoted in FBIS-NES, July 13, 1993, p. 64, and September 9, 1993, p. 62, respectively.

38. The above two paragraphs are based on Serhii Danylenko's article in *Holos Ukrainy*, August 27, 1993, as quoted in FBIS-SOV, September 1, 1993, pp. 33–34.

39. *Keyhan*, July 15, 1993, as quoted in FBIS-NES, July 21, 1993, p. 51.

40. *Pravda* (Moscow), July 24, 1993, as quoted in FBIS-SOV, July 28, 1993, pp. 50–51; and Kyiv Radio, July 23, 1993, as quoted in FBIS-SOV, July 26, 1993, p. 54. In the confrontation between Odesa and Kyiv, the latter prevailed. In March 1994, it was announced that the construction of the new terminal had begun. Kyiv Radio, March 14, 1994, as quoted in FBIS-SOV, March 16, 1994, p. 36. The Ukrainian government reportedly approved the construction of a tanker fleet by German firms in January 1993. For some details see Moscow Television, January 28, 1993, as quoted in FBIS-SOV, January 29, 1993, p. 50.

41. See Premier Kuchma's interview with *Molod' Ukrainy*, August 31, 1993, as quoted in FBIS-SOV, September 2, 1993, p. 44.

42. Kyiv Radio, March 14, 1994, as quoted in FBIS-SOV, March 16, 1994, p. 36.

43. For more details, see Tehran Radio, October 14, 1993, and February 7, 1994, as quoted in FBIS-SOV, October 15, 1993, p. 38; and FBIS-NES, February 8, 1994, p. 42, respectively.

44. Tehran Radio, April 17 and 18, 1994, as quoted in FBIS-NES, April 18, 1994, pp. 66 and 67.

45. Tehran Radio, April 18, 1994, as quoted in FBIS-NES, April 19, 1994, p. 63, and April 18, 1994, p. 67, respectively.

46. Moscow Radio, April 20, 1994, as quoted in FBIS-SOV, April 21, 1994, p. 57.

47. N. Kalashnikova, *Kommersant-Daily* (Moscow), April 20, 1994, as quoted in FBIS-SOV, April 21, 1994, pp. 57–58.

48. *Hatzofe* (Tel Aviv), March 28, 1993, as quoted in FBIS-SOV, March 29, 1993, pp. 91–92; and Moscow Radio, May 12, 1993, as quoted in same, May 13, 1993, p. 1.

49. The above two paragraphs are based on A. Starostyn, *Ukrains'ki obrii* (Kyiv), no. 18 (November 1993), p. 3, as quoted in FBIS-SOV, November 24, 1993, p. 44.

50. For some details, see Elaine Sciolino, the *New York Times*, June 10, 1993. For details on the Clinton administration's "dual containment" policy, designed to isolate both Iran and Iraq, see Douglas Jehl in the *New York Times*, May 27, 1993.

51. Kyiv Radio, May 13, 1993, as quoted in FBIS-SOV, May 17, 1993, p. 60.

52. A. Sychev, *Izvestiia*, December 14, 1993.

53. *Al-Sharq al-Awsat*, December 24, 1993, as quoted in FBIS-NES, January 4, 1994, p. 48; and Kyiv Radio, December 21, 1993, as quoted in FBIS-SOV, December 22, 1993, p. 45, respectively.

54. *Sovetskaia Rossiia*, February 3, 1994, as quoted in FBIS-SOV, of the same day, p. 45; and *al-Sharq al-Awsat*, February 5, 1994, as quoted in FBIS-NES, February 8, 1994, p. 38.

55. Kyiv Radio, March 8, 1994, as quoted in FBIS-SOV, March 9, 1994, p. 23; and R. Khotin, *Izvestiia*, July 29, 1994, respectively. According to one of Kravchuk's advisers, the total amount earned from the sale of arms abroad in 1992 was $20 million. See *Hatzofe* (note 48).

56. See note 38.

4

Azerbaijan and Iran

Gareth M. Winrow

The disintegration of the Soviet Union, the end of the Cold War, and the death of Ayatollah Khomeini facilitated the development of relations between the newly independent former Soviet Republic of Azerbaijan and the Islamic Republic of Iran. Although there are now opportunities to further ties, the unresolved issue of national identity may still pose problems for future relations between the two states. Changes on the domestic scene may encourage or constrain the development of bilateral relations. The regional context must also be taken into account. The conflict between Armenia and Azerbaijan over the disputed territory of Nagorno-Karabakh and the security interests of Russia have influenced the policies of officials in both Baku and Tehran.

Iran and Azerbaijan have close historical, cultural, and ethnic links. The two share a mixed Persian-Turkic heritage. Of the former Soviet republics that are Muslim, Azerbaijan is the only predominantly Shiite Muslim state. Today's independent Azerbaijan was long a battleground between the Persian and Ottoman and later Persian and Russian empires. The border between Iran and Azerbaijan was basically drawn up by the treaties of Gulistan and Turkmanchai in 1813 and 1828 after Russian victories over the Persian Empire. Family ties across this border remain. A large Azerbaijani population is concentrated in northern Iran. However, even before the Russian conquests, the current border between Iran and Azerbaijan running largely along the Araks River had been a sort of dividing line between a northern and a southern Azerbaijan.

The Russian factor was clearly of crucial importance in the formation of modern Azerbaijan and Iran. Soviet Russia had attempted to exploit a local rebellion to establish the Persian Socialist Soviet Republic of Gilan in a part of northern (but in this case non-Azerbaijani) Iran between 1920 and 1921. In 1945–46, refusing to vacate northern Iran, which they had previously occupied in agreement with Britain in the Second World War, Soviet troops proceeded to promote the formation of an Autonomous Azerbaijani Republic (and also an Autonomous Kurdish Republic) in that territory. Significantly, lack of local support as well as international pressure had compelled Soviet forces to retreat, and the Autonomous Azerbaijani Republic swiftly collapsed. The Soviet Union remained firmly in control of the Azerbaijani Soviet Socialist Republic, however. Relations between Moscow and Tehran suffered because of the notorious Article 6 of the 1921 Treaty of Friendship between Soviet Russia and Iran, which gave the former the right to occupy Iran in the event of another power's making use of Iranian territory to threaten Soviet Russia.

Today, Iranian officials are still aware of actual and potential problems in maintaining the territorial integrity of the Iranian state, although Russia is now in much less of a position to exploit them. There are large Kurdish and Turkmen minorities, for example, some of whom may entertain ambitions of becoming part of a Kurdistan or Greater Turkmenistan. The substantial Azerbaijani minority in northern Iran may attempt to secede and unite with the Azerbaijanis of independent Azerbaijan. Current economic hardship may contribute to the growth of separatist feeling in Iran. With the slump in the price of oil, Iran's major export and primary source of hard currency, officials in Tehran will have grave difficulty managing a foreign debt of up to $30 billion and controlling an inflation rate of over 60 percent in spite of heavy subsidization of the economy.

There could also be wider implications here for Iranian foreign policy. Nowadays, the standard line is that since the death of Khomeini there has been a struggle for control of Iran's domestic and external policy between moderate and pragmatic forces personified and led by President Ali Akbar Hashemi Rafsanjani, and radical, revolutionary elements led by Ayatollah Ali Khamenei, out to continue the line adopted by Khomeini. This argument is too simplistic. In a country's external relations, a mix of various and not necessarily compatible policies may be pursued at different times and locations. Thus, on some occasions, Iran will appear as a normal state actor behaving in accordance with the precepts of international law. At another time and place Iranian officials may be seeking to spread the Islamic revolution through recourse to unorthodox and nondiplomatic channels. In the making of Iranian foreign policy, other factors must also be considered, such as the role of history, geography, regional dynamics, and what is in reality a complicated decision-making apparatus where competing groups such as the leading clergy, the Revolutionary Guards, the president, the parliament, and various ministers are all involved in negotiating compromises and trade-offs.[1] Nonetheless, one may argue that with regard to Iranian policy in Central Asia and in the Caucasus, since the death of Khomeini a more pragmatic course has been pursued.

As in Iran, the authorities in Azerbaijan are also experiencing problems in maintaining the territorial integrity of their state. Azerbaijanis do make up a substantial proportion of the population of Azerbaijan, although the figure of 83 percent given in the official 1989 census may be somewhat inflated. The problem with the Armenian minority concentrated in Nagorno-Karabakh is well known. In the north of Azerbaijan the Lezgins have been agitating for union with their co-ethnics in neighboring Daghestan. In the south, the Persian-oriented Talysh minority is attracted to Iran. Azerbaijan could possibly fragment along ethnic lines. The country could also split into various fiefdoms run by powerful local warlords. The state-building process in Azerbaijan is far from smooth, with a war-ravaged economy and internal instability at the center. President Mutalibov was overthrown in March 1992 and attempted an unsuccessful coup two months later. In June 1993, the elected president Abulfaz Elchibey was ousted from power following an armed uprising which eventually led to the surprising return of Haidar Aliev, a one-time Brezhnevite and Communist Party Politburo member. In early October 1994 Aliev himself narrowly survived a coup attempt. This was apparently organized by Prime Minister Suret Huseinov, who days later fled to Russia. With the country on a war footing, the Azerbaijani economy is unable to develop in spite of its oil and gas reserves. These circumstances have affected Azerbaijan's foreign policy. Changes in leadership at the center have resulted in noticeable shifts in policy toward Iran, Russia, and Turkey.

Recent Developments in Relations between Azerbaijan and Iran: An Overview

In the period 1990–94, relations between Azerbaijan and Iran can be examined in three distinct phases. The first phase, from 1990 to mid-1992, was one in which ties between the two states were gradually strengthened. Between mid-1992 and mid-1993, relations suffered as Elchibey pursued a pro-Turkish policy. Since mid-1993, Baku and Tehran have expanded contacts as Aliev embarked on a more balanced policy toward Azerbaijan's neighbors. Reacting to events in Azerbaijan, and eager to curb Turkish influence in the region, the post-Khomeini Iranian authorities have also had to take into account their relations with Moscow and Armenia. Concerned for political stability and economic prosperity in the Caucasus, officials in Baku have acted with caution and restraint rather than with revolutionary zeal.

In the first phase of Azerbaijani-Iranian relations the authorities in Tehran initially proceeded cautiously in order not to endanger expanding economic ties with the Soviet Union. Immediately after Khomeini's death in June 1989 President Rafsanjani had visited Moscow and negotiated agreements to obtain Soviet weaponry and technology. Consequently, Iran scarcely reacted when in January 1990 Soviet troops forcibly intervened in Baku to crush the Azerbaijani Popular Front (PF) using the pretext that local Armenians were being massacred. Ignoring past promises to come to the aid of oppressed fellow Muslims, the Iranian Foreign Ministry merely expressed its "deep regret" at these "erroneous actions" and urged for a peaceful solution.[2] Moreover, the Iranian authorities only recognized the independence of Azerbaijan in mid-December 1991, once the end of the Soviet Union was inevitable. Significantly, in late November 1991, Iranian foreign minister Ali Akbar Velayati, while on a trip to the Soviet Union that included a visit to Baku, had spoken of the need for a united and powerful Soviet Confederation in order to prevent "independent" republics from coming under Western influence.[3] Velayati's remarks were particularly striking bearing in mind that Turkey had already recognized the independence of Azerbaijan on November 9.

Although Iran opened an embassy in Baku in January 1992, the authorities in Tehran struggled to compete with Turkey's increasing influence in Azerbaijan. Mutalibov signed a Friendship and Cooperation Agreement in Ankara in January 1992, and Azerbaijan became the first of the Turkic republics of the former Soviet Union to decide to switch from the Cyrillic alphabet to the Latin rather than Arabic script. However, by the spring of 1992 Iran's active role as a mediator in the dispute between Armenia and Azerbaijan over Nagorno-Karabakh had boosted its prestige in the region.

Azerbaijani-Iranian relations nose-dived with the election of the PF leader Elchibey to the presidency in June 1992. Elchibey was well known for past speeches in which he had pressed for union with Iranian Azerbaijan to realize the dream of a "Greater Azerbaijan." He was also a staunch advocate of adopting the Turkish secular model. Thus, in this phase Iran's efforts at mediation were abruptly terminated, although the escalation of fighting in and around Nagorno-Karabakh and the seizure of further Azerbaijani territory by the Armenians would have made it much more difficult for any intermediary to broker a peace settlement. Politically, contacts between Azerbaijan and Iran were virtually suspended, but economic ties between the two were consolidated.

A new era in relations between Baku and Tehran opened when Aliev assumed the presidency after a rebellion by forces under a local warlord, Huseinov—later Aliev's premier until the attempted coup in October 1994—had compelled Elchibey to flee the capital. Under Elchibey's presidency, as head of the autonomous and geographically separated Azerbaijani Republic of Nakhichevan, Aliev had chosen to disregard the instructions of Elchibey and had maintained close links with Iran. Welcomed in Tehran in August 1992 and March 1993, Aliev had secured economic deals whereby Iran had promised to supply the beleaguered Nakhichevan (suffering from an economic blockade imposed by Armenia) with much-needed food, oil, and electricity. Upon his becoming president, Iranian newspapers were quick to point out how Aliev had erected around two hundred mosques in Nakhichevan and had made a pilgrimage to the tomb of Imam Reza in Mashhad, while overlooking the fact that in the early 1980s Aliev too had voiced his hopes of ultimately seeing the unification of then Soviet Azerbaijan with Iranian Azerbaijan.[4]

In October 1993 Rafsanjani made a highly publicized visit to Baku and signed fourteen agreements, protocols, and memoranda including a memorandum on Principles of Friendship and Cooperation.[5] At the end of June 1994, Aliev was received in Tehran. Documents were signed concerning the establishment of a joint border commission; the export of Iranian gas to Nakhichevan; bilateral cooperation in the fields of water, electricity, science, culture, medicine, radio, and television; joint economic investments; the completion of the Khoda Afarin Dam Project; and cooperation in the Caspian Sea.[6] Iranian officials also resumed an interest in seeking a peaceful solution to the Nagorno-Karabakh dispute, although Russia and the CSCE by this time had developed their own proposals, and Armenia was probably less eager to countenance an active Iranian mediatory role following Tehran's denunciations of Armenian attacks against Azerbaijani forces near the Azerbaijani-Iranian border. These attacks led to thousands of Azerbaijani refugees fleeing across the border to Iran before the Iranian Red Crescent erected tent camps on the Azerbaijani side of the frontier.

It appears, though, that the authorities in Tehran are not in complete agreement concerning their assessment of Aliev's regional policy. In January 1994 Radio Tehran had praised Aliev's "balanced" conduct in improving relations with Russia and maintaining close relations with other neighbors while preserving the independence of Azerbaijan.[7] But in June an editorial in the *Tehran Times* warned Aliev that his "very complex policy" vis-à-vis regional states and his tendency to tailor his remarks depending on whether his audience was Iranian, Russian, or Turkish could damage relations with Iran.[8]

Iran as Mediator in the Nagorno-Karabakh Dispute

At the time of this writing, in spite of the initiatives and overtures of Russia, Turkey, the United States, the OSCE Minsk Group, and Iran, a peaceful solution to the Nagorno-Karabakh dispute remains to be agreed upon. Hostilities between Azerbaijani and Armenian forces had escalated and had threatened to spill over Azerbaijan's borders with Turkey and Iran before a tentative truce was concluded between the warring parties in May 1994. Many peace proposals have floundered on issues such as the status of the self-proclaimed Republic of Nagorno-Karabakh, whether Armenian units should withdraw from all occupied Azerbaijani territory before negotitions on the future status of the enclave could begin, and where and how many Russians should be stationed in a future peacekeeping force. Even the current Aliev regime remains suspicious of Moscow's regional ambitions and accuses Russia of being biased in favor of Armenia. Close historical, ethnic, and cultural links between Turkey and Azerbaijan ruled out the possibility of Turkey's acting as an intermediary in the conflict. But what of Iran?

Until the fall of 1993 relations between Iran and Armenia were on the whole cordial. In Iran, the Armenian community of approximately 200,000—occupying an important niche in local business—had a guaranteed representation in the parliament. Armenia aimed to tap Iranian oil and natural gas and exploit Iran's Persian Gulf ports, while officials in Tehran regarded Armenia as an economic and political outlet to the wider international community. Each state has received visits from a number of high-ranking delegations representing the other, including a visit by President Levon Ter-Petrosian to Tehran. Close ties with Christian Armenia at a time when that country was involved in a bloody conflict with Shiite Azerbaijan was further evidence of the pragmatic line pursued by Iran in the Caucasus. These ties encouraged the authorities in Tehran to seek to mediate in the Nagorno-Karabakh dispute, even though such action, if unsuccesssful, could have jeopardized Iran's relations with either Azerbaijan or Armenia, or both.

With the support of Azerbaijan, Armenia, and the Armenians of Nagorno-Karabakh, and at a time when Baku and Tehran were establishing firmer ties, in the first months of 1992 Iran embarked on a concerted campaign to obtain a durable, peaceful solution to the Nagorno-Karabakh problem. In February, Velayati toured the area and held discussions with the Armenian and Azerbaijani presidents. Armenian and Azerbaijani officials were soon in Tehran, and on March 16 agreed to a temporary cease-fire by signing the so-called Tehran Memorandum. Iranian deputy foreign minister Mahmud Va'ezi left for Baku and Erevan to work out the details of the cease-fire and arrange for the exchange of POWs and the bodies of war victims.[9] The Iranian-brokered cease-fire enabled UN special envoy Cyrus Vance to tour the region. UN Secretary-General Boutros Boutros-Ghali sent a message of appreciation to Velayati for the efforts of Iran in seeking to mediate in the conflict.[10]

Following up on another trip to the region by Va'ezi in April, on May 8 in Baku, Rafsanjani brought together Ter-Petrosian and acting Azerbaijani president Yacub Mamedov. Another agreement was signed in Tehran whereby a cease-fire would come into effect within one week, the economic blockade of Armenia would be lifted, international observers would be admitted into the area, prisoners would be exchanged, and a joint decision would be made on the problem of refugees.[11] But the next day news arrived that Shusha, the last Azerbaijani stronghold in Nagorno-Karabakh, had fallen and Armenian forces were threatening Nakhichevan. Va'ezi was immediately dispatched to the region once again. The Iranian deputy foreign minister was soon publicly denouncing this "undisguised aggression" and declaring that Iran considered Nagorno-Karabakh as part of Azerbaijan and was totally opposed to any change of borders in the region.[12]

Unilateral mediation by Iran was effectively ended, although relations between Iran and Armenia would not dramatically deteriorate until later in 1993. It seems that both Baku and Erevan had sincerely appreciated Tehran's efforts, but the Armenians of Nagorno-Karabakh could not be restrained. Elchibey had less faith in mediation and had initially but mistakenly hoped that Turkey would become more actively involved in the dispute.

Since the fall of 1993 Iran has been forced to take a renewed interest in the Nagorno-Karabakh dispute, with Azerbaijani refugees flooding toward the Iranian border in the wake of a series of Armenian military successes. As a precaution, in September 1993 Iran had started to amass troops on its northern border.[13] There were also reports that Tehran had deployed troops in Azerbaijan in an attempt to protect the Khoda Afarin Dam, which Iranian construction workers had been building, and that Iran had considered creating a buffer zone between southern Azerbaijan and northern Iran.[14] The authorities in Tehran were also most probably alarmed that tensions along Iran's northern border could stir up ill-feeling among the large Azerbaijani minority within Iran. Relations with Armenia suffered and ties with Azerbaijan were strengthened. Speaking in Baku in October 1993, Rafsanjani warned Armenia that Iran would endeavour not to provide military aid to Azerbaijan, but the "Islamic world will not allow open Armenian aggression against Azerbaijan."[15] Under these circumstances Iran will find it difficult to mediate between the Armenians and Azerbaijanis, but Tehran could still provide some input concerning work on a peaceful solution to the Nagorno-Karabakh dispute. Significantly, in January and June of 1994, Vladimir Kazimirov, Russia's special envoy for Nagorno-Karabakh affairs, held consultations with officials in Tehran. However, it seems highly unlikely that Iran will contribute to a possible peacekeeping force in Nagorno-Karabakh. A Russian-dominated CIS force would probably be dispatched under an OSCE mandate, with OSCE observers in place. Iran, of course, is a member of neither the CIS nor the OSCE.

Azerbaijan and Iran: Economic Cooperation

Trade between Azerbaijan and Iran has expanded in recent years and has not been affected by changes of leadership in Baku. A business council has been established and free-trade zones in Caspian Sea ports for the use of one another's business communities created. Unlike Turkey, Iran is able to offer Azerbaijan technical expertise in the oil and gas industries. In December 1993, Iran's ambassador in Baku stated that Iran was Azerbaijan's largest commercial partner, and that trade with Azerbaijan—worth almost $400 million over the last year—comprised 47.5 percent of Iran's total trade with the CIS.[16] In 1993, Turkey's trade turnover with Azerbaijan totaled only $102 million, which amounted to barely 3 percent of Turkey's trade with the CIS.[17]

There is an element of competition between Turkey and Iran over whether Azerbaijan and the newly independent Central Asian states should use Persian Gulf ports or the Turkish Mediterranean coast as a conduit for the export of their goods. On the other hand, Turkey and Iran are prepared to cooperate over the possible construction of an oil pipeline across both their territories to transport Azerbaijani oil to Western Europe. But the Western members of the international oil consortium, willing to extract oil from the largely untapped Caspian Sea reserves, prefer to use alternative routes for the pipeline, such as through Armenia or Georgia and then Turkey, or through a modernized Russian pipeline network. Aliev, although reneging on a previous understanding of Elchibey by allowing Russian Lukoil to have a stake in oil production in the Caspian, appears also to prefer the Iran–Turkey route and is still opposed to a route through Russia where Azerbaijan would remain economically dependent on Russia.[18] On September 20 though, the international oil consortium finally signed an oil production sharing agreement with the Azerbaijani authorities to develop three offshore Caspian Sea oil fields.

Azerbaijan and Iran could also boost commercial relations and consolidate social and cultural ties through common membership in the Economic

Cooperation Organization (ECO) and the Caspian Sea Cooperation Council (CSCC). Iran, together with Pakistan and Turkey (the founding members of ECO), had played an instrumental role in securing the admission of Azerbaijan and the newly independent Central Asian states into a rejuvenated ECO in 1992. Recent ECO meetings have discussed enhancing cooperation in fields such as transport, energy, and industry. Talks have also been initiated concerning the planning of a network of pipelines and power grids to meet the requirements of ECO members. However, to the displeasure of Turkey and Pakistan, Iranian officials have also spoken of the need for ECO to build an Islamic Common Market. It seems that in seeking to create "issue linkages" with pan-Islamic and Palestinian causes, the authorities in Tehran have attempted to use ECO to promote Iran's own private agenda.[19] Iran may also have ambitions to make ECO a security organization. Interestingly, in August 1993, Velayati had proposed that ECO should dispatch a delegation to Baku to hold talks with Azerbaijani officials to discover in what ways the organization could assist Azerbaijan.[20] Being in effect still a "poor man's club," the prospects for ECO remain uncertain.

The CSCC was sponsored by Iran and its formation announced in February 1992. Its members—Iran, Azerbaijan, Russia, Kazakhstan, and Turkmenistan—promised cooperation in such fields as trade, shipping, fisheries, and environmental protection.[21] A charter was promulgated in Tehran in October 1992. The CSCC appeared to be Iran's response to the Turkish-sponsored Black Sea Economic Cooperation scheme (of which Azerbaijan was also a member), which had been planned since late 1990 and was eventually officially inaugurated in June 1992.

Little more was heard of the CSCC until October 1994, when Russian officials suggested that it should become a multilateral coordinating committee responsible for overseeing the common exploitation of the natural resources of the Caspian Sea.[22] This was in reaction to the oil production sharing agreement of September 20 between the Azerbaijani authorities and the international oil consortium (in which, ironically, the Russian oil company Lukoil had a 10 percent stake) to which the Russian Foreign Ministry in particular was vehemently opposed out of concern that Western presence in the region would be heightened as a consequence. Iranian officials were placed in a quandry. The reactivation of the moribund CSCC could lead to closer Iranian ties with Russia and other Caspian Sea littoral states, including even Azerbaijan in the longer term. However, a revived CSCC could force the cancellation of the oil production sharing agreement, which could be to Iran's serious economic and political disadvantage if the members of the consortium were prepared to support the construction of an oil pipeline from the Caspian Sea to Turkey via Iran.

The Problem of Azerbaijani Identity

Relations between Azerbaijan and Iran may still be subject to friction due to the problem of Azerbaijani identity. What does it mean to be an "Azerbaijani," and where do the boundaries of Azerbaijan really lie? In recent Western literature at least two conflicting arguments have emerged with regard to Azerbaijani identity. According to Audrey Altstadt, Azerbaijani nationalism was fostered among the intelligentsia in the Russian-occupied part of Azerbaijan by the end of the nineteenth century. These Azerbaijanis regarded themselves as "Azerbaijani Turks," in spite of the fact that until the Russian conquest earlier in the century, all Azerbaijan had been a part of the Persian Empire. Without the pressures of industrialization and Russian occupation, the "Azerbaijanis" remaining within the Persian Empire continued to identify themselves with Persia.[23] Shireen Hunter has argued, though, that Azerbaijani nationalism in the territory of today's independent Azerbaijan only really took shape as a result of Stalin's determination to stamp out the Iranian heritage in the area. In Soviet Azerbaijan a Turkish consciousness was artificially instilled in most of the inhabitants; previously their culture had been more Iran-oriented apart from a Turkified language that was also used by Azerbaijanis in northern Iran. The purpose of this cultural reorientation was to ensure that Iran would be unable to resurrect a Greater Azerbaijan on its terms.[24]

The debate between these two scholars may at first seem irrelevant to current policy making, but how the approximately 6 million Azerbaijanis in today's independent Azerbaijan regard Azerbaijanis in today's northern Iran (up to 15 million, according to some estimates) and vice versa is important, bearing in mind Tehran's concern that the inhabitants of northern Iran may attempt to secede and link up with Azerbaijan to form a "Greater Azerbaijan." However, the possibility that the Azerbaijanis of independent Azerbaijan will seek to unite with Iran is not seriously considered at present.

The Iranian authorities must have viewed with grave apprehension the events of late 1989 and early 1990 when Azerbaijanis in then Soviet Azerbaijan demolished the border fence separating Nakhichevan and Iran and mingled with Azerbaijanis in northern Iran. Here, the Soviet Azerbaijanis, in addition to demanding that fertile land in the military zone along the border should be reclaimed, had also raised the question of unification with northern Iran.[25] The election of Elchibey as president of Azerbaijan must have also heightened Tehran's fears, bearing in mind that the Azerbaijan PF leader had on at least one occasion referred to Azerbaijan as encompassing not only the territory of "north Azerbaijan."[26] Elchibey may have hoped that the relative political freedom available in Azerbaijan compared to the more stifling regime in Iran—where only in recent years had publications in Azerbaijani been tolerated—would appeal to the Azerbaijanis in northern Iran. It is important to note that even though the visiting President Aliev in the summer of 1994 stressed that the "territorial integrity of Iran is sacred to the Azerbaijani republic," Iranian officials apparently still forced Aliev to cancel a planned trip to Tabriz, the capital of Iranian Azerbaijan.[27]

Seemingly in line with Altstadt's argument, in 1918 when the Azerbaijanis briefly secured independence from Russia there was no evidence of strong mutual attraction between them and the Azerbaijanis of northern Iran. Later, in 1945–46, the local population did not welcome the continued presence of the Soviet occupying force in northern Iran even though this could have culminated in the formation of a "Greater Azerbaijan," admittedly within the Soviet Union. In marked contrast, in 1946 the Soviet-sponsored Kurdish Mahabad Republic in northern Iran did obtain grassroots support.[28] It is not clear whether the Azerbaijanis of northern Iran will in time become attracted to the idea of uniting with an independent Azerbaijan. No longer the victims of the repressive policy of the shah, it has been argued that with the 1979 revolution and the shift in identification within the Iranian state from language to religion, the Azerbaijanis of northern Iran have come to identify themselves more closely with Iran.[29] There is also the belief among many Azerbaijanis in northern Iran that the Azerbaijanis in Azerbaijan are arrogant and regard themselves as superior to their cousins to the south, and that if a Greater Azerbaijan were to be created, the Azerbaijanis from the north would attempt to stake a claim to all the leading positions in this new state.[30]

In mid-August 1994 there were reports that immediately following a football match in Tabriz there were violent street demonstrations for two days. Local government buildings were attacked and the demonstrators denounced Rafsanjani, Khamenei, and other officials.[31] It is uncertain whether this could be the harbinger of a more concerted campaign on the part of the Azerbaijanis of northern Iran to secure secession from Iran and unite with Azerbaijan. Earlier in the same month there were riots in the northern Iranian city of Qazvin, which seem in part to be attributable to the anger of the Persian Qazvinis who had been under the rule of the Azerbaijani Zanjanis in Zanjan province. The demands of the Qazvinis for an independent provincial status were still not met by the central authorities, although in August the Qazvinis were removed from Zanjani jurisdiction.[32] This second incident would seem to suggest that even if the Azerbaijanis do not press to secede, in the current economic and social climate of Iran ethnic differences still pose threats to the internal stability of the country.[33]

One may also question whether Iran, perhaps out of concern over the possible formation of a Greater Azerbaijan, has been involved in fomenting disturbances along ethnic lines within Azerbaijan. Between June and August 1993, in the midst of the chaos that culminated in Elchibey's demise, there was news of a separatist rebellion among the Persian-speaking Talysh minority in southern Azerbaijan along one part of the border with Iran. According to the 1989 census, the Talysh numbered only 21,000, but this number is thought to reflect a campaign of assimilation from the Soviet era; the real number could be over 200,000.[34] The uprising was led by Colonel Ali Ikram Gummatov, who had apparently mounted a similar attempt to seize power in the region in early 1990, which was crushed by Soviet troops.[35] In this second uprising, a Talysh-Mugan Republic was proclaimed. According to some reports, Gummatov had plans to incorporate this self-declared republic within Iran.[36] Popular support for the rebellion had crumbled by the end of August 1993, though, and after months of hiding, Gummatov was arrested in December 1993. In late September 1994 Gummatov escaped from prison, and at the time of writing his exact whereabouts are unknown.

Was Iran secretly officially supporting this uprising? Details of what exactly happened are not clear. In a debate in the Azerbaijani National Assembly in mid-August 1993, while the crisis was ongoing, Interior Minister Vagif Novruzov claimed that Gummatov had connections with Iranian Hezbollah. Aliev reported, though, that Velayati, who was actually in Baku at that time, had denied official Iranian involvement.[37] Later, on national television on August 24, in a tirade against Gummatov, Aliev contended that the rebel colonel was supported by "foreign administrators and treacherous individuals living on the periphery of Azerbaijan." The president stressed that "neither Russia nor Iran could establish ties with such a bandit," and that Gummatov and his supporters had drummed up a myth that Russia and Iran were providing them with support. Aliev added that the Iranian ambassador had prevented Gummatov from entering Iran.[38]

One likely scenario is that this episode was another example of a powerful local warlord attempting to take advantage of the internal instability within Azerbaijan, on this occasion by appealing to ethnic Persian sentiment. Gummatov had previously benefited under Mutalibov and appears to have borne a grudge against Aliev. There are reports that the rebel colonel had at one time demanded as a price for the end of his rebellion the resignation of Aliev and the return to power of Mutalibov.[39] Official Iranian involvement appears to have been exceedingly unlikely. Why should Tehran seek to destabilize Azerbaijan? This would only serve to open up further the question of what *is* Azerbaijan, which could then have serious repercussions for the territorial integrity of Iran. This leads one to speculate as to who were the "foreign administrators" Aliev had in mind if their nationality was not Russian or Iranian. This concern for stability and the importance of Azerbaijan as an economic partner also helps to explain why Iranian officials do not appear interested in inciting radical Islam within Azerbaijan. It would serve no end, as the Azerbaijanis within Azerbaijan are notorious for their staunch belief in secularism, especially in the cities. Attempting to promote such radicalism would also provoke a heightened Turkish and Russian interest in Azerbaijan's internal politics, and would place Aliev in an increasingly uncomfortable position. The Tehran authorities have continued to follow a pragmatic line with Azerbaijan. At most, Iran appears to have offered only limited support to the small pro-Iranian Islamic Party of Azerbaijan founded in October 1992.

Regional Dynamics: The Importance of Russia

After the collapse of the Soviet Union, Russia has maintained a keen interest in activities in the Caucasus. Some observers may argue that Moscow continues to harbor imperial ambitions and that Russia is up to mischief in the region. For example, according to Thomas Goltz, Russia is deliberately stirring up trouble in the Caucasus by encouraging local minorities to press for self-determination at the expense of the territorial integrity of existing states. The governments in these threatened states are then forced to appeal to Moscow for military and political support to maintain the status quo. The case of Georgia and the Abkhazians is cited as one instance. Goltz also notes that Russia has meddled in the region in other ways. For instance, withdrawing Russian troops left behind weapons that the local warlord Huseinov made use of to pressure Elchibey to flee and to allow the more pro-Russian Aliev to return to power.[40] This argument, however, does not fully explain Russian policy in the Caucasus.

Russia has legitimate security concerns in the Caucasus. Moscow fears that regional instability—which has already destabilized parts of Russian North Caucasus—may threaten the southern Russian provinces of the Kuban, the breadbasket of Russia. It would appear that most Russian officials favor regional stability, or at least an environment of only limited instability that can be controlled. This accounts for Moscow's pressure, in the face of fierce opposition from Azerbaijan and Turkey in particular, to secure a modification of the CFE (Conventional Forces in Europe) Treaty to enable more Russian military hardware to be deployed along Russia's southern borders. It also explains Russia's peacekeeping role in Georgia and Moscow's efforts to mediate a peaceful solution over Nagorno-

Karabakh. Certainly, though, Russia is determined to have a continued military presence in the Caucasus. In June 1994 Defense Minister Pavel Grachev toured the region and secured agreements whereby Russia would be able to maintain three military bases in Georgia, two in Armenia, and a radar station in northern Azerbaijan, thereby providing for a unified air defense system in the Caucasus.[41]

Russia is not prepared to allow Turkey and Iran to acquire enhanced influence in the Caucasus and Central Asia at Moscow's expense. Deep-rooted fears of pan-Turkism were rekindled with the accession to power of Elchibey, and to many Russians Iran is still closely associated with Islamic fundamentalism and the Muslim "threat from the south." It seems that in Russian decision-making circles, after an initial phase following the unraveling of the Soviet Union when an overtly pro-Western policy was adopted, a consensus is now emerging that recognizes the increasing importance of maintaining close relations with the former Soviet republics. It seems no longer to be the case that there are decisive splits among Russian decision makers between those who emphasize pursuing a policy in favor of the First World (pro-West), Second World (pro-CIS), and Third World (pro–developing countries).[42] A course of action appears to be taking shape that attempts to amalgamate each of these three approaches. The authorities in Moscow are concerned to preserve close links with the newly independent countries of the former Soviet Union without jeopardizing improved relations with the West and with developing states such as Iran.

In recent years relations between the Soviet Union and Iran, and then Russia and Iran, have improved in spite of historical rivalries and Soviet/Russian interference in Iran during this century. Immediately before the death of Khomeini and the revision of the official Iranian policy of "neither East nor West," the withdrawal of Soviet troops from Afghanistan had created a more positive atmosphere. In 1989 a number of delegations visited both capitals, including the state visit of President Rafsanjani in June 1989 shortly after Khomeini's death. This visit set in motion a beneficial economic partnership. Iran has become dependent on Moscow for arms procurements and technology. Between 1989 and 1992 Russia provided 64 percent of Iran's arms imports, with Moscow committed to deliver forty MiG-29s, twenty to thirty Su-24s (longer-range aircraft), three submarines, armor, artillery, and sea mines. In addition to providing a source of hard currency, the authorities in Moscow hoped to influence Iranian foreign policy through these arms transfers.[43] Certainly, Iran has pursued a cautious, pragmatic policy in the Caucasus.

In March 1993, Foreign Minister Andrei Kozyrev held consultations in Tehran and agreed to a Declaration of Principles of Cooperation between

Russia and Iran which Yeltsin and Rafsanjani were to sign at some future date.[44] The declaration remains to be signed. In September 1993 relations between the two states briefly deteriorated when the Russian Foreign Ministry was highly critical of reports of an Iranian incursion into Azerbaijan to protect the Khoda Afarin Dam.[45]

Russian military officers based in Azerbaijan may have decided on their own accord to leave behind a stockpile of weapons that Huseinov and his followers could conveniently use. Regardless of who made the decision, relations between Russia and Azerbaijan did improve for a while with, for example, Aliev renegotiating the oil production sharing agreement for the Caspian Sea oil fields to enable Lukoil to acquire a stake. However, Aliev is also eager to maintain ties with Turkey and Iran—as Tehran Radio had pointed out in January 1994. Thus, officials in Baku remain determined to resist the deployment of a Russian-dominated CIS peacekeeping force in Nagorno-Karabakh without proper OSCE supervision—a line supported by Turkey and probably not opposed by Iran.

Russia, Azerbaijan, and Iran are each interested in stability in the Caucasus. Moscow, therefore, is most probably supportive of the current close Azerbaijani-Iranian ties. An Iranian-Azerbaijani axis against Russia is not likely given that the still unresolved question of Azerbaijani identity places limits on the extent of cooperation between Baku and Tehran.

Regional Dynamics: The Importance of the United States

It appears that the Caucasus ranks relatively low in the priorities of American foreign policy in the post–Cold War era. U.S. officials seem to admit tacitly that the Caucasus, and indeed former Soviet Central Asia, are in effect Russia's backyard. Cognizant of Moscow's security concerns, the Clinton administration appears prepared to tolerate Russian activities in the region provided that they are not destabilizing. This lack of direct American, and more generally Western, concern for developments in the region resulted in the UN Security Council's approving the previously deployed Russian (in theory CIS) peacekeeping force in Georgia. In May 1993, the United States was briefly involved in a so-called tripartite initiative with Russia and Turkey which had sought ways to end the conflict over Nagorno-Karabakh. This initiative soon became part of the OSCE Minsk Group's proposals, although one should note that the United States is also one of the ten members of this group.

American involvement in the Caucasus is constrained by the absence of diplomatic ties with Iran, and by problems in relations with Azerbaijan. Even the more pragmatic Rafsanjani is not prepared to seek a rapprochement with the United States. American officials also continue to view Iranian policy with grave suspicion and mistrust. In the summer of 1994, U.S. Secretary of State Warren Christopher, for all intents and purposes, accused the Iranian government of masterminding the bombings of Jewish targets in London and Buenos Aires.

Official ties between the United States and Azerbaijan are severely impaired by the operation of Section 907 of the 1992 Freedom Support Act. Here, Congress has effectively prohibited all official U.S. aid to Azerbaijan because of the Azerbaijani blockade of Armenia—although Armenia has likewise blockaded Nakhichevan. This aid embargo is clearly the work of a highly organized Armenian lobby. Armenia continues to receive extensive American aid. In August 1994 Clinton pledged to visiting President Ter-Petrosian that the forthcoming aid package would be "very significant." American officials stated that the per capita level of current U.S. assistance to Armenia was the highest of all former Soviet republics.[46]

American companies do have an important commercial interest in Azerbaijan. Pennzoil, Amoco, Unocal, Ramco, and McDermott are members of the international consortium prepared to extract oil from the Caspian Sea oil fields, although for political reasons they are opposed to the construction of a pipeline through Iran. If Russia fails to block the work of this consortium, U.S. relations with Azerbaijan are likely to improve because of the high commercial stakes. Significantly, President Clinton did receive Aliev in the White House in late September 1994 after the latter had addressed the UN General Assembly.

The Clinton administration should not let a Pax Russica develop unchecked in the Caucasus. Even if not directly involved in the region, the United States could make use of the OSCE to keep a watchful eye on the Russians. American-Iranian relations will not improve in the foreseeable future. American-Azerbaijani relations could be upgraded if the U.S. Congress revised its policy in spite of the Armenian lobby. This would lead to a more balanced American position on the Caucasus. American officials should be made more aware that close Iranian-Azerbaijani ties at present are of value to regional stability.

Conclusion

Future developments in the region and the state of relations between Azerbaijan and Iran in the medium and long terms are impossible to predict. Personalities appear to be one important element. The situation could change dramatically if Aliev, Rafsanjani, or Yeltsin were suddenly removed from power. Under Zhirinovsky or Rutskoi, for example, Russia could become an unashamedly expansionist and imperialist state. As already observed, individual leaders have played a particularly prominent role in the fluctuations in the external policy of Azerbaijan. Aliev is old and it is by no means clear who will succeed him as president; at this stage the return of Elchibey is extremely unlikely. Although in Iran the decision-making process is more complex, the removal from power of Rafsanjani for economic failings, for instance, could have significant consequences for Iranian foreign policy in the Caucasus. Tehran could pursue a more aggressive policy—perhaps more in line with the goals of revolutionary Islam—although this could backfire if regional instability ensued. Under those circumstances the Azerbaijanis of northern Iran might be compelled to choose between union with a Greater Azerbaijan or continued membership of an avowedly Islamic republic.

It would seem, though, that whoever is in charge of government, neither Iran nor Azerbaijan is likely to play the role of regional spoiler. The risks for the territorial integrity of these states would appear to be too great. Recent events in Qazvin and Tabriz must have alerted the Iranian authorities to these risks. However, one cannot guarantee the long-term stability of a region when a conflict within that region remains unresolved. The dispute among Armenia, the Armenians of Nagorno-Karabkh, and Azerbaijan should be settled to the satisfaction of all parties. In spite of the endeavours of Russia and the OSCE to find a solution, Iran might still have a role to play and should not be entirely excluded. Armenia would still prefer to deal with Iran rather than Turkey, despite a cooling in the relationship between Tehran and Erevan since the fall of 1993. With Iran's repeatedly expressed concern that the territorial integrity of Azerbaijan be respected, any Iranian contribution to a possible future peace settlement would thus seem likely to solidify further relations between Azerbaijan and Iran.

Notes

1. See Shireen Hunter, *Iran and the World: Continuity in a Revolutionary Decade* (Bloomington: Indiana University Press, 1990), pp. 6–20; and Shahram Chubin, *Iran's National Security Policy: Capabilities, Intentions and Impact* (Washington, DC: Carnegie Endowment for Peace, 1994), pp. 65–68.

2. *BBC Summary of World Broadcasts* (hereafter *SWB*), January 22 ,1990 ME/ 0668A/1.

3. *SWB*, November 19, 1991 ME/1242A/5.

4. Tadeusz Swietochowski, "The Spirit of Baku," *Central Asia Monitor*, no. 4 (1993), p. 19.

5. *Current Digest of the Post-Soviet Press* (hereafter *CDPSP*), vol. 45, no. 44 (December 1, 1993), pp. 27–28. Originally published in Russian in *Segodnia*, October 30, 1993, p. 4.

6. *SWB*, July 5, 1994 ME/2039MED/9.

7. *SWB*, February 2, 1994 ME/1911MED/3.

8. *SWB*, July 2, 1994 SU/2037F/1.

9. *SWB*, March 20, 1992 ME/1334A/11.

10. R.K. Ramazani, "Iran's Foreign Policy: Both North and South," *Middle East Journal*, vol. 46, no. 3 (Summer 1992), p. 410.

11. *Turkish Daily News* (hereafter *TDN*), May 9, 1992.

12. *CDPSP*, vol. 44, no. 20 (17 June 1992), p. 12. Originally published in Russian in *Izvestiia*, May 20, 1992, pp. 1 and 5.

13. "Iran—Azeri-wary," *The Economist*, November 6, 1993.

14. *Foreign Broadcast Information Service*, Central Eurasia (hereafter FBIS-SOV) 93-227, November 29, 1993, p. 83. Iranian-Armenian relations further nose-dived after reports that Armenian forces in Nagorno-Karabakh had downed an Iranian air force Hercules C-130 over Nagorno-Karabakh in March 1994, resulting in the deaths of those on board.

15. *CDPSP*, vol. 45, no. 44 (December 1, 1993), pp. 27–28. Originally published in Russian in *Segodnia*, October 30, 1993, p. 4.

16. FBIS-SOV-93-240, December 16, 1993, p. 81.

17. *Nisan 1994'te Turkiye Ekonomisi Istatistik ve Yorumlar* (Ankara: T.C. Basbakanlik Devlet Istatistik Enstitusu, 1994), p. 105.

18. For more background to the oil pipeline dispute, see Gareth M. Winrow, "Turkish Relations with the Newly Independent Republics in the Caucasus," *The Oxford International Review*, vol. 5, no. 1 (Winter 1993), p. 48.

19. Kaveh L. Afrasiabi, "The Economic Cooperation Organization (ECO)," *Central Asia Monitor*, no. 4 (1993), p. 30.

20. *TDN*, August 31, 1993.

21. Ramazani, "Iran's Foreign Policy," pp. 408–9.

22. *Radio Free Europe/Radio Liberty* (hereafter *RFE/RL) Daily Report*, nos. 194 and 195, October 12 and 13, 1994, by Liz Fuller.

23. Audrey L. Altstadt, *The Azerbaijani Turks: Power and Identity under Russian Rule* (Stanford, CA: Hoover Institution Press, 1992), especially pp. 70–71.

24. Shireen T. Hunter, "Azerbaijan: Search for Identity and New Partners," in Ian Bremmer and Ray Taras (eds.), *Nations and Politics in the Soviet Successor States* (Cambridge: Cambridge University Press, 1993), pp. 225–60.

25. Altstadt, *The Azerbaijani Turks*, p. 211.

26. Rajan Menon and Henri J. Barkey, "The Transformation of Central Asia: Implications for Regional and International Security," *Survival*, vol. 34, no. 4 (1992–93), p. 78.

27. *CDPSP*, vol. 46, no. 27 (August 3, 1994), pp. 21–22. Originally published in Russian in *Nezavisimaia gazeta*, July 5, 1994, p. 1.

28. Richard W. Cottam, *Nationalism in Iran* (Pittsburgh, PA: University of Pittsburgh Press, 1964), p. 133.

29. Patricia J. Higgins, "Minority-State Relations in Contemporary Iran," in Ali Banuazizi and Myron Weiner (eds.), *The State, Religion and Ethnic Politics: Afghanistan, Iran and Pakistan* (Syracuse, NY: Syracuse University Press, 1986), pp. 188–90.

30. Hunter, "Azerbaijan: Search for Identity," pp. 232–33.

31. *Cumhuriyet* (in Turkish), August 23, 1994.

32. *The Independent*, August 6, 1994.

33. There were reports earlier in 1994 that the violence in Zahedan—a predominantly Baluchi region near the Iranian-Pakistani border—which erupted after a Sunni mosque had been demolished, could have had an ethnic dimension.

34. Suzanne Goldenberg, *Pride of Small Nations: The Caucasus and Post-Soviet Disorder* (London and New York: Zed Books, 1994), p. 128.

35. Elizabeth Fuller, *Azerbaijan at the Crossroads* (London: Royal Institute of International Affairs, 1994), p. 29.

36. Robert V. Barylski, "The Caucasus, Central Asia and the Near-Abroad Syndrome," *Central Asia Monitor*, no. 5 (1993), p. 23.

37. *SWB*, August 20, 1993 SU/1772C1/1.

38. *SWB*, August 27, 1993 SU/1778C1/1–2.

39. Goldenberg, *Pride of Small Nations*, p. 128.

40. Thomas Goltz, "Letter from Eurasia: The Hidden Russian Hand," *Foreign Policy*, no. 92 (Fall 1993), pp. 92–116; and, "Still on the Prowl," *The Economist*, August 28, 1993.

41. *RFE/RL Daily Report*, no. 110 (June 13, 1994), by Liz Fuller.

42. For a discussion of these three schools, see Fred Wehling, "Three Scenarios for Russia's Middle East Policy," *Communist and Post-Communist Studies*, vol. 26, no. 2 (June 1993), pp. 182–204.

43. Chubin, *Iran's National Security Policy*, pp. 33–34 and 40–41.

44. *SWB*, March 31, 1993 ME/1651A/8–9.

45. *CDPSP*, vol. 45, no. 36 (October 6, 1993), p. 8. Originally published in Russian in *Nezavisimaia gazeta*, September 8, 1993, p. 2.

46. *TDN*, August 11, 1994.

5

Iran and Tajikistan

Mohiaddin Mesbahi

The collapse of the Soviet Union in December 1991 and the subsequent emergence of the new independent states in Central Asia and the Caucasus have presented Iran with a host of challenges and opportunities unprecedented in the contemporary history of its foreign policy, especially in the most recent stage since 1979. While the traditional focus of Iran's foreign policy has always been a southern thrust (Persian Gulf and the Middle East), the new northern tier openings in Central Asia and the Caucasus have presented Iran with significant breathing space and have opened up possibilities for political influence and economic and ideological gains. The new northern frontier also presents Iran with an opportunity to break out of its regional isolation in the south. This seems particularly critical in view of U.S.-Iranian hostility and Washington's dual containment policy, which has focused, in addition to Iraq, principally on Iran.

While the overall direction of the U.S. containment policy against Iran has been stretched recently to cover Central Asia—as Washington clearly prefers and advocates a distance between Central Asian states and Tehran—Iran will look to Central Asia as a new space through which to break out from isolation and containment. In addition, Central Asia (and the Caucasus) and especially its linkages with the Middle East, from Tehran's perspective, present important changes and modifications in both the political and cultural dynamics of the "new" Middle East. The inclusion of more non-Arab, Islamic ethnic elements further dilutes the predominantly Arab character of the Iranian regional subsystem.

These political opportunities are nevertheless accompanied by equally significant challenges and vulnerabilities. The comfort and stability of long and secure borders with the Soviet Union are being replaced by considerable anxiety over implications of ethnoterritorial dynamics and conflicts, competitive rivalries with neighbors, and "great power games"; thus, instead of a breathing space in the north, we see the emergence of a new pressure front for already taxed foreign policy responsibilities and concerns in the south. This study will look first into the key conceptual characteristics of the Iranian vision and policy in Central Asia and will then analyze the Tajik-Iranian relations in the framework of those general and conceptual principles.

Iranian Foreign Policy toward Central Asia: Conceptual Characteristics

Iran's view of Central Asia—that is, its place in the Iranian foreign policy framework and objectives—is generally affected by the interactive dynamics of three issues: first, the role of the *Russian factor*—Russian-Iranian relations or *Russian-centric* aspects of Iranian foreign policy in Central Asia; second, the *Islamic factor* or the geopolitics and geocultural role of Islam; and finally, a vision of *Iran's centrality* in shaping Central Asian (and Transcaucasian) developments. Iran's foreign policy toward Central Asian states is driven and informed to varying degrees by a mix of these three general themes; however, relations with each state—given the historical and geopolitical particularities of each—will require a different level of emphasis on these general principles and concerns.

Geopolitics and Balance of Power: The Russian Factor

Iran embraced the collapse of the Soviet Union with "mixed emotion." The collapse of the Soviet Union relieved Iran in one stroke from the threat of both the military presence of a superpower and the ideological challenge of Marxism as a historical universalist rival claim in the Muslim world. For more than a century, Iran's geopolitical calculation had been informed by the threat of Russian/Soviet imperialism and its considerable weight against a vulnerable and long Iranian border. Iran's historical gravitation toward alliance with distant powers like the British Empire up to 1945 and the United States in the postwar years was a result of this historical vulnerability and the perception of Russian expansionism. Iran became the buffer state between the presumed Russian southward thrust and the Western powers' historical geopolitical and economic interest (i.e., British India, and Persian Gulf oil). Iran's territorial integrity was to a large extent dependent on the great powers' implicit understanding of its position as the buffer state.

The Iranian revolution of 1979 and the subsequent hostility between Iran and the United States signaled the beginning of change in the historical fixation of the "buffer" concept and the balancing context of Iranian geopolitics. Somewhat unique in its foreign policy consequences, the anti-Western orientation of the Iranian revolution in 1979 did not translate into a pro-Soviet stand. In fact, Iran, especially in view of the Soviet presence in Afghanistan and Moscow's support for Iraq, remained distant from and critical of the Soviet Union through most of the 1980s. Iran's independent position vis-à-vis the superpowers, beyond its ideological motives, was a calculated position by Tehran underlining a message of nonalignment and thus perpetuating the notion of Iran maybe not as a buffer, but as a neutral zone.

Viewed from this perspective, Iran had a stake in the maintenance of a certain balance in the regional and international structure and distribution of power. Given the increasing hostility between Iran and the United States in the 1980s, and the gradual and thus decisive consolidation of U.S. power in the Persian Gulf, the presence of the less aggressive, yet functioning, "Gorbachevian" Soviet superpower seemed to serve Iran's overall geopolitical interests. The fear of a U.S.-led unipolar world system was thus the underlying reason behind Iran's cautious and tamed attitude toward the unfolding process of the Soviet collapse in the 1990–91 period. A major editorial in the *Tehran Times*, the semi-official mouthpiece of Iran's Foreign Ministry, assured the Soviet leadership that Iran, in contrast to other countries in the region, has a stake in the territorial and political integrity of the Soviet Union and will not utilize Soviet vulnerability.[1]

This consideration of Iran's vulnerability in a U.S.-dominated regional/international order is the key underlying factor in the development of Iran's Russian-centric policy toward the new independent states of Central Asia and the Caucasus. To have a correct, if not warm, relationship with Russia remains critical to Iran's regional foreign policy. This Russian-centric policy is designed to respond to three sets of Iranian concerns and objectives: namely, the importance of bilateral Russian-Iranian relations; the impact of Russia on Iranian–Central Asian relations; and the impact of the emergence of new states for Iran's domestic, i.e., territorial, integrity. First, bilaterally, Russia has been and will continue to be a source for purchasing arms and technology and for economic, trade, and political cooperation.[2] The Russian-centric policy, however, is not based on single issues or purely bilateral considerations, but includes the impact on Iran's multilateral and bilateral relations with Central Asian states.

Second, this Russian-centrism reflects Iran's recognition of Moscow's geopolitical influence in the former republics and its impact on Iranian–Central Asian relations. An anti-Russian policy in Central Asia on the part of Tehran thus will not serve Iran's immediate and long-term interests. Such a policy will create impediments against regional receptivity and will further pave the way for a more intensive U.S.-Russian cooperation against Iran.

Third, Iran's vulnerability against regional conflicts in Central Asia and Transcaucasia and its needs for regional stability demand a closer cooperation or understanding with Moscow. This is particularly important in view of the prominence that Iran has attached to its own role as a peacemaker and mediator.

This regional perspective does not exclude conflicts of interest and competitive policies, as will be shown later in Tajikistan's case, but illustrates the continuous attempt by Tehran to accommodate the Russian factor, to minimize Moscow's obstructionism, and to solicit its acquiescence or cooperation. Furthermore, the multiplicity of issues concerning the Russian–Iranian–Central Asian triangle does not lend itself to a uniformity of interests in all situations. Conflicts of interest—for example, in Tajikistan between Iran and Russia—are simultaneously accompanied by a general convergence of interests of the two countries in the issues concerning the geopolitics of the Caspian Sea, Iran's "second Persian Gulf," the sovereignty over Caspian Sea energy and food resources, and especially the long-term and very serious impact of the Caspian environmental crisis on Iran's northern provinces. Thus, the nature and impact of Russian-centrism in Iranian–Central Asian policy will be decided at the nexus of the bilateral and multilateral dimension of Russian-Iranian relations.

Islamic Geopolitics

The second factor in Iranian–Central Asian relations is the impact of Iran's particular characteristics as an Islamic state, one with a revolutionary/revisionist ideology perceived by a host of regional and international actors as destabilizing and threatening. This particular image of Iran has been the central and defining element in shaping its opportunities and constraints, and affecting Iranian foreign policy behavior. It is this uniformity in the Iranian image in the eyes of others—both friends and enemies—that has created an inescapable context for Iranian foreign policy in its bilateral or multilateral dimension.

Iran's foreign policy, pragmatic or revolutionary, will be measured within the confines of the level of sensitivity of other actors toward the geopolitics of the Islamic factor. Central to these geopolitics is, of course, the attitude of the great powers, above all the United States and Russia. U.S. attitudes toward the Islamic threat now dominate Iran's relations with its southern tier—the Persian Gulf, the Middle East, and even North Africa. Given the Islamic character of Central Asia and its linkage with the Middle East and Iran's geographical location, it will be an important consideration in shaping Iran's position in Central Asia as well. In Central Asia, in addition to the newly independent states and the United States, Russia will also look into the Islamic factor as one of the cornerstones of its policy formulation, options, and strategy.

A discussion of the role of Islam in Iran's future and its impact in Central Asia is beyond the scope of this paper; what is important here, however, is the role of the "threat" of Islam in shaping the attitudes of multitudes of actors with divergent interests who usually converge on the issue of "containment" of the Islamic threat. Whether Islam is a real threat in Central Asia or whether it is conveniently imagined as such remains largely irrelevant, as regional and international actors act upon the "Islamic factor" as one of the key threats to their domestic and external security in the post-Soviet period.

While the general culture and religious characteristics of Central Asia make it a region of opportunity and influence for Iran, the same factors are nurturing resistance and obstacles—a dichotomy that has characterized Iran's policy in the Middle East and the Islamic world in general. This dichotomy originates from the divergent impact of Iran in its relations with other states on the one hand, and its real or perceived impact or influence on social movements (i.e., Islamic activists/groups, etc.) on the other. In Central Asia, as will be shown in Tajikistan in particular, and as is the case in Iranian relations with Islamic states elsewhere, the inherent tension between state-to-state relations (i.e., Iran–Tajikistan) and state-to-social movement relations (i.e., the Tajik Islamic opposition) will be a continuous source of challenge and opportunity for Iran, notwithstanding its repeated assertion of its noninvolvement in revolutionary Islamic movements or its lack of interest in exporting the revolution.

Iran's policy toward the role of Islam or Islamic movements in Central Asia is fundamentally pragmatic, a pragmatism that reflects Tehran's appreciation of the underdeveloped nature of both political and orthodox Islam in Central Asia, the strength of the Soviet secular legacy, and, above all, the strength of the local and regional coalition that fear of Islam generates. This coalition not only targets Islam as a domestic challenge, but more importantly targets Iran and attempts its isolation. Iran's pragmatism is challenged by a combination of interdependent and mutually reinforcing dynamics, including the inertia of a self-proclaimed Islamic metropolis in Iran, domestic ideological pressure, and above all, absence of international and regional mechanisms willing to reward Iran's pragmatism. The absence of this "reward structure" erodes support and legitimacy at home while resulting in the loss of credibility with potential friends abroad.

Iran's Centrality

The third factor shaping Iran's policy in Central Asia is Iran's self-image as a central player in the region's international dynamics. This self-image is rooted in Iran's perception of its assets and liabilities. Iran's unique assets include its geographical contiguity with the former Soviet Union (Iran has land borders with Azerbaijan, Armenia, and Turkmenistan and sea borders with Russia and Kazakhstan); its natural role as the key transit link of Central Asia to the Middle East, the Persian Gulf, and the open sea; and its political importance as a major actor in the Middle East and Southwest Asia. Iran thus sees itself as a nexus and center of regional economic and political activities. This centrality, in addition to Iran's assets, also reflects appreciation of its resultant vulnerabilities.

Concern over territorial integrity, a traditional preoccupation, has now been strongly reinforced by the emergence of surrounding states with active and significant ethnoterritorial problems—problems magnified by the multi-ethnic nature of Iran itself. A prime regional refugee hub, Iran hosted more than 4 million refugees, 14 percent of its population in the 1980s and early 1990s, as a result of conflicts on its western border (Iraq) and on its eastern border (Afghanistan), and is now receiving refugees from the north (Azerbaijan). Regional conflicts are a major challenge to Iranian security and a direct consequence of its central location. This centrality has generated certain perspectives and attitudes in Iranian foreign policy toward Central Asia, which are not very different from those adopted toward the Persian Gulf. These attitudes and perspectives include an *anticontainment* strategy (a desire to undermine any attempt at Iran's isolation) and proactive diplomacy to enhance Iran's political, security, and economic strength and leverage.

In addition to bilateral relations, there are two themes in the anti-containment and proactive diplomatic posture that are essential to Iran's foreign policy in Central Asia, namely *regional multilateralism* and *diplomacy of conflict resolution and mediation*. Iran's multilateral policy is reflected in its promotion or creation of regional organizations such as the

Economic Cooperation Organization (ECO) and the Caspian Sea Littoral States Organization, and multilateral economic projects focusing on transit and energy.[3] Building transit linkages with Central Asia through an expanding shipping line in the Caspian Sea, and more significantly through the railroad with Turkmenistan (Sarakhs-Tezhen) will be a significant component of Iran's multilateral and regionalist approach toward Central Asia. This policy is also reflected in regional cooperation in the areas of energy and the transport of oil and gas to Europe via multilateral pipeline projects such as the one involving Turkmenistan, Iran, and Turkey.[4] These multilateral relations will provide a regional cross-current network that is hoped to provide Iran with economic benefits and to solidify its role as an integral part of the regional community, making isolation or containment unlikely or unworkable.

Iran's consistent effort in conflict resolution initiatives and mediation diplomacy in conflicts in Central Asia and the Caucasus is driven by concern over the negative impact of regional conflicts on Iranian security and their propensity to invite great-power intervention. An effective mediation would enhance Iran's prestige and its regional leverage, and would thus contribute to the overall notion of Iran's *centrality* in regional affairs. Iran's continuous mediation in the two major regional conflicts in the former territory of the USSR—Nagorno-Karabakh and especially Tajikistan—is underscored by the significance of mediation as a method in promoting Iran's security and political relevance to important regional dynamics—a *positive* central role that neutralizes the complex or *negative* impact of the "Islamic factor." Iranian foreign policy in Central Asia and the Transcaucasus, while reflecting these main themes, nevertheless has an evolving nature as the region itself is still in a transitional stage. The conceptual or even historical fixation of actors, including Iran, will thus be subjected to evolutionary or sudden changes or modification.

Iranian-Tajik Relations: 1992–1994

Iran's relationship with Tajikistan since the initiation of official relations on January 8, 1992, is in fact a microcosm of the interaction of the three prominent elements of Iranian–Central Asian policy: Islamic geopolitics, Russian-Iranian relations, and Iran's efforts in remaining a major player through an intimate engagement in the diplomacy of mediation. Iranian-Tajik relations will thus be analyzed in the context of these three interactive dynamics. The following section will first look into the role of Islam and the cultural factor in shaping the relations, and then will discuss other themes in the context of Iran's diplomacy in the Tajik civil war.

Islamic Geopolitics: Symbiosis of
Culture and Ideology

Among the newly independent states of Central Asia, Tajikistan occupies a special place for Iran. While Tajikistan lacks the economic significance of Turkmenistan and Kazakhstan and Uzbekistan's political weight, for the combined reasons of culture and ideology its relations with Iran carry a special role in shaping Iran's overall foreign policy in Central Asia. Of all the new "Muslim" states, Tajikistan is the only Farsi-speaking state with a strong and specific linkage with the Iranian cultural milieu. While Iran continues to claim a cultural/religious relevance in the whole of Central Asia, Tajikistan's linguistic connection with Iran separates it from others and gives it a certain level of closeness and importance to Iran that does not exist with other Central Asian states. In fact, it is this cultural element that presents Tajikistan not only as an opportunity but as a "burden" or "responsibility" for the Iranian leadership. (The intermingling of culture and religious affinity has created a complex and at times confusing element in Tajik-Iranian relations.) In fact, and in the long run, this cultural element may prove to be the most enduring element in Tajik-Iranian ties. Furthermore, the Tajik significance also lies in the fact that it clearly was the bastion of the most politicized or active Islamic tendencies among Central Asian states.

Tajikistan's Islamic movement started in the mid-1970s and grew under the impact of the Soviet invasion of Afghanistan and the gradual indirect influence of the Iranian revolution through Iranian radio broadcasts to Central Asia throughout the 1980s.[5] The fact that the majority of Tajik Muslims, with the exception of the Badakhshan Ismailis and an insignificant number of Ja'fari Shiites, are Sunni Hannafi was not without some significance in relations with Shiite Iran. Not only have the Tajik Muslims been separated from the Islamic world for decades, they and other Muslim societies of the former Soviet Union have gone through intense anti-Islamic state propaganda and socialization resulting in the general ignorance of the public about Islam, either in its Orthodox forms or the politicized "Iranian" version.

Furthermore, the structure of authority, leadership, and relations between the community and religious leaders generally and historically has differed between Shiite and Sunni Islam. Qadi Akbar Turajonzoda, the Qadi Kalan of Tajikistan and key Islamic leader of the Tajik opposition, has on several occasions referred to differences between Iran's Islamic experience and Tajikistan's and significantly specified two key obstacles to repeating the Iranian model in Tajikistan: first, the general ignorance of the public about

Islam and especially its role as a well-defined political ideology;[6] and second, the general disadvantage of a Sunni religious leadership in not enjoying the position of imam among their adherents as has been done by Shiite religious leaders such as Ayatollah Khomeini. In an interview with *Moscow News* in September 1992, during the heyday of the Islamicist surge to power, Turajonzoda warned against the premature comparison between Iran and Tajikistan and specifically addressed key differences. Indicating that the Iranian model is not likely to fit Tajikistan, he argued that Iran's Shiite Muslims have a "unifying factor—the imamate—which they obey without demur. We the Sunnis have no such centralization, and each mullah and parish can exist on their own, not obeying anyone's ecclesiastical authority."[7]

Turajonzoda's qualification about leadership problems, especially when the Islamic-democratic coalition seemed to be gaining ground against Nabiev's government, underlined one of the key problems facing any attempt by Iran or other actors to push for a nationwide Islamic takeover in Tajikistan. This structural impediment to the leadership of the Tajik Muslim community was further complicated by significant political differences rooted in the region/class nature of the distribution of power between the more urbanized and traditional ruling classes coming from the northern regions of Kulob-Qurghonteppa and Leninabad with strong procommunist or secular tendencies, and the more rural and poor inhabitants of the less developed regions as well as some of the lower socioeconomic groups in Dushanbe, which largely supported the Islamicist movement.

It is clear that the idea of establishing an Iranian model never became the foundation of a political strategy for the Islamicists and democratic allies. The appearance of more specific Islamic slogans in the critical and bloody days of September and December of 1992 indicated a definite radicalization of Islamicists regarding the idea of establishing an Islamic state. This was also reflected not only in the appearance of proto-Iranian slogans in Dushanbe, but the creation of some ad hoc revolutionary organizations based on the Iranian models. The appearance of slogans such as "Long Live the Islamic Republic" and "Death to America" was reminiscent of the Iranian revolutionary days of 1979, and the establishment of Nehzat-e Javanaan-e Dushanbe (Dushanbe's Youth Movement) brought to mind the *Komiteh*, Iran's revolutionary committees, one of the ad hoc grassroots legacies of the Iranian revolution that played a significant role in that revolution. The Dushanbe Youth Movement had an important role in Nabiev's resignation in September 1992, his eventual downfall, and the early defense of Dushanbe in October and December of 1992 against the onslaught of procommunist factions of the Jebhe Khalq, the People's Front.[8]

This symbolic or real radicalization of the pro-Iranian Islamic agenda reflected not a shift to a well-thought-out or externally inspired takeover strategy, as was claimed by the communist opposition and their Russian and Uzbek supporters, but haphazard, reactive sloganism of a grassroots nature, largely outside the realm of planning or direction of the coalition leadership. The Islamic-democratic coalition neither believed in the possibility or desirability of an Islamic alternative nor were even united in a preference for an ideologically tainted political model for Tajikistan. The general principles of the coalition platform referred to a democratic political system based on a new constitution and close relations with Iran and Afghanistan as well as other Islamic states.[9]

The role of democratic and nationalist groups and the intelligentsia in shaping the opposition platform and in defining the role of Islam in it seemed to be rather significant, though the intelligentsia and democrats numerically did not and do not carry a significant organized weight in comparison to the Islamicists or Communists. Their significance lies in the fact that they represent the general political flavor in Tajikistan, which does not support the creation of an Islamic state—at least not in the immediate future. This attitude is either due to a lack of understanding or ignorance of political Islam, or to a preference for a secular Tajikistan in which Islam as a religion and culture will have its proper and even flourishing place.

It is important not to confuse this secular tendency with the positions of the procommunist factions/clans of the Tajik traditional ruling elite, which, either because of ideological conviction, the inertia of Soviet socialization, or political convenience, have a definite anti-Islamic and anti-Iranian orientation. The "secular fundamentalists" who fought their way back to power in December 1992 and now hold power rely on their anti-Islamic posture as a strategy not only for coming to power, but for perpetuating their political hold in Tajikistan. In contrast, democratic tendencies—those active in the opposition underground, those in exile in Russia and in Iran, and those now silenced in Dushanbe—generally prefer a democratic polity with Islamic Tajik-Iranian cultural substance to a politicized ideological Islam. The theme of cultural Islam or the linkage with Iran on cultural grounds has been, from the initiation of relations with Iran in January 1992, a significant element shaping Iran's relations with the opposition, the intelligentsia, and even elements in the Tajik government, especially under Nabiev's rule.[10]

During most of the Tajik official contacts with Iran, the cultural theme has been emphasized while the issue of political Islam, politely or openly, was ignored or rejected. The visit of Nabiev to Tehran in June of 1992 was in this regard rather symbolic. This was the first trip of the president of

Tajikistan to any foreign state and took place in the midst of a severe political crisis at home and the initial stages of the armed clashes among the opposition groups. Among the variety of protocols signed by the two countries, the cultural agreements were the most extensive and far-reaching.[11] These included cooperation in the areas of language, publication of Persian education books for Tajik schools, student exchanges, scholarships, book exhibitions, and rebroadcasting of Iran's television programs.[12] In his report to the Tajik Supreme Soviet after the visit to Iran, Nabiev was very particular about the cultural emphasis in the shaping of relations with Iran, with which "until the 15th century we lived in a single state."[13] In an interview with *Narodnaia gazeta*, Nabiev characterized Iran and Tajikistan as two countries closely linked "by hundreds of threads of joint history and culture, unity of language and literature. . . ."[14] Particularly symbolic was Nabiev's trip to Shiraz, where he "conversed in the poetical language of Farsi" and "worshiped at the holy sepulchres of Shaykh Sa'adi and Khaji Hafiz, whose immortal works long since conquered the hearts of people of East and West."[15]

Similar emphasis on cultural links was expressed by Khudoiberdy Holiqnazarov, the Tajik foreign minister, who argued that while Iran's Islamic model remains a "complex issue"[16] given Tajikistan's diversity and lack of homogeneity, Iran as a "cultural standard" in "its broadest sense" has captured the "imagination of the greater part of the Tajik intelligentsia."[17] The same view was again expressed even after the resignation of Nabiev in September 1992 and during the short-lived government of Akbarsho Iskandorov. At the conclusion of the all-world forum of Tajiks, Iskandorov emphasized that Islamic fundamentalism will not be a determining factor in the domestic and foreign policy of Tajikistan.[18] Holiqnazarov, the foreign minister, reiterated the point that relations with Iran "will not be based on religious principles" but on historical "cultural and spiritual roots."[19]

The separation of the cultural from the ideological in the interpretation of the linkage with Iran was not only visible at the official level. It is important to note that the emphasis on cultural rather than religious/ideological links by the Tajik officials reflected the need to manage the Iranian factor in a less threatening way by channeling it into the less politicized contingencies of the Iranian model. It also signified a genuine need on the part of Tajik officials to deal with critical questions of Tajik national identity and its role in defining Tajik sovereignty. This is particularly important in view of the presence of more than 1 million Uzbeks in Tajikistan and clear pressure from Uzbekistan on the Tajik cultural life inside Uzbekistan, especially those in Bukhara and Samarkand where attempts at "cultural cleansing" are being made.[20]

The issue of Iranian culture as a source of linkage and support has survived to a certain degree even the deterioration of Iranian-Tajik relations after the takeover of the government by procommunist factions in December 1992. The government continued to support the teaching of Persian in elementary schools and Iran provided the core of the educational support and facilities, including 250,000 Persian books for elementary and high school students.[21] In addition, 120,000 Persian alphabet books have been provided by Iran.[22] Several Iranian book exhibits in Dushanbe, a project for the joint publication of a weekly journal, and the continuous support of Iran for the development and progress of the Persian language and annual conferences in Persian literature are part of the joint cultural protocol signed between the Iranian Ministry of Guidance and the Tajik Ministry of Media and News. Babakhanov, the Tajik minister of media and news, specifically emphasized the important role of Iran in supporting the solidification of the Persian languages, especially in view of the Tajik decision to replace the Cyrillic with the Persian alphabet in Tajik language training.[23] Rajab Amanov, the famous Tajik literary figure, also emphasized the significance of Tajikistan's access to "contemporary Iranian culture."[24]

It is worth noting that the issue of cultural linkage with Iran, though still a central theme in Tajik-Iranian relations, especially during the coldest period of Tajik-Iranian relations in late 1993 to early 1994, may still for political reasons not be welcomed by some of the hardliners in Dushanbe, especially those with close political connections to Uzbekistan. In a recent and somewhat bizarre parliamentary maneuver, the Tajik Supreme Council passed an unusual amendment to the 1989 Language Act. The amendment states that the Tajik language is no longer Farsi (Persian). Put forward by Shukhrat Sultanov, chief of the Organizational Department of the Communist Party of Tajikistan, "who himself speaks Tajik with great difficulty," this amendment was "clearly playing up to the current anti-Iranian mood."[25]

The emphasis on Iran as a cultural link nevertheless has been dialectically affected both positively and negatively by the Islamic components of the Iranian model or message. The fact that Iran is an Islamic republic, an *umm ul-qura* (Islamic metropolis), and a self-proclaimed custodian of Islamicism[26] is an inescapable reality and a central factor in shaping the relations between the two countries on bilateral (governmental and societal), regional (Russia and the Central Asian states), and international (primarily the United States) dimensions. The "Islamic threat" has affected these relations in a fundamental way. In Tajikistan, as elsewhere in Central Asia, the fight against Islamic fundamentalism was the critical factor that brought together a variety of domestic, regional, and international actors. The procommunist factions, regional clans, and political and social forces that feared losing their historical grip on political power in Tajikistan—either on ideological grounds or on purely utilitarian considerations—portrayed the crisis of authority in Tajikistan since 1992 as an externally inspired Islamic takeover and fought their way back to the top in December 1992 on an anti-Islamic platform.[27] One of the first decrees issued by the new government in Dushanbe in December 1992 was to outlaw any Islamic activities and to ban Islamic parties.[28]

Uzbekistan's policy of military and political support for the new government was formulated and supplemented under the notion of concern over the Islamic threat and the need for its containment. In fact, President Karimov has been the most outspoken of the Central Asian leaders on the threat of Islam and the most significant player in the creation of a regional consensus, as might be witnessed from the Uzbek-Russian intervention in the Tajik civil war. The discussion of the Uzbek role in this regard is beyond the scope of this study and has been dealt with elsewhere.[29] What is important to note is that the Uzbek anti-Islamic and anti-Iranian stand in Tajikistan has also become a key factor in shaping Uzbek-Iranian relations and the source of underlying tension in Tashkent–Tehran relations. Karimov's policy toward Tajikistan's civil war is intimately connected with his concern over Islamicist-democratic political challenges in Uzbekistan itself, where the suppression of the Islamic threat has repeatedly been used as a justification to curb political opposition to authoritarian rule, a general attitude characteristic of other Central Asian states, including Kazakhstan and Kyrgyzstan.

The containment of the Islamic/Iranian threat was also carried out by Russia. In fact, the Islamic threat in general has become a central defining element in Russian foreign policy toward the entire former Soviet South in addition to its role in shaping the debate about safeguarding Russia's own state security.[30] Russia not only played a delicate yet decisive role in shifting the balance of power during the domestic struggle in Tajikistan—especially in the two turning points of the civil war in September and December 1992—but it is now, through economic, political, and military support and presence, in reality the sole guarantor of the survival of the Imomali Rahmonov regime in Dushanbe.[31]

The regional "anti-Islamic" consensus has been riding on a significant U.S.-led international post–Cold War trend that perceives political Islam as a significant challenge to international security. Containment of the Islamic threat and Iranian influence is the cornerstone of the U.S. policy in the Islamic world (the Middle East and North Africa), which now also includes

Central Asia. U.S. policy in Central Asia has other dimensions such as economic interest and concerns over nuclear proliferation,[32] and is influenced by considerations over the expansion of political Islam. It is not an accident that other U.S. considerations—both traditional and proclaimed—such as promotion of democracy, the linkage between foreign aid and trade, and democratization and marketization have at least temporarily taken a backseat. U.S. regional allies in Central Asia and the Caucasus, namely Israel and Turkey, not only share and advocate the same policy but are instrumental in implementing U.S.-sponsored pilot projects and economic plans in Central Asia, and more specifically in Tajikistan.[33]

Tajikistan was officially included in discussions of U.S. concerns over Islamic fundamentalism and Iranian penetration in January 1994. During a U.S. Senate Intelligence Committee Hearing, James Woolsey, director of the Central Intelligence Agency, accused Iran of supporting terrorism in Tajikistan.[34] The charge was repeated in Woolsey's address in September 1994 to the Washington Institute for Near East Policy, where he again accused Iran of supporting "terrorist organizations and groups operating today from Algeria to Tajikistan."[35] The inclusion of Tajikistan in the realm of the political world of Islam, and the fact that it was discussed in the same context as Lebanon, Algeria, and Egypt by the United States, had several significant ramifications. First, it signaled the nature of U.S. policy in Central Asia in general and in particular in Tajikistan. Second, it gave moral and political legitimacy to those in power in Dushanbe by labeling the opposition as terrorists. Third, it demonstrated a general acquiescence to, if not approval of, Russia's intervention in Tajikistan and its participation in the containment of the Islamic threat.

Izvestiia reported the discussion of the Tajik crisis in a Moscow meeting between Evgenii Primakov, head of the Russian Foreign Intelligence, and James Woolsey in August 1993.[36] Some Russian sources raised concerns about the negative impact of Russian-U.S. collaboration against Islamic movements in Tajikistan on the future of Russian relations with the Islamic world.[37] Semen Bagdasarov, a leading Russian specialist on interethnic relations, argued that Tajikistan was the key to control of Central Asia and that the United States prefers to see Russia as a key player, instead of Iran, and a partner in the containment of Islamic fundamentalism.[38]

The coincidence of U.S. and Russian objectives in containing the Islamic/Iranian influence helped facilitate Russia's military and political involvement, which was not only geared toward cutting off the opposition from its supporters in Afghanistan, but also toward carrying its military campaign against opposition forces inside Tajikistan. U.S. reaction to the political repression exercised by the Tajik government against the opposition was, thus, understandably subdued. The U.S. policy toward the Dushanbe regime was generally supportive and even included providing some direct aid, which, according to the U.S. ambassador in Tajikistan, was a recognition of "the government's further progress in the area of democracy and human rights."[39] The opposition groups, especially those with democratic credentials, were particularly surprised by and critical of "the U.S. indifference" to human rights violations and the tacit support of the procommunist regime in Dushanbe by Washington. The passivity of international organizations such as Amnesty International was also perceived by the opposition as a function of U.S. policy.[40]

The presence of such wide-ranging and formidable regional and international consensus on the issue of the Islamic threat and Iranian influence in Tajikistan has been a major element in shaping Tehran's attitude toward the Islamic alternative, as well as Iran's relations with the opposition. Thus Iran's overall policy toward the Islamic factor—that is, an Islamic state or revolution in Tajikistan—could be characterized as *skeptical optimism*, reflecting skepticism in practice and substance and optimism in the realm of possibilities.

Iran's skepticism further reflected the subtle yet important shift in Iranian foreign policy approach after the war with Iraq, which indicated some adjustment in the interbalance and relationship between Iran's national interests and its internationalist/Islamic aspirations or obligations. Protecting the Islamic experiment in Iran and safeguarding the territorial integrity were to be given more explicit emphasis, an emphasis that was clearly reinforced by concerns over the severe domestic need for postwar economic reconstruction, the change in the international balance of power, and increasing instability all around the Iranian borders. While the Iranian postwar (1989–present) policy has reflected the continuous tension and difficulty of creating the "right" mix between principles of pragmatism and revolution, especially in the Middle East, it has been much more consistent in the Central Asian/Caucasian front, and most clearly so in the Tajik case.

In Tajikistan, Islamic possibilities clearly existed, yet Iranian policy, especially in the critical months between May and October 1992, when the opposition might have had a chance, was hesitant if not passive. This hesitation not only reflected Iran's awareness of Central Asian geopolitical realities, but further signified the general belief in Tehran that the clash in Tajikistan, as elsewhere in Central Asia, while couched in ideological terms, reflected tribal, regional, and ethnic differences, rather than an immediate receptivity to an Islamic alternative.[41] The promotion of an Islamic revolution, given the "unreadiness" of Tajikistan, could have undermined the less threatening and unique instruments of Iranian influence, namely the cultural linkage with Tajikistan. The pragmatic argument in Tehran was driven by the fact that Iran, through its cultural linkage, is Tajikistan's natural partner—a window of opportunity that a risky revolutionary strategy threatened to close.

Iran's hesitation regarding revolutionary experimentation was also reflected in the peculiar absence of a serious attempt at tactical ideological mentoring of the Tajik Islamic opposition by its "Iranian big brother." While some cosmetic similarities in slogans and organizations appeared in the heyday of the crisis in mid-1992, the tactical approaches adopted by the opposition in terms of obtaining power were anathema to an Iranian model or preference. This was particularly evident in the opposition's cooperation with the government during 1992 and reliance on the communist reformers, and especially the calculation of getting support from democratic Moscow and the international community against the old communist forces in the republic.

These were strategically wrong calculations and mistakes now repeatedly admitted by the leadership of the opposition, both Islamic and democratic, as key contributing factors in their setback.[42] Cooperation with communists and reliance on international support for "democracy" might have sounded like a reasonable strategy for the opposition, but not an acceptable and advisable strategy to Iran. Islamic models of revolutionary struggle, especially the one practiced by Iran itself, have historically been fundamentally based on self-reliance and the assumption of hostility of international forces (Russian or American). This strategic mistake indicated an absence of mentoring, tactical disconnection, and independence of opposition forces from Iran. Iran's skepticism was also clearly reflected in the tension between the opposition and Tehran in terms of unmet expectations. Iran refused to provide arms to the opposition when it mattered most,[43] and was clearly deficient in providing direct rhetorical support for the opposition through diplomatic means, media coverage, or polemics against the Dushanbe regime. Iran continued to portray the crisis in Tajikistan in non-ideological terms as an internal conflict with disturbing regional consequences. This absence of ideological support became the subject of continuous open criticism of Iran's Ministry of Foreign Affairs by the more "radical" Iranian press, which accused the official policy of being defensive, ineffective, and lacking in its moral standing in view of Iran's Islamic internationalist obligations. The radical press further provided a forum for the Tajik Islamic opposition to voice its frustration with the lack of adequate support from Iran, by reference to the *ghorbat* (an emotionally loaded Persian word for loneliness) of the Islamic opposition and the absence of any support from the Islamic countries for their cause.[44]

Iran's lack of support for pushing an Islamic revolution as a strategic choice thus entailed certain costs in further alienating the domestic constituency in addition to losing credibility with Islamic opposition groups. In fact, the cost in credibility is one of the intricate dilemmas of Iran's pragmatism as a *reluctant revolutionary* state. This dilemma is compounded by the ambiguity of the *reward structure* of pursuing a pragmatic moderate foreign policy. Pragmatic or revolutionary, Iran continues to have difficulty in reaping the benefit of the former, while still feeling the overwhelming weight and the baggage of the latter. A pragmatic Iran will still be perceived and treated as revolutionary. This dilemma is in general and, in the case of Tajikistan, driven by the twin factors of the inherent tension between the revolutionary symbolism of Iranian imageries and the pragmatic substance of its policy on the one hand, and the utility of a revolutionary and threatening Iran for a host of regional and international actors as an organizing concept and policy justification in Tajikistan on the other. The Iranian/Islamic threat is an instrumental force for building consensus, overcoming differences, and making strange bedfellows a political normalcy.

Significantly, and in spite of this dilemma, Iranian policy in Tajikistan during the 1993–94 period indicated a strategic commitment to project a pragmatic approach through Iran's commitment to continuous state-to-state relations, thus nourishing cultural links and above all positioning Iran for a *central* role in Tajik dynamics through its *mediating* role in conflict resolution.

Diplomacy

Iran's diplomatic relations with Tajikistan evolved within the complex and delicate confines of the geopolitics of the Islamic factor and its overarching impact on deciding the balance and relations among domestic and regional forces involved in Tajikistan. In addition, however, two other critical themes or characteristics of Iranian policy in Central Asia also played their respective roles in shaping Iranian-Tajik relations—namely the *Russian-centric* aspect of Iran's regional policy and the notion of *Iran's centrality* in affecting and influencing the region.

The first implies that Iran's policy in Tajikistan will not be anti-Russian and that it will be cognizant of the realities of Russia's interests and influence. Iran will accommodate the Russian factor in its own strategy by demonstrating the coexistence of interests and, more importantly, by cooperating in conflict resolution. A Russian-centric policy does not imply following Moscow's lead, but rather assuring Moscow that Tehran does not aim to replace Russia in Tajikistan. It does not imply partnership, though it leaves the door open for much tighter cooperation in the future. In the words of Foreign Minister Velayati, the resolution of regional crisis in Central Asia is directly dependent on "tight [*tanga-tang*] Moscow–Tehran cooperation."[45] Cooperation with Russia is obviously predicated on the assumption of Moscow's willingness to recognize Iran's interest and role in Tajikistan—a willingness that might not be forthcoming unless Moscow is convinced of the "centrality" of the Iranian factor in the stabilization of Tajikistan.

The second theme, "centrality," implies that Iran's legitimate interests and influence in Tajikistan cannot be denied or ignored. Though Iran is not the "center of the universe,"[46] it perceives itself to be a central actor in Tajikistan. In addition to its cultural significance, Iran's influence with the opposition made it an important player in the conflict resolution and eventual domestic dynamics of Tajikistan. While Iran, based on a realistic calculation of balance of forces on the ground, was skeptical of the opposition's armed struggle as a strategic option, it nevertheless appreciated and supported the Islamicists' military operation in a tactical sense. This was perceived to be the only way of convincing the Dushanbe regime and its regional supporters to take the opposition seriously and to look into negotiations, not as a vehicle for the opposition's surrender, but as a bridge toward some form of *national reconciliation*.

The definition of national reconciliation is a matter of some significance for all actors, including Iran. The Tajik government, Russia, Uzbekistan, and possibly others, like the United States, saw national reconciliation as being limited to disarming the opposition and a general amnesty—thus excluding any real participation by the Islamicists in the political process and power sharing. Tehran, on the other hand, perceived national reconciliation as a real vehicle for potential power sharing in Tajikistan between the opposition and the regime. Tehran thus advocates a free election and a new constitution, not necessarily because it is ideologically committed to Western-style democracy, but because it is convinced—as the opposition is—that the Dushanbe regime will either not survive real and free elections or at least will end up sharing political power with a genuine opposition. Iran's definition of national reconciliation in Tajikistan seems "politically correct" and quite comparable with the position taken by the UN and the CSCE while somewhat at odds with the Russian, Tajik, Uzbek, and U.S. preference.[47]

Iran's centrality was thus manifested in the diplomatic arena through its active and fundamental commitment to its role as a key mediator, at times facilitator, and at times guarantor or spokesperson for the opposition.

Mediation and diplomacy of conflict resolution were the substance of Iranian-Tajik relations, especially since 1992, and reflected the significance of Iranian relations with Russia and Iran's determination to remain a central player. Iran's mediating role in fact started even before the onset of the civil war in November–December 1992. In the famous showdown of the Islamicist-democratic forces with procommunist factions, reflected in the days of the demonstrations in Shakhidon and Azadi squares, the Iranian Embassy initiated mediation. During the visit of Nabiev to Tehran in June 1992, Nateq Nuri, Speaker of the Majlis (Iranian parliament), and Hashemi Rafsanjani, the Iranian president, suggested Iran's readiness to become involved in negotiations with the opposition.[48] During the April–May 1992 crisis, in a telephone conversation between Nabiev and Rafsanjani, the Iranian president suggested a peacemaking mission to Dushanbe led by himself. Nabiev declined the offer.[49]

It is conceivable that the Islamic opposition had requested Iran's mediation while refusing to accompany Nabiev on his trip to Tehran in late June of 1992. Nabiev criticized the opposition's appeal to "foreign countries"[50] and repeatedly blamed the opposition, especially Akbar Turajonzoda, for its noncooperative stand as reflected in the refusal to participate in his visit to Iran.[51] The opposition was critical of Nabiev's foreign policy, especially in view of his reluctance to engage with Iran more closely, although Nabiev had indicated during his trip to Tehran that Iran will be a major foreign policy priority.[52] During the negotiations among various opposition groups before the onset of the civil war, which led to the ill-fated Khorog Agreement, the Iranian Embassy again played a mediating role. In a telegram to Imomali Rahmonov on December 3, 1992, Iran's Speaker of the parliament offered Iran's mediation; it was again rejected by the new Tajik government.[53] In a meeting with Vladimir Gudev, the Russian ambassador in Iran, Mahmud Va'ezi, Iran's deputy foreign minister, expressed Tehran's apprehension about the instability in Tajikistan and suggested a joint effort by Moscow and Tehran toward resolution of the conflict.[54] Iran, fearing the expansion of Russian involvement, opposed the deployment of CIS troops on the Tajik-Afghan border and argued that the conflict should be resolved through political means.[55]

Iran's opposition to the deployment of Russian/CIS troops was a reflection of Tehran's deeper concern that Dushanbe, with the support and encouragement of Russia and Uzbekistan, had chosen a military option in dealing with the opposition—that is, a strategy of military elimination of the Islamicist-democratic coalition that was staging its guerrilla warfare not only from inside Tajik territory but from its bases and support stations in Afghanistan. Considering the Tajik-Afghan border, the border of the CIS,

Russia was acting in the context not only of protecting its client in Dushanbe, but performing its role as the key guardian of the CIS's exterior border, especially in the south, as envisioned under the CIS Collective Agreements.[56] The extraordinary summit of leaders of Russia and Central Asian states (with the exception of Turkmenistan) in Moscow in August 1993 ended with a firm and collective decision to strengthen the CIS troops on the Afghan-Tajik borders. The strong show of unity behind Tajikistan by Russia was also accompanied by diplomatic gestures, especially from Yeltsin, indicating that the door to negotiation with the opposition should be opened and Iran's influence in this regard should be utilized.[57]

The Russians, taking credit for the diplomatic opening, indicated that they have been successful in pressuring the Tajik government to modify its uncompromising position toward conducting negotiations. Anatolii Adamishin, Russia's first deputy foreign minister and one of the key architects of Russia's Tajik policy presenting the "moderate" side of Moscow's approach, argued that Moscow was not "master of the situation in Tajikistan" and that national reconciliation needed serious commitment to a political solution.[58] The Russian-Tajik-Uzbek view concerning a political solution did not, however, entail taking the Islamicist opposition as a serious partner for political power sharing, but was rather a vehicle for achieving the peaceful disarming of the opposition and their return to Tajikistan. Iran's mediation will be sought for this purpose.

Russian foreign minister Andrei Kozyrev, representing the more ideological and hard-line position of Russian policy in a news conference held in the Russian Foreign Ministry after a meeting of an Interdepartmental Commission on Tajikistan, told reporters that Russia will support diplomatic dialogue in general; however, a totally "different dialogue" (i.e., military) had to be used against the armed opposition.[59] At the end of his Central Asian tour and after the meeting with President Rahmonov, Kozyrev reiterated Russia's commitment to Tajikistan, obviously having the opposition and Iran in mind: "There is no question of leaving Tajikistan or abandoning Tajikistan. This is the clear-cut position of the Russian President, Boris Yeltsin."[60]

Iran's approach toward Tajikistan throughout 1993–94 indicated Tehran's desire: (a) not to become a "mediator" in the eventual destruction of the armed opposition—that is, to become by default the diplomatic arm of the Russian-Tajik strategy of victory over the Islamicists; and (b) to continue generally normal relations with the regime in Dushanbe—again underlining Tehran's desire and objective of convincing all other actors of its prominent role in Tajikistan. The diplomatic "tug-of-war" in Russian-Iranian and Iranian-Tajik relations surrounding the issue of negotiations and mediation reflected the conflict between Tehran's objective to remain "central" and the Russian and Tajik desire to utilize Iran without granting it a significant reward and keeping its role as peripheral as possible.

In a highly publicized and generally successful Central Asian tour in October 1993 by Iran's President Hashemi Rafsanjani, the leaders of Kazakhstan, Kyrgyzstan, Uzbekistan, and Turkmenistan reiterated the positive role that Iran can play in the settlement of the Tajik crisis while the Iranian president indicated Iran's readiness for "meaningful" negotiations and mediation. He deliberately avoided a trip to Tajikistan, a clear sign of tension in the relationship and Iran's gesture in questioning the legitimacy of the leadership in Dushanbe—a gesture not welcomed in Moscow. Rafsanjani's successful diplomacy was seen as a serious attempt to fill the Central Asian vacuum at the expense of Russia,[61] and its "nonideological" and mediating role in Tajikistan was perceived as an attempt to exclude the key role that belonged to Russia.[62] While Iran's claim of not supporting the Tajik guerrillas was considered to "completely comply with reality,"[63] Iran was still criticized for avoiding warmer relations with Tajikistan and indirectly supporting the guerrillas by creating a "specific moral-political atmosphere" within which "financial assistance by non-governmental organizations" has been extended to the opposition.[64]

During the period of general inactivity in Tajik-Iranian relations (1993 to mid-1994), some of the cultural activities continued in addition to occasional Iranian humanitarian assistance in providing medical aid,[65] fuel,[66] and the continuation of previously agreed-upon projects such as air links, banking cooperation, and student and diplomatic training.[67] Meanwhile, the leadership of the opposition announced that the conflict could only be resolved by direct talks between Russia, representing Dushanbe, and Iran, representing the opposition.[68] A more active Iranian mediation in Tajikistan, however, had to await changes in the military situation on the ground. By mid-1994 it became clear that Dushanbe had been unable not only to eliminate the armed Islamic opposition but even to solidify its position within the republic. Furthermore, the Russian forces and especially the border guards increasingly became the main targets of military operations. On the eve of the second round of Tajik negotiations, which took place in Tehran in June 1994 (the first round was conducted in Moscow in April), the military situation in Tajikistan according to Russian military sources had become "extremely complex."[69]

The second round of negotiations was slow, difficult, and in the end unsuccessful. These negotiations took place with the participation of UN representative Ramero Piriz-Ballon, observers from Russia, Iran, Pakistan, Kazakhstan, Kyrgyzstan, and Uzbekistan, opposition representatives led by

Otakhan Latifi, and the Tajik delegation led by Shukurjon Zuhurov, minister of labor. The low rank of the Tajik delegation was an indication of Dushanbe's reluctant attitude and a reflection of the recent military victories that the government forces had achieved against the opposition in Pamir.[70] Ten days of negotiations failed to produce a cease-fire agreement. The two sides' positions, especially on issues such as elections, were simply too far apart.[71]

Frustrated by the failure of its highly publicized diplomatic attempt, Tehran blamed Moscow for its behind-the-door machinations in undermining the resolution of the conflict in Central Asia.[72] While Iran's criticism was delivered in the form of an editorial in *Tehran Times*, Moscow's response came from the Russian Foreign Ministry. A top Russian Foreign Ministry official blasted Iran's criticism of Russia and argued that Iran's failure to promote revolution in Central Asia, and its inability to solve the Tajik problem, has led to political dissention in Tehran. This has created an Iranian "inferiority complex" and thus the search for a scapegoat in Russia.[73] Moscow demanded that Tehran use its influence instead to modify the opposition's unrealistic demands.[74] Several important issues separated the positions of the opposition and Tehran from the positions of Russia and Dushanbe, the most important of which were the issues of elections, the constitutional referendum, and arrangements for an interim government.

On the question of elections and the constitutional referendum, Iran's position closely resembled that of the UN and the CSCE: without some form of opposition participation in a freely held election, the motives for continuing the civil war will not disappear.[75] Russia initially shared the same opinion—a protocol to that effect had been signed in Moscow during the first round of Tajik negotiations in April 1994—but did in fact support Dushanbe's decision to go ahead with the presidential elections.[76] While the UN had hoped to receive support from the United States on this issue— the U.S. ambassadors in Tajikistan and Russia had been intimately involved in the Tajik developments—this support was not forthcoming. In fact, U.S. ambassador Stanley Escudero's suggestion to the Tajik opposition that they should participate in the elections by nominating a joint candidate with authorities in Leninabad oblast indicated that the United States generally supported Moscow's and Dushanbe's position for early elections.[77] It seemed that "neither the leadership of Tajikistan nor the Russian Foreign Ministry were serious about the negotiations with the opposition."[78] The toughening of the Russian and Tajik positions and the rush for the presidential elections were accompanied by a campaign of intimidation of the Tajik opposition figures in exile in Moscow.[79]

The Islamicist response to the Moscow–Dushanbe position was a new wave of military campaigns inside Tajikistan and continuous attacks against the Russian border guards on the Tajik-Afghan border. On the eve of the important military advancement in Tahvil Darya—which eventually brought the government to the negotiation table[80]—Akbar Turajonzoda announced that "the opposition would continue fighting on the Tajik-Afghan border and inside the country until the Dushanbe government signed a ceasefire agreement."[81] Russian-Tajik media reports also indicated participation of volunteers from Afghanistan, Iran, Pakistan, and Arab countries.[82] The Iranian position regarding the situation was indirectly reflected in an editorial in *Tehran Times*. While raising concerns over the focus of the opposition on the military option, the editorial gave the opposition its implicit support, outlined the opposition's demands, and warned that past experience in the suppression of Islam has led to the radicalization and militarization of Islamicists, inviting Moscow to look at similar crises in Algeria and Egypt.[83]

It was in this atmosphere that the second round of intra-Tajik negotiations resumed in Tehran in September 1994 with the participation of UN representatives, the vice president of Tajikistan, the leader of the Islamic opposition, Russia's representative, and the Iranian foreign minister. Iran clearly had placed high hopes on the success of these negotiations, and thus the delivery of the opposition to the negotiation table with a modified position seemed essential. This task was achieved by dropping some of the key demands of the Islamicists, such as legalization of political parties.[84] The cease-fire agreement in the Tehran accord signed on September 18, 1994, was the first serious agreement reached by both sides toward conflict resolution and paved the way for the third round of talks in Islamabad, Pakistan, which led to the extension of the cease-fire for another three months and an agreement on the release of some of the political prisoners. Iran's delegation in the Islamabad talks reportedly played an important role again in modifying some of the opposition's demands.[85]

Iranian press reports indicated Tehran's general satisfaction and reported the positive comments of officials from Russia, Tajikistan, Uzbekistan, the UN, and other sources as to Iran's key diplomatic role, underlying Iran's clear need for diplomatic success and recognition.[86] The progress in negotiations might have increased the chance of an improvement in Tehran–Dushanbe relations. During the negotiation period in Tehran, the Tajik vice president and head of the Tajik delegation met with President Rafsanjani when the two sides emphasized the need for renewed economic trade and diplomatic activities between the two countries. Rafsanjani specifically referred to the Sarakhs–Tajikistan railway connection project as part of the effort to link Tajikistan through Iran to the outside world.[87] Given

the financial cost of such a project and its lack of feasibility, it nevertheless symbolizes the importance of Iran as a key linkage for Tajikistan in
the mind of Iran's leaders—a reassertion of Iran's positive centrality in
Central Asia.

Conclusion

The civil war in Tajikistan is far from over, though there now exists a
prospect for a negotiated settlement on the political horizon. The political
settlement, when and if it comes, will not, however, be the end of the
political crisis in Tajikistan as different regions and political groups will
engage in political intrigue and infighting for power and security. The
bloody and brutal memory of the civil war will continue to cast its considerable weight on the future development of political alignment in the republic.
To the extent that Islamicist groups remain united and a viable political
force, Iran will remain an important political player, either as a peacemaker
or as an important source of external support. In a peaceful Tajikistan,
Iranian diplomatic relations will be enhanced by a higher level of state-to-
state relations, while on the societal plane, in addition to Islamic groups,
those social-political forces that value Iran on nonideological but cultural
grounds will become the source of Iranian attention and effort.

One of the key obstacles to Iran's further influence in Tajikistan, in
addition to challenges from other actors, will continue to be Iran's economic and technical limitations. The most tangible economic assistance so
far to Tajikistan was a 50-million-dollar credit that Dushanbe received in
1992.[88] This limited level of economic and financial assistance to Tajikistan
was driven by both Iran's own financial difficulties, especially in the area of
hard currency, and its unwillingness to provide such assistance to a regime
with an opposing, if not hostile, ideology. An effective and influential role
by Iran in Tajikistan will continue to depend not only on Iran's cultural
linkage, but on its ability to become a source of material and developmental
support for an impoverished state. A friendlier regime in Dushanbe will
facilitate further financial commitment and aid, though the essential
weakness of Iranian economic resources is likely to remain a major
obstacle for the rest of the 1990s. Iranian officials have complained on
occasion about the lack of interest among Iranian business circles to engage
in economic trade activities in Tajikistan. In comparison, however, Iran's
business community is much more active in other Central Asian republics
such as Turkmenistan.[89] Iran's economic limitations, especially in view of a
significant Russian role in the economic survival of Tajikistan, will be an
important modifier of its influence. In fact, in this regard not only Russia,

but other actors such as the United States, Uzbekistan, and China may play a more significant role than Iran.

Tehran will thus try to compensate its limitations on bilateral economic assistance by developing trade and through involvement in multilateral projects. In the final analysis, however, Iran's limited material resources are hoped to be compensated for by its unique cultural, linguistic, and religious ties to Tajikistan, a new state in search of not only economic development but an independent national sense of identity.[90] Islam will continue to be an important factor affecting Iranian-Tajik relations. To the extent that Islam remains a viable political force in Tajikistan, relations with Iran will be affected by a sense of apprehension. This negativity has proven to be a useful tool in the hands of the Tajik leadership to cultivate support from other actors who share concerns over the Islamic threat; in addition to traditional likeminded players such as Russia and Uzbekistan, the role of the United States in this regard could become increasingly important. The United States may not have a particularly significant interest in Tajikistan to justify an active presence. Its determined policy of containment of political Islam in addition to the ability to provide or facilitate financial assistance, however, will increasingly make it a distant yet significant player. While Russia shares with the United States a common ground in the ideological threat perception, Moscow will be wary of U.S. penetration in Russia's historical sphere of influence. Is it not thus ironic that Russia will simultaneously look to Iran's anti-Americanism as a base for political cooperation in blocking the expansion of the U.S. presence?[91] The Cold War ideology might have been buried, but the elements of great power competition that have roots in geopolitical calculations have survived in the Russian policy toward the southern region. In fact, Russia's view of the U.S. presence in Central Asia/the Caucasus and the adjacent regions, like the Persian Gulf, does not significantly differ from that held by Iran.[92] Given the significance of Russia in the overall Iranian foreign policy and the continuous hostility between Iran and the United States, Tehran may prefer a Russian rather than a U.S. presence in Tajikistan. Recognition of Moscow's interests in Central Asia is also shared by the Islamicist opposition leaders who have been categorical in recognizing Russia's interests and the necessity of close relations with Moscow.[93]

The overall and long-term impact of the Islamic factor in the final analysis, however, in addition to the role of external actors and their preferences, will be the function of the domestic sociopolitical impact of Islam in shaping Tajik society and polity, and will determine whether Islam is a viable political and social force or transient hype.[94] The role of Islam in politics has been categorically rejected and legally banned by the Tajik government and the ruling elites, as it has been in other Central Asian states. According to Tajik officials, the Islamic leaders of Tajikistan should look to Pope John Paul II and Patriarch Aleksei of Russia as models for their civic responsibility, and not to their Iranian counterparts.[95] The political platform of the two presidential candidates in Tajikistan was marked by the conspicuous absence of direct reference to the word "Islam"; instead the candidates made reference to the need for "spirituality" in personal life.[96]

Like elsewhere in the postcolonial Muslim world, Islam as an ideology will continue to have an appeal for those sociopolitical forces in Tajikistan that either through conviction or convenience look to religion as a principal organizing vehicle for political mobilization. The Iranian revolution and its political model are to a large extent particular to Iranian history and political culture and may not be mechanically imported or emulated. The significance of the "Iranian model" for Tajikistan, in this context, should therefore be measured not necessarily for its direct relevance, but for its atmospheric meaning and implications. The Tajik Islamic movement—weak or strong—in general is part and parcel of similar trends taking place elsewhere in the Islamic world where authoritarian secularism is under attack by religious activists.

In Tajiksitan, as elsewhere in the Islamic world, secularism—or one might say secular fundamentalism—is in power and there is little indication that in the short run, especially given external support, its hegemony could be effectively challenged. Its long-term domination and control, however, requires more than just repressive measures; it calls for breaking out of its authoritarian political culture and venturing into risky yet more promising ways of broadening political representation. This will be a large task, one that given both distant and recent authoritarian history (reinforced by the not exactly democratic presidential elections of 1994 in Tajikistan) has proven to be too challenging for the Tajik ruling forces. In the absence of a broadening political base of representation, and under repressive measures, political Islam, though unproven as a successful model of economic and political development, could be an effective source in political mobilization and change. Iran, pragmatic or not, may be a peripheral factor in such an eventuality.

Notes

1. *Tehran Times*, January 8, 1990, p. 2. The Iranian press was replete with warnings to Gorbachev of the trappings of too close relations with the United States and the danger of disintegration of the Soviet Union.

2. In this context, the issue of Russia's arms sales to Iran and the transfer of so-called "dual use" technology, especially in the area of nuclear technology, given the

U.S. sensitivity, will remain a complex one; it is an issue shaped by the interaction of multiple factors and dynamics such as its impact on U.S.-Russian relations, its financial and political utility for Russia, and perhaps above all the level of Iran's sensitivity. Iran's reaction to President Yeltsin's announcement of no more sales of arms to Iran during his trip to Washington in October 1994 was remarkably low-key.

3. For an official elaboration of Iran's views on Central Asia and on the issue of regionalism see Abbas Maleki, "Cooperation: Iran's New Foreign Policy Objectives," in *Majal'leh Motale'ate Asia-ye Markazi va Qafqaz, The Journal of Central Asian and Caucasian Review* (Tehran), vol. 1, no. 2 (Fall 1992), pp. 336–37.

4. For a report on the pipeline project, see "Central Asia Turning South," *The Economist*, October 29, 1994, p. 40.

5. On the role of Iran's Islamic broadcasts and their impact on Central Asia and Tajikistan, see *Ettela'at* (Persian), July 16, 1992, pp. 2–3, interview with Iran's ambassador to Tajikistan, Ali Muhammed Shabestari; *Al'Alam* (Arabic, London) September 1993 interview with leaders of Tajik opposition including Qadi Akbar Turajonzoda (partially reproduced in *Hamshahri* [Persian], September 29, 1993, p. 9).

6. *Al'Alam* (Arabic), September 7, 1994, interview with opposition leaders. This point was specifically reiterated by Shodmon Yusuf, the leader of the Democratic Party of Tajikistan.

7. *Moscow News*, no. 36 (September 6–13, 1992), p. 1.

8. For an interesting discussion of the Tajik crisis in September–November of 1992 and comparison between the *Komiteh* and the Dushanbe Youth Movement see "Tajikistan: Uncertain Developments and Ambiguous Future," *Keyhan Hava'i* (Persian) November 11, 1992, p. 22. It is perhaps noteworthy that this weekly publication usually reflects a much more radical position than that taken by the Iranian official policy.

9. See interviews with Qadi Akbar Turajonzoda, Dr. Shodmon Yusuf, and Dr. Taher Abduljabbar (head of the Rastokhez Party) in three issues of *Hamshahri* (Persian), September 29, October 3, and October 4, 1993.

10. During the Nabiev period, Iran's cultural activity flourished very quickly. Some Iranian sources argued that Nabiev's accommodation was due more to his vulnerable political base than to a general interest in cultural links with Iran. See *Salam*, October 8, 1993, p. 8.

11. For coverage of the Nabiev trip to Iran, see ITAR-TASS, June 30, 1992, in Foreign Broadcasting Information Service, Soviet Union (hereafter, FBIS-SOV), July 1, 1992; IRNA, June 28, 1992, in FBIS-SOV, June 24, 1992, pp. 28–29; IRNA, June 30, 1992, in FBIS-NES, July 6, 1992, pp. 66–67.

12. For issues concerning the cooperation on TV programming and also technical cooperation, see *Keyhan Hava'i*, July 29, 1992, p. 3.

13. "We should develop our ties mainly in literary, culture and scientific areas," *Narodnaia gazeta*, July 18, 1992, pp. 1–2.

14. *Narodnaia gazeta*, July 7, 1992, pp. 1, 2.

15. *Narodnaia gazeta*, July 7, 1992, p. 1. Shiraz, a city in the south of Iran, the capital of Fars Province, is one of the most traditional Iranian cities and famous for its romantic and literary traditions and contribution to Iranian culture. Hafiz and Sa'adi are the two greatest Iranian poets with influence not only among Iranians, but in the Iranian cultural milieu of Central Asia and the Asian subcontinent—India and Pakistan. It is interesting that Nabiev at Hafiz's tomb completed his cultural journey by taking a "fall" (fortune telling) from the Divan (collection of poems), where he received a "good sign" indicating the fruitfulness of his trip to Iran and a better relationship between the two countries; *Narodnaia gazeta*, July 7, 1992, p. 2.

16. See his interview with *Nezavisimaia gazeta*, July 11, 1992, p. 3.

17. *Holos Ukrainy*, August 12, 1992, p. 8.

18. *Interfax*, 18 September 1992, in FBIS-SOV, September 21, 1992, p. 56.

19. Ibid.

20. The Uzbek authorities are sensitive to this issue in particular, in view of strong influence of Tajik/Persian culture in Samarkand and Bukhara where more than a million Tajiks reside. Examples include the establishment of Turkish cultural complexes, the prevention of Tajik TV broadcast to Uzbekistan while transmitting Uzbek programming to Tajikistan, and other activities signifying the subtle cultural tension between the Uzbeks and Tajiks, a tension that goes beyond limited local cultural conflict and points to the larger picture which involves the power relationship between the two ethnic groups, and issues of sovereignty and nation-building. For a reflection of Iranian awareness and sensitivity on this issue see *Ettela'at*, July 16, 1992, p. 7.

21. *Keyhan* (Persian), September 25, 1993.

22. *Hamshahri* (Persian), August 20, 1993, p. 10.

23. According to Babakhanov, the government plan has envisioned a complete "Persianization" of the alphabet (i.e., conversion to the Arabic alphabet) by 1995–96. See *Hamshahri* (Persian), August 28, 1993, p. 10.

24. Amanov, who made the remarks at a special ceremony of his seventieth birthday at Dushanbe, specifically reiterated the uselessness of the negative "atmosphere" surrounding Iran in the republic and emphasized the cultural and literary and educational links, especially in the area of children's books. Iranian cultural work in this area also includes the translation of Persian books to Tajik (in Cyrillic) for immediate use. See *Jumhuri-ye Islami* (Persian), September-29, 1993. Also see *Salam* (Persian), August 29, 1993, p. 2.

25. Oleg Panfilov, "Officials Are Conducting a New Experiment with the Tajik Language," *Nezavisimaia gazeta*, July 27, 1994, p. 3.

26. For a discussion of the concept of *umm ul-qura* (the Islamic metropolis), see Mohiaddin Mesbahi, "Gorbachev's New Thinking and Islamic Iran: From Containment to Reconciliation," in H. Amirahmadi and N. Entessar, eds., *Reconstruction and Diplomacy in the Persian Gulf* (London: Routledge and New York: University Press, 1992).

27. For an early account of this view, especially just before the start of the main stage of the civil war, see V. Belykh and N. Burbyga, "Hostages of Terror," *Izvestiia*, September 9, 1992, pp. 1–2, which includes an interview with Sangak Safarov, the leader of the armed groups of the People's Front; and Oleg Blotskii, "Tajikistan: The Green and the Red," *Literaturnaia gazeta*, November 4, 1992, p. 11.

28. *Keyhan Hava'i* (Persian), December 16, 1992, p. 4.

29. See Mohiaddin Mesbahi, "Russian Foreign Policy and Security in Central Asia and the Caucasus," in *Central Asian Survey*, vol. 12, no. 2, 1993.

30. For a review of the discussion of the Islamic factor in Russian foreign policy debate, see Mohiaddin Mesbahi, ibid.

31. For the Russian policy, see ibid.

32. The issue of Tajik uranium and the possible interest of Islamic countries in it was raised in January 1992 in the Russian press. Nabiev's government, however, categorically denied the reports of any negotiations with Pakistan, Iran, Libya, and other countries on selling uranium and reiterated his government's position in a no-sale policy. *Interfax*, January 7, 1992, in FBIS-SOV, January 8, 1992, p. 70; and A. Komrakov, "Was There a Bomb?" in *Trud*, January 9, 1992, p. 3.

33. For a good overview of Israeli policy in Central Asia, see A. Ehteshami and E. Murphy, "The Non-Arab Middle East States and the Caucasus/Central Asian Republics: Iran and Israel," in *International Relations*, vol. 12, no. 1, April 1994. For views of Tajik Islamic and democratic opposition groups, see *Al'Alam* (Arabic), September 7,

1993, partially reproduced in *Hamshahri* (Persian), September 29, 1993, p. 9; for an Iranian commentary on Israel's policy in Tajikistan, see *Salam* (Persian), 16 October 1993, p. 3, and *Ettela'at*, November 2, 1994, p. 2.

34. For James Woolsey's testimony, see the Hearing of the Select Intelligence Committee, United States Senate, January 25, 1994, cited in Federal News Service (FNS) in Nexus databank.

35. R. James Woolsey, "Challenge to Peace in the Middle East," in *MEES* 38:1, October 3, 1994, pp. D2–D3.

36. *Izvestiia*, 10 August 1993, p. 3.

37. See, for example, Russia's former Minister of Justice Nikolai Fedorov's article in *Rossiiskaia gazeta*, May 14, 1993, p. 4, which criticizes the use of force against Islamic movements by Russia as counterproductive; also see Vladimir Koznechevskii, "Victim of the Islamic Roulette Desperately Wanted," or "In Search of Those Threatened by Islamic Fundamentalism," *Rossiiskaia gazeta*, August 6, 1993, p. 1.

38. Semen Bagdasarov, "There Is a CIS Border in Tajikistan. It Is a Russian Border, Too," *Rossiiskaia gazeta*, September 3, 1994, pp. 1, 6.

39. This remark was made by Stanley Escudero, U.S. plenipotentiary and extraordinary ambassador in Tajikistan at the ceremony of the signing of the Cooperation Agreement between Tajikistan and the United States. Dushanbe Radio, Tajikistan Network in Russian, July 29, 1994, in FBIS-SOV, August 1, 1994, p. 51.

40. For the opposition groups' position on U.S. policy, especially their critical attitude toward the U.S., see Akbar Turajonzoda's, "Tajikistan: Lonely and Alien," in *Salam* (Persian), August 22, 1993, p. 12; Akbar Turajonzoda, "Tajikistan: Burning in Bolshevik's Fire of Animosity," *Jehan-e Islam* (Persian), August 19, 1993, p. 4; Ajami, "A Letter from a Tajik Muslim to the Custodians of Human Rights," *Jumhuri-ye Islami* (Persian), August 8, 1993, p. 12; and *Al'Alam* (Arabic), September 7, 1993.

41. For a good elaboration of this view, see the article, "Ethnic Conflict in Central Asia: An Inheritance from Blind Nationalism," *Ettela'at* (Persian), 24 August 1993, p. 7.

42. For a detailed and interesting elaboration of key mistakes of the opposition in their political strategy, see the interview with A. Turajonzoda, S. Yusuf, and T. Abduljabbar (head of the Rastokhez Party) in *Hamshahri* (Persian), September 29, October 3, October 4, 1994.

43. Iran's Deputy Foreign Minister Mahmud Va'ezi informed the Russian ambassador in Iran, Vladimir Gudev, that Iran had refused to accept the requests for arms of several opposition groups in Tajikistan, ITAR-TASS, 28 October 1992 in FBIS-SOV, 30 October 1992, p. 11.

44. For a sample of this theme, see A. Turajonzoda, "The Lonely Tajikistan: Burning in the Fire of the Bolshevik Animosity," *Jehan-e Islam* (Persian), August 8, 1993, p. 4; Shamsol'haqh, "The Painful Diary of a Tajik Muslim," *Jumhuri-ye Islami* (Persian), August 12, 1993, p. 14; Ajami, "A Letter from a Tajik Muslim to the Custodian of Human Rights"; A. Turajonzoda, "Tajikistan: Lonely and Alien," *Salam* (Persian), August 22, 1993, p. 12. Turajonzoda's articles are specifically replete with bitter complaints about the absence of media coverage and the lack of "even humanitarian" support for the Islamic opposition.

45. "Territorial integrity and regional security of Central Asia and the Transcaucasus will be fundamentally dependent on a tight Moscow–Tehran cooperation," *Ettela'at* (Persian), August 19, 1993. A similar opinion had been expressed repeatedly by other Iranian officials. See the comments made by Mahmud Va'ezi, Iran's deputy foreign minister, ITAR-TASS, in FBIS-SOV, October 30, 1992, p. 11.

46. A notion that implies an Iranian historical illusion of self-importance in world

politics. Also the title of a good book by Graham Fuller, *"The Center of the Universe":*
The Geopolitics of Iran (Boulder, CO: Westview Press, 1991).

47. For example, on the critical issue of the Tajik presidential elections and the new
constitution scheduled for November 1994, Moscow, Tashkent, and Dushanbe strongly
pushed for excluding the opposition, a position that was at least implicitly supported by
the U.S., while Iran, the UN, and the CSCE saw this position as a recipe for the
nonresolution of the conflict. See Timur Varki, "A Blow at Russia's Prestige," *Obshchaia gazeta,* 12 August 1994, p. 2; and especially Oleg Panfilov, "The UN Accuses
Tajikistan Authorities of Undermining Negotiations: Otakhan Latifi Was Beaten in Moscow," *Nezavisimaia gazeta,* 6 August 1994. Otakhan Latifi is chairman of the Board of
Coordinating Center of Democratic Forces of Tajikistan in the CIS.

48. Voice of the Islamic Republic of Iran, June 29, 1992, in FBIS-SOV, 29 June
1992, p. 29.

49. *Interfax,* August 12, 1992, in FBIS-SOV, August 13, 1992, p. 55.

50. *Interfax,* August 12, 1992, FBIS-SOV, 13 August 1992, p. 55.

51. See *Narodnaia gazeta,* July 7, 1992, pp. 1, 2; and *Gazeta,* July 19, 1992, pp. 1–2.

52. For a view of the Islamic opposition on this issue, see *Interfax,* June 18, 1992,
interview with Davlat Usmon, the vice chairman of the Islamic Revival Party (IRP), in
FBIS-SOV, June 19, 1992, p. 69. Also see the interview with Muhammad Asimov,
president of Payvand (a society of Tajiks living abroad), who criticizes Nabiev's luke-
warm attitude toward Iran. *Interfax,* July 10, 1992, in FBIS-SOV, July 13, 1992, p. 20.

53. ITAR-TASS, December 7, 1992, in FBIS-SOV, December 8, 1992, p. 43.

54. *Keyhan Hava'i,* December 23, 1993, p. 6.

55. *Tehran Times,* September 5, 1992, also cited briefly by *Moscow Mayak Radio
Network,* in FBIS-SOV, September 10, 1992, p. 2.

56. For a discussion of the Russian role in CIS collective security, see M. Mesbahi,
"Russian Foreign Policy and Security."

57. *Jumhuri-ye Islami* (Persian), 8 August 1993, p. 76.

58. See the interview with Anatolii Adamishin in *Kommersant-Daily* (Russian), November 4, 1993, p. 4. Adamishin referred to serious differences with the Dushanbe
regime. He also reiterated Russia's historical role and mission in Tajikistan in bringing
not only "civilization" to Tajikistan but also security, without which the Central Asian
"bubbling cauldron will boil right to our own borders—next to the Volga."

59. *Moscow Mayak Radio Network,* November 10, 1993, in FBIS-SOV, November
12, 1993.

60. ITAR-TASS, 17 November 1993, in FBIS-SOV, November 18, 1993, p. 66.

61. *Moscow Radio* (in Persian), October 31, 1993, in FBIS-SOV, November 2,
1993, pp. 19–20.

62. Konstantin Eggert, "Iran Proposes to Export Construction Workers, Not Revolution," *Izvestiia,* October 29, 1993, p. 3, citing a Russian diplomat.

63. Moscow, *Radio Moscow in Persian,* October 25, 1993, in FBIS-SOV, October
28, 1993, p. 7.

64. Ibid. The commentary also points to the radical position taken by some influential circles and their newspapers in Iran toward the Tajik conflict. A report in *New Times*
cites an unnamed Russian intelligence source who claims Iran's financial support for the
opposition to be approximately 3 to 4 million dollars.

65. On Iran's assistance in building a medical center in Tajikistan, see ITAR-TASS,
June 18, 1992, in FBIS-SOV, June 19, 1992, p. 6.

66. ITAR-TASS, 3 December 1992, in FBIS-SOV, December 4, 1992, p. 44.

67. An agreement on the twelve-week diplomatic training of Tajik diplomats had
been signed during Nabiev's visit to Tehran in June 1992; Tehran, *Voice of the Islamic*

Republic of Iran, June 29, 1992, in FBIS-SOV, June 29, 1992, pp. 28–29.

68. *Hamshahri* (Persian) interview with the leaders of the opposition, September 29, 1993, p. 10.

69. Interview with Lieutenant General Anatolii Chechulin, the commander of Russian border troops in Tajikistan in ITAR-TASS, in FBIS-SOV, June 9, 1994, pp. 65–67.

70. ITAR-TASS, June 22, 1994, in FBIS-SOV, June 22, 1994, p. 62.

71. *Interfax*, June 23, 1994, in FBIS-SOV, June 24, 1994, pp. 62–63.

72. *Tehran Times*, July 22, 1994, p. 6.

73. ITAR-TASS, July 25, 1994, in FBIS-SOV, July 26, 1994, pp. 8–9. For the position of Grigorii Karasin, director of the Russian Foreign Ministry's Press and Information Department on the same subject, see ITAR-TASS, August 18, 1994, in FBIS-SOV, August 19, 1994, p. 7.

74. *Interfax*, August 20, 1994, in FBIS-SOV, August 22, 1994, p. 14.

75. On the UN, CSCE, and intriguing issues surrounding the Russian position, see Oleg Panfilov, "The UN Accuses Tajikistan's Authorities of Undermining Negotiations," *Nezavisimaia gazeta*, 6 August 1994, pp. 1, 3.

76. Ibid.

77. Ibid.

78. Interview with *Rossiiskaia gazeta*, September 3, 1994, pp. 1, 6.

79. For reports on beatings of opposition figures, especially Otakhon Latifi, chairman of the Coordinating Center for Tajikistan's Democratic Forces in the CIS, which took place in Moscow after his meeting with UN officials, see Timur Varki, "A Blow at Russia's Prestige"; and the interview with O. Panfilov with *Obshchaia gazeta*, August 26, 1994, p. 12.

80. On the importance of these operations, see Boris Vinogradov, "Our Man in Tajikistan," *Izvestiia*, September 20, 1994, p. 4.

81. *Interfax*, September 12, 1994, in FBIS-SOV, September 13, 1994, pp. 62–63.

82. Ibid; and ITAR-TASS, World Service, August 6, 1994; in FBIS-SOV, September 7, 1994, p. 8.

83. "Practical Ways for Achieving Peace in Tajikistan," *Tehran Times* (English), September 13, 1994, p. 2.

84. On concessions made by the opposition, see Turajonzoda's interview with ITAR-TASS, September 18, 1994, in FBIS-SOV, September 20, 1994, pp. 62–63.

85. For a view on the role of Iran's delegation, especially in arranging a special meeting between opposition leader Abdullah Nuri and the Tajik representatives in Iran's embassy in Islamabad, see *Ettela'at* (Persian), October 291994, p. 2.

86. For a sample of these types of reports, see *Ettela'at*, 22 September 1994, p. 8; on Russia's UN perspective on Iran's role, see *Ettela'at*, September 23, 1994, p. 7, and *Ettela'at*, September 26, 1994, p. 7.

87. The idea of a rail link had come up earlier in 1992 when the two countries had discussed the possibility of connecting Gorno-Badakhshan (via Faizabad) to lower Pyandzh (via Qonduz) with Herat-Mazar Sherif in Afghanistan to be linked to Mashhad in Iran. For an earlier discussion, see the interview with Khudoiberdy Holiqnazarov (the foreign minister) in *Nezavisimaia gazeta*, 11 July 1992, p. 3. For the Rafsanjani-Dostiev meeting, see *Tehran IRIB Television Second Program* in FBIS-SOV, September 20, 1994, p. 56.

88. For a polite expression of Tajik disappointment about the level of economic aid by Iran, see *Nezavisimaia gazeta*, July 11, 1992, p. 3 interview with Holiqnazarov.

89. See the interview with Muhammad Shabestari, Iran's ambassador in Tajikistan, in *Ettela'at*, September 8, 1993, p. 8.

90. The issue of cultural linkage seemed to have survived the critical political differ-

ences between Dushanbe and Tehran. A short yet impressive list of these links included the establishment of three schools to teach the Persian script, a major cultural center, providing copies of Persian translations of the Koran, 200 language-teaching manuals, 7,000 books for Tajik scholars, the opening of a 20,000-volume reading library, and the hosting of more than seventy delegations from Tehran (about 1,200 academics, artists, athletes, and so forth). Interestingly, these cultural activities also include 20,000 copies of Ayatollah Khomeini's famous collection of poetry, "The Wine Goblet and the Confidante." See *Ettela'at*, September 8, 1993, p. 8.

91. The concern over a U.S. activist role in Tajikistan and the need to court Iran has been expressed in Russia during the talks in Islamabad. See *Izvestiia*, November 2, 1994, p. 3.

92. See especially an exclusive and significant interview with Tertiakov, the Russian ambassador in Iran, with *Abrar* (Persian), August 10, 1993, pp. 2, 4, where the ambassador clearly outlines the common aspects of Russian-Iranian relations and views about the U.S. military and political presence in the Persian Gulf and the southern regions of Russia.

93. See, in particular, Abdullo Nuri's interview with *Izvestiia*, June 18, 1994, p. 4. Nuri argues that Russia could be a friend as well as the guardian of the Tajik border, but not an actor in the internal affairs of Tajikistan.

94. In this regard, while Tajikistan has its own particularities, the politics of its Islam resemble in general the rest of the Islamic world, of which Central Asia is now part and parcel.

95. See Imomali Rahmonov's address to an extraordinary session of the Supreme Council in Dushanbe, *Dushanbe Radio Tajikistan*, in FBIS-SOV, September 8, 1994, p. 48.

96. For Rahmonov's presidential manifesto, see *Narodnaia gazeta*, October 19, 1994, p. 1. For the views of the only other presidential candidate, Abdullojonov, who is Tajikistan's ambassador to Russia, see *Narodnaia gazeta*, October 19, 1994, p. 1.

Part III
The Turkish Factor

6

Iran and Turkey
Confrontation across an Ideological Divide

Henri J. Barkey

Iran and Turkey, brought together by geography and separated by ideology and regime interests, have had a long history of conflict and cooperation. The territories they inhabit serve as gateways for both Europe and Asia and as a result straddle more than one natural geopolitical subset: the Middle East, the Caucasus, the Indian subcontinent, the Balkans, the Black Sea, the Caspian Sea, Central Asia, and the Eastern Mediterranean. At the same time, each regime, because of its fundamental ideology and identity, represents an existential threat of sorts to the other. The Turkish-Iranian divide goes back to the end of the fifteenth century when the Sunni–Shiite division was the single most important ideological fault line. Today, the respective regimes interpret the secular-religious divide in very much the same way. In turn, this divide impacts their relationship in many areas, including Central Asia and the Caucasus.

In many respects, the two countries face parallel concerns: they inhabit what they perceive to be a hostile region where real and imaginary enemies abound. Despite the self-confident image of unity of purpose, nationhood, and ideology that Iran and Turkey project to the outside world, each remains mired in self-doubt and perceives its importance and role as being insufficiently appreciated by the international community.

Part of the self-doubt is a function of the recent emergence of ethnic nationalism among their own minorities. This is complicated by the fact that the post–Cold War era has been marked by rising ethnic awareness not only around the globe but also in these countries' immediate neighborhoods. If, for the time being, the impact of this development appears to be perhaps more acutely felt in Turkey than in Iran, the potential for similar developments in Iran is greater and more explosive given that country's ethnic and sectarian composition.

The two countries differ fundamentally in one important aspect: Turkey has been led by a status quo–oriented elite whose main fear was the Soviet Union. By contrast, the Iranian revolution installed a religiously inspired revisionist regime which, like all revolutionary regimes, has difficulty accepting an existing order it characterizes as being illegitimate and unjust. With the dissolution of the Soviet Empire, the Iranian regime is de facto today's primary revisionist power challenging—even if this challenge does not extend too far beyond the Middle East and adjacent regions—the only remaining superpower and status quo power par excellence, the United States. Both Turkey and Iran are straining to adapt themselves to the new post–Cold War environment: Turkey because previous strategic calculations that gave it prominence are no longer valid, and Iran because it finds itself ever more isolated and uncomfortable at having to face the United States alone. Iran's problems are compounded by having experienced the first post–Cold War confrontation, the Gulf War against Iraq, from a ringside seat.

This chapter will analyze Turkish-Iranian relations since the 1979 Iranian revolution within the context of changing geopolitical and ideological considerations. Postrevolution relations between Turkey and Iran have been marked by a significant degree of tension and suspicion. The mutual hostility emanates more from an ideological divide that separates the respective regimes than differences over identifiable "national interests." Unlike Greece and Turkey, which disagree over the use of the Aegean, the division of Cyprus, and their ethnic kinsmen living as minorities in the other, Iran and Turkey have few concrete issues that divide them. Each regime, however, stands in distinct contrast to the other and feels threatened by what the other represents. However, in Turkey, Tehran sees not just another neighboring state but an ally of the United States, a primary upholder of the regional order, and an example of a relatively well-established secular regime. Hence, what would otherwise be characterized as ordinary competition for markets in Central Asia is transformed into a rivalry about competing ideologies.

Although this chapter argues that the source of the tension rests with the revisionist ideas that are held by the regime in Tehran, this does not mean that Iran's foreign policy behavior is solely motivated by ideological concerns. Rather, Iranian foreign policy behavior is the outcome of the need for the regime in Tehran, albeit a revolutionary regime, to protect and preserve itself. Therefore, despite its rhetoric, Iran can behave in a conservative manner as it has in a number of areas, such as post–Gulf War Iraq, where it has sought to retain the status quo. Not unlike the foreign policies of other revolutionary regimes, Iran's is also nuanced and exhibits a combination of cold strategic thinking with ideological passion.

Of Revisionist and Status Quo Regimes

Because so much of the argument in this chapter depends on the impact of the Iranian regime's revolutionary character on Turkey and the region in general, it is important to focus briefly on the nature of the regimes in both of these societies. The two regimes stand in complete opposition to one another not just on the primary ideological question of secularism versus Islamic fundamentalism, but also over alliance relationships and modes of international behavior.

A revolutionary regime represents a threat to its neighbors because it refuses to accept the principles "on which states conduct their relations with each other."[1] Revolutions also increase the level of uncertainty in a region because following a revolution, not only are existing balances of power upset, but well-established communication links are damaged and, therefore, neither side can correctly identify the intentions of the other.[2] The resulting distortions in perceptions affect the revolutionary regime and the status quo power equally. In the Middle East these difficulties are compounded by the fact that the states are often weak and superficial in nature, thus vulnerable to challenges. "The superficial nature of states means that interaction between them will generally be strongly marked by the immediate present or immediate future, not by strategic considerations of old nations."[3]

This does not mean that traditional considerations based on geography, economics, and other strategic aspects do not play a role in the formulation of foreign policy. In fact, newly established revolutionary regimes may elect to follow some and sometimes all of their predecessors' policies. The classical example in this regard was the assertion that Soviet foreign policy was an extension of czarist foreign policy into the twentieth century. Similarly, revolutionary Iran, it is often argued, has continued some of the shah's foreign policy.

While similarities and continuities with the *ancien régime* undoubtedly remain in foreign policy, for the regime in Tehran, revolutionary ideology is the principal source of legitimation and internal discourse. Because the present Iranian regime came to power as a result of a fundamental societal and political transformation, it cannot depend solely on the prerevolutionary means of rule, whether they be patronage networks or authoritarian controls. It has to devise new means of establishing its authority over society, especially in view of the economically conservative aspect of the revolution: fundamental economic relations such as private property or profit have not been altered. The revolutionaries' main focus has been the political and ideological realm. Therefore, the particular version of Islamic theology that unites its leadership also sets limits beyond which foreign policies cannot stray too far. In fact, foreign policy is used by the regime as a source of legitimation. In other words, I accept Iranian revolutionary rhetoric for what it is: a shared set of ideas that is deeply ingrained within the regime's elite. Questions of security are, therefore, interpreted through this shared set.

A shared conceptual view of the world is, of course, the rule rather than the exception. However, what distinguishes Iran from other countries is the degree to which this conception is at variance with that of the rest of the world and its immediate region. The Islamic revolutionaries were intent not only on overthrowing the shah but also on severing his regime's links with the West and the United States in particular. From the beginning, Iran's new rulers did not hide their desire to export their revolution, whether by force or example.[4] Khomeini's insistence on the destruction of Saddam Hussein's regime during the Iran–Iraq War robbed Iran of the chance to conclude a cease-fire when it had the upper hand. Similarly, Iranian support for terrorism abroad has undermined the government's efforts at securing financing for developmental projects at home. Distortions in a revolutionary regime's perceptions of the world, especially a regime that perceives itself to be vulnerable, are likely to lead to incorrect interpretations of its neighbors' behavior. This is further accentuated by the fact that the regime has yet to institutionalize itself despite suggestions by some that the revolution has entered its Thermidorian stage.[5] Although existing divisions within the regime's elite may be the result of simple old-fashioned power struggles among cliques jockeying for position, the fact remains that often these are conducted along ideological lines. In turn, the resulting ideological sharpening bears a direct impact on the conduct of foreign policy. There is, in other words, a contradiction between Iran the state and Iran the revolution.

Turkey, which in the wake of World War I had to reinvent itself, also sought legitimacy in a set of ideas. In contrast to Iran, the Turkish regime attempted to construct an identity more attuned to the international status quo order even though this may have been at variance with the then existing Turkish societal norms. The ideas of nationhood, secularism, and modernity conflicted with the multicultural character and religiosity of the population residing in the new Turkish Republic. By hitching itself to a status quo order, the Turkish regime ensured that its new identity would be taken for granted. If over the decades Turkish foreign policy has, to a remarkable degree, been risk averse it is because the regime has sought to avoid confrontations that could upset the delicate balance it had constructed between regime and society. Over time, the Turkish system through a series of adaptations—opening up of the political sphere to competitive elections, corrective military interventions, and so forth—had thought that it had successfully institutionalized some of its ideas.

For Turkey as well as for the more established regimes in the Middle East, the advent of the Islamic revolution in Iran represented a profound shock. In Turkey it coincided with the beginnings of rumblings in society with regard to two of the more sensitive issues: religion and the Kurds. The state's secularist principles had already been challenged with the advent of the National Salvation Party of Necmettin Erbakan in the 1970s, although this party's growth had been stymied by the end of the decade. The Kurdish question was reawakened within the context of civil strife that pitted the left- and right-wing student groups and workers against each other. Kurds were prominent within the left wing. It is no surprise, therefore, that the government of the social democrat Bulent Ecevit recognized the new Khomeini regime in Tehran within twenty-four hours of its inception. As he publicly acknowledged later, Ecevit was more worried about the consequences of a possible breakup of Iran than about a revolutionary regime intent on exporting its ideas after assuming power.[6] Clearly, the Turkish regime had enough confidence in its population's acceptance of secularist ideas.

Nonetheless, the Iranian and Turkish regimes found themselves at odds with each other precisely because the underlying principles governing their establishments could not have been more opposite. In point of fact, each regime is the antithesis of the other, and by just being there, each represents an existential threat to the other. The new regime in Iran forced Turkey to confront issues it thought had been long buried; partly in reaction to the Iranian challenge, adjustments were made. These came principally during the leadership of Turgut Ozal, who pushed for a new Turkish synthesis that would be more tolerant of religious activities, beliefs, and norms without making a complete break with the secularist underpinnings of the republic.

This is not to say that classical state interests as determined by more objective issues such as geography and economics have become secondary to ideological concerns, or that Iran, in particular, is incapable of making cold, calculated decisions.[7] Rather, the case in Iran and Turkey is that the respective regimes' suspicions of each other have permeated all levels of relations between them. For Turkey what matters is the expansive obscurantism of Iran, while Iran views Turkey as being ruled by a heretic regime subservient to the Great Satan, the United States. These are the filters through which they approach each other and their common problems.

The Foreign Policies of Opposite States

Historical Context

Turkish-Iranian relations during the reign of the Pahlavis were always at a low level and "more or less superficial" despite the outward appearance of friendship and alliance.[8] Yet Kemalist Turkey's and Pahlavi Iran's commitment to modernization and secularism had created a basis for a shared ideological affinity.[9] They were also members of the same treaty organization, CENTO, the Central Treaty Organization (also known as the Baghdad Pact).

CENTO represented Turkey's first foray into the Middle East. Designed as an anticommunist alliance, it sought to bring like-minded states like Iraq, Iran, Pakistan, and Turkey together. Iran and Turkey shared common misgivings regarding the Arab world, the rise of radical regimes, and the Soviet Union. With the failure of the Baghdad Pact in 1958 following the overthrow of the monarchy in Iraq, CENTO lost much of its raison d'être. It was eventually replaced in 1964 by the RCD, Organization for Regional Cooperation for Development, which comprised only Iran, Turkey, and Pakistan. The RCD was a purely regional organization with none of CENTO's grand strategic design. As a result, Turkish interest in the Middle East declined. By contrast, the shah of Iran pushed to replace Britain after the latter's 1971 withdrawal from the Persian Gulf. In effect, with its attempts to meddle in Iraq, specifically in the Kurdish regions, Iran was a great deal more engaged in the Middle East than was Turkey. Turkey was content with seeking support for its position on Cyprus and later, following the dramatic rise in oil prices, access to Middle East markets.

Revolution and Its Aftermath

Soon after recognition of the new regime of Ayatollah Khomeini in Tehran by Ankara, the first test of the relationship materialized. Turkey refused to go along with the U.S. sanctions against Iran following the seizure of the U.S. embassy in Tehran in November 1979. This refusal was motivated by promises from Tehran of extensive future Iranian economic cooperation.[10] The decision paid off handsomely during the Iran–Iraq War that would start soon afterward.

The Iran–Iraq War

Hostilities between Iran and Iraq commenced some ten days after the military in Turkey assumed power on September 12, 1980, amidst one of the severest economic and political crises faced by the country in its modern history. Not only was political violence tearing the society apart, but years of economic mismanagement had resulted in bringing Turkish industry to a standstill. New and initially successful economic measures instituted in January of that year were blocked from further implementation by a deadlocked parliament.

Although in temperament and feelings closer to Iraq, Ankara maintained a strict neutrality during the war. The war proved to be a stroke of immense luck for Turkey. Both Iran and Iraq over the course of the eight-year war would turn to Ankara as a reliable supplier of goods and a transit route for imports from Europe and elsewhere. Strapped for cash and anxious to have access to relatively cheap consumer goods, both Iran and Iraq became significant consumers of a Turkish industry that had become moribund and was laden with large inventories. In fact, the export explosion toward the two belligerents and the revenues derived from transshipments of goods provided Turkey with sufficient foreign exchange revenues to bring economic reform measures to fruition.[11] Turkey, in other words, had the war to thank for its economic turnaround.

Turkish exports to Iran mushroomed from $45 million in 1978 to $1,088 million in 1983, or 19 percent of all exports, surpassing Germany that year, traditionally Turkey's largest customer. Turkish imports from Iran increased significantly, but perhaps not as dramatically: from $489 million in 1978 to $1,548 million in 1984. Concurrently, Iraq too had become as major a trading partner as Iran. However, the never-ending war and the significant decline in oil prices finally caused Iran to suffer from foreign exchange shortages that led to a curtailment of its purchases from Turkey. Another factor that helped sour Turkish-Iranian trade relations was the perception in Iran that Turkish middlemen reexporting third-party products significantly overcharged their Iranian customers. This led to the cancellation in August 1985 of a barter trade agreement signed in 1981 and 1982. The president of the Iranian Chamber of Industry admitted that the only reason these practices were condoned for so long was because of the war and dependence on Turkey.[12] Turkish exports to Iran declined to $440 million by 1987[13] and hovered around the $500 million mark until 1993 when they declined once more.

As much as the post-1980 export expansion to Middle Eastern countries suited the Turkish leadership, trade with Iran never recovered from the

decline it experienced toward the end of the Iran–Iraq War. President Suleyman Demirel's July 1994 visit to Tehran aimed, among other major goals,
at reviving the volume of bilateral trade to a yearly total of $2 billion. Three
characteristics define and affect future trade: first, the complementary nature of the two economies reduces the number of tradable goods available;
second, Turkish imports from Iran have traditionally been dominated by oil;
and finally, where Turkey's exports are competitive, such as in certain types
of industrial products, Iran has alternative markets to choose from, primarily in
the Far East. Excluding possible future pipeline connections and transit traffic,
the prospects for an enhanced economic relationship are not encouraging.

Relations since the End of the Iran–Iraq War

The relations between the two countries since the conclusion of the Iran–
Iraq War have been characterized by deep mutual suspicions. Nevertheless,
the Turkish approach to Iran has been a careful one, designed not to escalate
tensions along lines that pit "Islam against the West"; and Ankara has held
the belief that Iran ought to be constructively engaged in order to cultivate
good relations with those pragmatic elements in its power structure.[14] But,
as this chapter will try to demonstrate, the relationship is a tense one that
has assumed an element of competitiveness, punctuated by periods of outright hostility or cooperation.

Regime Insecurities and Foreign Policy

Western Connections

With the demise of the Soviet Union, Iran perceives itself to be exposed to
possible United States moves against it. It is worth remembering that it was
the downing of the Iranian civilian airliner by the United States in the
summer of 1988 that ultimately provided Iran with a justification to agree to
a cease-fire with Iraq.[15] U.S. policy has aimed to isolate the Iranian regime
diplomatically and economically.[16] Although some U.S. allies, most notably Japan and Germany, have maintained their economic dealings with Iran,
U.S. pressure has made it difficult for Tehran to obtain loans or trade easily
with the rest of the world. Thus, as a revolutionary or revisionist power confronting the United States, Iran is uncomfortable with the idea that its Western
neighbor, Turkey, is a member of the very alliance led by its main antagonist.

Turkey, by contrast, has viewed relations with Iran within the context of
its own domestic political and economic priorities and not from the perspective of Iran's confrontation with the West. Ankara's approach with respect

to the Middle East in general has until recently been reactive, avoiding of taking initiatives. Ever since the ascendancy of the Kurdish question, security considerations have come to dominate the Turkish side of the agenda. It was Iranian support for Kurdish groups starting in the early 1990s, specifically for the PKK, the Kurdish Workers' Party, that attracted Ankara's ire. (This issue will be dealt with in greater detail below.)

Though mistrustful of Iranian intentions, Ankara has attempted to demonstrate that its connections to the West do not determine its policy vis-à-vis Tehran. Turkish leaders are also cognizant of the fact that in the post–Cold War era, Washington's uneasiness with Tehran's regional ambitions endows Turkey with some strategic importance—admittedly nowhere near what the Soviet Union used to provide. In the Turkish-Iranian competition for influence in Central Asia, the Turks made the best of their connection with Washington and received an early endorsement from then Secretary of State James Baker, who acknowledged Turkey to be in the vanguard of halting the spread of fundamentalism among the newly independent Central Asian states.

Not surprisingly, this dual role—distancing itself from the West on policymaking vis-à-vis Iran while seeking U.S. support in Central Asia to halt Iranian expansion—has not gone unnoticed by Tehran. One Iranian newspaper ironically suggested that Iranian diplomats should instruct Turkish officials that, in the midst of its identity crisis, Turkey cannot always seek a balance that favors it in carrying out its Western role against Iran and in meeting its long-term political and economic interests regarding the world of Islam and the Islamic Republic.[17]

Also of concern to Iran have been Turkey's relations with Israel. Again interpreting these with the idea of a Western coalition against Tehran, the Iranian leadership has grown increasingly wary of the improving Turkish-Israeli relations in the aftermath of the September 13, 1993, signing of the Israeli-Palestinian Declaration of Principles. Preceding this event, the misgivings and lack of trust in Turkey's role in the region extends to the help Turkey has been providing Israel at the behest of the West in establishing diplomatic relations with Azerbaijan. As one Iranian newspaper argued, "Turkey has played a treacherous role in aiding Israel's infiltration into the Islamic world."[18] Even intra-Kurdish clashes that pit the Iranian-supported Islamic Movement of Kurdistan, IMK, against Talabani's forces belonging to the Patriotic Union of Kurdistan (PUK) are interpreted in Tehran as part of a secular attack on northern Iraq by Europe and Turkey.[19]

Ironically, the pressure maintained by the U.S. administration on Iran has pushed Tehran to cooperate more with Turkey despite all its anti-Turkish rhetoric, misgivings about its neighbor, and serious disagreements with Ankara. Turkey, after all, represents a conduit to those European states that do not completely support U.S. policy on Iran. As a result of U.S. pressure, as one Iran watcher commented, "Tehran needs the outside world more than the outside world needs Tehran."[20]

The Regional Context

Next to the Gulf War, the Arab-Israeli peace process is potentially the single most important development that will affect Iran's regional role and ambitions. The successful conclusion of the process threatens to isolate the regime in Tehran not only from its forward base in Lebanon but also from its ally Syria. More ominously for Tehran, the peace process will marginalize and isolate it from the region as new configurations—both economic and political—emerge. The implacable hostility of the regime in Tehran to Israel makes it difficult for Iran to reconcile itself with those countries that are in the process of establishing and extending their links with Israel, notwithstanding President Rafsanjani's declaration that Iran would not "physically" attempt to disrupt the process.[21] Whereas in 1992, Iranians interpreted the Turkish-Israeli rapprochement as a means for Turkey to obtain more aid from Washington,[22] in 1994 they began to view the increasing collaboration between these two states, which Egypt wants to participate in, as attempts at blocking "the rising Islamic tide."[23] Iranian perceptions are not completely inaccurate: Islamic fundmentalism and Iran were on the agenda during Tansu Ciller's November 1994 visit to Israel, the first by a Turkish prime minister.

Tehran, which has paid a price in its commercial dealings with the Arab countries because of its deteriorating political relations with them, will find itself further isolated as a result of improving Arab-Israeli ties. Trade with all Arab countries, including Syria but excluding the UAE, has declined dramatically over recent years.[24] Part of the decline is a reflection of Iran's poor economic conditions and the resultant diminution of its purchasing power. Clearly, in light of its relations with the Arab world, Tehran worries about the incursion of countries such as Turkey into what it jealously regards as its own turf. Iran reacted angrily to suggestions by then Prime Minister Demirel during a visit to the Gulf countries that Turkey wanted to participate in regional security arrangements in the Persian Gulf.[25]

Ideology and Domestic Politics

Some of the severest ideological clashes between the two countries manifested themselves over Turkish domestic politics and the issue of secularism. Secularism is not a purely domestic issue as it spills over into areas such as relations with the Central Asian republics. Soon after the revolution, Ayatollah Khomeini criticized the Turkish regime by arguing that it held on to power only through the force of bayonets. As Graham Fuller argues, "Ataturkism [to Khomeini] was worse than communism, for it was imposed by a nominal Muslim on his own Islamic state—a state that had gloriously led the Islamic world for centuries."[26] Iranians were perceived and accused by Turkish officials of interfering in the Turkish domestic political debate, helping antisecularist organizations, and even participating in assassination attempts—failed and successful—of Turkish intellectuals and, in one failure, of a Jewish businessman.

When in 1990 the Iranian ambassador to Ankara intervened in the domestic debate about the ban on wearing a head scarf and even took part in street demonstrations against the policy, he was declared a persona non grata by the Turkish government.[27] Almost from the beginning, Iranian officials on state occasions in Ankara made a point of never visiting the most obligatory of sites: Ataturk's mausoleum. They made no attempt to hide Iran's displeasure at the secularist reforms initiated by the founder of the Turkish republic. Turkish officials now make use of their opportunity to reciprocate by refusing to visit Khomeini's tomb.[28]

Both sides have complained about the vitriolic attacks directed at them by the opposing press. While the Iranian press and authorities blame the Turkish media's hostility to Iran and poor Turkish-Iranian relations on simple "Zionist control," Turks have been more sanguine about attacks on them. While the mainstream press in Turkey is overwhelmingly hostile to Iran, primarily because journalists see themselves as being part of a secular establishment, there are those close to the religious Welfare Party (Refah) who do not harbor similar attitudes. In Iran, the divisions between the radical and "pragmatic" wings of the revolution are often reflected in differing approaches to Turkey, while the mistrust of Iran in the Turkish press is widespread. In turn, this accentuates Turkish suspicions regarding the assassinations of some prominent journalists.

Tehran's unrelenting pursuit of its dissidents among the relatively large expatriate Iranian community living in Turkey has made both Turkish officials and especially the press wary of the regime's capabilities. In the aftermath of the revolution, a large number of Iranian exiles first found refuge in Turkey. Estimated at close to 1.5 million at its peak in 1987, the number has diminished significantly as many found other homes. Those remaining constitute fertile ground for exile politics and infiltration by Iranian agents, providing Iran with a capability for mischief.[29]

In Turkey, it is only Necmettin Erbakan, the leader of the Refah Party, who subscribes to the kind of views advanced by Iran regarding the United States and Israel. Zionism is Refah's bête noire; his opposition to Turkey's joining Europe and to Provide Comfort, the Allied-run operation based in southeastern Turkey protecting the Kurds in northern Iraq, is often formulated in the form of anti-Zionist anti-Western discourse. The party leaders and associated columnists will often repeat Iranian accusations. For example, in response to widespread speculation regarding the killing of Ugur Mumcu, a well-known secularist and columnist, Refah leaders echoed Iranian accusations regarding Israeli complicity.[30]

The electoral successes scored by the Refah in the March 1994 municipal elections, when it garnered nearly 20 percent of the votes cast, have served to uphold the Iranian belief that the Islamic segment in Turkey is growing and getting stronger. These electoral results also sent shivers through Turkey's secular establishment. If Rafsanjani in his declarations is careful not to upset either the Refah Party leadership or the Ankara government,[31] it is evident that Tehran sees Refah as a countervailing force in Turkish politics. Is Tehran misunderstanding the Refah phenomenon? Its leader Erbakan is first and foremost a Turkish nationalist: his Islamic orientation reflects his desire that Turkey not play a secondary role in a Western-run world order. Therefore, he thinks Turkey can improve its relative position in the Middle East and the world by "dominating" the Islamic world economically and politically.[32] His refrain that all Muslim countries want Turkey to lead the way, and his party's constant propaganda that Erbakan is the leader of the world's downtrodden and that he is not just the hope for salvation of the 1.5 billion Muslims of the world but for humanity's 6 billion,[33] are indications that Erbakan does not see himself as a follower of Iran's model. Such self-perceptions are not likely to help Erbakan or his party endear themselves to Tehran's leaders, especially since they make the same claims. In addition, Refah has been quite adept at manipulating Sunni–Shiite tensions in Turkey to its benefit.[34] This comes at a time when the Iranian leadership is facing an increasingly vocal domestic Sunni opposition.[35]

Geopolitical Concerns

If from an ideological perspective Turkey and Iran appear to be at loggerheads, their geopolitical position offers them many more reasons to cooperate than to mistrust each other. The three immediate areas of mutual concern are northern Iraq, Central Asia, and the Caucasus. With respect to both the Caucasus and the Kurdish question, they each share the same fears and problems. They both fear the dismemberment of Iraq, which could encourage the Kurds living in Iran and Turkey to seek similar outcomes. Similarly, despite the specter of Turkish irredentism in Azerbaijan, both countries would prefer to have stability along their borders because they cannot afford to be distracted by these issues. In Central Asia, the newly independent republics offer Iran and Turkey different possibilities that are not mutually exclusive.

Despite the prospects for collaboration in these regions, Iran and Turkey have shown little genuine interest in working together. The sensitivity of these areas for Iran can be seen in the apprehension with which it has approached them. Tehran has not championed the cause of Iraq's Shiites, who constitute that country's majority, and has not sought to inflame passions in Tajikistan where a democratic and Islamic opposition battles a communist *nomenklatura* regime left over from Soviet days. In effect, its behavior resembles that of a status quo power rather than a revolutionary one. It is Turkey, by contrast, that has made a great deal of emotional investment in Central Asia; the opportunity to extend secularism and Turkish identity at a time when the Kurdish rebellion led to a serious questioning of domestic identities provided a boost to the Turkish regime. As a result, Turkey has been far more aggressive than Iran in Central Asia and Azerbaijan.

One area of genuine difference is over Saddam Hussein's regime: whereas Turkey has been anxious, for economic and political reasons relating to northern Iraq and its own domestic Kurdish problem, to normalize relations with the regime in Baghdad and to see the revocation of the UN-sanctions regime, Iran remains quite mistrustful of Saddam Hussein. For Tehran, therefore, the continued isolation of Iraq as long as Saddam rules Baghdad is preferable. Although the regime in Tehran has recently called for the revocation of the sanctions, it is not clear whether this is a tactical move in view of Washington's opposition to such an outcome, since it allows the regime to appear supportive of "fellow co-religionists" without having to carry the resulting encumbrance.

What the following sections attempt to demonstrate is that the occasion for closer collaboration in these areas is impeded by a sense of mistrust that is the direct result of issues treated above—that is, the secular-Islamic dimension, the Western connections, and so forth.

The Kurdish Question and Northern Iraq

With significant Kurdish minorities in their midst, the leaders of both Ankara and Tehran have watched the developments in northern Iraq with alarm. The coming of age of the Kurdish administration in the coalition-protected zone of Iraq, and the elections and convening of a Kurdish parliament have been roundly criticized by Iran and Turkey as well as by Syria. These three states have met routinely to devise strategies against the burgeoning Kurdish autonomous zone and to make their vehement opposition known in any attempt by Iraqi Kurds to seek independence from Baghdad.

Iran, unlike Turkey, is opposed to the continuation of the Provide Comfort operation. For Tehran, Provide Comfort represents a vehicle through which the United States can maintain troops and military equipment close to its borders. It may also represent a precedent for Iran should its own Kurdish problem get out of hand. Iran's uneasiness with Western forces is a reflection of its belief that they are there to create a Kurdish state; the Iranian leadership finds the Turkish position contradictory.[36] Iranian and Turkish anxiety over each other's purported designs in northern Iraq precede the current difficulties over the fate of the autonomous region. During the Iran–Iraq War, while Turkey watched Iranian advances against Baghdad but especially in northern Iraq with apprehension, the possibility of intervening to block these advances was openly discussed. In turn, this caused consternation in Iran and confirmed Tehran's suspicions regarding Turkish intent to annex the area.[37]

By contrast, Turkey, which has been uneasy about the presence of foreign troops on its soil, faces a dilemma in that if these troops were to be removed, the refugee flow that led to the establishment of the force in the first place may repeat itself. In fact, Demirel is reported to have said precisely this to his Iranian hosts critical of Provide Comfort during his visit to Tehran in July 1994.[38]

Complicating Turkish-Iranian relations is the perception that Iran has allowed the PKK to use its territory to launch attacks on Turkey. In 1991, Turkey even detained an Iranian-flagged vessel, the *Cap Maleas*, transiting from Bulgaria on suspicion that it was carrying arms for the PKK. Officials in Ankara have routinely complained about the lack of cooperation on this front, although in the recent past Iran has been more forthcoming on the PKK question, leading to a slight improvement in bilateral relations.[39] Iranian worries about the revival of Iran's own domestic Kurdish question may account for the recent change in its stance. Iran may also have used the PKK as a means of countering what it perceived to be a pan-Turkic design on Azerbaijan during the rise of Abulfaz Elchibey and his Popular Front. Hence, the decline in Turkish fortunes following the overthrow of Elchibey may account for Tehran's recent lessening of its support for the PKK. These maneuverings do not disguise a deeper strategic need to preserve the Kurdish card for future use.

In the past, Iran always countered Turkish complaints about PKK activities by arguing that Turkey ought to do more to stop the activities of Iranian opposition groups on its territory, although there is little evidence that any of these have ever engaged in armed action against Iran. The *Cap Maleas* affair and a massive Turkish air force attack in January 1994 on a PKK camp deep in northern Iraq that killed nine Iranian villagers have only served to highlight anti-Turkish sentiment. Still, the two countries signed a protocol on September 5, 1994, promising to cooperate in "the fight against terror."[40]

The Slow Race for Central Asia

Soon after the dissolution of the Soviet empire, the looming Turkish-Iranian competition for influence in Central Asia became one of the most heralded bilateral conflicts of the post–Cold War era. The essence of this new rivalry is not difficult to fathom: accordingly, secular Turkey would intervene economically and culturally to block "fundamentalist Iran's" advances into the region. This was encouraged by both the United States, which has sought to limit the extension of Iranian influence, and the Turks themselves, who, in their search for markets and political influence in a new world order, found a post–Cold War mission.

From the outset, the new republics of Central Asia offered Iran and Turkey similar opportunities. For Iran it was a means of escaping a geographic isolation imposed on it by a hostile West and the Gulf Arab countries. Similarly for Turkey, increasingly shut out from the European Community, Central Asia provided a tantalizing chance to be the leader of a bloc of countries; in other words, it too would no longer be isolated in the post–Cold War world. In effect, the opening of Central Asia provided a strategic depth of sorts for both countries, and an arena where each thought it could exert a significant amount of influence, effectively increasing its relative importance in the eyes of the international community. Economically, both countries expected to benefit from the region. Iran offers the most direct access to international transportation networks through the Persian Gulf. The relatively underdeveloped markets of the Central Asian countries could also absorb the cheaper and unsophisticated products of Iranian industry. Not surprisingly, Turkey also sought access to these new markets. While some of its consumer goods may have been out of reach for individual Central Asian consumers, its large industrial firms were well poised to engage in engineering or construction projects such as pipelines. In short, tempered only by the small sizes of their markets, Central Asia states offered Iran and Turkey economic advantages that were of considerable significance.

Although Turkey was perceived to have important advantages—four of the five Central Asian countries and Azerbaijan were Turkic-speaking and only one Persian-speaking; Turkey had a more dynamic and better integrated economy, and access to Western capital and support—Iran benefited from its close proximity to the area. Access to Central Asia, even for Turkey, is through either Iran or Russia. A third route through South Asia is severely constrained by war-torn Afghanistan. Under these circumstances it is easy to see why Iran and Turkey would seek to compete in the region. Yet their competition has for the most part been tame with occasional difficulties. From the outset, the new republics were invited to join the Economic Cooperation Organization, ECO, the renamed Cold War relic formerly known as the RCD, which joined Iran, Pakistan, and Turkey. ECO's goals are not very ambitious; it is designed to facilitate trade and other types of cooperation among its participants. It mostly serves as a forum where Turkey and Iran can make public their intention to cooperate in regional endeavors and, perhaps more importantly, where the two countries can keep a watchful eye over one another.

If Turkey thought it could lead Central Asia into a new world, it soon found out that its capacities did not suffice to undertake this momentous project. But it was not Iranian moves that defeated Turkish aspirations as much as the Central Asians themselves who maneuvered politically so as to avoid one dominant patron, the Soviet Union, from being replaced by another, whether Turkish or Iranian. In four of the former Soviet republics, the new rulers are former Communist officials who have little sympathy for the kind of Islamic ideology Iran has to peddle. The Kyrgyz leader (the only one not to have been a Communist Party leader in the Soviet days) shares his counterparts' viewpoint. In addition, both Iran and Turkey underestimated the enduring Russian interest in its Near Abroad and the Central Asian regimes' desire for cordial relations with Moscow.

Nonetheless, Turkish-Iranian competition did manifest itself in such questions as rights to transit. Turkey, dependent on Iran for land access to Central Asia, has continuously complained of difficulties created by Iranians. At times it has retaliated, as when it closed its borders to Iranian trucks en route to Europe in response to Iranian insistence that goods going to Azerbaijan be transferred to Iranian trucks for transshipment.[41] Although Demirel raised the issue of roadblocks to Turkish transit trade in his visit to Tehran, Ankara expects to see improvement only in the long run, primarily because some of the difficulties are locally created rather than ordered by the central government in Tehran.[42] Transportation will remain a contentious issue in the future, primarily because, as Iranian foreign minister Velayati clearly stated, Central Asian states can trade with Turkey, but Iran would remain their "main link."[43]

Despite the low intensity of the competition over Central Asia, the regime in Tehran continues to worry about Turkey's "Western agenda." The refrain that Turkey in conjunction with the West is trying to impose secularism and pan-Turanism in Central Asia is often heard in the Tehran press. For Iran what is most important is not to export revolutionary Islam to Central Asian republics, but rather to impede the establishment of Western-oriented regimes to its north. This means it will compete with both Turkish and Saudi Arabian efforts to extend their influence there.[44] As argued earlier, Western and especially American apprehensions about the prospective Iranian role in that region in the aftermath of the Soviet Union's dissolution provided Turkey with the encouragement to step into the vacuum. At stake are not only the considerable economic investments but also psychological ones. Neither regime is willing to concede them to the other. In a way, the sheer presence of the other drives each of them to seek more clout and linkages. Both Turkey and Iran have tried to build regional groupings and alliances that, while excluding the other, nonetheless increase their own bargaining power. Turkey was the primary instigator of the Black Sea Economic Cooperation Zone, which includes Azerbaijan, Russia, Armenia, and Georgia but excludes Iran. Similarly, in the organization that joins together the littoral states of the Caspian Sea, Turkey is not a member.

The moderation of the competition between Iran and Turkey in Central Asia is also due to the fact that the two states can cooperate in some specific arenas. If geography appears to give Iran a distinctive advantage, it is not a complete one. One area where the two countries share a common interest is the construction of a gas pipeline from Turkmenistan through Iran to Turkey and then to Europe. The largest gas producer in the region, Turkmenistan, would like to diversify both its export routes and its customers. Access to Europe through Iran and Turkey would achieve this goal while also providing Turkey with a new source of gas for its burgeoning population and industrial base, and Iran with a conduit to export its own gas by hitching its network to this new one. While discussions to build such a pipeline have been conducted, it is U.S. recalcitrance that stands in the way of its progressing from the design to implementation stage. U.S. objections to extending credit to Iran will limit both U.S.-based companies and the World Bank from taking an active role in the project. Hence, in this case the two countries are dependent on each other and will presumably continue to seek common solutions to this and similar types of problems.

The rivalry in Central Asia could be inflamed if either side were to suddenly make gains at the expense of the other. The return of a pan-Turkic ideology that appeared at the end of the Ottoman Empire would threaten Iran both domestically and regionally by exposing its only direct cultural allies, the Tajiks, who have lost sizable chunks of their territory to the

Uzbeks during Stalin's era, to more Uzbek domination.[45] By contrast, the fall of the Uzbek strongman Islam Karimov, and his replacement by an Islamic regime, would undermine Turkish efforts in the region given Uzbekistan's influence there.

Azerbaijan

For both Turkey and Iran, Azerbaijan represents potentially the most explosive flash point in their relations. Yet they have succeeded in managing it despite the varying intensity of their competition. Azerbaijan's importance to Iran is due to the large number of Azeris living in Iranian Azerbaijan, creating the potential for an irredentist conflict. Of all the former Soviet republics, Azerbaijan is culturally and ethnically the closest to Turkey. The ethnic dimension is compounded in importance by the fact that the Azeris are locked in conflict with the Armenians—Turkey's age-old foe. In addition, Azeri oil and its potential transit through Turkey promises to be economically very rewarding to Turkey. Iran too stands to benefit from a pipeline crossing through its territory into Turkey; the Azeri government's decision to award Iran a 5 percent share of the consortium, worth an estimated $300–$350 million, angered Turkish officials, whose oil company was accorded only 1.75 percent.[46] By March 1995 intensive lobbying by Ankara succeeded not only in increasing its share to 6.75 percent, but also in receiving Washington's blessing to construct the pipeline through Turkish territory—preferably bypassing Iran.

The relative moderation (after an initial burst of enthusiasm) of the Iranian and Turkish roles in Azerbaijan has come about for four reasons: First and most important, Russia has continued to exercise its influence in the region with the aim not only of securing the allegiance of the republics in the Caucasus but also of forcing them to join the CIS and allowing Russian troops to man the Turkish and Iranian borders. Russia has succeeded in enticing Azerbaijan back into the CIS by helping the Armenian war effort in Nagorno-Karabakh and, thereby, indirectly forcing out the pro-Turkish president of Azerbaijan, Abulfaz Elchibey. Russian involvement has deterred both Iran and Turkey from taking a more active role.

Second, as Oles Smolansky argues, if Russia has emerged as the most successful contender in the three-cornered competition in Transcaucasia, it is in part due to the fact that many of the economic ties between Russia and the Transcaucasian republics have survived the collapse of the USSR.[47] Russia has aggressively sought to disrupt Azeri oil deals with third-party consortiums and especially with Turkey. Third, Turkey has been constrained by the following factors: Despite its closeness to Azerbaijan, Turkey does not possess a direct land corridor to Baku. It has a sliver of a border with Nakhichevan which, in turn, is separated from Azerbaijan proper by Armenia. Also, Turkish intervention against Armenia runs the risk of evoking the bitter memories of the 1915 massacres. By contrast, this very last fact allowed Iran to take a more active role and attempt to become an honest broker and intermediary. Finally, Iran fears the impact of domestic instability, caused either by the spread of the war or foreign intervention, on its own delicate domestic ethnic balances. Turkey's initial self-confident and buoyant entrance into Central Asia and especially Azerbaijan evoked precisely the threat of Turkish-Azeri intervention in Iran's domestic ethnic mosaic. Tehran's support for the PKK was, in fact, a means of cautioning Turkey against such interference and demonstrating its own similar capabilities by striking at its neighbor's Achilles' heel. Once the Turkish threat subsided with the ascendance of Russian power and the demise of Elchibey, Iran proved to be more cooperative on border issues.

In the Caucasus (as in Central Asia), Iran and Turkey share the same concern over resurgent Russian influence. Some Iranians, however, suggest that in "blocking U.S. infiltration," Russia and Iran share common security interests in Central Asia.[48] Although Iran has had more amicable dealings with Moscow, in part because the Russians have been anxious to sell large quantities of unused military equipment for cash, Russia's attempts at regaining its former sphere of influence have not been comforting. The Russian fear of "fundamentalism" on its southern borders, which has led to its involvement in the Tajik civil war, is an added constraint on Iran's activities in the region as a whole and a potential source of friction. As the Azeri ambassador to Tehran openly stated, Iran should not be worried about Turkey's influence in Azerbaijan, but rather about the return of Russian influence.[49] If the present regime in Moscow prevails, its pro-Western tendencies will preclude it from cozying up to Tehran beyond an acceptable level. In fact the Kremlin could even be forced to turn its back on Iran. If the right wing gains power in Moscow, it too will make sure that the former Soviet republics toe a closer line. In either case, both Iran and Turkey would be the principal losers since they will see their access to potentially very lucrative markets denied to them or at least severely constrained.

Conclusion

In Central Asia and the Caucasus, Turkey, Iran, and Russia are engaged in a competition that requires crisscrossing alliances. Russia and Turkey have a common interest in responding to Iranian Islamic influences, however mild they may be at present. Iran and Russia have tried to combat pan-Turkish ideas and thus contain Turkey's influence throughout the region. Finally, Iran and Turkey have yet to make common cause against Russian moves designed to limit both of their influences.

In this triangular game in Central Asia and the Caucasus, which dyad emerges will depend on the following factors: First, let us consider developments in the regions adjacent to Iran and Turkey. As a result of the Arab-Israeli peace process and if recent Turkish moves to join a form of antifundamentalist alliance with other status quo countries in the Arab world, and especially with Israel, continue, Iran may turn increasingly to Central Asia to compensate for its forced isolation in the Middle East and may even seek to make common cause with Russia. The likelihood of this possibility is high since Turkey, forced by the post–Cold War strategic changes, is in pursuit of a regional role that will regain some of its importance in the Western alliance. This could unwittingly be aided by a U.S. policy that is acrimonious toward Russia.

Second and alternatively, Turkish-Russian cooperation against Iran would materialize if a rise in Islamic movements occurred—not necessarily engineered by Iran—sprinkled with some limited successes in which such movements manage to come to power in the region as a whole. The determination with which Russia has tried to block Turkish ambitions in Azerbaijan and Turkish-Azeri oil deals makes this unlikely in the short term.

Finally, Turkish-Iranian cooperation against a resurgent Russia is quite unlikely because of two reasons. First, it would require a radical policy shift on Moscow's part—one likely to be adopted by a hostile right-wing nationalist regime. Even then, Iran and Turkey's timid reaction to the Chechnya crisis, dictated by their own domestic priorities and concerns, demonstrates how difficult it is for them to openly challenge Moscow. The second reason entails the deep mistrust with which each regime approaches the other. While there are many reasons the two states ought to cooperate, their respective regimes perceive each other as ideological opposites. The range of the Turkish-Iranian mistrust is not limited to any particular area, such as Central Asia or Iraq, but rather encompasses a wide variety of issues including domestic politics, ideology, and religion. Strengthening of one in any area reduces the perceived security of the other. Hence, any attempt at genuine cooperation between the two will remain hostage to other influences emanating from different aspects of their relationship.

Notes

I would like to thank the United States Institute of Peace for its support of this project.
1. David Armstrong, *Revolution and World Order* (Oxford: Clarendon Press, 1993), p. 3.
2. Stephen M. Walt, "Revolution and War," *World Politics*, vol. 44, no. 3 (April 1992), p. 341.

3. Ghassan Salamé, "The Middle East: Elusive Security, Indefinable Region," *Security Dialogue*, vol. 25, no. 1 (March 1994), pp. 17–35.

4. See R.K. Ramazani, "Iran's Export of the Revolution: Politics, Ends, and Means," in *The Iranian Revolution: Its Global Impact*, ed. John L. Esposito (Miami: Florida International University, 1990); and Farhang Rajaee, "Iranian Ideology and Worldview: The Cultural Export of Revolution," in the same volume.

5. Jean-François Bayart, "Republican Trajectories in Iran and Turkey: A Tocquevillian Reading," in *Democracy without Democrats: The Renewal of Politics in the Muslim World*, ed. Ghassan Salamé (London: I.B. Tauris, 1994).

6. Süha Bölükbası, *Türkiye ve Yakinindaki Orta Dogu* (Ankara: Dıs Politika Enstitüsü, n.d.), pp. 11–12.

7. Johannes Reissner argues that Turkish-Iranian relations are characterized on the Iranian side by a mix of "cold calculations and revolutionary gesticulation"; Johannes Reissner "L'Iran et les changements au Moyen-Orient," in *La nouvelle dynamique au Moyen Orient: Les relations entre l'Orient Arabe et la Turquie*, ed. Elisabeth Picard (Paris: Editions L'Harmattan, 1993), p. 132.

8. Ihsan Gürkan, "Turkish-Iranian Relations: Dynamics in Continuity and Change," *Turkish Review of Middle East Studies*, vol. 7 (1993), p. 73.

9. Shireen T. Hunter, *Iran and the World: Continuity in a Revolutionary Decade* (Bloomington: Indiana University Press, 1990), p. 133.

10. Philip Robins, *Turkey and the Middle East* (London: Chatham House, 1991), p. 54.

11. For detailed analysis of Turkey's gains and losses during the Iran–Iraq War, see Henri J. Barkey, "The Silent Victor: Turkey's Role in the Gulf War," in *The Iran–Iraq War: Impact and Implications*, ed. Efraim Karsh (London: Macmillan, 1989).

12. Bölükbası, *Türkiye*, pp. 25–26. Also, after the war Western companies provided credits and technologies Turkey was unable to match. Ibid., p. 35.

13. Barkey, "The Silent Victor," p. 136.

14. Atila Eralp, "Facing the Iranian Challenge: Turkey's Relations with Iran after the Islamic Revolution," paper presented at "The Reluctant Neighbor: Analyzing Turkey's Role in the Middle East," United States Institute of Peace, June 1–2, 1994, Washington, DC.

15. At the time, President Khamenei asserted that the war had "gained unprecedented dimensions, bringing other countries into the war and even engulfing innocent civilians," quoted in Thomas L. McNaugher, "Walking Tightropes in the Gulf," in Karsh, ed., *Iran–Iraq War*, p. 191.

16. The United States does not export any military or dual-use equipment to Iran. It also tries to ensure that no official credit, especially concessional financing, is extended to Iran by allies or by international financial institutions, such as the World Bank.

17. *Ettela'at*, February 23, 1993, in Foreign Broadcast Information Service, Near East and South Asia (hereafter FBIS-NES), 93-034.

18. *Salaam*, "Commentary Views Turkish Role in Israeli Affairs," July 29, 1992, in FBIS-NES and Asia 92-146. Similarly, Tehran blames Turkey for helping Israel to develop cordial relations with Azerbaijan; see Hamid Haidar, "The Israelis Are Coming," *al-Wasat*, May 9, 1994, in *Mideast Mirror*, same date, p. 17.

19. *Resalat*, January 30, 1994, in FBIS-NES, 94-027, February 9, 1994.

20. Amir Taheri in *Asharq al-Awsat*, in *Mideast Mirror*, August 15, 1994, p. 16.

21. *Mideast Mirror*, June 8, 1994, pp. 15–17.

22. *Voice of the Islamic Republic of Iran*, July 18, 1992, in FBIS-NES, 92-139.

23. *Voice of the Islamic Republic of Iran*, January 31, 1994, in FBIS-NES, 94-023 February 3, 1994.

24. *IRNA*, August 10, 1994, in FBIS-NES 94-154.

25. *Abrar* (Tehran) in Persian, February 9, 1993, p. 16. Ruzbeh Buolhari, "Blackmail—Ankara Style," in FBIS-NES, 93-034.

26. Graham E. Fuller, *The Center of the Universe: The Geopolitics of Iran* (Boulder, CO: Westview Press, 1991), p. 203.

27. Gürkan, "Turkish-Iranian Relations," p. 79.

28. Mehmet Ali Birand, "Iran'da ne oldugunu merak etmiyorsanizi, bu yazıy i ıokumaydn," *Sabah*, July 28, 1994, p. 10.

29. This problem is exacerbated by the absence of visa regulations on Iranians coming to Turkey. Estimates of Iranians in Turkey vary from 600,000 to 2 million. Gürkan, "Turkish-Iranian Relations," p. 81.

30. *Mideast Mirror*, February 11, 1993.

31. Mehmet Ali Birand, "Iran'ın Türkiye'ye bakısı neden degisiyor?" *Sabah*, July 23, 1994, p. 14.

32. Ruşen Çakır, *Ne Şeriat ne Demokrasi: Refah Partisini Anlamak* (Istanbul: Metis Yayınları, 1994), p. 163.

33. Ibid., p. 165.

34. In September 1994, the Refah mayor of Istanbul ordered the demolition of an Alevi meeting and prayer house, engendering a strong reaction in this community. For details, see *Cumhuriyet*, September 12, 1994.

35. Sami Shourosh, "The Coming Sectarian Conflict in Iran," *al-Hayat*, translated in *Mideast Mirror*, September 9, 1994, pp. 19–22.

36. Editorial in *Resalat* (Tehran), January 30, 1994, in FBIS-NES, 94-027, February 9, 1994.

37. Barkey, "The Silent Victor," pp. 144–45.

38. He is reported to have said: "What would you do if a million Iraqi refugees came to your borders and a million to ours?" *Hürriyet*, July 28, 1994.

39. Mehmet Ali Birand, "Iran'ın Tükriye'ye," *Sabah*, July 23, 1994.

40. *Reuters*, September 5, 1994.

41. Cengiz Çandar in *Sabah*, August 4, 1993, p. 16.

42. Author's interview with Turkish Foreign Ministry official in Ankara, July 29, 1994.

43. Interview with Ali Akbar Velayati, *as-Safir*, November 27, 1993, in FBIS-NES, 93-228. See also Ali Akbar Velayati, "The Shape of Trade and Economic Relations between Iran and Central Asia," *Turkmenskaya Iskra* (Ashgabat), August 8, 1994, in FBIS-NES, 94-159.

44. Reissner, "L'Iran et les changements," p. 139.

45. Mohammad-Reza Djalili, "L'Iran face aux développements en Transcaucasie et en Asie centrale," *Cahiers d'études sur la Méditerranée Orientale et le monde Turco-Iranien*, no. 16 (1993), p. 251.

46. Hàyrettin Uzun, head of the Botas pipeline firm, is reported to have said, "We have been surprised. How can we tell our public the situation that the Turks are close relatives of the Azeris, but have the smallest share in the deal?" *Reuters*, November 16, 1994.

47. See Oles Smolansky, "Russia and Transcaucasia: The Case of Nagorno-Karabakh," chapter 8 in this volume.

48. *Hamshahri*, August 23, 1994, in FBIS-NES, 94-168.

49. *Resalat*, February 25, 1993, in Foreign Broadcasting Information Service, Soviet Union (FBIS-SOV), 93-045.

7

Turkey and Central Asia
Reality Comes Calling

Patricia M. Carley

The "discovery," upon the opening-up of the Soviet Union, of more than 60 million Turkic people in the republics of Central Asia unleashed a flurry of debate about the implications for the world's only independent Turkic country at that time: Turkey.[1] The discourse about the future of the two regions ranged from the possible reorientation of Turkey's foreign policy eastward in a substantial departure from its general western alignment, to the rise of a Turkic-based grouping of states destined to become a formidable new regional power in the world. This latter speculation caused a considerable stir, with its parallel assertion of the "re-emergence" of "pan-Turkism," an ideology and movement from the late nineteenth century in the Ottoman Empire which sought the political union of the world's Turkic peoples, the majority of whom, outside the Ottoman Empire, lived under Russian tutelage.

Latent pan-Turkist sentiment, some said, lurked beneath the surface of all the Turkic-speaking peoples, making it only a matter of time before Turkey and Central Asia (together with Azerbaijan) formed a federation of some kind based on this Turkic kinship. This development, some even claimed, would evince the reappearance of the Ottoman Empire, albeit in a slightly altered form, as if Central Asia had once been part of that empire (which it had not).[2] There were claims to the effect that the main Central Asian languages of Uzbek, Kazakh, Kyrgyz, and Turkmen were mutually intelligible with Turkish, even that they were in fact dialects of Turkish. In the late 1980s, there seemed to be little doubt that the Turks would be taking a leading role in the development of the newly independent Central Asian states, not least by being an economic and political model based naturally on the ethnic and linguistic kinship of the Turkish and Central Asian peoples, and that this new relationship was bound to alter both Turkey's foreign policy and the strategic alignments of the entire region.

Much of this discussion transpired in spite of what can only be called complete ignorance—perhaps not so much about Turkey, but about Central Asia, its relations with Turkey, and, most certainly, about pan-Turkism. In fact, much of it happened precisely *because* there was so little knowledge of Central Asia in the West or in Turkey—it truly was "discovered" at that moment in time by many otherwise well-informed people. (Much of the discussion was in fact not a little patronizing to the Central Asians themselves, who, after all, did not feel themselves to be discovered.) Furthermore, speculation on the Turkish–Central Asian relationship often occurred as if the matter existed in a vacuum, as if the only influencing factors in the equation were events of the late 1980s. There was little or no attempt made at the time to look into the historical or even practical validity of the assertions made, whether about the actual nature of the ethnic and linguistic kinship between the Turks and Central Asians, their historical relationship, or the history and content of pan-Turkism—all factors that might have helped to determine if the claims had any basis in reality.

This essay will attempt to fill in that space, albeit somewhat belatedly, for there is much background that rarely managed to get a hearing above the clamor of the time. Now that the furor about Turkey and Central Asia has abated somewhat, and the relationship has run aground into some sober realities, it is possible to get the attention of those once caught up in the more sensational proclamations and explain how many factors—historical, linguistic, political, ethnic—could have predicted from the start the cooling in relations. Missing in the original discussion, and hopefully provided here, was an understanding of the *overall* picture of the relationship between the two predominant regions of Turkic peoples in the world: a brief history; a short analysis of pan-Turkism, its development in the Ottoman Empire, the reaction in Central Asia, and the way it developed in Turkey after the establishment of the republic; Ataturk's legacy on Turkish foreign policy; developments in Central Asia since the creation of the USSR; and finally, against this background, a review of the Turkish–Central Asian relationship as it developed from the late 1980s to today. It will be seen that history, the legacy of Ataturk, the nature of pan-Turkism, and the realities of twentieth-century development in the USSR indicated quite clearly that a wider political or economic union between Turkey and Central Asia would have been extremely unlikely, and that even a closer relationship between the two regions would run into trouble very quickly.

It should be stated at the outset what this chapter is not. It is not aimed at providing specific details of the content of Turkey's current relationship with Central Asia, as these kinds of basic facts are fairly readily available. Nor will it examine Turkey's relationship with Azerbaijan, which for many historical and linguistic reasons is really a very different case from the Central Asian countries and requires a separate analysis altogether. The relationship among the Central Asians, though a factor in the Turkish–Central Asian relationship generally, is simply outside the scope of this chapter. To avoid having to write "with the exception of the Tajiks," or "with the exception of Tajikistan," throughout, the term "Central Asia" here will refer to the majority Turkic peoples of the region. Finally, this chapter does not, for obvious reasons, pretend to present an in-depth analysis of the factors described below. Generalizations are, alas, necessary.

Historical Background

Origins of the Turkic Peoples: How Great the Ethnic Kinship?

Though the exact birthplace of the original Turkic tribes seems destined to remain obscure, the scholarly consensus suggests that the first people to be known as the Turks, called "Tu-kiu" in Chinese sources, emerged in the sixth century from the Altai Mountains, having occupied an area that is now Mongolia.[3] The first migration south and west occurred after the Hunnic and then Chinese invasions, leaving a branch of Turkic tribes in areas adjacent to and on top of the settled population (mainly Iranian peoples such as Soghdians) in what is now called Central Asia or Turkestan.[4] Both the original Iranian population, largely settled in the oases, and the newly arriving Turkic groups, both sedentary and nomadic, were subject to invasion from Arab groups from the south, so that by A.D. 716, the entire sedentary population of Central Asia, what the Arabs called Transoxiana (south of the Syr Darya River), was converted to Islam.[5] Turkic tribes farther east were converted by the mid-eighth century, after which the Arabs retreated south, never again to rule over this part of the world. The tenth-century incorporation of Transoxiana into the Persian Samanid empire left a lasting legacy of Persian cultural, administrative, and linguistic influence on a population increasingly Turkicized ethnically by constant tribal migrations. Some Turkic tribes settled in the outer areas of Central Asia, such as the Kyrgyz in the Altai Mountains, and the Uighurs in the Tarim Basin in present day Xinjiang.

The Turkic tribes who first occupied the predominantly settled areas of Central Asia were those whose leading tribe was called the Oghuz. As other Turkic tribes from farther east moved into Central Asia, the Oghuz continued to move west until, at the end of the tenth century, the Oghuz tribes made a major migratory thrust west, taking them almost completely out of Central Asia. This process eventually produced three famous Turkic peoples: the Khaljj, who later established themselves in Afghanistan; the Seljuk; and the Osmanli or Osmans, better known to the West as Ottomans.[6] From this time in history, the Oghuz tribes and their descendants no longer maintained strong ties with the peoples who remained in Central Asia. The Turkic groups from the eastern parts of Central Asia, still migrating into the region to such places as the lands around Lake Issyk-Kol (in present-day Kyrgyzstan), were seen to occupy the "true land" of the "Turks," and memories of the Oghuz soon "faded from these regions."[7]

The Seljuk branch of the Oghuz pressed into Khorasan in northern Iran, moved into Baghdad, and soon conquered much of Anatolia (then Byzantium), making their capital at Konya. Though the Seljuks could not maintain control over all their domains, their foray into Anatolia was the beginning of what would prove to be the permanent Turkification of that region. Many disparate Turkic tribes settled in Anatolia and intermarried with the indigenous Christian population.[8] In the fourteenth century, a Turkish khan from the Osman tribe enjoyed a series of military successes in Anatolia and eventually established the hereditary line of the house of Osman. The massive western migrations of Turkic tribes ended about this time, and the Osmans, or Ottomans, built an empire which, with few exceptions, focused its military and commercial horizons toward the empires of Europe. By the beginning of the fifteenth century, Anatolia was fully in Ottoman control and the Turks there experienced a course of history quite divergent from that of the Turkic tribes remaining in Central Asia.

In Central Asia

After the Oghuz tribes moved west, the Turkic and Persian tribes in Central Asia endured centuries of invasions from the east and northeast. Tribes such as the Kara Kitai, who were ethnic Chinese, moved first into the Kashgar region (Chinese Turkestan) and then into western Central Asia. The Kara Kitai left not only considerable Chinese influence for several centuries (in Samarkand and other cities a number of the local dignitaries were "Kitai," completely Chinese in culture), but also the word "Kitai" itself, which means "China" in several Muslim languages as well as Russian.[9] Before the thirteenth-century Mongol invasion, a group of Turkic tribes called Kipchak held power on the northern steps of Central Asia. The Kipchak formed one of the main ethnic components of eastern nomadic Turkic tribes, such as the Uzbek and Kazakh clans that would later migrate into the heart of Central Asia and greatly affect the ethnic makeup of the people. The Oghuz tribes who had migrated west centuries earlier did not incorporate these Kara Kitai/Chinese or Kipchak/eastern Turkic ethnic elements to any great degree.

One of the most famous events in Central Asian history—also after the out-migration of the Oghuz—was the invasion by Mongol leader Genghiz Khan at the beginning of the thirteenth century. Genghiz crushed the rule of the Kara Kitai, the Kipchak, and other tribal leaders, and set up Mongol political and military domination from as far west as the Urals, throughout Central Asia, east through Mongolia, and as far east as Peking.[10] The Mongol raiders often recruited warriors from the Kipchak and other Turkic tribes and, as there was a relatively rapid mixing of population, their ethnic influence on the Central Asians was significant. Mongol linguistic influence also remained, especially among the eastern parts of Central Asia.[11] Genghiz and his Mongol armies were the last significant tribal movement west across Central Asia, though nomadic tribes continued to conquer and mingle for centuries after.

At the end of the fifteenth century, an Islamicized nomadic group known as the Uzbeks (or Usbegs) moved south from Siberia. The Uzbeks brought back the dominance of the eastern Turkic nomadic tradition to a region returning, after the Mongol invasion, to Persian cultural—but not ethnic—dominance.[12] Though the tribe was known as "Uzbek," the name did not denote a linguistic or ethnic unit but rather a kind of political one, for the tribal composition included Turkic groups, Mongols, Kara Kitai, Tangut (a Tibetan group), and others.[13] These nomadic conquerors soon mingled and intermarried with the city dwellers, as have all conquerors of Central Asia, leaving their ethnic mark on the settled peoples and becoming Persianized in the cities in culture and tradition in turn. The rule of the Uzbek khans lasted until the mid-seventeenth century, and was followed by a period of political breakdown and anarchy in Central Asia.[14]

Probably the word used most often to describe Central Asia after Tamerlane's (a descendent of Genghiz) rule in the fourteenth century is "isolation." Beginning in the fifteenth century, intellectual and cultural contacts between Central Asians and their co-religionists and ethnic kin elsewhere in the world, already slight, virtually ceased, resulting in the steady cultural, political, and economic decline of the region. The isolation was sustained in part by the terrain: Central Asia is cut off to the north by a vast, empty steppe, and in the south by harsh mountain ranges. Though direct communications with Persia in the south were not always difficult, the sixteenth-century conversion of that empire to the Shia branch of Islam effectively severed religious links, and there were few contacts with the Ottoman Empire. Constant intertribal feuds and pillages, petty wars and raids solidified the decay and retreat into obscurity. By the beginning of the nineteenth century, there was no unified power in Central Asia, no clearly defined frontiers; the various khans and other rulers were at almost constant war with one another, and fairly regular incursions from the nomadic Kazakhs or Turkmens, as well as regular rebellions from Tajiks and others, provided almost constant instability.

In the Ottoman Empire

The situation throughout those centuries was quite different for the Turks in the Ottoman Empire. The Oghuz Turks who migrated to Anatolia mixed with Balkan peoples, Greeks, Bulgars, and Serbs, especially the Ottoman ruling classes, as intermarriage became increasingly common.[15] The anthropological features of the Oghuz Turks have thus been characterized by their non-Altaic features, as the Mediterranean influence became the dominant aspect of their ethnic makeup.[16] Even the Turkish peasants of Anatolia lost much of the "Asiatic character" they once possessed centuries before due to their intermixing with the indigenous Byzantine population.[17] Thus the ethnic and anthropological distinctions between the western Turks of Anatolia and the eastern Turks of Central Asia diverged centuries ago, as the Ottoman Turks absorbed the ethnic features of those they conquered and the Central Asians absorbed the ethnic makeup of those they were conquered by, including the Mongolians and Chinese.

Furthermore, and in contrast to the almost total isolation of Central Asia, the western Ottoman Turks were, by the time of the fall of Constantinople in 1453, firmly entrenched in Europe. Though the caliph in Istanbul was the titular head of all of the world's Muslims, and a great part of the Ottoman Empire was made up of conquered Islamic lands in Egypt and Arabia, it was with European armies that the Ottomans were in competition, both militarily and commercially. Italian, French, English, and Dutch merchants and their families grew in number in Istanbul, the Ottoman capital, throughout the centuries of Ottoman rule. The weight of European influence was felt in many other ways, not least from the sway of European modernized institutions and ideas of nationalism, which were finding their way to the upper ranks of Ottoman society. Clearly, in addition to their separate and disparate ethnic development, the historical experiences of the Central Asian and Anatolian peoples for centuries overlapped little, if at all.

Pan-Turkism

Despite this historical and ethnic divergence, the late nineteenth century saw the development of a movement known as pan-Turkism, which promoted the unity of the Turkic peoples of the world, primarily located in the Ottoman and Russian empires. Pan-Turkism emerged as a reaction to several other developments at the time, including: the growing strength and increasingly hostile demands of nationalist and separatist movements among other, non-Turkish, ethnic groups in the Ottoman Empire; the increasing bellicosity of Russian-led pan-Slavism; and the continuing decline of Ottoman power vis-à-vis Europe. The pan-Turkist movement "peaked" in the second (and into the third) decade of the twentieth century, when it became the battle cry of several revolutionary Young Turk leaders in an attempt to save the empire from imminent dismemberment after World War I.

When, in the late 1980s, the emergence of the Central Asian republics from the obscurity of the Soviet Union aroused great excitement in Turkey, the notion of "pan-Turkism" was historically resurrected, this time largely by outside (mostly Western) observers, and presented as a force to be reckoned with in the future, one that would inevitably challenge regional power arrangements. Most spoke of the movement's "re-emergence" in the assumption that the ideology was once widespread, popular, and potentially powerful.

Yet, a glance back to the time of the movement's heyday would have demonstrated that even then, the pan-Turkist movement consisted primarily of the dreams of a few elites in the Ottoman and Russian empires who disregarded some very basic historical, ethnic, and linguistic realities. The movement hardly resonated among the vast majority of the Turkic peoples in the Russian Empire, the objects of Ottoman pan-Turkist aspirations who, with little or no consciousness of ethnic identity, identified themselves primarily as Muslims before the establishment of the Soviet Union.

Following the establishment of the Turkish republic in 1923, the pan-Turkist movement there became the cause of a few extreme Turkish nationalists who saw themselves as the natural leaders of all the Turkic peoples, or of Tatar émigrés from the USSR determined to keep alive the struggle against the Soviet state. Whatever influence the movement may have had among Anatolian Turks was overwhelmed by the authority of Ataturk who, as part of his plan for Turkey, systematically severed ties between his nation and the rest of the Turkic world. And finally, the Turkic peoples in the Russian Empire (albeit under Soviet manipulation) developed distinct ethnic identities of their own, which, after more than three generations, have largely gained dominant allegiance. Thus, even a brief understanding of the history of pan-Turkism and modern developments in Turkey and Central Asia could have demonstrated the unlikelihood that pan-Turkism could emerge in the late twentieth century as a popular movement, or even that the ethnic and linguistic kinship of the Turks and Central Asians would somehow become the basis of a special relationship between them.

The History and Content of Pan-Turkism

At the end of the nineteenth century, there was little understanding among Ottoman Turks of their ethnic identity. The word "Turk" was rarely used as an identifier, except perhaps pejoratively to denote a backward peasant. The pan-Turkist movement took some of its initial inspiration from an Ottoman Turk named Ziya Gokalp who aspired to arouse the Turkish people from their "national unconsciousness" and to glorify in their Turkish national identity. For some in the movement, these ideas evolved into an elaborate myth of Turkish racial and ethnic purity—and superiority—coupled with romantic visions of a legendary homeland of all the Turks, claimed loosely to be somewhere in Central Asia. Generally, pan-Turkists in the Ottoman Empire, and later those in Turkey also, envisioned a great unity of the Turkic peoples under their own leadership. The other Turkic peoples, it was expected, would naturally fall in line behind the authority of the greater Ottoman Turks.[18]

Yet even at this early twentieth-century cathartic moment in history, brought about by the collapse of the two large empires containing the Turkic peoples, their political and ethnic affiliations to a certain extent "up for grabs," pan-Turkism never captured popular allegiance in either Anatolia or Central Asia. There were simply too many realities working against it. In aiming to unite in some form the world's Turkic peoples, the movement sought to bring into a "Turkish empire" peoples who were in fact widely scattered geographically, had conflicting goals and interests at the time, and who were at varying stages of development and civilization. Pan-Turkism hoped to cut through numerous layers of the differing cultures that had settled over these vast areas from Turkey to Central Asia, including mixtures of Persian, Islamic, and Arabic, to combine all the Turkic-speaking peoples into one supranational nation; yet in the end, it struggled in vain against the strength of these differences.

In the case of language, the pan-Turkists insisted that one Turkic language could unite all Turkic peoples. Yet even in 1918, there were so many variants of the Turkic languages that it was impossible to unite them. One author writing at the time describes that, "just as at one time Latin was understood from the mouth of the Danube to the Atlantic . . . and dialectical differences resolved themselves into the Rumanian, French or Spanish languages, so the Turkish language developed. The notion that original community of speech constitutes a bond of union is a weak reed on which to lean."[19] Another wrote, "Complex linguistic gymnastics could not unite a multi-linguistic empire."[20] Similarly, the Turkic peoples of the world were no more united in ethnicity than in language. An author, again of the period, wrote:

> to speak of the Osmanlis [Ottomans] and the Turanian Turks [of Central Asia] as a racial and cultural unity would be by a stroke of the pen, or by means of a propagandist pamphlet, to wipe away all in the invasions, migrations, massacres and fusions which for twenty centuries played havoc with that part of the world. The fact remains that if there is no other community than a distant relationship in language, there need be no community of interest at all.[21]

It became clear, even to its adherents, that pan-Turkism was failing in its attempt to promote a wider nationalist identity among the world's Turkic peoples. After the disintegration of the Ottoman Empire, the pan-Turkist movement lost its prime impetus. And, as Ataturk's nationalist independence movement resolutely rejected all pan-Turkist aspirations, the movement lost virtually all its force—and its relevance. Pan-Turkist ideologists like Ziya Gokalp soon focused their ideas on a more narrowly based national consciousness specific to the Ottoman Turkish population, with the aim of buttressing the goals of Ataturk. By 1920, at the start of the struggle against the allied armies occupying Anatolia, talk of engaging in adventures outside of Anatolia essentially ceased.[22]

Ataturk, "Outside Turks," and Relations with Russia

The legacy of Ataturk, the founder of the Turkish Republic, is a principal reason pan-Turkism not only failed to materialize at the time, but remained unlikely to do so in the future. Though long dead and of perhaps waning relevance, Ataturk's persisting influence cannot be dismissed. He was, after all, more than just the military leader who defeated the British, French, Greek, and Italian forces then occupying much of the area of modern Turkey at a time when no one would have thought it possible. He went on, after establishing the republic, to define its parameters territorially, politically, socially, ethnically, and linguistically. More than is usually the case with a founder of a modern nation, Ataturk crafted an entirely new society from the ruins of an old empire.

Toward his goal of making Turkey a modern, Westernized nation, Ataturk implemented a series of radical social and political reforms, including: the secularization of the political system and, to a great extent, of society; the transformation of the alphabet of the Turkish language from Arabic to Latin and purging many Arabic and Persian words; and the modification of modes of dress and behavior. These were more than reforms, however, as they became part of the very fabric of the Turkish state and society. There was no state before Ataturk, nor would one have emerged without him; thus, his legacy is greater than simply "influence." Furthermore, his legacy has been greatest among the groups that have held power in Turkey since his time—the government and the military—who doggedly support Ataturkist ideals. Indeed, the military elites have more than once intervened in the political system to uphold them. Thus it can be said that Turkey does not embark lightly on policies that roll back or contravene Ataturkist ideas.

Most relevant to this discussion is Ataturk's strictly territorial definition of Turkey, and his firm rejection of pan-Turkism. In establishing Turkey's borders around Anatolia, he shifted the focus of the country away from empire to nation-state, and molded a new kind of patriotism specific to the new, territorially bound Turkish nation-state.[23] Shifting the focus to a previously nonexistent form of legitimacy, the Turkish nation and Turkish nationalism, Ataturk replaced the old ideas of empire, dynasty, and even religion as the basis for a state. From the start of his nationalist movement, Ataturk aimed to instill pride in specifically Anatolian Turkish national identity, a pride that had not existed before. Thus, for the first time, Ataturk articulated a new sense of specifically Turkish ethnic identity and language, which involved the partial if not complete abandonment of the old loyalties and ways of self-identification as Ottomans and Muslims.[24]

Ataturk fully rejected all forms of pan-Turkism. It was the pan-Turkists and their slogans, Ataturk declared, that were responsible for the Ottoman Empire's participation in World War I and its humiliating defeat.[25] He went further to proclaim that "it was illusions and sentiments which were the origin of the actions which brought this nation to the foot of the gallows. . . . Instead of increasing our enemies and pressure upon us by adopting ideas we did not accept and we are unable to accept, let us return to our natural limitations, to our legitimate limitations."[26] To Ataturk, pan-Turkism was for the Turks only an "ideological bind" that would not serve the aim of creating an independent, sovereign, Westernized, and modern nation for the Turkish people. Ataturk remained throughout his life suspicious and even contemptuous of pan-Turkist ideology, which he stated was full of "illusions" and had no practical value, and he was firmly opposed to encouraging vague sentiments about some "nebulous pan-Turkist homeland."[27]

Ataturk's rejection of pan-Turkism incorporated a refusal to become involved in any way in the fate of other ethnic Turkic groups outside the frontiers of the new republic, groups known as "*dis* Turkleri" or "outside Turks." He also fully repudiated any irredentist aspirations in connection with them. After the establishment of the republic, Ataturk cast the new country's foreign policy orientation toward Europe, and in renouncing concern for outside Turks, Ataturk rejected the very essence of pan-Turkism.[28] Ideas such as these became a cornerstone of Turkish foreign policy, particularly for its ensuing generations of government elites.

One reason fueling Ataturk's rejection of pan-Turkism was the need to secure friendly relations with the (then new) Soviet Union. It is a rather ironic aspect—and one not often acknowledged—about Soviet-Turkish relations, especially in view of the historical enmity and sharply conflicting ideologies, but the Soviet Union and Turkey generally maintained what can be called "good neighborly" relations throughout most of their modern history. This was not in contradiction to Turkey's Western orientation, but was aimed at avoiding any unnecessary conflicts on its borders, and it became a tenet of Turkey's foreign policy that has been maintained to today. The mutually pragmatic relations established between Turkey and the USSR were grounded in the March 1921 Treaty of Friendship, which contained a pledge by both sides not to interfere in the affairs of the other—a pledge which was studiously adhered to throughout the decades, with only few exceptions. Each side agreed to forbid the formation of organizations that might operate to the detriment of the other, and in this capacity, Ataturk proscribed pan-Turkist organizations (and ignored the existence of Turkic peoples in the Soviet Union), and the Soviet government abandoned (at least officially) its support for underground communist parties in Turkey and accepted Ataturk's banning of such parties.[29]

Even during the Cold War years, Turkey by and large maintained this unwritten understanding with the Soviet Union. The most notable interruption in this state of affairs was in the months immediately after World War II, when Stalin made bellicose demands on the Bosporus Straits and on regions of eastern Turkey. Tensions between the two heightened to such a degree as to propel Turkey into joining the NATO alliance. Stalin's actions were regretted by subsequent Soviet leaders, and within two months of Stalin's death in 1953, the demands were unequivocally dropped in the hope of rectifying the situation. Though Turkey was by this time squarely a NATO member, the position of unspoken but mutual "tolerance" between Ankara and Moscow was renewed, despite ideological differences. Over the years, there was never talk of mutual trust or ideological understanding; it was simply a practical stance for both countries and beneficial for both. Ataturk's belief that cordial relations with the Soviet Union were more important than the fate of that country's sizable Turkic population remained a central tenet of Turkey's foreign policy.

Pan-Turkism after Ataturk

Ataturk's repudiation of pan-Turkism's ideals and its implicit irredentism relegated the movement to the periphery of Turkish political life. Until World War II, pan-Turkism was relatively dormant in Turkey, kept alive on the fringes largely by refugees from the Soviet Union whose pan-Turkist activities contained a virulently anti-Soviet and anti-Russian hue. In the 1930s, the mainly Tatar émigrés were joined by a number of Anatolian Turks influenced by German notions of racial superiority and anticommunism, eventually leading to a split in the movement between the fascist wing, which denied that the "racially pure" Turks of Turkey had any connection with the racially inferior "Mongolian Turks" in the East, and the traditional pan-Turkists, whose goals of Turkic unity were focused precisely on the eastern Central Asians. It was the creed of even the traditional pan-Turkists, however, that the Anatolian Turks had a leading—and superior—part to play in the Turkic world, that the Turks had created many states and empires in Asia, and that "the present Turkish Republic is the last and the most perfect state."[30] That Turkish chauvinism, present since the early days of the movement, is significant, for it reappeared again in Turkey's relations with the Central Asian republics in the late 1980s.

The Turkish establishment's strict adherence to Ataturk's dictums about "outside Turks" and relations with Russia are demonstrated in the events during World War II, the only time in Turkey's history that pan-Turkism became even moderately prominent. At that time, pan-Turkist activists, still primarily Tatar and Azeri émigrés, managed to scrape—but not reach—high echelons in government. The hope of the movement was a German victory over the USSR that would free the Turkic peoples, making possible the long-dreamed-about union or confederation (led by the Turks). Contacts between pan-Turkist groups and German officials, which included discussions of the creation of Turkic states upon the collapse of the Soviet Union, were prevalent, and the pan-Turkists aided Germany in conducting an intense propaganda campaign in Turkey throughout the war.[31]

There was sympathy for Germany in Turkey, including in the government—a sentiment dating back to their alliance during World War I. Pan-Turkist activists succeeded in gaining the attention of government officials, and some of the latter were flirting with the idea of abandoning their neutral stance in the war. However, in the end, German officials were not able to penetrate senior government levels, and their discussions regarding plans for the Turkic groups in the USSR never went further than with the pan-Turkists. The government, after some initial wavering, quickly reasserted its Ataturkist traditions by maintaining officially throughout the war that it had no irredentist ambitions and would not move from its position of neutrality.[32] (Turkey did not in fact declare war on Germany until March 1945, when it did so largely in order to participate in the forming of the United Nations.)

As the war progressed, the government grew less tolerant of pan-Turkist activities. In May 1944, when there were large anticommunist demonstrations in Istanbul and Ankara incited by pan-Turkist propaganda, the government responded by arresting thirty pan-Turkist leaders. A campaign against the movement was initiated, and 195 Soviet refugees, most of Tatar origin, were forcibly repatriated. Pan-Turkist leaders were accused of conspiring to overthrow the Turkish government and their organizations were banned.[33]

After the May 1944 protests, President Inonu made a critical speech in which he declared that: pan-Turkism unequivocally represented a danger to the Turkish Republic; the Turkish people desired no part in any adventurist policy and rejected irredentism altogether; and the Soviet Union was the historical friend of Turkey.[34] (These very arguments are present in the current debate in Turkey regarding its relations with the Central Asian republics.)

After the war, pan-Turkism returned to the fringe of Turkish politics. Less overt pan-Turkist strains were incorporated into the right-wing Nationalist Action Party (NAP), led by Alparslan Turkes. While a review and analysis of the NAP is not possible here, it should be said that the party, virulently anti-Soviet and Turkish nationalist, routinely gained less than 10 percent of the vote over several decades, though occasionally gaining the spotlight as part of a ruling coalition. The nationalist attentions of the NAP were focused primarily on areas such as Cyprus, and later Bulgaria, rather than on the Turkic peoples of the USSR. The party, shut down along with all other political parties after the 1980 military intervention, re-emerged in the late 1980s, at the same time as Turkey began developing relations with the former Soviet republics, a process in which NAP leader Turkes has played a prominent role. The party, however, has remained on the relative periphery of Turkish political life.

In Central Asia

At its peak in the Ottoman Empire, in the years leading up to World War I, the pan-Turkist movement elicited little response from among the Turkic peoples of the Russian Empire. To a degree even greater than in the Ottoman Empire, the Muslims in Central Asia had little consciousness of ethnic or national identity, making remote the success of an appeal on this basis. The exception to the absence of national identity was among the relatively more educated and urbanized Tatars living in Russia "proper," from whom what pan-Turkist sentiments that were espoused primarily came. The Tatars, however, were in many ways the furthest removed—linguistically and culturally—from other Turkic groups in the Russian Empire, and even their enthusiasm for these ideas drew little reaction. Among those Muslims who did aspire to raise the national consciousness of their fellow Muslims in the Russian Empire, the essential goal was political and social reform among the Muslims. Wider goals included either independence for the Muslims, or some kind of political autonomy within a federation with Russia. Political union or confederation with the Turkic peoples outside the Russian Empire was hardly mentioned, except among a small group of Tatars who eventually relocated to Constantinople before and during the war years (World War I). In any case, it was to the peoples' Muslim consciousness that the reformers mainly appealed, and not their ethnic or national one.

Identity

Ethnic or national identity was almost unknown in Central Asia until well into the twentieth century. In relations with others, ethnic considerations rarely came into play. That which differentiated people was not ethnicity—or even language for that matter—but way of life, that is, whether one was a sedent or a nomad. Even Uzbeks and Tajiks, who were of different ethnic and linguistic groups, did not separate along ethnic lines. The population in the cities was frequently mixed and bilingual in both Uzbek and Tajik, and people often had no awareness of which ethnic group they belonged to. Individual loyalties among both the settled and nomadic groups rarely went beyond family or kinship ties, or perhaps to a particular village.[35] (Even the terms "Uzbek" and "Tajik" were not used by the people themselves until the Soviet period.)

The strongest cultural influence on the settled people, regardless of their ethnicity, was from Persia, and the Turkic tribes that settled in the oases soon adopted the Persian and Tajik (Iranian) cultures while retaining their Uzbek (Turkic) language.[36] In fact, the Russian colonization of the region in the mid-to-late-nineteenth century was facilitated by this almost total absence of national identity and the presence of only narrow family and tribal loyalties. Islam was the only common thread among all of the peoples in the region, and even that was not a unifying factor, since religious practices among the settled and nomadic peoples differed greatly.[37] Thus, before the 1917 revolution, the idea of belonging to a particular nation, of being an Uzbek, a Turkmen, or even a Tatar, simply did not exist in the consciousness even of most Muslim intelligentsia and still less of the masses.[38]

The Reformers

Ideas from the outside world came into the Russian Empire largely through the more educated Tatars. Aided by the large Crimean Tatar minority living in the Ottoman Empire (refugees from the 1854–55 Crimean war), the Tatars in Russia began to learn, by means of Ottoman texts and newspapers, of nationalist ideas germinating among the Ottoman Turks. This influence, plus increasing czarist repression, galvanized a small group of Tatar intellectuals in the late nineteenth century, led by Ismail Bey Gaspirali (or Gasprinskii in Russian), a modernizer who promoted the unity of all of Russia's Muslims.[39] His famous journal *Tercuman* (Translator) was written in what he called a "pan-Turkic language" in the hope that it would be understood by the Tatars and the Central Asians. Gaspirali would eventually influence the development of a reform movement in Central Asia known as the Jadids, a small group of relatively liberal-minded, Western-oriented Islamic nationalists.

However, Gaspirali appealed mainly for religious and not national unity. In addition, his "pan-Turkist language," an amalgamation of Crimean Tatar and Ottoman Turkish, though claimed by some scholars to be "fairly comprehensible" in all the Turkish world,[40] was, other scholars maintain, one of the reasons *Tercuman* could not reach its intended audience. The journal was simply "unable to create a common Turkic language understandable to all Turks," as the combination language was not understood by most Central Asians.[41] This was primarily because Crimean Tatar is not comprehensible to most other Turkic groups, and Ottoman Turkish is understood easily only by the Azeris in the Caucasus.

The Central Asian Jadids also based their appeal almost exclusively on religious consciousness and called for radical religious and social reform among the Muslims of the Russian Empire. The reformers held several "All-Muslim" congresses in 1905–6 aimed at promoting Muslim unity.

Though there were delegates present from the Crimea, Kazan, Central Asia, and the Caucasus, the meetings were dominated mainly by Tatar intellectuals. Debate at the congresses covered aims such as social reform and gaining political equality with Russia, and, from a few delegates, independence for the Muslims.[42] There was, however, virtually no discussion of political unity—or even cooperation—with ethnic groups outside the Russian Empire, including the Ottoman Turks. While pan-Turkists in the Ottoman Empire were dreaming of one nation of all Turkic peoples that would include Anatolian Turks, this was not being considered by most of the Muslim nationalists in Russia, who spoke more often of a federation with Russia or independence. There was simply no strong tie with Anatolia.

After being refused substantive political representation in the Russian Duma, in the years leading to the 1917 revolution some among the Muslim reformers turned outside for help. It was this group that can be called the Russian empire's pan-Turkists, though they remained a small part of the Muslim nationalist movement there. Most of these nationalists transferred their activities to Constantinople (and it would in fact be these Tatar émigrés from Russia who would keep the pan-Turkist movement alive in Turkey in the ensuing decades). Others looked to the revolutionary movement in Russia, convinced that a socialist revolution would secure them autonomy within a Russian Federation, or independence. In the end, however, the work of the relatively Westernized and educated Tatars and Central Asian Jadid leaders met with little response from the vast majority of the Muslims in the empire. This is especially true for those in Central Asia, who were the most isolated.

Obviously, this subject is far more complex than what can be described in a few short pages, and many other factors, personalities, and events require illumination. Yet it is clear that even had the Red Army not moved in and forcibly joined the region to the USSR, the probability that a pan-Turkic-based union would have been formed was even more remote from the Central Asian side than the Ottoman. And that was at a time when strong and *local* national feelings were not developed in Central Asia, as they are today. Thus even at a juncture in history when the future of the Turkic peoples in the world was in its most extreme state of flux, pan-Turkism had little popular support.

The Soviet Period

After the incorporation of Central Asia into the USSR, the Soviets set about filling up the ethnic identity vacuum, with the quite deliberate aim of breaking up the potential Muslim unity the Jadids had been seeking. It is not necessary, nor within the scope of this paper, to describe the Soviet nationalities policy; the important point in this context is that separate ethnic identities were established in Central Asia, primarily through the drawing of boundaries and the promotion of separate literary languages. The Soviet government created distinct territorial units in Central Asia, some with the status of republic, others autonomous regions within a republic, and supplied each of these territorial units with an official language—and a separate alphabet.[43] It is true that the Soviets virtually *created*, at least in some cases, ethnic identities where none had before existed, or hardly so, yet today, after three or more generations, these identities have largely stuck. This is the case not least because, despite the arguable artificiality of their origins, the borders, languages, and ethnic names applied were not based on total fantasy or unreality, but in fact did reflect some basic ethnic and linguistic distinctions between the different groups in Central Asia.

Clearly, the developments over most of this century in Central Asia—and in Turkey—did much to make pan-Turkism a nonstarter, relegating it to a moment in history, and the moment of a few intellectuals. The development of separate ethnic identities and official languages in the Central Asian republics, and their orientation, albeit forced, toward Moscow, together with the Turkish government's policy of essentially ignoring the existence of Turkic groups in the Soviet Union in deference to harmonious relations with Moscow, did much to make an unrealistic notion—however romantic—that much more improbable and illusory.

The End of the Cold War

For most of their premodern and modern history, Turkey and Central Asia have essentially had no relationship to speak of. This state of affairs changed rather radically in the late 1980s. When the Soviet Union opened its doors and the republics began peeking out from behind the proverbial curtain, Turkey seemed literally to pounce on the Central Asian republics. In an apparent state of euphoria upon the discovery of (or newfound opportunity to acknowledge) linguistic kinship with the Central Asians, Turks from highest-level officials to businessmen to scholars visited the region, where they were ecstatically received both officially and popularly, amid cries of *"kardes!"* (brother!) Cultural and economic agreements were signed with each republic, and diplomatic activity approached whirlwind proportions; Turkey rushed to recognize all of the republics upon gaining independence and quickly set up diplomatic representation. Furthermore, Turkey declared itself to be the natural link between Central Asia and the rest of the world, and encouraged other countries to support it in this role.

This period of euphoria gave rise to all kinds of claims, assumptions, and speculation in Turkey, Central Asia, and the West about the future of the world's Turkic peoples. Turks (from Turkey) contended that the ethnic and linguistic kinship was so strong that, for example, Anatolian Turkish could be easily understood throughout Central Asia. In the hope of strengthening those linguistic ties, Turkey initiated a campaign to encourage the Central Asians to make a rapid shift from the Cyrillic to the Latin alphabet. The Turks also set up satellite TV programming in Turkish to Central Asia. Taking on the leadership of the "Turkish world," as the Turks invariably called it, Turkey also promised considerable economic and cultural assistance to the Central Asian republics. The world would soon see, it was heralded, the "era of the Turk."

The Central Asians, for their part, seemed only to encourage the Turkish feelings of elation. They did not dispute such assertions as the mutual intelligibility of their languages with Turkish, nor did they argue even with Turkey's claim to leadership of the "Turkish world"—or at least they did not counter such claims publicly. And in the West, particularly the United States, there was a torrent of articles about the "resurgence" of pan-Turkism from observers who themselves were just discovering the linguistic ties between the Turks and Central Asians. Journalists, politicians, experts, and nonexperts proclaimed that the world would soon see radical shifts in political allegiances and alliances, possibly even the formation of new, ethnic-based political unions. All appeared convinced that Turkey and Central Asia were bound inevitably to develop their relationship into a strong, ethnically based regional grouping. Those who attempted to suggest a more sober, certainly less "sexy" analysis of the future for the Turks and Central Asians were, at least for a time, almost completely drowned out.

Yet, hanging around in the background were some fairly straightforward reasons behind these initial, enthusiastic claims. Turkey, for most of its modern existence, has experienced a proverbial identity crisis of several dimensions. Though it strives to be Western, it is Muslim, and though it is Muslim, it is not Arab. Almost uniquely, Turkey has at various times simultaneously been included as part of Western Europe, the Near East, the Middle East, and the Balkans—belonging to several regional groupings but never to one unequivocally. Therefore, in many ways it is essentially alone. Its language is (or was) not closely related to that of any other state. Furthermore, the one region to which it aspired the most to be included, the West, has remained tepid in its response, especially Western Europe. Turkey has long felt insulted by this indifference, which sometimes takes on an uglier hue in the form of European attitudes toward Turkish guest workers, for example. These attitudes are particularly galling to Turks when they recall their past as the rulers of a great empire, a past of which they are deeply conscious and in which they retain great pride.

When Central Asia was finally able to come out from behind the Soviet wall, these and other factors combined to induce Turkey to test the waters outside the established Ataturkist foreign policy structures—and they were elated with what they found. As if for the first time, they discovered other languages related to theirs—Turkish was no longer the "odd language out." This of course was always the case, and it was perhaps known to at least some of them, but it came alive to Turks as never before. After decades of the humiliation of running after others, pleading for acceptance, here was a region where Turks were welcomed as kin, as brothers, by people who looked up to them. Central Asia was a region so obviously meant for them to lead. For many Turks, it represented a chance to recapture the greatness of their past, and could perhaps lead to a time when the "Turks" of the world would once again be a force not to be dismissed, a force with Turkey at the helm. (Another important dynamic at work was the worsening Kurdish problem in Turkey, in that the discovery of other "Turks" seem to fortify anti-Kurdish sentiment. This is an important aspect of domestic politics that, unfortunately, cannot be dealt with in detail here.) It is hardly a wonder, then, that the Turks got carried away with the almost romantic possibilities awaiting them in their relations with Central Asia, and that they were convinced that these developments were a matter of destiny.

The Central Asians had a somewhat different—and more concrete—agenda. After centuries of Russian colonization, and decades of Soviet totalitarian rule that severely limited their relations with the outside world, the Central Asians were thrilled to receive the Turks' enthusiastic attention. Once it was apparent that there would be no overt repercussions, the Central Asians wanted to demonstrate to the world that they were peoples with languages, cultures, histories, and traditions distinct from the Russians, something of which the rest of the world was barely aware. Upon gaining independence, the Central Asians began the process of decolonization, making the desire to define themselves on their own terms even greater. In this, attention from Turkey was very welcome. After decades of being forced to view the world through Moscow's eyes and the medium of the Russian language, and to repeat the Soviet ideological line that their colonization by Russia was a "positive" step that brought them only great benefits, here was a country that enthused about their own Central Asian languages and cultures. This was a relatively new experience. And on a more important and more pragmatic level, of course, the Central Asians were very hopeful about the practical aspects of Turkey's attention, and many economic benefits were desired and expected from the relationship.

In the West, what was behind the belief in the rise of pan-Turkism was more prosaic: ignorance. Few areas of the globe were as completely unknown to most of the world as was Central Asia before the breakup of the Soviet Union. Even otherwise very well informed people had barely *heard* of this region; still fewer knew anything about Uzbeks and Kyrgyz, since Central Asia seemed to drop off the map sometime in the fifteenth century to all but a handful of outsiders. With the opening of the USSR, Central Asia was truly "discovered" by many in the West. Articles proclaimed the existence of millions of Turkic-speaking Muslims in the former Soviet Union as if this fact alone were a new development. And unfortunately, since so little was known about the region, there was a tendency, for a time at least, to accept virtually anything that was said or written, and to fall for the more sensational claims, of which pan-Turkism was one. Similarly, since the nature of Turkey's relations with other Turkic peoples was almost equally unknown, many were inclined to affirm the Turks' vision of Central Asia, in the mistaken assumption that since they were linguistic kin, the Turks must have a real insight into the people and events in the region. This is certainly the case of the U.S. government, which, for a time, sanctioned Turkey's "special role" in Central Asia—without, apparently, any understanding of whether such a role actually existed. During this period it was as if the normal processes of analysis were abandoned, as Western commentators seemed to take everything that was said about Central Asia at face value.

Reality Sets In

Now that the initial euphoria has waned, it has become apparent that cooperation between Turkey and Central Asia is not going to take on the form of a Turkic-based regional grouping, and that Turkey's relations with this part of the world are not necessarily going to be as strong as once proclaimed. Certainly no political union, federation, or confederation is foreseen. Even the political cooperation has died down. Turkish satellite TV, though still broadcasting, is reportedly not very popular, and few in Central Asia tune in. Of the numerous economic and cultural agreements signed, many have not been fulfilled. Within the Turkish Foreign Ministry, there is considerably less enthusiasm for close cooperation with the Central Asian countries, and the Central Asians themselves have for a while now eased up in looking to their "Turkish brothers" for any particular or special relationship. Western observers, learning that perhaps they spoke too soon, have largely fallen silent on the matter.

Always present, of course, were essential realities that were either unknown or ignored. One is the difference in language. Though related, the Turkic languages are in fact not all mutually intelligible, any more than the Slavic, Germanic, or Romance languages are; this was the case when pan-Turkism first emerged a century ago and even more true now. The Turkic languages divide up into several different branches. Anatolian Turkish belongs to the western Oghuz branch, together with Azeri and Turkmen, the latter being the only Central Asian language in this group. Gagauz, the language of the Turkish minority in Moldova, is also found in this group. (Turkish is most closely related to Azeri, the two being essentially mutually intelligible, though not perfectly.)[44] According to Turkic scholar Karl Menges, the other major Turkic language groupings are: the "Turki" group, which includes "sedentary" Uzbek (spoken in the cities) and "village" Kyrgyz, as well as some ancient Turkic languages such as Chagatai; and the Kipchak group, which includes Kazakh, Karakalpak, literary Kyrgyz, nomadic or village Uzbek, and Tatar.[45] Current literary Uzbek, the language used by the largest Turkic group in Central Asia, is based on the dialect formerly used only in Tashkent. Profoundly influenced by Persian, Uzbek has assumed many non-Turkic and non-Altaic features, including the loss of vowel harmony—one of the hallmarks of the western Turkic languages, especially Turkish.[46] Kazakh and Kyrgyz generally have many fewer Arabic and Persian loan words than does Uzbek, having instead a larger number of Mongolian words not found in the western Turkic languages.[47] Turkish also has many fewer Arabic and Persian influences, the result largely of extensive language reform in Turkey's early decades.

Despite these differences, many Turks—and some western Turkish speakers—maintained that they could use their language and be understood in all of Central Asia. However, if this was their experience, it was likely the case largely because the people they met very much *wanted* to communicate with them. Related languages generally are mutually intelligible to varying degrees, when both speakers are willing to listen and deduce. One can, for example, use a knowledge of Russian to get by in Poland, but that does not make those two languages mutually intelligible. Once again, enthusiasm seemed to overwhelm reality. The Central Asians for the most part never pretended to speak the *same* language as the Turks—except when it was in their interest to do so. An article about the experience of the new Central Asian students at Turkish universities admitted, "they have trouble with the language."[48] One of the main reasons that Turkish satellite television has never gained much popularity in Central Asia is that the audience simply does not easily understand it, even the "simplified" Turkish that is often used. Central Asians have generally remained tuned in to Russian TV for the plain reason that they can understand it more readily.[49]

Except for the fact that their languages are in the same linguistic branch, there are not many other factors that necessarily unite the Turks and Central Asians. As outlined above, they are ethnically quite diverse, since the Turks were not ethnically influenced by the waves of Tatar, Mongol, and Chinese migrants that have become a strong component of the ethnic makeup in Central Asia to varying degrees. Similarly, their histories have not overlapped for centuries, essentially since the last Osman tribes moved westward in the eleventh and twelfth centuries. From the time of the establishment of the Ottoman Empire, of which Central Asia was never a part, the Turks' focus was, to a great extent, toward Europe.

There were other sobering realities for the Turks and Central Asians that soon became evident. After decades of studiously ignoring the existence of the Turkic peoples in the Soviet Union, it turned out that, with the exception of a handful of scholars, few in Turkey—including in the Foreign Ministry—actually knew anything about Central Asia. Many Turks went there with the expectation of discovering people like themselves; many were equally surprised—and disconcerted—to meet total strangers. The Central Asians are not in fact "Turks," as the Turks invariably insisted on calling them; they have their own histories and languages about which the Turks, like the rest of the world, in fact knew very little. In addition to those differences, the Turks encountered a foreign—very Soviet—mentality among the Central Asians, the result not least of having been part of a totalitarian system for their entire existence within their current frontiers. They may have been speaking related tongues, but they were not speaking the same language. Even more important, both the Turks and the Central Asians quickly realized that Turkey simply did not have the financial resources to fulfill the many agreements signed during the "euphoric" years. Clearly, the Turks severely overestimated the state of the Central Asian economies—and the ability and inclination of the Central Asians genuinely to change the economic status quo of the Soviet days—and underestimated the level of political, economic, and social devastation resulting from the Soviet period. Certainly no one country has the resources necessary to address the economic problems of the Central Asian countries, but Turkey's own economic difficulties quickly made it apparent that Turkey was not in a position even to try.

The Turks' unfamiliarity with Central Asia was apparent in other ways also. Their desire to help their "Turkish brothers" there quickly revealed a paternalism not lost on the Central Asians. This paternalism, reminiscent of the original pan-Turkist movement's ideology, reflected the Turks' general presumption of their superiority over the more backward "outside Turks," who presumably seek Turkish leadership to introduce them to the modern world. Regarding Turkey's role in Central Asia, the Turkish popular press frequently spouted such headlines as "Turkey is the new savior" and "Turkey is the star of the Turkish World." Even the Turks' insistence on calling the Central Asians "Turks" rancored, though the Central Asians at first did not object to it, especially when it was thought that making the Turks happy would yield economic gains. The Central Asians, though, do not generally call themselves "Turks," but "Uzbeks" or "Kazakhs," national identities that have largely taken root there. Finally, though grateful for whatever the Turks wanted to offer by way of financial or cultural aid, the Central Asians were not prepared, having only just gained their (at least nominal) independence, to tuck themselves under the wing of another outside power, not even a Turkic one.

What the Turks overlooked, at least initially, was the necessarily mercenary stance of the Central Asians. Their relative obscurity and economic chaos left them in no position to choose alliances on the grounds of ethnic kinship. If Turkey was going to help, then they could act the part of Turkic "little brothers." Otherwise, they could as easily turn to Iran or the United States and take a commensurate pose. While Turkey was building its relationship with the Central Asians, they were as busy cultivating ties with any other interested countries. This is not to suggest that there was nothing genuine in the Central Asians' declarations of brotherhood with the Turks, only that motivations other than just kinship were coming into play.

There were political problems that interfered with the relationship. Turkey was hailed as the model of secular democracy for the newly independent countries. However, it was soon clear that several of the Central Asian states were not as interested in democracy, even Turkish style, as originally thought. Talk in Uzbekistan or Turkmenistan of following the "Turkish model" (as President Karimov stated at the first Turkic summit in October 1992 in Ankara) soon ceased. The leaders of those countries have more recently cited the "Asian model," referring to countries such as Korea, but also to China, which boasts economic development without political reform.[50] The forced flight of several Uzbek opposition leaders to Istanbul in the past two years has also caused tension between the Uzbek and Turkish governments. Turkey has increasingly found itself in an awkward position in this regard, attempting to juggle its roles of beacon for the opposition and ally of the Uzbek government.

Finally, both the Turks and the Central Asians, linguistic kinship not withstanding, were quickly made to acknowledge the critical import of their relations with Russia, relegating their relations with each other to secondary importance. The situation has, in fact, fallen back into its traditional pattern.

The recent tension between Turkey and Russia over passage through the Bosporus Straits was just one reminder to Turkey of the possible consequences of neglecting relations with Russia. It is Russia, after all, and not the Central Asian countries, that directly impinges on Turkey's security. Seyfi Tashan, director of the Foreign Policy Institute in Ankara, put it succinctly when he said, referring to the Central Asian countries, "We are not going to enter into a war with Russia for their sake."[51] The same article quoted Turkish prime minister Ciller's declaration that the "basis for relations between Turkey and Russia will be cooperation, not competition." Even more telling, Nationalist Action Party leader Alparslan Turkes, the strongest proponent of Turkish–Central Asian ties on the current political scene in Turkey, stated that "Turkish governments are very sensitive to Russia. We have suffered 14 great wars with the Russians. . . . We don't want to have any military confrontation with them."[52]

For the Central Asians, like it or not, Russia remains the main force to be reckoned with. Their political and economic interdependence, built into the Soviet system, together with Russia's determination not to relinquish control over the region's resources, means that relations with no other country can command greater priority for the Central Asians. This was clear even before the "sobering period" between Central Asia and Turkey, for example, when, at the first summit of Turkic leaders in Ankara in October 1992, several of the Central Asian presidents refused to sign a joint communiqué. The tendency to eschew any binding agreements among them was displayed most adamantly by Kazakhstan's President Nazarbaev, who expressed his concern that, according to one newspaper, "the restructuring of the region along ethnic and religious lines would impede their integration with the rest of the world."[53] The article went on to note that Nazarbaev specifically wanted the CIS—that is, Russia—to be part of the process of economic integration discussed at the summit, a reservation seconded by Turkmen president Niiazov and Uzbek president Karimov. Nazarbaev repeatedly stated that while he favored developing economic relations with Turkey, this must not damage his country's "previous obligations to the CIS." Two years later, when Kazakhstan and Turkey signed a military agreement in August 1994, Nazarbaev, still of the same mind, was quick to point out that the agreement did not contradict Kazakhstan's military agreements with other countries, including Russia.[54]

Conclusion

The cooling in relations between Turkey and Central Asia was clearly "in the cards" from the very start; this would have been obvious had more attention been given to both the historical factors and the practical realities affecting the relationship. There of course remains talk about the "special relationship" between them, but while there is genuine sentiment in such talk, much more is going on behind it—more than was understood by even the players themselves a few years ago. The Turks, perhaps caught up in the enthusiasm and elation of the moment, made grandiose claims about, and plans for, the momentous rise of the Turkish world, of which they would be the leaders. The Central Asians, probably not so caught up in the more romantic notions, were certainly ready to reap what they hoped would be the economic benefits of Turkey's attention. Westerners, in a flurry of excitement and stimulated by the thrill of historical conspiracy, proclaimed the imminent rise of pan-Turkism. All of these plans, hopes, and claims have been blunted to some extent by the prosaic realities. The more sensational notions could have been easily refuted with a little background information.

It is true that the Turks have made a commitment to the Central Asian countries, a commitment that is genuine and continuing. Turkish businessmen have invested (in some cases) very heavily in the region, presumably in the expectation of great economic benefits. Political and military agreements are still being signed between government leaders. In addition, and curiously, one other way in which the Turks are heavily involved in some of the Central Asian countries is in the building of religious schools, though the precise source of funding for these activities remains unclear. And, for the first time in Turkey's history (and perhaps in recognition of the limited understanding of the region in Turkey), an official institute has been established for the study of Central Asia—TIKA (Turk Isbirligi ve Kalkma Ajansi), the Turkish acronym for the Turkish Cooperation and Development Agency (which in English is rendered as TICA, or the Turkish International Cooperation Agency).

Clearly, a strong relationship is developing, a relationship that, nonetheless, must be seen in a wider context. The situation can best be illustrated by a statement from Uzbekistan's Foreign Minister Abdul Aziz Kamilov, who, in response to a question on his country's relations with Turkey at a meeting in Washington in October 1994, noted that ties with Turkey were developing very well, as were relations with other countries. If however, the questioner was suggesting that Uzbekistan "should have some special relationship with Turkey, the answer is no, this is not the case."[55]

United States Interests in the
Turkey–Central Asia Relationship

When the Central Asian countries first gained independence at the end of 1991, the United States did not have a well-defined policy toward the region. Turkey quickly stepped in to offer itself as official bridge between the United States and the new states, submitting that its linguistic and ethnic links to the region, and its own secularist and West-oriented political and economic policies, made it an obvious choice. Perhaps due to the over-whelming foreign policy agenda facing the United States at the time—the other superpower having just collapsed—the United States agreed to let Turkey assume this intermediary role to promote the West's agenda in the Central Asian states.

It became clear, however, that leaving Turkey to conduct U.S. policy in Central Asia was not a practical course. For many of the reasons outlined above, the role Turkey was presuming for itself in the Central Asian states was not without problems. In addition, the Central Asians themselves quickly made it apparent that they did not wish to have their relations with the United States routed through Turkey. There was the further problem of Turkey's inability to come up with the resources necessary to play such an extensive role.[56] The original U.S. policy was not without its domestic critics also, many of whom viewed it as ill-advised. Typical of the comments to that effect were those of then Senator Alan Cranston, who, after a visit to Central Asia declared that "the Central Asians do not see Turkey as an appropriate model for their political and economic development. The cultural and ethnic ties between the Central Asian countries and Turkey are far less significant than the Bush administration seemed to believe." He went on to cite American embassy workers in the Central Asian countries admitting that "promoting the Turkish model for the Central Asian republics is short-sighted and condescending."[57]

The United States quickly rectified the situation, beginning with the swift opening of embassies in all five countries through which it began pursuing its policies in the region directly. U.S. interests also became more defined and included, among others things, the promotion of political stability, non-proliferation, democratization, and human rights, the development of market economies, and pro-Western foreign policies.[58] These interests have not always coincided with Turkey's, particularly in such areas as human rights. For although sometimes forced to react to the most egregious violations, Turkey does not make human rights as central an issue in relations with the Central Asians as does the United States. However, the two countries' policies are not generally at odds.

Clearly, it is not in the interests of the United States to become a rival to Turkey's pursuance of broad relations with the Central Asian states, not least because the United States would prefer to see Turkish influence para-mount there than the influence of other neighboring countries such as Iran. There is thus no incentive for the United States to pursue any policies that could be construed as an attempt to undercut, thwart, or too intensely compete with Turkey's efforts in the region.

In the end, it is very likely that Turkey's relations with Central Asia, after shifts in various directions, will settle somewhere in the "normal" range, that is, they will be stronger than some relationships and weaker than others. Especially since the ideological barrier has fallen, Turkey will certainly continue to cultivate good relations with Moscow—relations that will, in many if not most instances, ultimately take greater priority. Similarly, it will be a generation at least before the Central Asians will be in a position to step back from their relationship with Russia—and Russia will certainly not make it easy for them in any case. Americans, for their part, would be wise in the future, should a similar development occur elsewhere in the world, to resist the temptation to embrace dramatic claims, engaging though they may be. Now that the excitement has passed in the case of Turkey and the Central Asian countries, the United States has recognized that it must deal with each of them as the separate entities that they are.

Notes

1. The word "Turkic" here refers generally to the people who speak languages in the Turkic family of languages (a branch of Altaic languages).

2. See, for example, "Fire, Fury and Nationalism," *U.S. News and World Report,* July 6, 1992, which states that the Turks are discovering in Central Asia "both their origins and reminders of their own lost Ottoman Empire," and a November 24, 1991, *Washington Post* article that describes Central Asia as a region of the world which "consists mostly of Turkish-speaking Muslims, a legacy of their days as part of the Ottoman Empire."

3. Karl H. Menges, *Introduction to Turkic Studies* (New York: American Council of Learned Societies, Research and Studies in Uralic and Altaic Languages, 1962), pp. 24–27.

4. Karl H. Menges, "Peoples, Languages and Migrations," in *Central Asia: Century of Russian Rule*, ed. Edward Allworth (New York: Columbia University Press, 1967), p. 87. The term "Turkestan" was commonly used after the region became Turkicized, though not by the people in the region but by outsiders. There are many different definitions of what exactly constitutes "Turkestan," and "Central Asia" for that matter (i.e., whether it includes parts of China, Afghanistan, and so forth). For the sake of simplicity, this paper will use the term "Central Asia," referring to the area of the former Soviet republics.

5. Ibid., p. 88.

6. Olaf Caroe, *Soviet Empire* (London: Macmillan, 1953), p. 51.

7. W. Barthold, *Histoire des Turcs d'Asie Centrale* (Paris: Librairie d'Amerique et d'Orient, 1945), p. 84.

8. Roderic H. Davison, *Turkey* (Englewood Cliffs, NJ: Prentice Hall, 1968), p. 20.

9. Barthold, *Histoire des Turcs*, p. 153.

10. Elizabeth E. Bacon, *Central Asians under Russian Rule: A Study in Cultural Change* (Ithaca, NY: Cornell University Press, 1980), 2nd ed., p. 4.

11. Barthold, *Histoire des Turcs*, p. 128; Bacon, p. 4.

12. M.A. Czaplicka, *Turks of Central Asia in History and Present Day* (Oxford: Clarendon Press, 1918), p. 17.

13. Menges, *Introduction to Turkic Studies*, p. 69.

14. Barthold, *Histoire des Turcs*, pp. 188–89.

15. Davison, *Turkey*, p. 24.

16. Menges, *Introduction to Turkic Studies*, p. 21.

17. Czaplicka, *Turks of Central Asia*, p. 11.

18. There are a number of books and articles on pan-Turkism that describe these trends in full detail. They include: Jacob Landau, *Pan-Turkism in Turkey: A Study in Irredentism* (Hamden, CT: Shoe String Press, 1981); Louis L. Snyder, *Macro-Nationalism: A History of the Pan-Movements* (London: Greenwood Press, 1984); Edwin Pears, "Turkey, Islam and Turanism," *Contemporary Review* (London), 114, October 1918; Charles Hostler, *Turkism and the Soviets: The Turks of the World and Their Objectives* (London: George Allen and Unwin, 1957); Czaplicka, *Turks of Central Asia*; A.C. Edwards, "The Impact of the War on Turkey," *International Affairs* (UK), vol. 22, no. 3, July 1946. There are also several Russian articles on the subject, though the Soviets obviously had political motives in their "scholarship" on this issue. They include: D.E. Eremeev, "Kemalizm i Pan-Tiurkizm," *Narody Azii i Afriki* (Moscow), 1963, no. 3; and E.F. Gasanova, "Ob ideologicheskikh osnovakh kemalizma i ikh sovremennom tolkovanii v Turtsii," *Narody Azii i Afriki*, 1968, no. 3.

19. See Pears, "Turkey, Islam," pp. 375–77.

20. Snyder, *Macro-Nationalism*, p. 123.

21. Czaplicka, *Turks of Central Asia*, p. 108–9.

22. F. Kazemzadeh, "Pan-Movements," *International Encyclopedia of Social Sciences*, vol. 11 (1968), pp. 369–70.

23. Jacob Landau, ed., *Ataturk and the Modernization of Turkey* (Boulder, CO: Westview Press, 1984), p. xi.

24. Frank Tachau, *Turkey: The Politics of Authority, Democracy and Development* (New York: Praeger, 1984), p. 33.

25. Hostler, *Turkism and the Soviets*, p. 109.

26. Kili, Suna, *Kemalism* (Instanbul: School of Business Administration and Economics, Robert College, 1969), p. 38.

27. Jacob Landau, *Radical Politics in Modern Turkey* (Leiden: E.J. Brill, 1974), p. 194.

28. Daniel C. Matuszewski, "Empire, Nationalities and Borders: Soviet Assets and Liabilities," in *Soviet Nationalities in Strategic Perspective*, ed. Enders Wimbush (London: Croom Helm, 1985), p. 89.

29. Donald Everett Webster, *The Turkey of Ataturk* (Philadelphia: American Academy of Political and Social Science, 1939), pp. 92–93.

30. Hostler, *Turkism and the Soviets*, p. 171.

31. Landau, *Pan-Turkism in Turkey*, pp. 108–10.

32. Ibid., p. 111.

33. Ibid., p. 112; Hostler, p. 185.

34. For this and other aspects of Turkey's foreign policy during World War II, see Edward Weisband, *Turkish Foreign Policy 1943–1945: Small State Diplomacy and Great Power Politics* (Princeton, NJ: Princeton University Press, 1973).

35. For a description of this question in Central Asia, see Alexandre Bennigsen and Chantal Lemercier-Quelquejay, *Islam in the Soviet Union* (London: Pall Mall Press, 1967).

36. See Caroe, *Soviet Empire*, on this point.

37. Bennigsen and Lemercier-Quelquejay, *Islam in the Soviet Union*, pp. 19–21.

38. Alexandre Bennigsen, "Islamic or Local Consciousness among Soviet Nationalities?" in *Soviet Nationality Problems*, ed. Edward Allworth (New York: Columbia University Press, 1971), pp. 168–75.

39. For a more comprehensive discussion of this, see Alan Fisher, "The Crimean Tatars, the USSR and Turkey," in *Soviet-Asian Ethnic Frontiers*, W.O. McCagg and B. Silver, eds. (New York: Pergamon Press, 1979).

40. Shirin Akiner, *Islamic Peoples of the Soviet Union* (London: Kegan Paul International, 1983), p. 92.

41. Serge A. Zenkovsky, *Pan-Turkism and Islam in Russia* (Cambridge, MA: Harvard University Press, 1960), p. 31.

42. Ibid, p. 45.

43. It is by now well known that the alphabet chosen initially was the Latin, until it was apparent to Moscow that the Asian areas could potentially drift away from under its influence. By 1940, all of the Central Asian region was using a modified Cyrillic alphabet. Perhaps had the second alphabet change not occurred, this essay would have quite a different conclusion. That, however, is left for speculation.

44. At a conference the author attended in Turkey in September 1991 in which Azeris participated, the Turkish translators were periodically unable to translate the Azeris.

45. Menges, "Peoples, Languages and Migrations," p. 74.

46. Ibid., p. 69.

47. For more on languages in Central Asia, see Geoffrey Wheeler, "Turkic Languages of Soviet Muslim Asia: Russian Linguistic Policy," *Middle Eastern Studies*, vol. 13, no. 2 (May 1977), pp. 208–17.

48. "The Boys from Bishkek, Baku and Samarkand," *Turkish Times*, January 1, 1993.

49. By way of a small anecdote, in an Uzbek language class attended by this author, the few Turks in the class were having only a slightly easier time learning the langauge than the Westerners.

50. See Cassandra Cavanaugh, "Uzbekistan Looks South and East for Role Models," *RFE/RL Research Report*, vol. 1, no. 40 (October 9, 1992), for some citations in the Uzbek press on this.

51. "Old Clash of Empires Still Echoes," *Christian Science Monitor*, September 13, 1993.

52. Ibid.

53. "Ankara Summit Reveals Strains between Leaders," *Turkish Times*, November 15, 1992. For other Turkish press on the summit, see FBIS-WEU-92-212, November 2, 1992.

54. *RFE/RL Daily Report*, August 9, 1994.

55. Carnegie Endowment for International Peace, October 7, 1994.

56. See Steve Coll, "Turkey: A Modern Role for an Ancient Land?" *Washington Post*, May 24, 1993.

57. Alan Cranston, "Out of Focus: U.S. Policy toward Central Asia," *Harvard International Review* (Spring 1993), p. 61.

58. For an outline of U.S. policies in the Central Asian states, see Jim Nichol, "Central Asia's New States: Political Developments and Implications for U.S. Interests," Congressional Research Service Issue Brief, November 22, 1993.

Part IV

A Russian "Monroe Doctrine" in the Making?

8

Russia and Transcaucasia
The Case of Nagorno-Karabakh

Oles M. Smolansky

The Nagorno-Karabakh Conflict: Origins and History

In 1921, after Soviet troops overran Transcaucasia, Stalin—a Georgian—acting in his capacity as the commissar of nationalities, ordered the incorporation of the enclave of Nagorno-Karabakh, inhabited mainly by Armenians, into the territory of the Azerbaijani Soviet republic. In 1922, the latter, along with Armenia and Georgia, joined the USSR as members of the Transcaucasian Soviet Federated Republic. In the reorganization of 1936, all three became separate union republics of the USSR.

In its most recent reincarnation, the dispute between the Armenians and the Azeris, whose historical enmity has also been powered by religious and cultural differences, erupted into the open in 1988, when the Armenian inhabitants of Nagorno-Karabakh, complaining about economic and cultural discrimination, rebelled against Baku's overlordship. Initially, they demanded autonomy and, after their request was turned down, the Armenians asserted their right to secede from Azerbaijan and, eventually, proclaimed the independence of the Nagorno-Karabakh Republic. In the wake of the dissolution of the USSR, there occurred a widespread arming of the sides involved in the conflict and it was gradually transformed into a full-fledged war. Moreover, in 1992, the Nagorno-Karabakh problem attracted the attention of outside parties interested in its outcome, among them Turkey and Iran, complicating efforts to regulate the Azeri-Armenian confrontation by political means. In 1992 and 1993, as the conflict intensified, killings, deportations, and the flight of the civilian population from the war zones changed the demographic makeup of the region, making a return to the *status quo ante bellum* unlikely and, perhaps, impossible.

In any event, the Azeris held their ground until 1992, when the Armenians went on the offensive, gained control over the entire enclave (including its capital, Stepanakert), and evicted some 30,000 Azeris who had resided there. The Armenians also captured the strategically vital Lachin corridor that links Nagorno-Karabakh to Armenia. Azerbaijan instituted an economic blockade of Armenia and, in late 1992, announced that it would not agree to a cease-fire while parts of its territory were occupied by Armenian troops.[1]

By April 1993, the Armenians had captured approximately one-tenth of Azerbaijan's territory, including the town of Kelbajar, thus opening a second corridor between Nagorno-Karabakh and Armenia. They had also advanced toward the town of Fizuli in the southwestern part of the country and, in the process, effectively sealed off the Azeri region of Nakhichevan from the rest of the country. It was reported at the time that some of the weapons used by the Armenians had been handed over to them by the units of the 7th Russian Army, stationed in Armenia.[2] Baku accused Erevan of aggression and asked the United States and the United Nations to intervene. Washington condemned the escalation of hostilities and renewed its call for a peaceful settlement, to be negotiated within the framework of the peacemaking efforts undertaken by the fifty-two-member Council on Security and Cooperation in Europe (CSCE). Turkey and Iran warned Armenia that further incursions into Azerbaijan were not acceptable to them, but the fighting continued later in the spring and summer of 1993, as did various ineffective efforts at a negotiated settlement of the Armenian-Azeri conflict.[3]

As Baku's position softened—it no longer demanded unconditional Armenian withdrawal before negotiations could begin—Armenia and Azerbaijan, in May 1993, agreed to a plan worked out by the United States, Russia, and Turkey. Under its terms, the Armenians were to withdraw from the recently captured Azeri territory. This would be followed by a sixty-day cease-fire, the continuation of the peace talks, and the lifting of the economic blockade of Armenia. As it happened, however, the peace plan was rejected by the government of Nagorno-Karabakh on the grounds that it did not "guarantee the safety of Karabakh's civilians."[4]

The reverses suffered by the Azeris at the hands of the Armenians resulted in major political changes in Baku. In June, the final contingent of Russian forces, which had been stationed in Azerbaijan, withdrew ahead of schedule, leaving a huge arsenal of weapons under the control of Colonel

Suret Huseinov, a bitter political enemy of the strongly nationalist, anti-Russian, and pro-Turkish President Abulfaz Elchibey. As Huseinov's well-armed troops approached Baku, Elchibey fled to Nakhichevan. Concurrently, Haidar Aliev, former KGB chief in Azerbaijan and member of Brezhnev's Politburo, assumed the post of the Speaker of the parliament and, eventually, the presidency. For a time, Huseinov became the prime minister. Also in June, the Armenian forces broke the cease-fire and attacked the town of Agdam, situated in western Azerbaijan.[5]

In July 1993, Agdam fell to the Armenians, followed by Fizuli in August and Goradiz, situated near the Iranian border, in September. The Armenians now held about one-fifth of Azerbaijan's territory and had caused some 1 million civilians to flee their homes. These events occurred in spite of the UN Security Council Resolution 822, passed in August, which called for "immediate, complete and unconditional withdrawal of Armenian forces from recently occupied areas of Azerbaijan" and warned that "appropriate steps" would be considered in case of Armenian noncompliance.[6] As the Armenians continued their offensive, Turkey and Iran repeated their warnings and, after the fall of Goradiz, Iranian troops did in fact cross into Azerbaijan, provoking a strong reaction by Moscow.[7] In mid-December, Azeri troops staged an offensive designed to force the Armenians to retreat from some of the conquered territory. It fizzled out in early 1994. After several unsuccessful attempts and three more Security Council resolutions, a cease-fire was finally brokered in Moscow later in the year. It has held, but a resolution of the differences separating the combatants is not in sight.

The difficulties encountered by potential peacemakers have resulted from a head-on collision of principles that are essentially irreconcilable:

- the principle of the inviolability of established borders (promoted by Azerbaijan);
- the right to national self-determination;
- the right of national minorities to independent existence—i.e., statehood (this and the point above espoused by Armenia); and
- the need to establish stability as a prerequisite to securing respect for human rights of individual citizens.

However, the main reason for the failure to regulate the Nagorno-Karabakh conflict has been the lack of political will on the part of all the contending parties to reach a mutually acceptable compromise. For this reason, all attempts to broker a negotiated settlement have failed. This includes efforts by the United Nations and the CSCE (particularly its "Minsk group," set up in 1992); by the "Alma-Ata initiative" of Kazakhstan's president Nursultan Nazarbaev; and by the United States, Russia, Turkey, and Iran. The major problem with these initiatives, which occasionally got into each other's way, has been the lack of mechanisms for adoption and enforcement of binding decisions.

Russia and the Nagorno-Karabakh Conflict

Initially, the Russian Federation, which had sanctioned peacekeeping operations in some parts of the former USSR (Southern Ossetia, Moldova, Tajikistan), turned down the Armenian request to become involved in Nagorno-Karabakh. As Air Marshal Evgenii Shaposhnikov, commander-in-chief of the Commonwealth of Independent States (CIS) armed forces, put it in 1992, the troops under his command would never be used to "separate warring tribes."[8] However, since Russian units were subsequently sent to Tajikistan to perform precisely that task, Shaposhnikov's statement sounds rather hollow in retrospect. A more convincing, though unstated, explanation was that, at the outset, the Russian Federation preferred not to become directly involved in the Nagorno-Karabakh conflict. Freedom of maneuver between the warring parties offered Moscow better opportunities to advance its interests than siding with either combatant and becoming enmeshed in one of the most intractable ethnic conflicts to erupt in the territory of the former Soviet Union.

Moreover, the initial hesitation to become involved in Nagorno-Karabakh was also influenced by the indecision at the highest levels of the Russian government as to the basic course Moscow was to follow in foreign policy. It will be recalled that, in 1992, the debate on this issue was conducted by the "Westerners" and the "Eurasians." The former argued that Russian interests were best served by close cooperation with the industrialized and democratic members of the Western bloc and that other regions of the world were much less important to Moscow. According to this school of thought, the Russian Federation, which had acquiesced in the dissolution of the USSR, should pay little attention to the former Soviet republics that were not inclined to cooperate with Moscow. This applied particularly to Transcaucasia as well as to Central Asia, hence Shaposhnikov's curt dismissal of the "warring tribes." Initially, this position appears to have been held by President Boris Yeltsin and his associates, including Foreign Minister Andrei Kozyrev, who emerged as one of its most eloquent proponents.

Opposed to the "Westerners" were the "Eurasians," who objected to what they perceived as Russia's subordination to the West. Instead, they argued that the Russian Federation, as a great power, had interests of its own and that these interests did not always correspond to, and were sometimes in conflict with, those of the Western powers. This made it imperative for Moscow to advance its interests regardless of whether such a course of action was acceptable to its Western partners or not. For the "Eurasians," this meant, in part, reestablishing and maintaining Russian influence over the former Soviet republics—the Near Abroad, as the non-Russian portions of the dissolved Union were now called. As the Communist-nationalist-dominated Foreign Affairs Committee of the former parliament put it in late 1992: "Russian foreign policy must be based on a doctrine that proclaims the entire geopolitical space of the former Union a sphere of vital interests. . . . Russia must secure . . . the role of political and military guarantor of stability on all the territory of the former USSR."[9]

By 1993, it became evident that the Yeltsin team had shifted from its original foreign policy approach. While retaining its basic pro-Western orientation, Moscow also embarked upon a much more assertive course of action in the Near Abroad. In February, Yeltsin suggested that Russia should have "special powers as guarantor of peace and stability" on the territory of the former Soviet Union. The United States objected to what some Washington officials referred to as the Russian version of the Monroe Doctrine, and Moscow quietly backed off.[10] But in April, Russian defense minister General Pavel Grachev announced that the "main threat to Russia's security emanates from the south"—a clear indication that the military establishment was strongly in favor of actively defending Russian interests in Transcaucasia and Central Asia.[11] And in the fall, Kozyrev stated repeatedly that Transcaucasia as well as Central Asia were a "part of Russia's strategic sphere of influence" and that no "international organization or group of states can replace our peacekeeping efforts in this specific post-Soviet space." *Izvestiia* commentator Melor Sturua aptly referred to Kozyrev's statement, made in a speech before the UN General Assembly, as "an abbreviated version of the Brezhnev Doctrine, which asserted Moscow's right to intervene in the former Communist world." Undeterred, both Kozyrev and Grachev continued to make these claims throughout 1994.[12]

Moreover, in September 1993, Russia formally requested Western approval of a plan to increase the number of tanks and other heavy weapons that the USSR had been permitted to station in the Caucasus under the terms of the 1990 Treaty on Conventional Forces in Europe. (Among other things, this treaty had imposed a limit of 220 tanks for the Caucasian region.) Since the accord was not to go into effect until 1995, Russia could, in the meantime, do whatever it wished.[13] Although the West refused to comply with Moscow's request, the latter was clearly designed to reinforce the Kremlin's claim to supremacy in the region and to indicate that it was prepared to use force to defend its interests. In short, in 1993, Russia decided to reassert itself in the Transcaucasian republics. In the case of Georgia, this was done directly, but the situation Moscow faced in the conflict between Azerbaijan and Armenia was more involved and complex. It is to this subject that we now turn.

Factors Influencing Russia's Position

The collapse and breakup of the USSR was greeted with enthusiasm by the Western powers, including the United States. The emergence of newly independent republics in the former Soviet territory, including Transcaucasia, was seen as a positive development that not only did not harm Western interests but might, in time, serve some of them, particularly in the economic sector. Possible, indeed likely, access to the rich oil and natural gas deposits of Azerbaijan, Kazakhstan, and Turkmenistan was the most obvious case in point. Transcaucasia's immediate southern neighbors, Turkey and Iran, were also ecstatic over the demise of the Soviet Union and the emergence of friendly independent states along their northern border: Ankara and Tehran no longer shared a common frontier with Russia, an ancient and bitter enemy.

Initially, Moscow did not seem to mind, accepting the fact that the USSR's southern neighbors as well as the West had become involved in the affairs of the Transcaucasian and Central Asian republics. However, as noted, in 1993, Russia's attitude began to change and the Kremlin stepped up significantly its efforts to reestablish preeminence in the territory of the former Soviet Union. As already mentioned, one of the most intractable problems that Moscow has faced proved to be the Armenian-Azeri struggle over Nagorno-Karabakh. Among other things, the disappearance of a strong center contributed to the internationalization of the conflict and to an increase in the number of (mostly indirect) participants in it. This turn of events made the Nagorno-Karabakh dispute even more difficult to control and to regulate.

In addition to the above-mentioned general policy considerations, Russia's decision to play a major role in the Nagorno-Karabakh conflict has been influenced by several other factors. As seen from Moscow, they include the following:

1. The Russian Federation regards itself (and has been recognized by the rest of the world) as the legal successor of the USSR and has thus felt some responsibility for the Soviet failure to resolve the conflict in its early stages.
2. The conflict has occurred in a region adjacent to the Caucasian frontier of the Russian Federation, thus affecting Russia's security and

national interests. For example, Daghestan, an autonomous republic within the Russian Federation, has what has been described as an "ethnically complex" border with Azerbaijan. Moreover, the northern Caucasus, with its mosaic of hostile ethnic and religious groups, contains many other potential conflicts that could be ignited under the impact of the continuing chaos in Transcaucasia.

3. Approximately 400,000 Russians reside in Azerbaijan, and 50,000 more live in Armenia. Although the numbers are not as large as those in many other republics, the potential exodus of close to half a million Russians was enough to attract Moscow's attention. By supporting Armenia, Moscow risked incurring the wrath of Baku, leading to possible persecution and flight of hundreds of thousands of Russians. In contrast, there was little likelihood of anti-Russian reprisals in Armenia—Erevan, unlike Baku, simply had nowhere else to turn. (It might be noted in passing that, in terms of the existing Armenian and Azeri communities in Russia, the picture is reversed. The former is significantly larger—60,000 as against a much smaller number of Azeris. It is also more important politically, because many Armenians hold high positions, especially in the economic life of Russia, and exert an influence on Russia's policies.)

4. Ethnic Muslim nationalism within the Russian Federation—in the autonomous republics of Tatarstan, Bashkorostan, and others—has made it difficult for the Kremlin to disregard Nagorno-Karabakh. It has also complicated Moscow's position by curtailing its freedom of maneuver.

5. Moreover, the five Muslim members of the Commonwealth of Independent States (Kazakhstan, Uzbekistan, Turkmenistan, Tajikistan, and Kyrgyzstan) have strongly supported Baku. Hence, by adopting an anti-Azeri position, Moscow has risked destabilizing the political situation not only in the Russian Federation but also in the Commonwealth.

6. At the same time, Moscow cannot abandon Armenia, a Christian nation with strong historical ties to Russia. In fact, Armenia has been what a Gorbachev Foundation report described as Russia's "guaranteed ally" in the Caucasus and, unlike Azerbaijan and Georgia, a founding member of the CIS. It is also one of the relatively few former Soviet republics to have signed a mutual assistance treaty with the Russian Federation. Consequently, Russian troops, stationed in Armenia at the time of the dissolution of the USSR, have remained and have, significantly, continued to guard the border with Turkey.

7. Last but not least, as already mentioned, Russia's position has been complicated by Turkey's and Iran's involvement in the Nagorno-Karabakh conflict primarily on the side of Azerbaijan. While Turkey, in an attempt to counterbalance the Russian position in Armenia and in a show of solidarity with the ethnically related and Turkic-speaking Azeris, has played the role of a "guaranteed ally" of Azerbaijan, Iran, with a large Azeri population of its own and with the shared adherence to the Shiite brand of Islam, has adopted a more even-handed policy. As part of its competition with Turkey, Iran has unsuccessfully attempted to mediate the dispute by maintaining working relationships with both Azerbaijan and Armenia. The rivalry among Russia, Turkey, and Iran has served as an additional powerful impetus for Moscow to try to reestablish its once dominant position in Transcaucasia.[14]

The Three-Cornered Competition

Initially, Moscow saw Turkey as being at a distinct advantage in its relations with Transcaucasia and Central Asia. It was ethnically and linguistically related to the Azeris and the inhabitants of the Central Asian republics, except the Tajiks, and it shared with many of them adherence to the Sunni branch of Islam. In addition, Turkey prided itself on the secular nature of its political system, which differentiated it sharply from the Islamic Republic of Iran and made Ankara more attractive in the eyes of the mostly secular, former Communist elites in the newly independent Muslim republics. Finally, Turkey could boast of a successfully developing economy, which contrasted sharply with the state of "stagflation" characteristic of the economies of most of the CIS member states, and which could serve as a model to be emulated by the Muslim republics. In Transcaucasia, all of these factors combined to render Turkey a very attractive model for Azerbaijan's nationalist, anticommunist, and anti-Russian National Front. It came to power in 1992 and, under the leadership of Abulfaz Elchibey, went out of its way to cultivate the Turkish connection as a counterweight to Moscow. For its part, as noted, Ankara adopted a strongly pro-Azeri position, supporting Baku and publicly condemning what it termed "Armenian aggression in Nagorno-Karabakh and Nakhichevan." (Given the historic antagonism between the Turks and the Armenians, Ankara's decision to side with the Azeris was a virtual certainty anyway.) Under these circumstances, Russia publicly professed adherence to an evenhanded policy but, in reality, tilted toward its "guaranteed ally," Armenia.

The other "southern" participant in the three-cornered competition in

Transcaucasia and Central Asia has been the Islamic Republic of Iran. Compared to Ankara, and for reasons cited above, Tehran's position has been relatively weaker. Nevertheless, Iran has been able to exercise some influence due in part to its geographic proximity to, and hence its potential ability to serve as a transportation link between, Azerbaijan and Central Asia on the one hand and the Persian Gulf or Turkey's Mediterranean ports on the other. Moreover, the Persians are ethnically and culturally related to the Tajiks and share the Shiite brand of Islam with the Azeris. In fact, western Azerbaijan has historically been under Iranian control. In any event, in its competition with Moscow and Ankara, Tehran, because of its relatively weaker position, has played the peacemaking card more persistently than its rivals, but it has also been the least successful; the most serious proposals for a peaceful resolution of the Nagorno-Karabakh conflict have resulted from the efforts mounted by Russia and the CSCE, from which Iran had been excluded. At the same time, it bears repeating that all the international peacemaking activity has so far proved futile.

Initially, Russia emerged as the most successful outsider in the three-cornered competition that developed in Transcaucasia (and, for that matter, Central Asia) following the demise of the USSR. In retrospect, this was not surprising. Although in 1992–93 Moscow's positions in the Transcaucasian republics were badly shaken, Russia managed to reverse the unfavorable trend and to advance its interests significantly, particularly in Georgia and, to a lesser extent, in Azerbaijan. The Kremlin succeeded in this difficult task because of a confluence of several factors. Thus, many of the existing economic ties between Russia and the Transcaucasian republics survived the collapse of the USSR. In a similar fashion, both antagonists in the Nagorno-Karabakh conflict depended on Russia for military supplies, as well as for at least some training of their military personnel. In this respect, it has been estimated that, by late 1993, Armenia received from Russia more than 250 tanks and 350 artillery pieces, while the corresponding figures for Azerbaijan were 400 and 450, respectively.[15] It is also significant that most members of the national elites in Transcaucasia had been trained in the former USSR and that many of them are not uncomfortable with the notion of close cooperation with Russia. Last but not least, the presence of sizable Russian communities in Armenia and especially in Azerbaijan, coupled with Moscow's stated concern about their safety, has been a factor in the regional leaders' decision making.[16]

A discussion of outsider involvement in Transcaucasia would be incomplete without a brief reference to the Western powers. In early 1993, the West, as a whole, was not seen in Moscow as overly interested in the outcome of the Nagorno-Karabakh conflict. Having demonstrated their impotence in the Yugoslavian crisis, the Western powers were not expected to become involved in a war between Armenia and Azerbaijan. They expressed their concern in the form of passing strongly worded resolutions at the UN Security Council and supporting the diplomatic efforts mounted by the European Community, but they were not prepared to intervene militarily in Transcaucasia, where no vital Western interests were at stake.

Yet in late 1993, as part of a general stiffening of Yeltsin's foreign policy, Moscow became openly critical of Washington's posture in the Nagorno-Karabakh conflict. Specifically, according to unnamed Ministry of Foreign Affairs officials, the Europeans, and particularly the Americans, had recently exhibited a "clear dissatisfaction" with the initiatives pursued by the Russian diplomats. This was interpreted to mean that the United States and some of its allies resented Russia's stepped-up activity and rising influence in Transcaucasia. As the Ministry of Foreign Affairs saw it, the primary task of the Russian diplomacy was to end the hostilities and to institute a cease-fire on the assumption that other important problems—such as refugees and the economic blockade of Armenia—could not be resolved until the fighting stopped. In contrast, the United States and its European allies were "coldly and academically" developing a plan for an overall settlement, a task which, the Kremlin argued, would take years to complete.

Moreover, after the Minsk group of the CSCE was set up in June 1992, with Russia, the United States, and Turkey as its moving forces, Moscow offered Washington to dispatch joint missions to Baku and Erevan. The State Department refused, leading the Russian Ministry of Foreign Affairs to conclude that the Americans were not interested in an "equal partnership." Instead, Washington forced Moscow to agree to the creation of an "informal *troika*: the United States, Russia, [and] Turkey." In this type of arrangement, the Americans had evidently hoped "to become an arbiter, a superior judge." Secret meetings of the group did not continue for too long—it soon became evident that Turkey saw as its primary task total rejection of all Armenian proposals. In the end, the events on the ground—Armenian advances and Azeri retreats—overtook the tripartite diplomatic efforts.[17]

The perceived Turkish and American reluctance to cooperate with Moscow on equal terms may thus have been another factor prompting the Kremlin to seize the initiative and to try to reestablish its dominant position in Transcaucasia. However, it bears repeating that the joint U.S.-Russian-Turkish peace plan of May 1993 was turned down not by the Azeris but by the Armenians, albeit those of Nagorno-Karabakh, claiming to act independently of Erevan.

Russian Involvement

In the initial (i.e., Soviet) stage of the conflict, the Kremlin backed the Azeri position because it was based on the principle of the sanctity of borders. Gorbachev correctly equated acceptance of the right to redraw frontiers (no matter how unpalatable to one or more parties) to opening a "Pandora's box" of ethnic strife. Given the Soviet opposition to Armenian demands for full autonomy and, subsequently, independence, the Azeris usually had the better of the fighting. However, in 1992, the Russian Federation began to support Armenia. The main reason for Moscow's change of heart, as indicated above, was the coming to power of Azerbaijan's National Front, headed by Abulfaz Elchibey, and Baku's subsequent shift away from Russia and toward Turkey.

By the end of 1992, the Armenians captured all of Nagorno-Karabakh and continued their offensive in 1993 in spite of the fact that in May, Erevan and Baku had accepted a peace plan worked out by the United States, Russia, and Turkey. At that time, as noted, Nagorno-Karabakh turned down the plan and the Armenian government claimed that it was in no position to change Stepanakert's mind. At this juncture, it seemed that the key to the solution of the Nagorno-Karabakh conflict was not to be found in Washington, Ankara, or Tehran but in Moscow—the only party capable of decisively influencing Armenia and, through it, Nagorno-Karabakh, by means of extending or withholding political and material support. Therefore, it may be safely assumed that Stepanakert's refusal to compromise had to enjoy the tacit support of Erevan, and Erevan's position, in turn, had to have been sanctioned by Moscow. The purposes of the exercise were to demonstrate the Kremlin's ability and willingness to act independently of the United States and Turkey, and to secure the downfall of Elchibey and the National Front. Moscow was successful on both counts. By May 1993, it became obvious that Russia's continued insistence on protecting its sphere of influence in Transcaucasia and on blocking outside encroachments into the region were no empty words. It was equally telling that Ankara and Washington, both strong backers of Elchibey, eventually bowed to the inevitable.

As the Armenian offensive continued in the summer and early fall of 1993, the forces of Nagorno-Karabakh, as noted, reached the Iranian border, leading Tehran to order its army units to cross into Azerbaijan. The move elicited a strong reaction from Moscow. Kozyrev announced that "no matter what . . . [Iran's] motives are, [the move] cannot meet with our understanding or support."[18] In short, having earlier rebuffed Turkey and the United States, Russia now formally notified Iran that its foray across the old Soviet border was not acceptable and that is forces would have to be withdrawn. They were. Transcaucasia began to look more and more like part of the Russian sphere of influence.

In September 1993, President Aliev visited Moscow and announced that Azerbaijan would join the CIS and its economic union and would sign a collective security treaty with Russia—steps Elchibey had consistently refused to take. A good analysis of these events was offered by Armen Khanbabian, who described the removal of Elchibey and his replacement by Aliev as a "major achievement of Russian policy." Under Elchibey, Azerbaijan had served as an important link between the former Soviet Muslim republics on the one hand, and Turkey (and, to a lesser extent, Iran) on the other. All that had now come to an end. Russian interests once again reigned supreme in the southern regions of the former USSR, and the vehicle Moscow used to score this major political victory was the Nagorno-Karabakh conflict. In fact, Khanbabian disclosed, now it was Erevan's turn to become concerned about a possible "return of Russian forces to the conflict zone" in the guise of peacekeeping units because their appearance might "hamper Armenian interests."[19]

However, having "cleared the deck," Moscow has found it difficult to resolve the Nagorno-Karabakh dispute on its terms. To be sure, Aliev and Armenian president Levon Ter-Petrosian came to Moscow in late September 1993 for another round of negotiations, but no breakthrough was achieved on that occasion. Pointedly, no representatives of Turkey, Iran, or the United States were invited to attend these sessions.[20] Aliev and Ter-Petrosian met again in Ashgabat (Turkmenistan) in December 1993, where they were attending a conference of the CIS heads of state. Both expressed themselves in favor of a peaceful settlement of the Nagorno-Karabakh conflict, but made no progress in that direction.[21]

The Azeri offensive of December 1993 gave rise to new efforts to assert Russia's primacy in Transcaucasia. In January 1994, Yeltsin's special representative on Nagorno-Karabakh, Vladimir Kazimirov, conducted negotiations with officials of the Iranian foreign ministry. In Moscow, his visit was regarded as a success: Iran conceded that Russia should "play first violin" in efforts to resolve the Nagorno-Karabakh dispute. Significantly, the sides objected to the "internationalization" of the conflict. The term referred to both "direct intervention by Turkey" and the recruitment of foreign mercenaries from such countries as Afghanistan, Russia, and Ukraine.[22]

Be that as it may, in early 1994 Moscow began to treat Azerbaijan as the main stumbling block to Russian efforts to mediate the Nagorno-Karabakh conflict and as a main obstacle to the reestablishment of Russian preeminence in Transcaucasia. At this juncture, the emboldened Kremlin was seeking Baku's compliance with the following requests: establishment of Russian military bases on Azerbaijan's territory; use of Russian border troops to guard Azerbaijan's frontiers; recognition of Russia as the sole mediator in the Nagorno-Karabakh conflict; some form of recognition by Azerbaijan of the Nagorno-Karabakh Republic; and recognition by Baku of a twelve-mile zone in the oil-bearing Caspian shelf, accompanied by renunciation of the fifty-mile exclusion zone on which Azerbaijan had insisted. Since these demands were unpopular in Baku, and since its bargaining position had been weakened as a result of the Armenian victories, some commentators suggested that Aliev had ordered the winter offensive to improve Azerbaijan's ability to negotiate a better deal.[23]

Russian pressure on Azerbaijan intensified in February 1994, after Moscow and Tbilisi signed a treaty of mutual assistance. Among other things, it provided for the establishment of Russian bases on Georgian territory and the stationing of Russian border troops along the frontier with Turkey. Commenting on these developments, Grachev noted that Moscow wished "to establish military bases throughout the Transcaucasus" and to station Russian frontier guards along Azerbaijan's border with Iran. Partly in response to these events, Aliev traveled to Ankara. Since Turkey, as noted, had been a staunch supporter of Elchibey's, Aliev's first foreign visit after being elected president was clearly intended to strengthen his hand in the difficult negotiations with Moscow and Erevan.[24]

Undeterred, the Kremlin continued its efforts to seize the diplomatic initiative in Transcaucasia. A new factor was the heavy-handed intrusion of the Russian military into the negotiating process. On February 18, 1994, the defense ministers of Armenia, Azerbaijan, Nagorno-Karabakh, and Russia signed a protocol that provided for a cease-fire and a staged resolution of the conflict. As envisaged by Grachev, who presided over the proceedings, the stages included: disengagement of the combatants; the creation of a neutral corridor (ten to twenty kilometers wide); and the establishment in it of thirty-five control posts, commanded by Russian officers and manned by observers from all the involved parties. These measures would be followed by the withdrawal of Armenian forces from the occupied Azeri territory.[25]

Though praised in Moscow and approved by Ter-Petrosian, the protocol was rejected by Aliev. A government spokesman explained that the cease-fire, the creation of the neutral zone, and the negotiations should take place simultaneously with the withdrawal of Armenian troops from Azeri territory and the return of the refugees to their homes in Azerbaijan and Nagorno-Karabakh. Equally significant was Aliev's "categoric opposition to the deployment of Russian troops in Karabakh." He believed that their presence in the war zone would prolong, not shorten, the conflict because it would "obstruct the withdrawal of Armenian armed groups from . . . occupied [Azeri] territory."[26] Concurrently, Baku showed new interest in the activity of the CSCE. On the same day that he refused to approve the Moscow protocol, Aliev met with the head of the Minsk group delegation and urged the group to continue its efforts. Aliev's attitude made sense: Azerbaijan and the CSCE agreed that negotiations concerning the status of Nagorno-Karabakh should begin only after the withdrawal of Armenian troops from the occupied territories.[27]

Brushing off the initial setback, Grachev, in May 1994, called another meeting of the defense ministers at which he proposed that they sign a document regulating the "first stage of the implementation of the Russian plan." This entailed troop withdrawals, followed in quick succession by the "liberation of the territories, return of the refugees, exchange of prisoners, restoration of communications," and the determination of the future status of Nagorno-Karabakh. Grachev also insisted that the number of observer posts be increased to forty-nine and that they be manned by 1,800 Russian military personnel. He felt that there was no need to introduce observers from the CIS ("CIS is Russia," as he put it) or from the CSCE, and added that Russia alone should guarantee the implementation of the cease-fire and of the eventual peace settlement. (It is noteworthy that no unanimity on this subject prevailed at the highest levels of the Kremlin hierarchy. Touring Transcaucasia, Yeltsin's representative Kazimirov expressed a preference for a multinational peacekeeping force which would include units from such neutral European countries as Austria, Sweden, and Finland.)[28]

Grachev's second attempt at imposing a settlement failed also. Azerbaijan refused to sanction the introduction of Russian troops into Karabakh and let it be known that it would acquiesce in Grachev's plan only if the Russian peacekeeping units were placed under the "control of international observers." This counterproposal, it was widely understood, would be rejected by the Kremlin.[29] To understand Aliev's intransigence, it is important to note that by mid-1994 Baku had acquired staunch support among the Western powers, led by the United States. Thus, even before the collapse of the May round of negotiations, the U.S. ambassador in Azerbaijan announced that "any plan regulating the Karabakh problem . . . must be implemented within the framework of the Minsk group of the CSCE." He added that the "entry into the zone of conflict of CIS disengagement forces must be under the control of international observers." Moscow was not pleased. It recognized that the West had "its own regional interests and ambitions" that the parties to the conflict were endeavoring to use for their own purposes. At the same time, as Russia saw it, during the last two years the Minsk group had succeeded in preparing but one single document—the mandate of the CSCE observers—and even it had not yet been ratified. In contrast, Moscow had come up with a full-fledged peace plan.[30]

In July 1994, as Turkey expressed its willingness to participate in peacekeeping operations in Karabakh and generally supported Aliev's position, the Kremlin scored something of a victory in Transcaucasia when the UN Security Council approved the deployment of Russian peacekeeping units in Georgia. However, the major difference between the situation in that country and Azerbaijan was President Eduard Shevardnadze's official request for their presence. It is also noteworthy that the Security Council had "authorized United Nations military observers to monitor the . . . activities" of the Russian troops in Georgia.[31]

Azerbaijan's position on Nagorno-Karabakh was spelled out in late summer 1994 by Speaker of the Supreme Council Rasul Guliev. Baku insisted that Armenia withdraw its forces from all the occupied territories and that it do so in the following stages: complete and lasting cease-fire; separation of the combatants; their withdrawal from occupied enemy territory; lifting of the blockade on transportation and power transmission; return of the refugees to their home areas; and, only then, determination of the status of Nagorno-Karabakh. On the subject of the peacekeeping force, Guliev noted that it should be composed of representatives not of one country but of several. Baku also insisted that its introduction into Azerbaijan's territory be preceded by complete withdrawal of Armenian troops from all eight occupied Azeri districts (*raiony*). In contrast, Armenia and Karabakh, agreeing with Russia, demanded not only that the order of the above stages be reversed but also that their forces remain in the strategically and economically vital Lachin and Shusha districts, whose status was to be negotiated later.[32]

Another major bone of contention—this one involving mainly Russia and the West—had to do with the role of the CSCE in the Nagorno-Karabakh conflict. Given some of the differences at the highest levels of the Russian government, the Kremlin's position cannot be reconstructed easily. Nevertheless, it is safe to assume that Moscow has wished to minimize the peacemaking role of the outsiders and has preferred to remain the sole ultimate arbiter in the dispute. As one Russian commentator put it, the Kremlin was prepared to grant the CSCE the "right of signature" (*pravo podpisi*) in exchange for the UN Security Council's approval of its own peacemaking mission. In any event, as alluded to above, many in the Kremlin believed that such members of the Minsk group as Turkey and the United States had their own interests in Transcaucasia and that they desired to curtail Russia's freedom of action by forcing it to accept the CSCE framework for the resolution of the Nagorno-Karabalsh conflict. Hence,

Baku's refusal to subscribe to Moscow's proposals was attributed to American and Turkish pressure. To keep the record straight, it should be reiterated that both Erevan and Stepanakert had serious reservations about the Kremlin initiatives for fear that Russian military presence in Karabakh would enable Moscow to exert pressure on both sides. However, aware of Baku's uncompromising stance, the Armenians chose to have it bear the brunt of Russian displeasure.[33]

The signing of an oil deal between Azerbaijan and an international consortium in September 1994 did nothing to promote the cause of peace in Nagorno-Karabakh. Although all the parties continued to advocate peaceful resolution of the conflict, Russia inflamed the situation by sharply and openly critizing the petroleum accord. In fact, Moscow's pressure led Aliev to counterattack—he accused the Kremlin of engineering the escape of a group of incarcerated political prisoners and used the oppoprtunity to announce that Baku would not sanction the stationing of Russian border guards along the Iranian frontier.[34]

The signing of the new petroleum contract propelled Washington even more prominently into the Nagorno-Karabakh picture. The subject came up during the U.S.-Russian summit meeting of late September: while Yeltsin reiterated Moscow's insistence that it be recognized as the principal peacemaker in Transcaucasia, Clinton argued that Russia's actions must correspond to the established norms of international law and must be under the control of the United Nations and of the CSCE. This led one knowledgeable Russian commentator to conclude that Washington had moved into Transcaucasia and that the Clinton administration had let Yeltsin know that the United States was now prepared actively to pursue and to defend its interests. Moscow's previously "unlimited role" in Transcaucasia had thus come to an end.[35]

In October, representatives of the CSCE's Minsk group met in Vienna and agreed to dispatch an international peacekeeping force to Nagorno-Karabakh. Sources in Moscow, reflecting the view held in the Kremlin, described the decision as "clearly anti-Russian," designed to prevent the deployment of Russian troops in the conflict zone. This Western intrusion into the former Soviet territory, it was held, established a dangerous precedent and was motivated by the multi-billion-dollar deal recently concluded between Azerbaijan and a Western oil consortium.[36] The clear implication was that the Kremlin was not prepared to abandon its claim to ascendancy in Transcaucasia.

Moscow signaled its displeasure by informing Washington and London that it could not comply with the terms of the Treaty on Conventional Forces in Europe (CFE). The Kremlin explained that the unstable situation in the Northern Caucasus as well as in Transcaucasia made it imperative for Russia to maintain in the region larger forces than had been originally planned. The Western powers refused to sanction any changes in the CFE, but the Russian request was important in that it represented an escalation in the growing tension between Moscow and the Western allies.[37] Part of the general deterioration of Russo-Western relations, which occurred in 1994 and was marked by public disputes over the future of Bosnia and Iraq (to mention but the more prominent examples), the confrontation in Trans-caucasia was, in many ways, more serious than the other crises. Georgia, Armenia, and Azerbaijan were, after all, parts of the former empire, and the increasingly nationalistic Yeltsin leadership felt that the West was en-croaching into the Kremlin's exclusive sphere of influence.

Undeterred by Moscow's objections, the West continued to advance. In late October, UN Secretary-General Boutros Boutros-Ghali visited Baku and Erevan, presenting them with the following list of principles on which, he said, peacekeeping in the region should be based:

- maintenance of the territorial integrity of Azerbaijan;
- inviolability of Azerbaijan's borders;
- inapplicability of force as a means to resolve the Nagorno-Karabakh conflict; and
- liberation of all Azeri territory seized illegally during the conduct of military operations.

Boutros-Ghali explained that these principles rested on UN Security Council Resolutions 822, 853, 874, and 882. The Azeri officials were un-derstandably pleased but complained that these documents had not been implemented. They also called upon the United Nations to support the efforts by the CSCE to create an international peacekeeping force for Nagorno-Karabakh. Aliev in particular took the opportunity to reiterate Baku's above-mentioned position and added, significantly, that the rights of the Armenian population would eventually be guaranteed within the con-fines of the Azerbaijani state. For its part, Erevan had little use for the secretary-general's views or mission.[38]

In mid-November, the Russian Ministry of Foreign Affairs hosted an-other round of talks between the deputy foreign ministers of Armenia and Azerbaijan. They led nowhere. Concurrently, representatives of the Minsk group met in Moscow to discuss yet again the problem of peacekeeping in Nagorno-Karabakh. Before the meeting opened, the ministries of foreign affairs and defense issued a joint statement warning that "Any attempts to play down the obvious role of Russia would . . . [be tantamount to] wrecking the peace process." They also called on the United Nations, the CSCE, the CIS, and other involved parties to join efforts in order to solve the Karabakh problem. This meeting, too, produced no results.[39]

An important change in the international approach to the Transcaucasian conflict occurred in December 1994 at the CSCE general meeting in Budapest. (On that occasion, CSCE was renamed OSCE—Organization for Security and Cooperation in Europe.) In general terms, Moscow continued to demand that the West recognize the territory of the former Soviet Union as a Russian sphere of influence and that Russian troops be used as peacekeepers in conflicts emerging in the Near Abroad. In particular reference to Nagorno-Karabakh, the Kremlin objected to the dispatch of an OSCE peacekeeping force to Transcaucasia but was overruled by the majority of the member states. Instead, they decided that a 3,000-strong multinational force should be sent to Nagorno-Karabakh and that its Russian component should not exceed one-third of the force. However, several important issues remained unresolved. Among them were: the nature of the force's mandate; the exact number, composition, and the role of the peacekeepers; and, finally, its command.[40] Whether and how the issues will be resolved, only time will tell.

Evaluation

The examination of Moscow's record in Transcaucasia suggests that it deserves to be classified as a conditional success. This conclusion rests on the following assumptions:

1. Russia has retained Armenia and has brought a reluctant Georgia back into its political fold. It appeared to have done so with Azerbaijan as well, but in 1994, as noted, Moscow has run into some unexpected problems in its dealings with Baku.
2. These Russian gains have been achieved in spite of Iranian and particularly Turkish efforts to gain a degree of influence in Transcaucasia.
3. Russia succeeded in removing from power those local politicians inimical to Moscow's interests (Elchibey), or has reduced them to the role of supplicants who retain power because of Moscow's sufferance (Shevardnadze).
4. Finally, Russia has made some of the above gains—and, in the process, advanced its interests and influence in Transcaucasia—by fanning regional conflicts in Azerbaijan and Georgia while paying lip-service to regional security and stability. It might be noted parenthetically that, in pursuing this policy, Russia was not blazing any

new trails. Rather, it was adhering to Moscow's time-tested practice of utilizing ethnic conflicts to consolidate its influence in the non-Russian areas.[41]

Nevertheless, it is equally important to note that Moscow's successes in Transcaucasia have been achieved at a price and that they have created new problems (and redefined some old ones) whose resolution is not going to be easy and is by no means assured. In the price category should be listed the impetus to local nationalism, provided by the Russian policies, particularly in Georgia and Azerbaijan. Thus, it is true that in Azerbaijan, Elchibey's erratic behavior caused him to lose popular support and, combined with the battlefield reverses suffered at the hands of the Armenians, helped pave the way for Aliev's return to power. At the same time, anti-Russian sentiments are still very much in evidence in Azerbaijan, and nationalism remains a potent force in the country's politics. (This conclusion applies to Georgia as well.) Moreover, Moscow has discovered that the old apparatchik Aliev is more difficult to manipulate than the Kremlin had originally expected. To be sure, as noted, he did lead Azerbaijan into the CIS and signed a mutual defense treaty with Russia. But as of this writing, Aliev, unlike Shevardnadze, has refused to sanction the reintroduction of Russian forces into Azerbaijan. How this problem will be resolved remains to be seen. However, given the fact that Azerbaijan enjoys the support of the United States, Turkey, and Iran, Baku's position in its dealings with Moscow is stronger than that of Tbilisi, which, for all intents and purposes, has been abandoned by the international community.

Oil

Another problem that has caused strain in Azeri-Russian relations pertains to the Caspian petroleum deposits or, more specifically, to the extraction of the off-shore oil and its transportation to West European markets. In 1993, Elchibey signed a far-reaching agreement with a Western consortium, headed by British Petroleum, which provided for the exploitation of three major offshore fields. Once extracted, the Caspian oil was to be transported to Turkey's Mediterranean coast via either Georgia or Iran. Russia was totally excluded from participation in both facets of the original deal. Though not acknowledged publicly, this agreement was not acceptable to Moscow and no doubt strengthened its resolve to oust Elchibey. Significantly, one of Aliev's first official acts as the president of Azerbaijan was to inform the consortium that the original contract would have to be renegotiated.[42]

In February 1994, Azerbaijan and Great Britain signed a memorandum providing for cooperation in the exploitation of some of the Caspian off-shore oil fields. In late April, the Russian Ministry of Foreign Affairs deliv-ered a note to the British government, informing it that Baku had no right to dispose of these deposits because there existed "no sectoral demarcation of the seabed in the Caspian Sea." The latter was described as an "enclosed body of water with a single ecological system," which had to be managed jointly by all the littoral states.[43]

Disregarding Moscow's warning, Baku and London reiterated their de-termination to proceed with the February accord. Aliev noted that the Rus-sian government had not nullified the October 1993 agreement, signed by Minister of Fuel and Energy Iurii Shafranik, which recognized Baku's juris-diction over the Azeri and Chirag off-shore fields. Other Azerbaijani sources noted that the 1993 accord also granted Lukoil (Russia's national petroleum company) the right to exploit the developed part of the Guneshli field. In addition, Lukoil would receive 10 percent of the profits which Socar (the Azeri oil company) stood to earn as a result of its deal with the international consortium.[44] Interestingly, Prime Minister Viktor Chernomyrdin distanced himself from the position adopted by the Ministry of Foreign Affairs (MFA). On May 31, 1994, Aliev, who had emphatically rejected the MFA's interpretation of the status of the Caspian Sea, telephoned Chernomyrdin. The premier said that he had known nothing about the MFA's April 1994 note to the British government and was very surprised at its content. He then assured Aliev that he had no intention of challenging the legality of the February 1994 agreement.[45]

On September 20, 1994, Socar signed an agreement with an international consortium, which consisted of five U.S. companies, British Petroleum, Statoil (Norway), as well as the Turkish and Saudi national oil companies. According to the terms of what was immediately dubbed the "deal of the century," Azerbaijan would receive approximately 80 percent of the profits. The consortium, which was expected to invest some $8 billion over a thirty-year period, also undertook to pay Baku an initial bonus of $300 million. In addition, Azerbaijan would receive all the natural gas extracted in the pro-cess, with the result that its profits, for the life of the contract, were esti-mated at close to $35 billion. The initial daily production of some 80,000–90,000 barrels of oil a day could be pumped through the existing pipelines between Baku and the Russian Black Sea port of Novorossiisk. Eventually, as the volume of production increased, a new pipeline would be required.[46]

For Azerbaijan, in addition to enormous economic benefits, the oil deal also represented a major political gain. As indicated above, economic considerations prompted the West—and particularly the United States—to insert itself into the Transcaucasian picture and to play an important part not only in negotiating the petroleum accord but also in making efforts to block Russia from assuming the dominating role in attempts to resolve the Nagorno-Karabakh conflict. Thus, the final round of negotiations on the oil deal took place in Houston. After the contract had been signed, President Clinton assured Aliev that the United States stood squarely behind the petroleum agreement. Moreover, as noted, during the late September meetings between Clinton and Yeltsin, the U.S. president tried to persuade his Russian counterpart to withdraw the MFA's objections to the oil deal. Yeltsin countered by suggesting that the issue be considered by Russian and American experts.[47]

In the meantime, elaborating on its previous position, the Ministry of Foreign Affairs declared that the September 20 oil deal was "premature" and "illegal." A spokesman argued that the accord violated the Soviet-Iranian treaties of 1921 and 1940, which, in their economic aspects, had treated the Caspian Sea as a "unified whole" whose resources could be exploited only after an agreement to proceed had been reached by all of the littoral states. As already mentioned, the MFA argued also that the Caspian was an "internal sea," a fact that rendered international conventions regulating the use of the shelf inapplicable.

The ministry's position was initially rejected by Azerbaijan and Kazakhstan, as well as the Western powers. All maintained that the Soviet-Iranian treaties dealt only with "fishing resources and ecological problems" and had no relevance to the shelf and fuel extraction.[48] The MFA's arguments were also discounted by Lukoil, which insisted that its approach was based on the previously mentioned interstate agreement that Russia and Azerbaijan had signed in October 1993. In spite of the pressure from all directions, the ministry refused to concede the point. In October 1994, following bilateral negotiations with Iran, the MFA presided over a conference that was attended by representatives of the five littoral states and was intended to "examine all aspects of bilateral relations, focusing on the use of Caspian natural resources." A Russian diplomat tried to establish fresh groundwork for the MFA's position by noting prior to the opening of the conference that "the Caspian Sea regime could be altered only through negotiations between all sides concerned. . . ." Baku would have none of that. Foreign Minister Hasan Hasanov countered that the conference should concern itself only with such items as "shipping, the exploitation of bioresources, and the problem of the sea surface." He added that Azerbaijan would reject efforts to place on the conference agenda the issue of the exploitation of the fuel resources.[49]

In the end, the conference produced a draft Treaty on Regional Cooperation in the Caspian Sea. The question of the fuel deposits was discussed, and the concluding statement noted that no state had the right to act without consulting the others, but Azerbaijan refused to approve this provision. Moreover, while the conference was in session, Aliev telephoned Chernomyrdin, who assured the president that the Russian government had no objections to the September oil deal.[50] The premier repeated his assurances on October 21 during a meeting of the CIS heads of state. The timing was significant because, one day earlier, an MFA spokesman criticized those Russian industrialists who were collaborating with Baku in exploiting the Caspian fuel resources. The spokesman then dropped something of a bombshell: in defending Russia's rights, the ministry was acting on Yeltsin's orders.

This assertion, *Nezavisimaia gazeta* explained, was "only partially correct." On July 21, 1994, acting on Kozyrev's recommendation, Yeltsin signed a secret order (number 396) entitled "Protection of Russian Interests in the Caspian Sea." Among other things, it dealt with the application of economic sanctions against Baku should the latter go ahead with the oil deal. A short time later, in a letter to Chernomyrdin, Kozyrev suggested the imposition of economic, financial, and trade restrictions to induce Azerbaijan "to respect the interests of Russia and the norms of international law." Aware that adoption of these measures was tantamount to an imposition of an economic blockade, Chernomyrdin turned Kozyrev down. The situation was further complicated by the fact that the MFA's position had gained the support of the Foreign Intelligence Service, whose chairman Evgenii Primakov reportedly felt that the "oil contract represents a threat to . . . Russia's national security." In spite of that, Yeltsin did not order the implementation of secret order 396.[51]

In November 1994, Azerbaijan significantly strengthened its position vis-à-vis the MFA by concluding an important agreement with Iran. Under its terms, Tehran received 5 percent of the Azeri stake in the joint enterprise (or 1 percent of the overall profits). In return, it undertook to finance Baku's participation in the initial development of the oil fields. The understanding was generally regarded as tantamount to Iran's "recognition of the legality of the Caspian shelf deal." As such, it significantly weakened the position of the MFA, which had been trying to secure Tehran's support for its arguments.[52]

On November 17, Aliev met Yeltsin in Moscow. The Russian president reportedly told his Azeri counterpart that the "leadership of the Russian Federation intends to cooperate with Azerbaijan in developing the [Caspian Sea] resources. . . ." Given the MFA's opposition to the oil deal, Yeltsin's assurances were particularly important. He had to choose between the Ministry of Foreign Affairs on the one hand, and of Fuel and Energy on the other, and he seemed to have picked the latter.[53] Azerbaijan had won an important victory. It was marred in April 1995, when Baku, bowing to strong U.S. pressure, canceled the November 1994 deal with Tehran. Its action prompted Iran to endorse the postion of the Russian MFA and to challenge the legality of the Western oil agreement.

Pipelines

In a related issue, Moscow and Baku differed also on the location of the pipeline that would transport the Azeri petroleum to its West European destinations. With more than 15 billion barrels of oil located below the surface of the Caucasus, Central Asia, and the Caspian Sea, the producers, including Azerbaijan, Kazakhstan, and others, see their fuel resources as a means of escaping both relative poverty and Russian domination. Since a great deal of money is to be made not only from the extraction but also from the transportation of petroleum and natural gas, the neighboring states—Turkey, Iran, and Russia—have been vitally interested in having the pipelines from the Caucasus and Central Asia situated in their respective territories.

In the initial behind-the-scenes political tug-of-war, Azerbaijan, under Elchibey, expressed its preference for the "Turkish variant." As mentioned earlier, Russia's elimination from this project deeply perturbed Moscow, contributing to its decision to remove Elchibey. In December 1993, Natih Aliev, Haidar's son and president of the Azerbaijan Oil Company, disclosed that Baku was considering three different pipeline projects. One envisaged overland transportation of petroleum to the Georgian Black Sea port of Poti, where it would be loaded on the supertankers and shipped to Europe via the Turkish Straits. Aliev acknowledged that the main drawback of this project was Turkey's reluctance to sanction supertanker passage through the Straits. The other variant, initially favored by Elchibey and strongly backed by Ankara and, subsequently, also by Tehran, provided for the construction of an overland pipeline connecting Baku with the town of Ceyhan, located in southern Turkey near the Mediterranean coast. Significantly, Aliev did not judge this variant to be "ideal" either because the pipeline would have to cross the politically unstable Iranian Kurdistan. This left open the "Russian option"—overland transportation of petroleum to Novorossiisk from where supertankers could ship it to Europe via the Turkish Straits. According to Aliev, the problem with this variant was its cost. He denied reports that a secret agreement with Russia opting for the Novorossiisk route had already been signed, and added that, in Baku's opinion, the problems of extraction and transportation were "organically linked" and would, therefore, "ideally, be resolved simultaneously."[54]

In May 1994, the pipeline problem was discussed in Istanbul by representatives of the international consortium that had been negotiating the oil deal with Baku. No agreement was reached, but several alternatives were considered. One was to lay a pipeline directly from Azerbaijan to Turkey. It was rejected, in part, because of instability in Turkish Kurdistan. Another was to use the Iranian territory and to effect a hookup with the Iraqi pipeline, using its Mediterranean terminal near Iskenderun. This idea was abandoned because of opposition to Iran's involvement in the project and because the Iraqi pipeline remained closed due to the UN-imposed embargo. Still another (already mentioned) variant envisaged the use of the existing pipelines between Baku and Novorossiisk. From there, oil would be pumped to the Turkish port of Samsun via a pipeline to be laid on the bottom of the Black Sea. Petroleum would then have to be transported to the Mediterranean, a rather costly proposition. Hence, many experts concluded that the most promising alternative was to use the old pipeline, connecting Baku with Georgia's Black Sea port of Batumi. (At that time, this pipeline was closed due to the political instability in Georgia.) In due course, a new, parallel line would be built to supplement the old one. From Batumi, petroleum would be pumped to Samsun via a projected underwater pipeline. This variant was deemed less expensive than the Novorossiisk project but its drawbacks were substantial: Georgia was still in a state of turmoil, and Russia was bitterly opposed to any plans that bypassed its territory.[55]

After the signing of the oil deal in September 1994, as already mentioned, it was agreed that petroleum would be pumped to Novorossiisk via the old Soviet pipeline because there were no other alternatives. Time was not regarded as a major factor in developing the plans for a new pipeline, however, for it was assumed that some six years would be required to reach the stage of mass-production of the Caspian oil.[56]

It was at this juncture that the differences between Russia and Turkey surfaced anew. It will be recalled that relations between the old rivals had already been strained due to Ankara's decision to limit the number of supertankers using the Straits on their way to and from Novorossiisk and other Black Sea destinations. Moreover, in late September, Ankara disclosed that it now preferred laying a new pipeline across Armenia and eastern Turkey. It was also "categorically opposed" to the Novorossiisk variant and particularly to its current status as a terminal for the supertankers using the Straits. For its part, Moscow had no use for the new Armenian plan. As *Izvestiia* put it: "if the pipeline bypasses the territory of Russia, this would not only deprive our country of multi-millions in profits but would also significantly lower its political influence in the Transcaucasus."[57]

It was under these circumstances that Moscow unveiled its latest project—the construction of a pipeline between the Bulgarian port of Burgas and the Greek Aegean port of Alexandroupolis. The protocol to proceed with the construction of the "Trans-Balkan Pipeline" was signed in Saloniki at the beginning of September. Three hundred and fifty km long and capable of pumping 35–40 million tons of petroleum a year, the pipeline's cost was estimated at $700 million. From Novorossiisk, oil would be shipped to Burgas in supertankers flying the Greek flag.[58]

Responding to the Russian challenge, Turkey once again revived the Georgian variant. On a state visit to Tbilisi in mid-November 1994, President Suleyman Demirel expressed Ankara's strong preference for the Georgian pipeline. A "senior official" explained that this "route would cost half a billion dollars less than the Russian version" but neglected to mention that the political situation in Georgia remained in a state of flux. (The Armenian variant, previously pushed by Turkey, had in the meantime encountered the opposition of the U.S. oil companies because of the unresolved conflict in Nagorno-Karabakh.) That point was picked up in Moscow. *Izvestiia* objected to Demirel's proposal on the ground that political instability in Georgia would make it difficult to implement.[59]

It remains to be noted that the need to choose between Russia and Turkey placed Azerbaijan on the horns of a dilemma. In explaining its position, Foreign Minister Hasanov said that, in the search for solutions to its problems, Baku was determined not to manipulate its "closest partners." Instead, Azerbaijan was guided by the realization that it was obliged "to take into account the interests of both countries and to make sure that they will support . . . [Baku] not only in the economic plane but also in the solution of the Nagorno-Karabakh problem."[60]

President Aliev's efforts to promote Azerbaijan's military and economic interests have been governed by two major considerations. First, as already noted, Azeri nationalism is very much alive and its disregard by any political leader, particularly in the form of perceived weakness vis-à-vis Armenia, is likely to lead to the leader's downfall. (Moreover, transformation of faithful Communist functionaries into ardent nationalist leaders is not an uncommon phenomenon on the territory of the former Soviet Union.) One way or another, and notwithstanding his initial pro-Russian "tilt," Aliev has assumed an Azeri nationalist posture. At the same time, and second, having suffered a major defeat in the war against Armenia and aware that Russia may yet prove to be the only power capable of reversing that defeat, Aliev's Azerbaijan has attempted to recoup its losses by playing its two major trump cards, which address Moscow's main interests, namely the reintroduction of Russian troops into Azerbaijan and participation in the exploitation of Baku's oil reserves. Given these Russian aspirations, it is noteworthy that the Azeri government has remained silent about the permanent stationing of the Russian forces in the republic's territory. Instead, its officials have been saying that significant *economic* concessions could be secured by "any party" helpful in reaching a solution to the Nagorno-Karabakh dispute that would be acceptable to Baku. In other words, even Aliev has clearly hedged his bets and has shown determination to resist Moscow's pressure, unless Russia is prepared to force the Armenians to make concessions to Azerbaijan.

Conclusion

All of these developments have greatly complicated Moscow's peacemaking mission in Nagorno-Karabakh. The problem, which the Kremlin has faced since 1988, has been how to defuse the Azeri-Armenian conflict without totally alienating either Erevan or Baku. It will be recalled that, initially, Gorbachev attempted to use some force against the Nagorno-Karabakh Armenians and sanctioned Azeri military operations against the enclave. These measures failed. In 1992, the Russian Federation joined many members of the international community in paying lip-service to a "two-tier" approach to the settlement of the Nagorno-Karabakh conflict. A cease-fire was to be implemented first, followed by negotiations designed to resolve the outstanding differences between the combatants by peaceful means. Some in Moscow recommended going one step further and imposing an arms embargo on both Azerbaijan and Armenia. However, because of Erevan's, Stepanakert's, and Baku's determination to solve their differences on the battlefield, nothing came of these initiatives.

Another approach was attempted in the spring of 1993, when the foreign ministers of Russia and Azerbaijan explored the possibility of creating a "security zone" around Nagorno-Karabakh. The plan envisaged the withdrawal of Armenian and Azeri forces from the enclave and the deployment of Russian peacekeeping units around it. Moscow undertook to use its influence in Erevan and Stepanakert in an effort to persuade them to agree to the new plan. In return, Baku would recognize the Nagorno-Karabakh Republic as a full-fledged participant in the ensuing peace negotiations (something the Azeri government had been reluctant to do until then) and would lift the economic blockade it had imposed on Armenia. In the end, Elchibey rejected this Russian proposal.[61] A new peacemaking effort was mounted by Grachev in 1994. Baku again found it unacceptable because of Moscow's reluctance to pressure the Armenians into withdrawing their forces from all the occupied Azeri territory. For its part, the Kremlin has argued that "extreme solutions," such as full independence of Nagorno-Karabakh or its reabsorption into Azerbaijan, were not acceptable and therefore out of the question.[62] To this, it might be added that Moscow is unlikely to sanction a union between Nagorno-Karabakh and Armenia. Not only would such a step significantly strengthen Erevan, but it would also humiliate Azerbaijan, driving it away from Russia into the waiting hands of the West and Turkey.

Occasionally, the Kremlin also floated some trial balloons. One was an offer to Nagorno-Karabakh of a "confederate status" within Azerbaijan. The enclave's autonomy and an otherwise undefined "special status" would be protected and guaranteed by Russia.[63] If accepted by all concerned, this solution would establish Moscow as the dominant power in Erevan, Stepanakert, and Baku for a long time to come: all three would depend on Russia for the implementation of this plan and for the protection of their respective interests. For this reason, the proposal found no takers. Another reported possibility was the creation of a Transcaucasian Federation, with Russian bases in all three republics and Russian troops guarding their frontiers. It was rumored that Armenia and Georgia were inclined to accept this proposal but Azerbaijan was not.[64]

In the meantime, as evidenced by the continued occupation of a significant part of Azerbaijan, the Armenian objective is to weaken the adversary militarily and politically in order to force Baku to relinquish Nagorno-Karabakh in exchange for the conquered territory. Azerbaijan has so far refused to sanction such a transaction, an attitude which, in turn, has strengthened the intransigence of the Armenian hardliners. They argue, correctly, that the Nagorno-Karabakh military forces are stronger than ever and that they occupy, from the strategic point of view, ideal positions from which the pressure on Baku can be increased at any time of the Armenians' choosing. Concurrently, Aliev was reported to have complained to Moscow that, in spite of Baku's major political and economic concessions to Russia, the Kremlin has "delivered" little by way of Armenian concessions. He has also rejected any notion of exchanging captured Azeri territory for a new status for Nagorno-Karabakh.[65] Needless to say, these developments have greatly complicated Moscow's peacemaking efforts.

The Nagorno-Karabakh conflict has had a direct bearing on Russia's relations with Armenia and Azerbaijan as well as on its overall position in Transcaucasia. It has also demonstrated both the strength and the weakness of Moscow's position in Transcaucasia. On the one hand, the war has been used by the Kremlin to keep its hold on Armenia, while trying to reassert its influence in Azerbaijan. In this pursuit, as demonstrated above, Russia has been reasonably, but not uniformly, successful. On the other hand, both parties to the conflict understand that Moscow cannot openly embrace either of them because support of one side will automatically lead to the diminution of the Kremlin's influence in the other. (The combatants have occasionally publicly accused Russia of siding with their adversary. In retrospect, however, this appears to have been but a tactical device, designed to prevent such a tilt from occurring.) At the same time, since Moscow cannot afford to permit one side to defeat the other, it has become increasingly interested in the localization and eventual settlement of the conflict, provided that this be done on Russian terms. That is to say, the Kremlin wants to be the chief (if not the exclusive) peacemaker as well as peacekeeper in Transcaucasia. As noted, these efforts picked up steam in 1994 when it became obvious that the West, led by the United States, had decided to establish its economic and political influence in Azerbaijan. Having failed in its quest, the Kremlin will have to reassess its policy in Transcaucasia. Whatever it decides to do, however, Moscow will have to deal with Tehran's, Ankara's, and, above all, Washington's determination not to allow Russia to exercise unrestricted influence over this economically and strategically important region.

Notes

1. For more details, see David Binder, *New York Times*, April 2, 1993.

2. *Economist* (London), April 10, 1993, p. 58.

3. David Binder, *New York Times*, April 7, 1993. On Iran and Turkey, see ibid., April 13 and 15, 1993.

4. *New York Times*, May 27, 1993. On the softening of Azerbaijan's position, see Aidyn Mekhtiev, *Nezavisimaia gazeta* (Moscow), April 27, 1993.

5. For more details, see *New York Times*, June 7, 13, and 16, 1993; and *Sunday Times* (London), July 4, 1993.

6. *New York Times*, August 19, 1993. See also the *New York Times*, August 24, 1993.

7. See *New York Times*, September 5 and 8, 1993. On the Iranian incursion, see statement by Deputy Foreign Minister Sergei Lavrov, as quoted by V. Abarinov, *Segodnia* (Moscow), September 16, 1993.

8. As quoted by the *Economist*, November 14, 1992, p. 60.

9. As quoted in ibid.

10. See Steven Erlanger, *New York Times*, August 29, 1993.

11. As quoted by Aidyn Mekhtiev, *Nezavisimaia gazeta*, April 27, 1993.

12. Craig R. Whitney, *New York Times*, October 7, 1993; and Melor Sturua, *New York Times*, October 27, 1993. See also subsequent statements by Kozyrev and Grachev, as quoted by Aidyn Mekhtiev, in *Nezavisimaia gazeta*, December 23, 1994; and by Stephen Kizer, *New York Times*, September 25, 1994.

13. Signed by the USSR in 1990 and ratified by the Russian Federation in 1992, the treaty provided for major reductions in conventional forces in Europe. For more details, see Craig R. Whitney, *New York Times,* October 7, 1993.

14. The above section is based on a report prepared by the Gorbachev Foundation and entitled "Karabakhskii konflikt: sostoianie i puti uregulirovaniia," text in *Nezavisimaia gazeta*, February 5, 1993.

15. Lee Hockstader, *Washington Post*, weekly edition, September 20–26, 1993. In 1993, Armenia replenished its arsenals by capturing Azeri artillery and tanks.

16. Some of the above material, too, is based on the Gorbachev Foundation report cited in note 14.

17. Material in the above three paragraphs is based on the article by Leonid Mlechin, *Izvestiia* (Moscow), November 13, 1993.

18. As quoted by Serge Schmemann, *New York Times*, September 10, 1993.

19. Armen Khanbabian, *Nezavisimaia gazeta*, September 10, 1993.

20. *New York Times*, September 26, 1993.

21. Liana Minasian, *Nezavisimaia gazeta*, December 25, 1993.

22. Konstantin Eggert, *Izvestiia*, January 15, 1994.

23. Aleksandr Iskandarian, ibid., February 8, 1994.

24. *Economist*, February 12, 1994; and Tehran Radio, February 9, 1994, as quoted in Foreign Broadcast Information Service, Near East and South Asia (hereafter FBIS-NES), February 14, 1994, p. 74.

25. Viktor Litovkin, *Izvestiia*, March 2, 1994.

26. Baku Radio, March 2, 1994, as quoted in Foreign Broadcast Information Service, Central Eurasia (hereafter FBIS-SOV), March 3, 1994, p. 49; Moscow Radio, March 2, 1994, as quoted in same, p. 50; and Baku Radio, March 9, 1994, as quoted in FBIS-SOV, March 10, 1994, pp. 30–31.

27. Baku Radio, March 2, 1994, as quoted in ibid., March 3, 1994, p. 50.

28. Liana Minasian's and Armen Khanbabian's articles in *Nezavisimaia gazeta*, May 17, 1994.

29. Aidyn Mekhtiev, ibid., May 19, 1994. For more details, see Liana Minasian, ibid., May 18, 1994.

30. Nikolai Zheliabov, ibid., May 31, 1994.

31. For more details, see *New York Times*, July 22, 1994.

32. Aidyn Mekhtiev, *Nezavisimaia gazeta*, August 31, 1994, and Liana Minasian *Nezavisimaia gazeta*, September 3, 1994.

33. The above two paragraphs are based on Liana Minasian, ibid., September 3, 1994.

34. Armen Khanbabian, ibid., September 29, 1994.

35. Aidyn Mekhtiev, ibid., October 5, 1994.

36. *Kommersant-Daily* (Moscow), October 22, 1994, as quoted in FBIS-SOV, October 24, 1994, p. 9.

37. For more details, see James Adams, *Sunday Times*, October 23, 1994; and *Economist*, November 5, 1994, pp. 51–52.

38. The above two paragraphs are based on Aidyn Mekhtiev, *Nezavisimaia gazeta*, November 1, 1994. See also his article in *Nezavisimaia gazeta*, November 10, 1994.

39. See Baku Radio and Moscow Radio, November 15, 1994, as quoted in FBIS-SOV, November 16, 1994, p. 1.

40. For more details, see Jane Perlez, *New York Times*, December 7, 1994; and *Economist*, December 10, 1994, p. 46.

41. For some illustrations of this thesis, see Mark A. Uhlig, *New York Times*, October 27, 1993.

42. *The Economist*, December 11, 1993, p. 62.

43. See Gennadii Charodeev, *Izvestiia*, June 7, 1994.

44. Aidyn Mekhtiev, *Nezavisimaia gazeta*, June 15, 1994.

45. B. Filippov and Arif Useinov, *Rossiiskaia gazeta* (Moscow), June 11, 1994, as quoted in FBIS-SOV, June 14, 1994, p. 11.

46. The Azeri and Chirag fields are believed to contain some 4 billion barrels of oil,

with the extraction cost estimated at $118 billion; *New York Times*, September 20, 1994. See also Agis Salupkas, *New York Times*, September 21, 1994; and El'mar Guseinov, *Izvestiia*, September 22, 1994.

47. Aidyn Mekhtiev, *Nezavisimaia gazeta*, September 20 and October 5, 1994.

48. The above material is based on Gennadii Charodeev, *Izvestiia*, September 22, 1994; and Vladimir San'ko, *Nezavisimaia gazeta*, September 28, 1994. For more details on the MFA's position, see Moscow Radio, October 8, 1994, as quoted in FBIS-SOV, October 11, 1994, pp. 17–18.

49. Moscow Radio, October 10, 1994, as quoted in FBIS-SOV, October 11, 1994, p. 18, and Aidyn Mekhtiev, *Nezavisimaia gazeta*, October 11, 1994.

50. Aidyn Mekhtiev, *Nezavisimaia gazeta*, October 15, 1994.

51. The above material is based on Aidyn Mekhtiev, *Nezavisimaia gazeta*, October 27, 1994.

52. El'mar Guseinov, *Izvestiia*, November 17, 1994.

53. Aidyn Mekhtiev, *Nezavisimaia gazeta*, November 19, 1994.

54. As quoted by Aidyn Mekhtiev, ibid., December 17, 1993.

55. Aidyn Mekhtiev, ibid., May 31, 1994.

56. El'mar Guseinov, *Izvestiia*, September 22, 1994.

57. El'mar Guseinov, ibid., September 29, 1994.

58. Karen Hope, *Finansovye izvestiia*, October 6, 1994.

59. Paris Radio, November 15, 1994, as quoted in FBIS-SOV, November 16, 1994, p. 42; and El'mar Guseinov, *Izvestiia*, November 17, 1994.

60. As quoted by Aidyn Mekhtiev, *Nezavisimaia gazeta*, December 15, 1993.

61. For more details, see Aidyn Mekhtiev, *ibid.*, April 27, 1993.

62. See Leonid Mlechin, *Izvestiia*, November 13, 1993.

63. See Armen Khanbabian, *Nezavisimaia gazeta*, September 10, 1993. For a more recent version of this plan, see Liana Minasian, in same, September 3, 1994.

64. *Economist*, November 13, 1993, p. 61.

65. See Leonid Mlechin, *Izvestiia*, November 13, 1993; *Economist*, November 13, 1993, p. 61; and Aleksandr Bangerskii's interview with Aliev, *Nezavisimaia gazeta*, December 25, 1993.

9

Russia and Tajikistan

Sergei Gretsky

Historical Aspect

Russia's active interest and diplomacy in Central Asia in general, and in the part that is now Tajikistan, dates back to the beginning of the nineteenth century. It can be explained as a reaction to British aspirations in the region, which were viewed as a threat to the Russian empire.

At that time, the Emirate of Bukhara, which is currently part of the Republic of Tajikistan, became a matter of contention between the Russian and British empires. The first British-Afghan war tilted the balance to Russia's advantage. Emir Khaidar, concerned by British expansion in the region, sent an emissary to the court of Nicholas I, asking the latter for "protection of Bukhara from Englishmen, threatening to conquer it."[1]

But it was not until 1864 that growing rivalry between the two empires, and the ambitions of Russia's own elite, pushed Russia to send troops into Central Asia. Its expansion continued until 1895, when Russia and Britain signed an agreement on demarcation of the Pamir (Badakhshan). That agreement demarcated Russian and British possessions along the Panj River, thus virtually dividing Tajiks, specifically Badakhshanis, and Uzbeks between two states—Russia and Afghanistan. The Emirate of Bukhara and the Khanate of Khiva became Russian protectorates in the 1880s, but not until 1920 were they formally absorbed by Bolshevik Russia.

In 1867, Russia established a Turkestani Governership-General with Tashkent as its capital city to administer the new territories under its control. The choice of the governership's capital city proved to be very important for the subsequent political history of the region. Unlike Samarkand or Khwarazm, not to mention Bukhara and Khiva, Tashkent never was a major political, economic, or cultural center in Central Asia. The choice of Tashkent signaled two interconnected developments: the rise of Uzbeks as the region's dominant nationality, and Russia's policy of reliance on them to promote its interests in the region.

That policy received a further boost after the Bolshevik revolution and the 1920s campaign of national and territorial delimitation of Central Asia. Uzbekistan was virtually turned into a regional "big brother." Tashkent was proclaimed the "star city of the Orient," meant to serve as a raw model and a center of gravity not only for the Soviet Central Asian republics but for the Third World in general. Gradually, Tashkent institutions began to produce party, state, military, and cultural cadres for all Central Asian republics, thus placing Uzbeks in control of the cadre policy in the region.

The rise of Tashkent from the late nineteenth century onward objectively, if not intentionally, separated Central Asia religiously and culturally from the rest of the Muslim world, one of the centers of which for centuries was in Bukhoro-i Sharif, the Sacred Bukhara. Among other things, this separation resulted in the gradual supplantation of both Farsi (Tajik), which was the dominant language of court, administration, and culture and—more important—Arabic, the language of Islamic learning, by Uzbek. Even after the conquest of Bukhara, the national and territorial delimitation of Central Asia, and the establishment of the Republic of Uzbekistan, there was no move on the part of the Uzbeks to proclaim Bukhara or Samarkand their capital. Apparently, Uzbeks did not associate their national identity or pride with those world-famous cities where the Tajik population still prevails.[2] Nor did these cities become part of Tajikistan, but were instead reduced to the status of provincial centers within Uzbekistan.

On the other hand, Bolshevik ruling elites evidently feared that continuity of Bukhara as political, administrative, and cultural center would, if it were made the capital of Uzbekistan or Tajikistan, be fraught with keeping alive historical memory that could constantly attract forces of Islamic opposition or even resistance. Indeed, as is well known, anti-Bolshevik resistance in Tajikistan continued into the late 1930s. In this connection, one might recall the fate of St. Petersburg. For similar reasons, St. Petersburg was stripped of its glory as an imperial capital and a major European intellectual and cultural center and made to share the fate of Bukhara.

Thus, in accordance with its policy of reliance on the Uzbeks and its grooming them as "big brothers" for other Central Asian nations, in 1924–29, Moscow virtually rubber-stamped its plan of national and territorial delimitation. For Tajiks, the result was disastrous. Out of 1,200,000 Tajiks, only 400,000 found themselves within the confines of the Tajik Soviet Socialist Republic, of which 93 percent of the territory was mountains. Eight hundred thousand Tajiks were left in Uzbekistan. The only voluntary concession the Uzbeks made was the city of Khujand and a number of districts of the would-be Khujand province. This had far-reaching consequences for the politics of Soviet and post-Soviet Tajikistan.

Khujand and a number of neighboring districts had become part of the Turkestani Governorship-General in nineteenth century. This had promoted close ties with Tashkent and the Uzbeks, as well as the Russians. Already before the Bolshevik revolution, Khujand emerged as a city with some industrial and transportational infrastructure. In the eyes of Khujandis, this gave them an advantage over the rest of Tajiks, who were subsequently incorporated into Soviet Russia and then the Soviet Union much later. Thus, under the pretext of being more modernized and developed, and capitalizing on the fact that Soviet rule was installed in Khujand back in November 1917, which made Tajik Bolshevik leaders a part of the new political elite, Khujandis justified their claims for political power and leadership in the republic. Since Khujand became part of Tajikistan in 1929—whereas Tajik Autonomous Republic within Uzbekistan was established in 1924—it took Khujandis about twenty years to oust the already existing party and government leadership that consisted of Bukharians, Samarkandis, and Pamiris. From the mid-1940s, Khujandis exercised undivided rule over the republic until the early 1990s, when challengers emerged.

Khujand's inclusion into Tajikistan and its ascension to power was explained by the desire of the Uzbeks to maintain control over the republic whose separation from Uzbekistan was taken painfully in Tashkent. For the reasons mentioned above, the Khujandis were preferred by the Uzbek leaders over any other group in Tajikistan. Since Uzbekistan enjoyed favoritism from Moscow and was the training center for the bulk of Central Asian apparatchiks, Uzbek leaders could easily select cadres who would be loyal to them both in Tajikistan and elsewhere. So, it has been no secret that since the 1940s all nominees for top party and governmental jobs in Tajikistan, the overwhelming majority of them Khujandis, were first approved by Tashkent and only then by Moscow. This state of affairs continued until the breakup of the Soviet Union and the sudden advent of independence in 1991.

To Be or Not to Be?

The failed coup of August 1991 accelerated not only the transition to independence of the Soviet Republics but their internal polarization as well. Kahhor Mahkamov, first secretary of the Tajik Communist Party and president of the republic at the time, did not protest the coup; he hoped that the restoration of a hard-line communist regime in Moscow would save his shaky power and that of his fellow apparatchiks.

The united opposition, which included the Islamic Renaissance Party (IRP), the Democratic Party, the "Rastokhez" Popular Movement, the "La'li Badakhshon," the "Nosiri Khusraw" cultural societies, and supporters of Qadi Akbar Turajonzoda, spiritual head of the Tajik Muslims, in September–October 1991 organized a two-week demonstration in the center of Dushanbe in support of the Moscow democrats. Demonstrators in Dushanbe demanded sweeping changes and compliance with Gorbachev's decrees that banned the Communist Party and nationalized its property. They were backed by Anatolii Sobchak, mayor of St. Petersburg, and Academician Evgenii Velikhov, President Gorbachev's personal envoys to Tajikistan, who arrived in Dushanbe in early October. Their mediation bore fruit: "the activities of the Communist Party and its successor were suspended; its property was nationalized; the IRP was legalized; presidential elections were postponed, giving the opposition more time to pursue its campaign; representatives of three parties were included in all-republican and local election commissions; all presidential nominees were given access to TV and radio; and Rahmon Nabiev suspended his chairmanship of the Supreme Soviet for the period of the election campaign."[3]

The support of the Russian democrats was another manifestation of growing unity of all democratic, proreform forces in the Soviet Union. The ties between Russian and Tajik democrats had begun in 1989 when Nikolai Travkin, leader of the Democratic Party of Russia, came to Dushanbe to establish relations and coordinate activities of his party with similar Central Asian parties and movements. In 1990 Boris Yeltsin, chairman of the Commission on Construction and Architecture of the Supreme Soviet of the USSR at the time, had paid a visit to Dushanbe where he met and discussed cooperation with the Democratic Party of Tajikistan and the Rastokhez. Davlat Khudonazarov, Bozorali Safarov, and Gulruhsor Safieva, members of the USSR Supreme Soviet, became active in the Interregional Deputies Group (*Mezhregional'naia deputatskaia gruppa*), which united all bright democratic lights in the Soviet parliament under the leadership of Academician Andrei Sakharov. The Tajik opposition advanced Khudonazarov as its presidential nominee, and he received the backing of both Russian and other republics' democrats. That support and cooperation brought severe criticism of the Russian democrats from the Tajik apparatchiks, communists, and a proportion of Russians and the Russian-speaking population. This intensified after August 1991, when the democratic leadership of the Russian

Federation took political initiative into its own hands and greatly influenced the processes that were unfolding throughout the USSR.

Then came December 1991, and a dramatic turn in history for the nations that made up the Soviet Union. In December 1991, Tajikistan and other Central Asian republics were forced to face their independence after the three Slavic republics—Russia, Belarus, and Ukraine—disbanded the Union of Soviet Socialist Republics in Belovezhskaia pushcha. Paradoxical as it might have seemed—especially after months of bargaining and pressuring Gorbachev for more control over their own republics—the leaders of Central Asia did not rush to capitalize on their unexpected opportunity. Nor did they come forward with political platforms outlining guidelines and directions for their countries. Instead, they hurried to join the Commonwealth of Independent States (CIS) formed by Russia, Belarus, and Ukraine. The communist leaders of Central Asia feared that otherwise they would be left face to face with the force that was already seriously challenging their power.

That force was Islam. It was organized into the Muslim Spiritual Board of Central Asia and Kazakhstan, the All-Union Islamic Renaissance Party, and some other Islamic groups and organizations. The degree to which Islam exercised influence over politics varied from republic to republic, but developments in Tajikistan demonstrated the seriousness of the danger. Moreover, in Tajikistan, Islamic forces entered into a coalition with secular democratic parties and movements. In Uzbekistan, the possibility of such a coalition was under consideration.

Central Asian political elites understood that without Russian military, if not economic, support, their regimes would not last long. Joining the Commonwealth and specifically its military organization as well as signing a cooperation and extradition treaty between CIS ministries of interior and a cooperation treaty between ministries/committees of state security (former KGBs) provided the rulers of Central Asia with a secure rear and gave them much needed time to suppress all sorts of opposition to their rule. Thus, by joining the CIS, the leaders of Tajikistan—as those of other Central Asian states—were voluntarily inviting Russians to exercise control over their independence.

The Khujandi elite was particularly anxious to safeguard a Soviet Union–style relationship with Moscow. An almost seventy-year dependency on Moscow had completely atrophied political will and the ability to decide and act independently. With the emergence of the Islamic-democratic opposition, which questioned and effectively opposed the one-party and one-grouping (Khujandi) rule in Tajikistan, that impotence became evident.

In order to survive and continue to rule Tajikistan, the Khujandis had to overcome their sentiments toward the Russian democratic leaders and put right their relations with them. This they did by winning over the Tajikistani Russians and tarnishing the image of the Tajik opposition. That, by fall of 1992, the Russian democrats took the side of old Tajikistani Communist apparatchiks can be explained by a number of reasons: the old Tajik elite's misrepresentation of the opposition's intentions; mistakes made by the opposition itself that alienated Tajikistani Russians and Russian-speakers; and changes in Russia's domestic situation.

Russians in Tajikistan

Russia's policy toward Tajikistan, which eventually led to its intervention in the republic, should be divided into two distinct, yet intertwined and overlapping, segments—Tajikistani Russians' involvement, and the Russian Federation's policy, which in many respects was induced by that of the former.

Russian policy toward post-Soviet Tajikistan can be divided into three stages:

- December 1991 to August 1992, which was characterized by Russia's relative lack of interest in developments in Tajikistan: this coincided with the growing involvement of the Tajikistani Russians, and, specifically, members of the Russian military, in civic strife between the procommunist Khujandi–Kulobi alliance—with its paramilitary wing, the Popular Front of Tajikistan (PFT)—and the Islamic-democratic opposition (April–November 1992);
- the second period, from September 1992 to the middle of 1993, which witnessed Russia's increased involvement in civic strife and then military intervention in the civil war in Tajikistan;
- the third stage, from late 1993 to the present, marked by Russia's increased military presence in Tajikistan, accompanied by a gradual turning of the republic into a Russian protectorate, and by efforts to reconcile its one-sided policy with attempts to act as an intermediary at the UN-mediated inter-Tajik peace talks.

In Tajikistan, perestroika generated a process of national awakening. As it progressed, it produced a growing feeling of uneasiness among the Russians and the Russian-speaking population. The three-day demonstrations in February 1990, which ended in bloodshed, were interpreted by many Russians and Russian-speakers as the first call to leave. In December 1991, almost overnight, Russians and Russian-speakers in Tajikistan (as in Central Asia in general) found themselves a minority in a country whose historical orientation, culture, and religion were basically foreign to them. They realized that they were in the lands of Islam, which they viewed, as do many other Europeans, as alien and inferior.

Thus, the Tajik apparatchiks, who had their own reasons to fear an Islamic revival, found potential allies in Tajikistani Russians. They skillfully fanned the latter's Islamophobia, spreading rumors about the alleged plans of Islamists to take power by force, turn Tajikistan into an Islamic state, make women wear a *hijab* (veil), and expel all non-Muslims from the country. At the same time, the old political elite tried to save itself by advocating *druzhba narodov*—stability—and restoration of the Soviet Union. To soil the reputation of the secular part of the opposition, the elite cited the law that proclaimed Tajik the state language, adoption of which had been initiated by Tajik intellectuals, as the prime source of all the misfortunes of the Russians in the republic.

There was a certain irony in this. It would have been unthinkable for the Communist-dominated Supreme Soviet of Tajikistan to almost unanimously approve the law as they did in mid-1989, thus making Tajikistan the fourth republic after the three Baltic ones to proclaim the native language as the state language, if it were not to their advantage. In this law the apparatchiks saw the possibility of tightening control over the republic by peacefully driving Russians and Russian-speakers out of the party and state bodies—and, eventually, from Tajikistan—and by appointing their own nominees to the vacancies.

The campaign launched by the apparatchiks succeeded. The limited support that the opposition had from the Tajikistani Russians and Russian-speakers during the September–October 1991 demonstrations and in the Tajik November 1991 presidential elections gradually diminished. If in 1991 many Russians and other Europeans sided with the opposition and were speakers at its demonstrations, during the March–May 1992 opposition's demonstration, by contrast, their almost complete absence was evident.

This change, though, occurred not only as the result of a smear campaign, but because circumstances had changed: it was one thing to support the opposition in fall 1991 when the Russians in Tajikistan still lived in the Soviet Union; in 1992 they objectively felt differently.

Besides, what contributed to the change of heart were the numerous mistakes made by national democratic leaders after the opposition became part of the Government of National Reconciliation (GNR) in May 1992. Many of their statements and deeds aggravated the Russians and the Russian-speaking population, no matter that they were made after April–May 1992 when the Russian military stationed in the republic supported the procommunist Khujandi–Kulobi alliance. Shodmon Yusuf, chairman of the Democratic Party, expressed concern that this support might have an adverse affect on the Russian and the Russian-speaking population. His statement was interpreted as the opposition's declaration that the Russians had been taken hostage in the republic. In July 1992, Mullah Abdughafor, an influential radical Muslim figure, and his men took Russian schoolchildren and their teachers hostage, and made them protest against Russian military meddling in the civic strife that had begun after the formation of the GNR. The deputy chairman of Rastokhez, Dr. Mirbobo Mirrahim, who became chairman of the State Television and Radio Committee, voluntarily closed Russian and Uzbek television broadcasts and Russian "Mayak" radio channels to protest anti-GNR coverage of developments in Tajikistan. The effect was to frighten the Russians and Russian-speakers and push them into the arms of the old Khujandi apparatchiks and the newly formed Popular Front of Tajikistan, a predominantly Kulobi paramilitary organization that was armed and trained by the Russian and Uzbek military.

Another important factor that made the Tajikistani Russians and Russian-speakers politically active and sympathetic to the Popular Front's agenda was the impossibility of migrating to Russia or other "safe" CIS republics. Those who were financially well-off or had relatives in other republics had left Tajikistan by early 1992. Others either had no money or relatives, or psychologically were not ready to leave Tajikistan, which had been their motherland for several generations. Besides, those who had migrated—intellectuals, white- and blue-collar workers—communicated back all the typical difficulties that new immigrants encounter everywhere. Feeling abandoned by Russia, they had no other option but to fight for their survival in Tajikistan.

The key factor, though, that politically mobilized the Tajikistani Russians was the Russian military, notably the 201st motorized rifle division. Technically, division officers served in the Russian armed forces, but they were Tajikistani Russians. An overwhelming majority of them were born and had lived most of their lives in Tajikistan or some other Central Asian republic. They had no opportunity to continue their service in Russia, which already was cutting its armed forces and struggling to accommodate tens of thousands of homeless and jobless officers brought home from Europe and CIS countries. Thus, the 201st division's officers were actually trapped, and had no choice but to secure their survival, and that of their families, in Tajikistan. Unlike the civilian population, they had powerful means at their disposal—arms—which presaged later tragic developments.

Gradually, in the course of 1992, the 201st division evolved into an independent political force facilitated by its rather dubious status. After the collapse of the Soviet Union, despite calls from the opposition to take over the division—and 85 percent of the division's personnel were Tajiks, Uzbeks, and other Central Asian and non-Slavic nationalities—then President Rahmon Nabiev agreed with Russia to put it under "dual control." It was Nabiev who gave the ranks to senior officers of the division, including its commander, Mukhriddin Ashurov. Ashurov became major-general of the Russian army by the decree of the president of Tajikistan! That ultimately helped the Khujandis to win over the division to their side. However, as late as May 1992, some leading officers were still tilting toward supporting the opposition.[4]

By midsummer 1992 the growing unrest in Tajikistan began to attract Moscow's attention. At about the same time, the fate of the 201st division finally caught the eye of the Russian top brass. This was partially facilitated by the fact that many senior officers from Tajikistan had been promoted to key positions in the Joint Command of CIS strategic forces (including generals Farruh Niiazov and Anatolii Martovitskii) or in the Russian Ministry of Defense (notably Colonel Viacheslav Zabolotnyi, the 201st division's commander). Many KGB officers joined the central KGB office in Moscow, including two former chairmen of the Tajik KGB, generals Vladimir Petkel and Rezo Tursunov.[5] On the other hand, Moscow's attention coincided with growing anti-NIS (Newly Independent States) sentiments in Russia. These were caused by the increase in anti-Russian sentiments in newly independent states that followed the breakup of the Soviet Union and that were manifested in pressing calls to sever all ties with Russia and to drive out the Russians living in those republics. On top of that, by the end of 1992, the Russian military increasingly regarded Tajikistan as an opportunity to seek retribution for the lost Afghan war. By the fall of 1992, the military's independence in the republic was best demonstrated in September, when Russia's acting premier Egor Gaidar visited Dushanbe. It coincided with the supposedly unauthorized hijacking of two tanks from one of the 201st division's garrisons in Qurghonteppa. Gaidar gave orders to return or stop the tanks by all available means—orders that were met with laughter and never fulfilled.[6]

The Russian Federation and Tajikistan

After the collapse of the Soviet Union and the passage of the Soviet republics to independence, Russia lost interest in them for a period of time. This was due to a number of reasons. First, like any other former Soviet republic, Russia was absorbed by the euphoria over independence and by what was popularly referred to as finally leaving a cramped communal flat and enjoying the peacefulness of a private home. Second, the Russian leadership was preoccupied during the transition period with the need to institutionalize its independence, a task complicated by the vast Soviet bureaucracy. Third, President Boris Yeltsin had to deal with growing political opposition to his rule and to the political and economic reforms promoted by his government. Finally, Russia's diplomatic efforts were more concentrated on developing close relations with the United States and the West than on strategizing about the character of relations with NIS. For these reasons, Russia did not initially express interest in or press for establishing a well-integrated CIS, which probably many in its leadership now regret.

In May 1992, when the Tajik opposition became part of the Government of National Reconciliation (GNR), one of its representatives, Dr. Khudoiberdy Holiqnazarov, chairman of the Nosiri Khusraw Society, became minister of foreign affairs of Tajikistan. Shortly thereafter, he presented President Nabiev, Prime Minister Akbar Mirzoev, and the Committee on Foreign Relations of the Supreme Soviet of Tajikistan with the "Concept of Foreign Policy of the Republic of Tajikistan." For various reasons, the Tajik Supreme Soviet was unable to discuss or adopt the concept, and it was never published. However, in his own and his ministry's activities, Dr. Holiqnazarov tried to implement it as much as he could. While the concept envisaged the development of multilateral ties with ethnically, historically, culturally, and religiously fraternal countries of Afghanistan and Iran, the cornerstone of Tajikistan's foreign policy was seen in strengthened political and economic cooperation with Russia. "Geopolitically, Tajikistan needs Russia, and we understood perfectly well that only thanks to Russia can Tajikistan exist as an independent and sovereign state," said Dr. Holiqnazarov.[7]

Despite such clearly expressed intentions on the part of the new Tajik foreign minister, relations with Russia proved to be difficult. Initially, the Russian government was suspicious of the goals of the GNR and the opposition in general. Dr. Holiqnazarov believes this may be explained by the feeling expressed by Russian foreign minister Andrei Kozyrev that in Tajikistan the "people who came to power spoke more about sovereignty, independence and national renaissance" than the preceding government.[8] By mid-July 1992, after the two foreign ministers got to know each other better and Dr. Holiqnazarov was able to explain the opposition's agenda to Kozyrev, their relationship improved. In September, during the CIS summit in Bishkek, when the situation in Tajikistan was already grave, Russia's desire to support the democratic movement in the republic was still felt. Indeed, after the summit Yeltsin dispatched Gaidar to Tajikistan to restrain the 201st division's ardor, which he failed to do. Yet no matter how strong Kozyrev's and Gaidar's sympathies toward the opposition were, they could not save the GNR. The Russian military had already gained the upper hand in determining Yeltsin's policy vis-à-vis NIS.

Russian military meddling on the side of the Popular Front—which never prevented officers from the 201st division from selling arms to the opposition as well—led to protests on the part of the opposition's supporters and the GNR. In September 1992, there was a demonstration of refugees from Qurghonteppa in front of the Russian Embassy after the Popular Front, assisted by a regiment of the 201st division based in Qurghonteppa, took over the town. Russian ambassador Mechislav Senkevich fled the building in panic and could not be found for a couple of days, having found refuge in 201st division headquarters. The Ministry of Foreign Affairs of Tajikistan sent a strongly worded protest to the Russian foreign ministry. In October, when Sergei Shoigu, chairman of the Committee (now Ministry) on Extraordinary Situations, came to Dushanbe from Moscow to offer Russian humanitarian assistance to thousands of refugees from Qurghonteppa, Foreign Minister Holiqnazarov protested personally to this member of the Russian government. As he recalls, "I said sharply that until the time came when Russia stopped interfering in the internal affairs of Tajikistan, we would not take any humanitarian assistance from it."[9] Those words were taken out of context and widely publicized as an example of GNR's anti-Russian policy.

Given the factors and developments discussed above, a change in Russian policy in Tajikistan was inevitable. By mid-fall 1992, Moscow finally decided to support the Khujandi–Kulobi alliance, though on the surface it pretended to be neutral. In the second half of November, Russia even co-sponsored with other Central Asian states a proclamation of civic truce and a cease-fire agreement, which was adopted at the sixteenth session of the Supreme Soviet of Tajikistan in Khujand.

But ten days later special brigades of the Popular Front entered the republic from Termez, Uzbekistan, where they had been trained by the Russians and Uzbeks, with whose help they launched an offensive on Dushanbe, the Gharm/Karategin Valley, and some districts of Qurghonteppa province.

This signaled the birth and concrete manifestation of Russia's Near Abroad policy. At the same time, it should be noted that behind the Russian decision to intervene in Tajikistan stood President Islam Karimov of Uzbekistan, who was motivated by his desire to prevent the Tajik opposition from gaining any success that might ultimately challenge his power in Uzbekistan and the region.

Russia's Near Abroad Policy

Russia's initial indifference to defining the character of its relations with NIS was changed, to a great degree, by the flow of refugees from these countries. Hundreds of thousands of refugees began to flood Russia with their stories of nationalistic oppression that had forced them to flee. These generated public sentiment against some non-Russian newly independent states and could not help but affect Russia's domestic politics. Anti-democratic nationalistic and communist forces advocated the restoration of the Russian empire or the Soviet Union. Some, like Vladimir Zhirinovsky, leader of the Liberal-Democratic Party, cast himself as the chief defender of Russians in the Near Abroad, adapting his ideas and slogans in a way that resembled those of Sangak Safarov, the leader of the procommunist Popular Front of Tajikistan. Safarov's proclamation, "I will not let you be butchered," rallied around him Russians, Russian-speakers, and the Russian military. Communists picked up these sentiments and called for the restoration of the Soviet Union.

Gradually, the nationalists and communists stirred up emotions to a such degree that the Russian leadership could no longer ignore the issue. This forced President Yeltsin to turn his attention to the NIS, specifically to Moldova and Tajikistan, with their civil conflicts. These two countries and their Russian and Russian-speaking population became catalysts of what was termed as "Russian Near Abroad policy." To be more accurate, Boris Yeltsin and Andrei Kozyrev should thank the military in Tajikistan—as well as in Moldova—for launching what was later elaborated theoretically into the Near Abroad policy. Yeltsin acquired a powerful tool to counteract Zhirinovsky and other leaders of the Russian opposition who long had been criticizing him for an alleged lack of interest in the fate of fellow Russians "trapped" in the NIS. Kozyrev scored points at home by demonstrating that in at least one dimension of his foreign policy Russia could still behave like a superpower, flexing its muscles and regularly claiming success.

The Near Abroad policy proclaims the NIS a zone of Russia's vital interests. It postulates Russia's special responsibility for the protection of NIS borders. These Russia considers to be its own, and it aims to preserve stability in the NIS and to protect the interests of Russians and Russian-speakers living in NIS. Less eloquently but more straightforwardly, the essence of this policy was formulated by Konstantin Zatulin, State Duma CIS Committee, who said that "with all respect to these states [NIS], many of them are doomed to become our satellites or die—this is the degree to which I recognize their territorial integrity."[10]

Of all the states to emerge from the Soviet collapse, Tajikistan, apart from being the policy's birthplace, offers the most vivid illustration of the Near Abroad policy and its failure. In December 1992, when the Russian and Uzbek militaries were assisting the Popular Front of Tajikistan in pushing thousands of civilians, as well as armed supporters of the opposition, across the Panj River into Afghanistan, and then in conducting ethnic cleansing in Dushanbe and the Karategin Valley in the name of restoring civic peace and stability within Tajikistan and along the Tajik-Afghan border, they probably did not realize that they were pushing Tajikistan into civil war. Russia ignored lessons of the Afghan adventure: first, pushing a country into a civil war is no way to ensure stability; second, getting involved is easy, disengaging is difficult; third, undertaking a constantly increasing financial burden to maintain your troops and those of your client regime can have serious domestic consequences; and, fourth, civil war outlives outside interference. These considerations doom Russian Near Abroad policy in Tajikistan to failure.

Protection of Southern Borders

Stability has yet to be restored along the Tajik-Afghan border. Indeed, on the contrary, the Tajik civil war has become increasingly internationalized. As the result of a shortsighted policy, neighboring Afghanistan, with its own civil war, is now enmeshed in the Tajik civil war. Constant skirmishes on the border, shelling and bombarding of Afghan territory in attempts to stop the penetration of the opposition fighters into Tajikistan, killing of Russian officers and soldiers as well as of Tajik opposition fighters, and the taking of POWs by both sides can hardly be regarded as signs of stability. In this connection, another parallel with the Afghan war can be drawn: the same justification—the need to protect the stability of southern borders of the USSR—was used to justify Soviet intervention into Afghanistan. Yet such intervention in both cases only caused an escalation of instability not just in the country itself but in the entire region, each time bringing unstable southern borders closer to Russia. The argument that the Russian treasury does not have money for building a border infrastructure along the periphery of the Russian Federation does not forestall criticism—even now Russia is laying out money to erect three-echelon border defense facilities along the Tajik-Afghan border. Over the years, it will have to spend a considerable amount of money to maintain border troops and installations in Tajikistan as well as in the other NIS.

Russian intervention in Tajikistan sharply increased drug trafficking along the Tajik-Afghan border, and this adversely affected the whole world. It is estimated that 20 percent of the illegal drugs used in the United States are of Afghan origin. Now the civil war in Tajikistan is apparently repeating the Afghan pattern. The absence of a strong central government, the criminal past of many in the current Tajik leadership and among warlords on both sides, the breakdown of the economy, the uncontrolled borders, and the expansion of commercial ties and transportation links to other parts of the world all facilitate the expansion of the illicit drug business. A U.S. State Department report published in 1994 cites a claim by Tajik authorities that private opium buyers from Uzbekistan, Turkmenistan, and elsewhere are generating a dramatic increase in the production of Tajikistan-grown opium destined mainly for foreign markets. In 1993, the neighboring Badakhshan province of Afghanistan roughly doubled its opium poppy acreage and potential opium production.[11] There were several reports in the Russian press implicating the Russian military in Tajikistan in drug trafficking, as earlier the press had reported on Soviet military involvement in drug dealing in Afghanistan. In early 1994, one of the leaders of the Tajik opposition revealed that it was providing drugs for the Russian border guards in exchange for the right of passage inside Tajikistan.[12]

Restoring Stability inside Tajikistan

Since the beginning of 1993, the disparate regional and political forces that formed the procommunist bloc—and that form the current government—have been divided over their conflicting interests. This has produced a new surge of localism in a country that has already been divided regionally by the civil war. In the central government, forces from the regions of Kulob and Khujand have clashed, producing a paralysis that has prevented the central authority from governing effectively. There is also rivalry between Kulobis and their former partners in the Popular Front of Tajikstan (PFT)—the Laqais and the Hissori faction. Presidential elections held on November 6, 1994, only furthered political destabilization because they were rigged to ensure that the Kulobi faction would win. Had the elections been fair, it is likely that Abdumalik Abdullojonov, a candidate of the old Khujandi elite, would have won, according to the indications of independent pre-election polls.

This present situation is exacerbated by the almost complete criminalization of life and politics in Tajikistan. Since the PFT came to power in November 1992, politically and economically Tajikistan has been controlled by the Front's leaders, many of whom have a criminal past. Appointed to central and local governments, they have abetted criminalization, which negatively affects everyday life in the republic, depriving it of prospects for stability. The best illustration of the rule of crime in Tajikistan is the case of Yokub Salimov, the minister of interior with the rank of major-general. For years he has been a leading figure in Tajikistan's network of organized crime, in Dushanbe in particular, and in 1982–86 served time in prison for extortion. After his appointment, Salimov added many of his cronies in crime to the staff of the ministry.

Protection of Russians and Russian-Speakers

So far, the Russian government has not demonstrated a genuine concern for the fate of the Russians and Russian-speakers in Tajikistan. Official figures suggest that in 1993 and 1994 these groups left Tajikistan at a higher rate—7,000 a month—than in 1992. In May 1994, the figure for Russians and Russian-speakers remaining in the republic was about 100,000, quite a decline from the 600,000 Russians who lived there in 1990. At present, the high prices of air tickets and the low prices of real estate in Tajikistan restrain the flow of refugees somewhat.

The Russian government has done nothing to foster conditions that might persuade Russians and Russian-speakers to remain. With all of its power to influence Tajik politics, it did nothing to have the "Law on the Language" revoked or dual citizenship granted to the Russians. However, it should be kept in mind that this may not be easy to manage, since the majority in the Tajik Supreme Soviet is composed of Khujandis and Uzbeks, and the latter follow Uzbekistan's President Islam Karimov's policy on the matter, which is explicitly negative toward Russians. Interviews with refugees published in the Russian press suggest that they continue to be subjected every day to harassment by ultra-nationalists. The first half of 1994 also saw a sharp increase in the number of Russian officers murdered in Dushanbe and other towns of Tajikistan; significantly, these crimes are not attributed to the opposition, which denounces such acts.[13] On the contrary, several attacks on and insults of Russian officers were made by the special brigades of the ministry of interior, which consists of Kulobis with a criminal past.[14] On the eve of the presidential elections in November 1994, there were widespread instances of intimidation of the Russian population by these same special brigades. The Russians, who were generally expected to vote for Abdullojonov, were told to stay at home on the election day; many had their passport data taken, while others had their passports confiscated until after the elections.

Toward the Russian Protectorate of Tajikistan

As far as Tajikistan is concerned, the Near Abroad policy can be explained by Russian strategic interests in Central Asia rather than by apprehension over the plight of Russians or anything else. These interests are still in the process of being defined by Moscow, but they are directly connected to Uzbekistan's ambition to emerge as a regional superpower.

Reviving once influential ideas of pan-Turkic unity (reinterpreted by President Karimov as pan-Uzbekism), Uzbekistan seeks to reestablish the Turkestani Governorship-General, only this time not under Russian but under Uzbekistani control. Increasingly aware of this drive, Russia, or at least a constituency within the Russian government not connected with the military-industrial complex—which over decades has established close relations with the Uzbeks—is now departing from its century-old policy of reliance on Uzbeks. This has been facilitated by the fact that the power base of Uzbeks in Moscow lay primarily in the top leadership of the Communist Party, which disappeared after the abortive August 1991 coup and the demise of the Soviet Union.

In 1992, Karimov encouraged the old Khujandi elite and the regional leaders from the economically depressed Kulob province, whose population traditionally had been strongly anti-Khujandi and anti-Uzbek, to form an alliance against Tajikistan's Islamic-democratic opposition. Their coalition can be explained by the Khujandis' need for fighting manpower, which only the Kulobis could provide, to preserve their rule in Tajikistan. It was clear that the Khujandis would later have to share power with the Kulobis. The Kulobis' dominant role in the fighting allowed the Khujandis to pose as neutrals in the civic strife. The reward Kulob got was that for the first time in Soviet Tajikistan's history a Kulobi, Imomali Rahmonov, was elected as chairman of the Supreme Soviet. Also, the majority in the new government were appointees from Kulob. Still, the Khujandis kept the most important political and economic strings in their hands, ensuring that they would be able to maintain a firm grip on the country. They counted on having the Kulobi fighting forces do away with the opposition, after which the Khujandis would reinstate a Khujandi as head of state.

This has not happened. To secure its interests in Tajikistan, Russia threw its support behind Imomali Rahmonov and the Kulobis. By supporting the Kulobis, who have never held political power or enjoyed support from outside, the Russians are creating a whole new balance of power in Tajikistan. When Uzbekistan's President Karimov and the Khujandis tried to oust Rahmonov in December 1993, Russia provided the crucial backing that made his survival possible. A year later, in November 1994, it was again Russian support that made possible Rahmonov's election as president of Tajikistan, despite indications that an absolute majority of the population, Tajikistani Russians included, would vote otherwise.

The political dependency of the Kulobis on the Russians, and their inability to quell political unrest and provide the civil tranquility necessary for stable social and economic development, all draw Tajikistan further into the orbit of Russian domination. For its part, Russia has a price to pay, too. It has apparently assumed responsibility for running Tajikistan's wrecked economy, admitted the republic into a new ruble bloc, and provided it with loans—with strings attached. For admission to the ruble bloc and for the loans, Tajikistan had to transfer all its gold and currency reserves to Russia as a deposit. Since the republic's reserves were not that large, the government had to add some plants and factories to the list of deposits to meet Russia's terms. In all probability, Tajikistan will have to agree to the stationing of Russian troops even after completion of their present mission. According to Premier Abdujalil Samadov (dismissed in December 1994), the groundwork has been laid for the creation of a permanent Russian military presence. In fact, in early 1994, General Andrei Nikolaev, commander of the Russian Border Troops, announced at a press conference in Dushanbe that Russian troops will remain in Tajikistan indefinitely.

In a rare moment of candor, President Rahmonov admitted that the "consequences of the war were so dreadful that little was left of our independence. We can only speak of true and full independence when we are not dependent on others, when we are united, and when justice rules in our land."[15]

Yet, there is one reason why Tajikistan will need Russia for a long time: to counterbalance Uzbek hegemonistic ambitions. All political forces in Tajikistan acknowledge this underlying strategic principle of Tajik foreign policy. Opposition leader Akbar Turajonzoda said: "We understand that if Russia leaves, Tajikistan will cease to exist. But if Russia chooses to fight us, we have no other choice. . . ."[16] Badakhshanis, who predominantly support the opposition, are preparing to celebrate a centenary of their voluntary incorporation into the Russian empire in 1895 after their three successive emissaries sent to the court of Nicholas II were turned down.

Thus, what we are witnessing is Russia's attempt to turn Tajikistan into a protectorate—to give it a status comparable to the one the Emirate of Bukhara enjoyed before being conquered by Bolsheviks in 1920.

Russia and Peace Process in Tajikistan

With continuous fighting inside Tajikistan and across the Tajik-Afghan border, Russia was left with little choice but to permanently increase its military presence in Tajikistan throughout 1993 and 1994. It tried to raise peacekeeping forces among CIS members, but with limited success—the only countries to send small numbers of troops were Uzbekistan and Kyrgyzstan.

After the failure of what was to be a blitzkrieg operation in 1992, a number of successful military operations by opposition fighters in 1993, and the growing fear in Russia of being drawn into a "second Afghanistan," Yeltsin began to consider a peace settlement as a better solution. Besides, as General Grigorii Bessmertnyi, chief of staff of CIS peacekeeping troops in Tajikistan, acknowledged, support for the opposition inside Tajikistan was growing.[17] Moreover, a U.S. Information Agency opinion poll in September 1993 showed that almost 60 percent of Russians opposed the deployment of Russian troops in Tajikistan.

In November 1993, the Russian government made its first contacts with the opposition leaders, when Evgenii Primakov, director of the Russian Foreign Intelligence Service, traveled to Tehran to meet with Said Abdullo Nuri, chairman of the Movement for the Islamic Revival of Tajikistan, and Akbar Turajonzoda, his first deputy. These contacts were continued in March 1994, when Anatolii Adamishin, first deputy minister of foreign affairs and Yeltsin's envoy to Tajikistan at the time, traveled to Tehran and met with Akbar Turajonzoda. Those direct contacts and consultations convinced Russia to give the green light to UN-mediated peace talks between the Dushanbe regime and the opposition, and to put pressure on the government to agree to sit at the negotiating table with the opposition leaders.

In 1994, three rounds of talks were held—the first in Moscow in April, the second in Tehran in June, and the third in Islamabad in October. It is only natural to assume that Russia, which is one of several official observer countries, is highly visible at the talks. Among others, it is represented by Yeltsin's personal envoy to Tajikistan, Ambassador Aleksandr Oblov. A'lbert Chernyshov, deputy minister of foreign affairs of the Russian Federation for CIS, also, allocates a great deal of his time to Tajikistan and the peace talks. In September 1994, he spent twelve days in Tehran, trying to broker the agreement on a temporary cease-fire. In October 1994, he spent ten days at the third round of talks in Islamabad. With so much attention to the peace process in Tajikistan, why so little progress?

It is evident that the success of the talks and political resolution of the civil war, to a great degree, depends on the Russians. Why, then, is there not only a lack of Russian pressure on the Tajik government that would push the latter toward peace and national reconciliation, but also the presence of certain steps that would jeopardize the peace process? For example, in June 1994, during the second round of the peace talks, Ambassador Oblov had called off the signing of the agreement on a temporary cease-fire despite the intentions of both the Tajik government and the opposition to initiate a cease-fire. Furthermore, in June, Moscow apparently encouraged the Tajik government in its decision to hold presidential elections and a referendum on the new constitution, both of which violated the agenda that the government and the opposition had earlier agreed to in Moscow. This decision prompted UN Secretary-General Boutros Boutros-Ghali to suspend the activities of his special envoy to Tajikistan, Ambassador Ramiro Piriz-Ballon, and the preparations for the Islamabad round of talks. Only a successful offensive by the opposition forces in Tavildara in August–September 1994 persuaded Moscow and the Dushanbe regime to go back to the negotiating table.

These developments can be explained by a number of factors. First, Moscow is not rushing to bring peace to Tajikistan because it lacks a clear-cut understanding of what kind of settlement would be advantageous to it and would best guarantee its strategic interests in Tajikistan and the region.

Second, in all possible scenarios of the outcome of the peace process, Moscow still hopes to preserve the current regime, regarding it as the only one loyal to its interests. To this end, the Kremlin is trying to create international legitimacy for Rahmonov's government. Thus, to make presidential elections appear democratic, the ballot was postponed to allow Abdullojonov to register after he initially had been denied. Moscow continues to pressure the Tajik opposition to agree to re-enter political life without first obtaining a lifting of the ban on opposition political parties and mass media, and without the dropping of criminal proceedings against opposition leaders. In addition, Russian leaders put high stakes on creating a rift between Islamic and secular wings of the opposition, in hopes of winning over the latter and entering into separate negotiations with each. However, except for the leader of the Democratic Party of Tajikistan, Shodmon Yusuf, who had a change of heart and became Rahmonov's supporter after a September 1994 meeting in Tehran with A'lbert Chernyshov and Abdulmajid Dostiev, Rahmonov's first deputy and head of the government's delegation at the peace talks, all such attempts have failed.[18]

Third, Moscow is opposed to outside mediation in the Tajik civil war, as in other hot spots of the former Soviet Union. At the same time, Moscow aims to get the UN or CSCE endorsement of its special right to be the chief mediator and the chief, if not the only, peacekeeper in current or future conflicts between or within the newly independent states. When, in early 1994, Rahmonov supported the idea of Ambassador Piriz-Ballon, who promised to secure a UN Security Council resolution to send UN military observers to Tajikistan, this was rejected outright by General Boris Piankov, then commander of CIS peacekeeping forces in Tajikistan. Piankov said that he would never permit Western spies to sit in his headquarters.[19] The Russians are persistent in their attempts to confine the venue of the talks—which are now rotated between Moscow, Tehran, and Islamabad—solely to Moscow, where they feel it would be easier to induce the opposition's compliance. The Russians have rebuffed attempts to move the talks to one of the UN cities (Geneva, New York, Vienna), with Abdulmajid Dostiev going so far as to make openly anti-American statements in Islamabad concerning the matter. With initial Western acquiescence, the Kremlin considers the NIS its backyard, where no other country should be allowed to interfere.

Conclusion

With the breakup of the Soviet Union and transition to independence, Russian-Tajik relations are in for a period of a painstaking search for their underlying principles. The Tajik civil war obscures this search for Russia, which is tempted to capitalize on the current Tajik regime's political, economic, and military dependency on Moscow by turning the country into a Russian protectorate. This temptation, however, may jeopardize Russia's strategic interests in the region, which are to preserve its influence in Central Asia and to stymie Uzbekistan's aspirations to emerge as regional superpower. Tajiks, like other Central Asians, are wary of Uzbek ambitions, and prefer to have a counterbalancing Russian presence. But with the exception of the current regime, which seems ready to concede everything to guarantee its survival, Tajiks are unlikely to trade one form of external domination for another. Thus, by alienating them, Russians risk losing what limited support they can get in the region. For any democratically elected Tajik government striving to achieve real independence, good relations with Russia are a critical guarantor of existence. At the same time, to escape a firm Russian embrace such a regime will have to establish stable relations, primarily economic, with countries outside Central Asia and the former Soviet Union. These ties can only be with Western powers. As developments around Tajikistan explicitly demonstrate, neighboring Islamic powers like Iran and Pakistan, historically most close to Tajiks, have shown no inclination to support their Muslim brethren in Tajikistan and, in so doing, to oppose Russia. Should anti-Western hardliners prevail, Russia will be a potential ally for the Islamic world in its confrontation with the West. The same considerations may stimulate Russia to accommodate the Tajik opposition, especially its Islamic part, by procuring a power-sharing deal between the opposition and the Kulobis. Such a deal will also help to obstruct Uzbekistan's attempts to reinstate Khujandis in power in Tajikistan, a move that would restore Uzbek domination over Tajikistan and promote Uzbek influence in the region.

Yet for the time being, Russia seems to favor turning Tajikistan into a Russian protectorate—the same status the Emirate of Bukhara, part of what is now the Republic of Tajikistan, had at the end of the nineteenth century until finally falling to Bolshevik intervention in 1920. History seems to repeat itself, but Russian policymakers apparently forget a proverbial axiom: you cannot enter the same waters twice—the 1990s are not the 1920s, when Bolsheviks managed to defeat anticommunist opposition in Central Asia, conquer the Emirate of Bukhara, and drive tens of thousands of Tajiks, Uzbeks, and other Central Asians across the Panj River into Afghanistan. The world has changed dramatically, and the end of the twentieth century is the time of the fall of communism and imperialism and the revival of Islam and the Muslim world.

Notes

1. *Istoriia tadzhikskogo naroda*, vol. 2, Moscow, 1964, p. 79.
2. It is interesting that prior to the breakup of the Soviet Union and the appearance of independent Central Asian states, few people in the Middle East knew about Soviet Central Asia and its peoples. But when the name of Bukhara was mentioned it caused one and the same reaction among both intellectuals and common people: "Oh, Bukhara! Sure, we know. It is the birthplace of Imam al-Bukhari." "As-Sahih" of Imam Ismail al-Bukhari (810–870) has for eleven centuries been the prime and most authentic collection of the Prophet's *hadith*, sayings, for Sunni Muslims world over, and revered by them as the second most important book next to the Quran.
3. S. Gretsky, "Qadi Akbar Turajonzoda," *Central Asia Monitor*, no. 1, 1994, p. 21.
4. "Polkovnik Nikolai Dyomin: 'Eto voina mezhdunarodnoi mafii,' " *Nezavisimaia gazeta*, February 9, 1994, p. 3.
5. After KGB's reorganization into the Foreign Intelligence Service and the Federal Counterintelligence Service, generals Petkel and Tursunov joined the latter, where they head Central Asian operations.
6. "Chego zhe khochet rossiiskoe pravitel'stvo v Tadzhikistane," *Nezavisimaia gazeta*, August 25, 1994, p. 3.
7. Taped interview with Dr. Khudoiberdy Holiqnazarov in Islamabad, Pakistan, on October 27, 1994.
8. Ibid. It must be noted that out of more than twenty ministers of the Government of National Reconciliation, only three represented the opposition. Thus, in fact, an old government from the Soviet times was preserved intact.
9. Ibid.
10. Igor Rotar', "Stat' nashimi satellitami ili umeret'," *Nezavisimaia gazeta*, May 5, 1994, p. 3.
11. "International Narcotics Control Strategy Report" (Washington, DC: U.S. Department of State, 1994), p. 222–23.
12. *Moskovskie novosti*, no. 16, April 17–24, 1994, p. A10.
13. FBIS-SOV-94-119, p. 63; *Izvestiia*, June 29, 1994.
14. *Izvestiia*, February 22, 1994, p. 3.
15. FBIS-SOV-94-174, p. 47.
16. Phone conversation with Akbar Turajonzoda, May 15, 1994.
17. *Izvestiia*, July 7, 1994, p. 1.
18. In December 1994, Shodmon Yusuf's chairmanship was suspended at the congress of the Democratic Party in Moscow.
19. B. Vinogradov, "Prizrak 'vtorogo Afgana,' " *Izvestiia*, March 3, 1994, p. 3.

10

The Asian Interior
The Geopolitical Pull on Russia

Alvin Z. Rubinstein

Professor Firuz Kazemzadeh of Yale University has cautioned against expecting Central Asian states to develop into democracies in the near term:

> Democracy is a tender plant that has existed for only very short periods of time among very limited numbers of people even in the West. At present, Central Asian republics are governed essentially by the same men who ran them on behalf of Moscow. Whereas a particular leader may be overthrown or voted out, the old ruling apparat is in place and will remain in place for the foreseeable future. There is even less of an alternative to the old communist cadres in Central Asia than there is in Russia.[1]

This observation may well prove accurate with regard to the domestic politics of the five Central Asian republics—Kazakhstan, Kyrgyzstan, Tajikistan, Turkmenistan, and Uzbekistan—which are now independent after more than a century of tsarist and Soviet imperial rule. Geopolitically, however, their independence, international recognition as nation-states, and membership in the United Nations have far-reaching consequences for the region and for the great powers. To grasp the importance of the Central Asian republics, it is necessary to place their emergence on the international stage in a broader perspective.

The end of the Cold War and the collapse of the Soviet Union profoundly affected the international configuration of power. The bipolar era that dominated the international system from 1945 to 1991 is now history.

With its disappearance, virtually every government of the globe must re-think basic foreign-policy assumptions and approaches to national security. This is as true for the Third World as it is for the United States, Europe, and East Asia. A changed geopolitical environment mandates reassessment of long-established foreign-policy positions.

For the great powers, today's international environment more nearly re-sembles that of the 1920s than the 1940s: it is characterized by the absence of a serious military threat to any of them; the lack of a defining ideological adversary; uncertainty in Europe, the Far East, and the Middle East in the wake of collapsed empires; and the impulse to look inward to domestic problems and politics at the expense of any ambitious foreign-policy agenda. The passing of the bipolar era has ushered in a transitional acentric world composed of independent, asymmetrically equipped nations vying for advantage. Acentrism epitomizes the new diffusion of power in the multi-polar system of the post–Cold War era. New influential actors are emerg-ing—Japan, Germany, China, India—but they still lack the necessary mix of political will and economic and military capability required for a role as a world power. At the same time, the United States, although the world's most powerful country, finds its influence limited. Straitened economic conditions circumscribe the political leverage that should be the concomi-tant of such military superpower.

Relevance for Central Asia

All of the above bears on the situation of the Central Asian republics. Having unexpectedly and suddenly had independence thrust on them, the elites—both those in power and those in opposition—are growing accus-tomed to ruling in their own nation-state. Their attachment to sovereignty over their own domain may become strong enough to make permanent the arbitrary territorial framework that Stalin stitched together in the 1920s and 1930s, the better to rule the Soviet empire. No matter that the prospects of most of these new nation-states are bleak. Few have politically unified elites, all are economically vulnerable, and their security is an even more daunting problem. Notwithstanding all of this, the appeal of nationhood is a potent force. It suggests, for example, that none of the Central Asian repub-lics is likely to consider integration or merger with any other nation-state, even if there are strong affinities of language, ethnicity, religion, or combi-nations of these. Moreover, the longer these countries can function as na-tion-states, the more their elites will grow accustomed to self-rule, and the less likely Russia will find it feasible to reestablish its former imperial rule.

Having said this, it is necessary to stress how heavily dependent the

Central Asian nations are on Russia for economic necessities, trade, finances, expertise, and security; and how very limited is their access to the outside world. But this dependence does not make reincorporation into the Russian empire inevitable. The condition of obvious vulnerability need not in and of itself contravene the nation-building process; it is not tantamount to being without bargaining chips. Much will depend on regional stability and cooperation, and on the extent to which the personal ambitions and political skills of the Central Asian leaders are consonant with the advancement of domestic cohesion and development.

What was noteworthy during the period of U.S.-Soviet rivalry in the Third World was not the vulnerability of Third World regimes but rather their ability to obtain resources "ranging from economic assistance and advanced weaponry to political advisers and combat troops for the promotion of their regional ambitions, national defense, or internal consolidation; and their skill in doing so without relinquishing sovereignty or freedom of action on vital issues in foreign policy."[2] Thus, the Soviet Union was not able to dictate the foreign policy of Gamal Abdel Nasser or Anwar Sadat, nor was the United States able to impose its wishes on clients such as Iran (under the shah), Israel, or Pakistan, even though both superpowers served as generous patrons.

There are two lessons that seem relevant for Central Asia. First, Third World clients elicited support, in most instances far beyond their needs, because Washington and Moscow, utterly fascinated by each other, underestimated the extent to which they were being exploited by their clients. In their quest for strategic advantage, the two superpowers adopted a de facto de-ideologization that led them to take whatever clients became available instead of seeking them on the basis of their complementary political and ideological beliefs. But in today's emerging acentric international system, such generous and often uncritically provided assistance is likely to be the exception rather than the rule: the U.S.-Soviet Cold War is over and key Third World regimes can no longer exploit "The Great Game" for their own uses. As a consequence, local leaderships must look to their security and developmental needs without the luxury of a reliable patron-protector as a supplier of arms and a hedge against defeat at the hands of a regional rival.

The second lesson is that ambitions need to be tailored to capabilities. Excessive reliance on a great power can lead to the militarization of politics and foreign policy. Great powers are usually more willing to furnish swords than plowshares, in part because their defense industries produce far more than is essential for deterrence or defense. Any Third World leader wants sufficient weaponry to safeguard national interests. But heavy infusions of arms can warp a leadership's national priorities, causing it to focus on expanding its power at home and abroad at the expense of economic growth and political stability.

Too often in the past, Third World elites proclaimed their commitment to economic development, but then proceeded to act otherwise. They may have wanted to modernize, but when confronted with a choice of policy options, they opted for the securing of more power. To paraphrase what Harold Beglie (1871–1929) once said about Christianity, it is not that development was tried and found difficult, but that it was found difficult and not tried. The way to institutionalize power is to build a stable and growing socioeconomic system.

Thus, in groping for a successful foreign-policy orientation, Central Asian elites should take special care to avoid the mistakes of their Third World compatriots, many of whom mismanaged their affairs, squandered resources and opportunities in pursuit of overly ambitious agendas, and adopted grandiose economic plans whose consequences were inflated urban bureaucracies and sharply decreased output and efficiency. They need to look inward to the monumental tasks of nation building. The Soviet legacy is a doleful one: artificial boundaries divide ethnic groups; distorted economic development makes self-sufficiency, even in basic foodstuffs, almost an impossible dream; bureaucratic structures have always depended on Moscow for money, direction, and patronage; and there has been reckless waste of scarce water resources. For example, the problems caused by plowing up large expanses of steppe lands in Kazakhstan during the Khrushchev period (1954–64) led to a degradation of the land in such a short time that much of the acreage had to be removed from grain production altogether. Soil erosion and loss of fertility, dessication, severe wind erosion, and increased dust storms are continuing reminders to the leaders in Central Asia that the marginal lands over which they preside require special care if they are to help provide for the needs of a growing population. With Central Asia's population growth one of the highest in the world—an increase of more than 3 percent a year—there is a premium on job creation, resource maximization, and judicious investment. These tasks constrain and challenge even the best-intentioned of leaderships, and call for a foreign policy that is both affordable and security oriented.

In coming to grips with the parlous problems of security and survival in an inhospitable environment, the governments of Central Asia appear to be pragmatic and aware of the need to work together. Admittedly, early discussions on regionalism fell flat. Thus, at Bishkek (Kyrgyzstan) in April 1992, "the idea of a Central Asian confederation was decisively laid to rest. It was undermined by the president of Turkmenistan, Saparmurad Niiazov, who refused to sign the protocol to create a single investment fund and investment bank for the states of Central Asia, to adopt a common price policy, and to coordinate the program for economic development in the region."[3] That dispelled the notion of a special solidarity along ethno-religious-linguistic lines among the Central Asian Muslim republics of the former Soviet Union and strengthened their acceptance of the interrelated but sovereign nature of each of them. After the "failure" of Bishkek, the second regional summit meeting, held in Tashkent in January 1993, emphasized the importance of closer economic interaction and the urgency of adopting measures to tackle the environmental problems of the Aral and Caspian sea basins. But the ensuing year was more notable for economic deterioration than progress. There was also disenchantment with the economic benefits of the Russian-dominated Commonwealth of Independent States (CIS), reluctance of some members to remain in the ruble area, and realization of the West's limited interest in providing significant amounts of investment capital.

More recently, there have been indications of a move toward some form of economic unity. On January 10, 1994, Kazakhstan and Uzbekistan announced that they intended to push economic union. Shortly thereafter, Kyrgyzstan joined the new association, "which is far less ambitious than previous regional plans for cooperation and appears therefore to have a greater chance of success."[4] The announcement on February 1 of the removal of customs posts on the borders of the three countries was the first tangible move toward stimulating inter-republic trade. All the parties have reassured Moscow that their bilateral relations with the Russian Federation will not be affected, and each understands the importance of maintaining good relations with Moscow.

The pragmatism and prudence of the Central Asian republics in the realm of foreign policy is evident in their approach to three crucial issues: relations with Russia; standard setting by Kazakhstan; and diplomacy along the borderlands.

Relations with Russia

With the dissolution of the Soviet Union in late December 1991, 450 years of imperial Russian history came to an abrupt end. The termination of Russian rule in Central Asia and the Caucasus means that Russia is no longer a Middle Eastern power. Turkey, Iran, and Afghanistan are no longer threatened by the Russian and Soviet military with which they had contended throughout the nineteenth and twentieth centuries. The full foreign-policy and defense implications of this historic development have, understandably, not yet been absorbed by all the regional actors, or, for that matter, by the United States.

For the moment, Russia is pursuing modest goals in Central Asia. It has seemingly accepted the loss of the empire, although it is hard-pressed by various ultra-nationalist and imperial-minded political groups to assert Muscovite rule and project Russian influence in the areas of the Near Abroad, the *blizhnee zarubezhe*, an expression coined by Russians to distinguish between independent former imperial domains with Russian minorities and the rest of the world. Under President Boris Yeltsin and Foreign Minister Andrei Kozyrev, Russia's policy has been nonthreatening in Central Asia. Admittedly, tough border issues remain unresolved and could implode, with dire consequences for all the parties. For the moment, however, Yeltsin has been nonconfrontational. He has accepted the independence of the Central Asian republics, and has focused on the critical political and economic problems besetting the Russian Federation. His foreign policy has its roots in Gorbachev's approach and is likely to persist for as long as friendship with the West remains Moscow's prime goal.

Although Russian policy toward Central Asia "is still fairly vague," Moscow is actively involved on a number of fronts.[5] By way of illustration, it viewed with equanimity the discussions on inter-republic cooperation among the Central Asian republics at a meeting in Tashkent in January 1993. It knows that economic necessity is a strong cement, and that the Central Asians will be dependent on the Russian market, monetary system, and expertise for the indefinite future. Most of Central Asia's trade is still with the Russian Federation: despite erratic production and delivery schedules in both republics, the Russian Federation and Turkmenistan were each other's best trading partner in 1992.[6] Such economic relationships remain the norm between the Russian Federation and the individual Central Asian republics. Moreover, according to one Russian specialist on the region, "Russians and Ukrainians make up the bulk of the modern labor force and the senior technicians and managers of Central Asia. Their exodus would jeopardize all economic reform, so the governments of the region need to calm the fears of the Russians who dominate urban areas and often hold key jobs."[7]

Military ties between Moscow and the Central Asian republics also remain close, in great measure because republic leaderships want a residual Russian military presence as protection against *internal* challenges to their position, which they evidently fear more than external threats or even a return of Russian rule. When the Turkestan Military District, one of the largest in the former Soviet Union, was officially abolished on July 1, 1992, Russian troops stationed in Uzbekistan, Kazakhstan, and Kyrgyzstan were placed under the general jurisdiction of the authorities in these republics; those in Tajikistan and Turkmenistan, however, remained under Moscow's control.[8] Treaties of friendship and cooperation between Russia and the

Central Asian republics serve as the legal and institutional bases for close cooperation in the realm of defense. In Tajikistan and Turkmenistan, Russian troops play a major role in patrolling the borders with Afghanistan and Iran, and in March 1994, Russia and Uzbekistan signed a treaty strengthening their military cooperation.[9] The reaffirmation in all of the treaties of the existing borders between republics of the CIS is of considerable political significance. It suggests that at least for the foreseeable future, Russia has no designs on the sovereign status of the Central Asian republics.

In Central Asia, there is little to substantiate the thesis, increasingly heard in Western commentaries, that the empire is striking back, that a more forceful Russian policy seeks to reimpose Russia's rule. Moscow has not destabilized any of the republics (in contrast to its quite different behavior in the Caucasus), nor has it intruded itself directly into factional struggles, except in Tajikistan. Even there, Moscow may have been drawn into the civil war by the specter of Islamic fundamentalism raised by the pro-Moscow Tajik leader Imomali Rahmonov and Uzbekistan's President Islam Karimov, and by the increasing boldness of cross-border attacks from Tajik fundamentalists in Afghanistan. At present, Russian troops serving in the Muslim republics are there at the request of the host governments. According to President Karimov, Russia is today "a guarantor of stability in Central Asia."[10]

This does not mean that Moscow is averse to using economic leverage to obtain political and military concessions deemed essential for its security. Such an approach is consistent with the influence that a strong power can usually exercise over a weak power that is located in its perceived sphere of influence. Russia's preponderant strength and position make it a force to be reckoned with for the long term, but that is not tantamount to assuming that a repeat of its past territorial expansion is inevitable.

The most serious danger of conflict between Russia and the Central Asian republics inheres in the precarious situation of the approximately 9 million ethnic Russians living in the region. Several hundred thousand have already left Tajikistan to escape the civil war and endemic domestic instability. Similar exoduses have begun elsewhere in the region. One Russian deputy foreign minister noted that Russia could not intervene militarily on the spur of the moment without incurring international isolation and possible sanctions, nor could it repatriate beleaguered nationals, because Russia lacks adequate housing and employment for them. "We will have to remain, lingering on as we did in Afghanistan."[11] The way to protect ethnic Russians living in the former Soviet republics, he argued, was to draw attention to violations of their human rights and to negotiate agreements with the governments concerned, at the same time that democratization was being nurtured.

No doubt, Russian military officers who have spent their lives in Tajikistan, Uzbekistan, or one of the other republics have a vested interest in drawing Moscow's attention to the Near Abroad. And in Russia, domestic politics plays an important role in dramatizing the issue. Egged on by ultra-nationalists, such as Vladimir Zhirinovsky from Kazakhstan, people have linked the problem to the broader issue of "what is Russia," and what the limits of the Russian Federation should be. Considered in terms of security, the present borders are porous, makeshift, and difficult to imagine as permanent lines of demarcation between nation-states.

Yet, thus far, the exodus from Central Asia has not adversely affected efforts by Moscow and the Central Asian republics to normalize their relationships. Moscow is working with each of them to safeguard the rights of the Russian community, work out incentives designed to persuade trained personnel to stay on the job, and make the departures, when undertaken, as smooth as possible. There have been no attacks on Russians, no efforts to expel them forcibly, and no official manifestations of anti-Russianism. The Russian minorities are uneasy, however, and any palliatives are apt to be brief in duration.[12]

An important step toward staving off any dangerous surge of migration was taken on December 23, 1993, in Ashgabat, when President Yeltsin and President Saparmurad Niiazov of Turkmenistan signed agreements permitting dual citizenship and regulating migration.[13] These were the first of their kind between CIS members, and may well improve the situation. But according to American scholar George Ginsburgs, Turkmenistan "was not the best partner for such a test" because "its public track record in the treatment afforded the resident foreign community was good, especially in comparison with how outlanders fared elsewhere in the C.I.S. constituency." Moreover, he adds, "why a set of legal constraints on official behavior should succeed in sanitizing popular culture is not quite clear."[14] Notwithstanding the subsequent actions of the Kyrgyz and Tajik governments to adopt similar legislation, his skepticism is appropriate. Although accurate statistics are not available, Russians are leaving. An estimated 10 percent of Turkmenistan's population in 1991, they may well be less than 8 percent now. Ultraconservative Russian journalists deride the agreement on dual citizenship. One termed the ceremony "in which Boris Yeltsin was awarded a Turkmen passport, ordained 'an honored citizen of Turkmenistan,' and declared to be the first possessor of dual citizenship . . . a rare genre of political buffoonery."[15] Despite the calm situation in the country, Russia's ambassador to Turkmenistan acknowledged that "there is an exodus of the Russian-speaking population":

I consider it an entirely natural process. It began a while back, at the start of the 1970s, and the increase in migration following the disintegration of the Union is perfectly explicable: People have a certain feeling of estrangement from their historical homeland, relatives and friends. And there are, in addition, transport and currency barriers and difficulties over children's tuition in Russian higher educational institutions. The children are taking in their old folk. Having completed their service, servicemen are leaving. And despite the very warm, friendly relations between our two countries, it was important to put the resettlement process on a legal, controlled basis.[16]

The agreements on dual citizenship (which neither Uzbekistan nor Kazakhstan favor); the Treaty of Collective Security of May 15, 1992, which enjoins the signatories from participating in any grouping of states hostile to any of the members; the follow-up bilateral defense treaties; the presence of Russian troops in Tajikistan, Turkmenistan, and Uzbekistan along the 1,600-mile border with Iran and Afghanistan; the persistent pressure to create a ruble zone; and the periphery's close and dependent economic links to the center all testify to the centrality of Russia's position in Central Asia. Foreign Minister Kozyrev denoted Moscow's purpose: "We must not abandon those regions that have for centuries been spheres of Russian interests. And we must not be afraid to say so."[17]

On January 25, 1993, the Russian Federation Ministry of Foreign Affairs published "Concept of Foreign Policy of the Russian Federation," which set forth in general terms the country's foreign policy agenda.[18] With respect to Central Asia, the document sees an urgent need for protecting "the external borders of the Commonwealth [CIS]," Russia's assumption of responsibility "for ensuring stability and human rights and freedoms in the space of the former USSR," and the negotiation of "treaties and agreements guaranteeing the protection of the rights of Russian citizens living outside the limits of the Federation, on the basis of reciprocity and in full accordance with the standards of international law."[19] At the same time, the document insists "that it would be a mistake to believe that this conceals a claim to the role of the new 'center' of the Commonwealth, or that the Russian interest is so great that its realization may be paid for at any cost."[20] And Kozyrev has frequently contended that Russia's special role in maintaining stability in the former Soviet Union is not that "of a gendarme but of a peacekeeper." Moreover, this "special role does not signify Russia's claims to some 'free hand' in respect to its neighbors."

We are organizing our actions strictly in accordance with the principles of international law: respect for the sovereignty and independence of the states involved in conflicts, noninterference in their internal affairs, and recognition of their territorial integrity, with respect for the rights of national minorities.

In all cases where this is possible Moscow aspires to joint actions within the framework of the CIS.[21]

With respect to Central Asia, in contrast to the Caucasus, we may be witnessing the emergence of a kind of Russian Monroe Doctrine. Moscow's aims are a combination of security, traditional great-power influence over weaker neighbors, and strategic denial. The absence of an all-embracing neo-imperial ideology, the preoccupation with socioeconomic reform of flawed institutions, the need to foster Russia's integration into the world economy and attract foreign investment, the quest for stability on its periphery to permit the reconstruction of a strong state at home, and the increasingly intolerable costs of using military instruments to impose and manage political domination make it unlikely there will be a repetition of the Bolsheviks' success in mounting an imperial comeback in the post-1917 period.[22]

The government in Moscow is weak, and the system it administers fragmented and quasi-chaotic. Given the priorities of recreating a viable political system and developing a market-oriented economy, it has good reason to nurture friendly relations with the Central Asian republics and a step-by-step, pragmatic accommodation that institutionalizes their independence. For the Central Asian leaderships, Russia's weakened condition and uncertain strategic situation offer the opportunity to consolidate their sovereignty and normalize their relationships with Russia. The key to this process may well be found in Kazakhstan's experiment in international living.

Standard Setting by Kazakhstan

Larger than the other four republics of Central Asia put together, Kazakhstan is a vast area stretching from the Caspian Sea in the west to China in the east. Although the recipient of much attention internationally because of its vast oil reserves and the arsenal of nuclear weapons on its territory, Kazakhstan's full geostrategic importance derives from the fact that its independence:

- improves the prospects of Turkmenistan, Uzbekistan, Tajikistan, and Kyrgyzstan surviving as independent states;
- largely ends the likelihood that Moscow will soon resume an imperial-minded policy in Central Asia;
- strengthens the buffer zone between Russia and the Middle East;
- eliminates Moscow as a threat to the flow of Persian Gulf oil or to the key oil-producers of the region, and, in the process, precludes a revival of a major source of past tension between Washington and Moscow during the period of the U.S.-Soviet Cold War.

An essentially indefensible borderland region, Kazakhstan faces many of the classic problems of nation building, including the need to stabilize relationships with its neighbors, develop a national identity, train native elites, and find a way of building institutions suitable to its political culture and economic potential. Solutions to these difficulties must be accomplished without triggering an interventionist response from Russia, on which Kazakhstan remains heavily dependent. Thus far, President Nursultan Nazarbaev has shown impressive acumen. He favors the Turkish model, with its strong president, multiparty system, statist outlook on the economy leavened by a receptivity to private enterprise and foreign investment, and commitment to secularism. Unlike Turkey, however, Kazakhstan is constrained by its 4,000-mile border with Russia and its unusual ethnic mix. Nazarbaev, realizing that the Kazakhs are not a majority in their own country, nonetheless seeks to institutionalize power in the hands of the 42 percent of the population of 17 million that is Kazakh. The Russians (38 percent of the population), other Slavs (7 percent), and Germans (5 percent) dominate the northern half of the country. The contiguity of Russia mandates a policy of political prudence toward the Slavs. If Nazarbaev is to succeed in cementing national cohesion and keeping the levers of power in the hands of the Kazakhs, he must maintain close and friendly relations with Russia, which not only continues to dominate Kazakhstan's economy, but still provides many essential domestic and international services, including currency, passport and internal civilian documentation, external security, embassies, and representational functions.[23]

Kazakhstan may, in time, emerge as a regional power in its own right. For the moment, however, it must forge a common identity for all the inhabitants of the country and avoid polarization along ethnic lines. Nazarbaev wants good relations with Moscow, if only to buy time for his nation-building process. To this end, he has guaranteed all nationalities within Kazakhstan equal rights, even as he shrewdly and methodically concentrates power in the hands of strategically placed Kazakhs in the government. He senses the intense opposition of Kazakh nationalists to permitting Russians to wield power and fears that were that to happen, there could be a repeat of the political unrest that occurred in late 1986 when Gorbachev replaced the Kazakh party boss Dinmuhamed Kunaev with Gennadii Kolbin, a Russian.

At the same time, however, Nazarbaev has instituted a policy of "Kazakhification" that is quietly but steadily nudging Russians out of positions of power and patronage in favor of Kazakhs. Kazakh is being pushed as the official language: it is estimated that only 1 percent of the Russians in the country (Russians being about 6 million of the total population of 17

Kazakh.[24] On December 14, 1993, the Kazakhstani Ministry of Justice prohibited official recognition of all Russian community organizations.[25] Coming on the heels of changing Russian city names, placing restrictions on the Russian Orthodox Church, and curtailing Russian-language education, the move suggests that Nazarbaev's strategy of consolidating power at home may soon exacerbate tensions with Moscow. Reports of interethnic tensions are increasing. Supposedly, more than 200,000 Russians emigrated from Kazakhstan in 1993, and Nazarbaev's opposition to dual citizenship may have the intended consequence of encouraging a continued emigration of Russians. That will inflame ethnic relationships in Kazakhstan and give the Russian ultra-nationalists in the Russian Federation the fuel they need to fire mass support for ethnic Russians in the Near Abroad, and, in the process, feed secessionist dreams among Cossack groups in northern Kazakhstan. Seccessionist pressures (epitomized by the quip, "when we leave, we will leave with the land") would be difficult to contain, once released.

Ultimately, Nazarbaev's secularism, statism, and populism must rest on a sound economy. Kazakhstan has the energy and natural resources, and international investment and expertise are available. A loosening of government control of the economy and fostering of a market-oriented economy are needed, as are privatization and development that benefit the entire population, not just the clans loyal to Nazarbaev. Should economic divisions coincide with ethnic divisions, the situation could become volatile.

Meanwhile, at the diplomatic level, Russia and Kazakhstan have resolved the politically important issue concerning the joint use of the Baikonur cosmodrome, the largest space center in the world. This agreement helped ameliorate tensions arising from disputed issues relating to citizenship and the rights of Russians in Kazakhstan. Under the agreement, Kazakhstan agreed to lease the cosmodrome to Russia for twenty years with the option of an additional ten years. In turn, Russia will pay $115 million to Kazakhstan annually in lease payments. Under the terms of the agreement, Baikonur is considered "Russian territory for the duration of the lease period where all Russian laws will have equal force as in the rest of Russia."[26] Not too much, perhaps, should be read into the symbolism of Nazarbaev's making his first official visit as president to Moscow to sign the agreements. Still, the reports of the two presidents' concluding agreements on economic cooperation and integration, as well as a "memorandum of the basic principles for resolving issues concerning the civil and legal status of citizens of Kazakhstan living in Russia and Russian citizens residing in Kazakhstan," and an agreement on strategic Russian nuclear forces temporarily stationed in Kazakhstan suggest a realization in Moscow and

Almaty that the stakes for each are too momentous to tolerate a policy of drift and indecisiveness.

What happens in Kazakhstan will have enormous implications for the nations of Central Asia and the Middle East, for Kazakhstan is the buffer separating them from Russia. Stable Kazakh relationships with its neighbors will strengthen the sovereignty of all the new states, while the future of Russia as a "normal" great power, able to transcend its imperial past, also depends in part on the ability of Kazakhstan to thrive as an independent nation-state.

Diplomacy along the Borderlands

Forget the "Heartland" thesis. Popularized at the turn of the century by Halford Mackinder and his German rival, Karl Haushofer, the romantically attractive but dubious notion that control of Central Asia was the key to dominance of the Eurasian land mass cannot be shown even to have influenced (much less determined) the behavior of nations. Stalin's military-industrial buildup in Central Asia in the 1930s was "primarily determined by the critical situation in the Far East, where the Soviet position was weaker than elsewhere," while Hitler invaded the Soviet Union in contravention of "Haushofer's grand concept of a Eurasian Transcontinental bloc, rallying Germany, Soviet Russia, India, China, and Japan and stretching 'from the Rhine to the Amur and Yangtse.' "[27] Clearly, any strategic vision worthy of critical examination must be rooted in historical context. With respect to Central Asia, this means a view of the region as a vast borderland between Russia and the Middle East. Any policy that contributes to the viability of the new republics and that ensures their nonthreatening character to Russia must, by virtue of consolidating this strategic buffer zone, redound to the long-term security of Turkey, Iran, and the Arab states of the Persian Gulf region.

The political survival and future economic well-being of the Central Asian leaderships are highly interdependent: none of these nations can succeed without support from, or reliance on, the others. To this end, there is need for a network of meaningful (as opposed to symbolic) bilateral relationships; expansion of inter-republic trade; joint investment in projects of mutual benefit, especially in the areas of water resources and conservation, energy, transportation, and communications; and finally, reassurance to Moscow that the civil rights of the Russian minorities are being protected.

It is perhaps too early to discern a pattern in the foreign policies of the Central Asian states. But Kazakhstan, Uzbekistan, and Turkmenistan seem to be prompted by a sense of what is important. All three, to varying degrees, have taken steps to establish close political and economic ties with

Russia, as well as with Turkey and Iran; and all have been active farther afield, with China, India, the United States, and key West European countries. Bilateral trade and economic agreements, such as the ones concluded in November 1992 between Turkmenistan and Kazakhstan and Uzbekistan, have become commonplace. The Central Asian countries have agreed to keep import and export tariffs low, but such agreements are being "undermined by current formal and informal quantitative restrictions on trade."

> As under the Soviet regime, explicit tariffs are of little consequence when the trading mechanism effectively prevents the free flow of goods. For example . . . payments restrictions to balance trade have reduced trade volume. . . . In addition . . . participants have blatantly ignored other aspects of the common customs policy. Each, for example, is setting its own tariffs vis-à-vis outside parties without really consulting the others.[28]

Frequent summits notwithstanding, the Central Asian countries are not taking the decisive steps needed for economic cooperation. Their trade is still overwhelmingly with Russia, which is to be expected, but what is somewhat disappointing is the low volume of trade and investment with Turkey, Iran, and Pakistan, all of which are strongly committed to developing ties with Central Asia. Nothing better illustrates the gap between intentions and behavior than the case of the Economic Cooperation Organization (ECO), which was originally formed by Iran, Pakistan, and Turkey as the Regional Co-operation for Development in 1964 and expanded on November 30, 1992, to include the five Central Asian republics of the former Soviet Union. The agreement, hailed at the signing ceremony in Islamabad as a significant step toward strengthening multilateral ties among countries that share the Islamic faith and culture, called for lower tariffs, establishment of an investment bank, increased trade, and a joint airline for ECO members. But ECO has no funds, no permanent secretariat, and no credible political or economic agenda.

The critical views of two leading Pakistani journalists typify the generally dismissive assessment of ECO made by most analysts. According to Arif Nizami, editor of *The Nation*, "Pakistan, Iran and Turkey want to have strong economic ties with the Central Asian Republics and, in the process, are willing to offer the moon, but there are practical difficulties of enormous magnitude which have to be overcome even before a semblance of a meaningful basis for cooperation can be laid."[29] Najam Sethi, editor of *The Friday Times*, an intellectually lively and far-ranging weekly, noted that ECO compares poorly on any number of measures of economic cooperation to the European Union and ASEAN. Turkey, Iran, and Pakistan did not make much headway with ECO's predecessor (Regional Co-operation for

Development) at a time when they at least had common security concerns and alliances with the United States. They are therefore less likely to do so now. Today, according to Sethi, "Turkey's state is avowedly 'secular' as Iran's is 'Islamic.' Turkey is solidly behind the United States, Iran is implacably opposed to it. Pakistan is lost somewhere in between. Despite the pious rhetoric, chances are they will push and shove, rather than cooperate with, one another."[30]

Turkey and Iran have a potential for influencing Central Asia second only to Russia's. No two countries have benefited more from the dissolution of the Soviet Union and the independence of the five new nations of Central Asia. Both have been active in Central Asia and, for the most part, helpful. But Turkey and Iran need to do more to strengthen institutional linkages and present alternatives to Central Asia's excessive economic reliance on Russia. For the immediate future, Russia's weakness, more than their wisdom, has been Central Asia's principal security asset. Although a certain competition is inevitable, it would be tragic if they were to shortchange the political collaboration that could bring them more security than any they have known for centuries and certainly more than they could realize alone. Recent developments in Central Asia should occasion new thinking, not only in Turkey and Iran but also in the United States, on how best to safeguard the geostrategic and political environment of the post-Soviet period.

A Time of Testing for the United States

The Central Asian republics are, and will remain, of marginal interest to U.S. foreign policy, but their continued independence is nonetheless a windfall strategic development, and should be encouraged far more than has been the case to date. Russia's preeminent interests in the region must, of course, be recognized and respected, and nothing should be done to heighten its sense of military insecurity. But if China can pursue an active policy of nurturing political ties and expanding economic relations without jeopardizing its détente with Russia, so can the United States.[31]

At the diplomatic level, major embassies, not just a minimal representation, should be established and staffed with specialists who know the local language, not just Russian. The teaching of English should become a major project for each U.S. Information Agency post. It would signal America's long-term interest and encourage local elites to look beyond their own region to interaction with the global information and intellectual system.

Politically, America encourages democracy, pluralism, and market economies, but it needs to temper advocacy with understanding of the limits imposed by geography, culture, and weak political-legal structures. For example, President Askar Akaev of Kyrgyzstan allows a free press, but his close associates are reputedly as corrupt as in the Communist era, and he runs an unabashedly authoritarian system. Widely hailed for its efforts to democratize and develop a market-oriented economy, Kyrgyzstan faces serious economic problems, the result of a concatenation of natural disasters (earthquakes and mud slides), worsening terms of trade, and falling industrial production. It permits privatization of much of the commercial sector, which has brought support from the International Monetary Fund and international investment in mining and hydroelectric power development, but does not, in accordance with the constitution approved in May 1993, permit private ownership of land, thereby sending mixed signals. Moreover, there is a loss of trained manpower owing to the emigration of non-Kyrgyz groups: more than 10 percent of the 1 million Russians, about a third of the 110,000 Germans, and comparable numbers of the less numerous other European nationalities have left.[32] The result is growing uncertainty about the republic's democratic prospects.

Arguably, the United States government could do much more in the economic realm to strengthen the Central Asian republics economically and politically by lobbying for their membership in the international cotton cartel in order to decrease their dependency on the Russian market; organizing bilateral and multilateral irrigation and soil conservation programs for the ecologically traumatized Aral and Caspian sea basins; and supporting programs to train public health, pollution control, and market management specialists. U.S. government funds for new aid programs are limited, however, by both domestic priorities and budgetary constraints.

The U.S. private sector is prepared to invest in major projects, but in certain instances it needs Washington's political approval. One such proposal calls for the construction of a natural gas pipeline from Turkmenistan to Iran and then on to Turkey. A consortium involving Iran poses a political problem for Washington, as does, in a sense, the relatively poor human rights record of President Niiazov of Turkmenistan. But no government funds would be involved, all the parties would benefit, and, moreover, this is Turkmenistan's one opportunity to develop a degree of economic and political independence vis-à-vis Moscow.

The Clinton administration has expressed its reluctance to slight Russian sensitivities. But, in this case, that should not even arise. By its own official statement of foreign policy objectives, Moscow approves of projects that promote regional economic cooperation:

> The expansion of relations and the strengthening of positions of third states with the former union republics may be accompanied by aid for their eco-

nomic development, which in itself creates tangible plusses for Russia due to the retained interdependence between our production complexes.[33]

The indecisiveness is to be found in Washington, not Moscow. Any U.S. administration prefers to steer clear of involvement with Iran. But given that the U.S. Commerce Department has permitted the sale of certain advanced technologies and equipment to Iran, and that the proposed natural gas pipeline would contribute to the economic strengthening of Turkmenistan (and Uzbekistan and Kazakhstan as well), the political risk seems worth running. In the period ahead, Central Asia's prospects for developing stable internal systems will depend, in important measure, on timely and wise support from the United States.

Notes

1. Firuz Kazemzadeh, "United States Policy toward Central Asia," *Vital Speeches*, September 1, 1992, p. 679.

2. Alvin Z. Rubinstein, *Moscow's Third World Strategy* (Princeton, NJ: Princeton University Press, 1988), p. 227.

3. Boris Z. Rumer, "The Gathering Storm in Central Asia," *Orbis* (Winter 1993), p. 93.

4. Bess Brown, "Three Central Asian States Form Economic Union," *RFE/RL Research Report*, April 1, 1994, p. 33.

5. *Nezavisimaia gazeta*, May 29, 1992.

6. "Russian-Turkmen Trade Indicators Up," Foreign Broadcast Information Service, *FBIS Report: Central Eurasia* (hereafter, FBIS, *Report: CEur*), December 16, 1992, p. 8, from *Turkmenskaya iskra*, October 17, 1992.

7. George I. Mirsky, "Central Asia's Emergence," *Current History*, October 1992, p. 338.

8. "Grachev on Russian-Turkmen Military Agreement," Foreign Broadcast Information Service, *Daily Report: Central Eurasia* (hereafter, FBIS, *CEur*), June 12, 1992, p. 15, from *Izvestiia*, June 10, 1992. See also, "Officials on Military Treaty with Russia," FBIS, *CEur*, June 12, 1992, pp. 82–83, from Interfax (Moscow), June 11, 1992.

9. "Presidents Sign Accord," FBIS, *CEur*, March 2, 1994, pp. 15–16, from ITAR-TASS, March 2, 1994.

10. "Central Asian Presidents Hold News Conference," FBIS, *CEur*, February 1, 1994, p. 1, from Kazakh Radio Network (Almaty), January 31, 1994.

11. "Shelov-Kovedyayev on Western View of Russia, Rights in Republics," FBIS, *Report: CEur*, September 11, 1992, p. 31, from *Novoe vremia*, August 14, 1992.

12. *Izvestiia*, January 4, 1994.

13. "Bilateral Agreements Signed with Russia," FBIS, *CEur*, December 27, 1993, pp. 78–79, from ITAR-TASS, December 23, 1993.

14. George Ginsburgs, "The Issue of Dual Citizenship among the Successor States," *Ost-Europa Recht*, no. 1 (1995). The analysis is comprehensive, covering not just Russia's relations with CIS states but also its attempt to come to terms with the former autonomous republics of the Russian Soviet Federated Socialist Republic that now seek the status of sovereign states.

15. "Russian Diplomacy, Results of Ashgabat Summit," FBIS, *Report: CEur*, January 14, 1994, p. 1, from *Segodnia*, December 28, 1993.

16. "RF Envoy to Turkmenistan Cited on Improved Situation of Russians," FBIS, *Report: CEur*, April 4, 1994, p. 3, from *Rossiiskie vesti*, March 16, 1994.

17. "Neighbors Need Not 'Take Offense' over Shared Interests," FBIS, *CEur*, January 27, 1994, p. 8, from *Komsomol'skaia pravda*, January 26, 1994.

18. "Concept of Foreign Policy of the Russian Federation," FBIS, *Report: CEur*, March 25, 1993, pp. 1–20.

19. Ibid., pp. 4–5.

20. Ibid., p. 5.

21. "Kozyrev Details Russian Peacekeeping Effort," *FBIS Report: CEur*, February 16, 1994, p. 32, from *Novoe vremia*, January 25, 1994.

22. Mohiaddin Mesbahi, "Russian Foreign Policy and Security in Central Asia and the Caucasus," *Central Asian Survey*, vol. 12, no. 2 (1993), pp. 210–12.

23. Stephen C. Robb, "Lessons for Kazakhstan," April 30, 1993, p. 5 (typescript).

24. "Ethnic Russians in Central Asia Face Pressure," FBIS, *Report: CEur*, March 24, 1994, p. 69, from *Rossiiskaia gazeta*, February 19, 1994.

25. "Anti-Russian Campaign Reported in Kazakhstan," FBIS, *Report: CEur*, January 24, 1994, p. 75, from *Rossiia*, December 29, 1993.

26. "Yeltsin Terms Visit Successful," FBIS, *CEur*, March 29, 1994, p. 4, from Itar-Tass, March 28, 1994.

27. Milan Hauner, *What Is Asia to Us? Russia's Heartland Yesterday and Today* (Boston, MA: Unwin Hyman, 1990), pp. 196–97.

28. Sheila Marnie and Erik Whitlock, "Central Asia and Economic Integration," *RFE/RL Research Report*, April 2, 1993, p. 39.

29. Arif Nizami, "Competitors Promising Moon to Central Asian Republics," *The Nation*, February 9, 1993.

30. Najam Sethi, "ECO or What?" *Friday Times* (Lahore), February 18–24, 1993.

31. See Ross H. Munro, "Central Asia and China," in Michael Mandelbaum, ed., *Central Asia and the World* (New York: Council on Foreign Relations Press, 1994), pp. 221–34.

32. "The President's 100-Meter Dash," Joint Publications Research Service, *Central Eurasia*, August 25, 1993, p. 85, from *Komsomol'skaia pravda*, August 4, 1993; "Akayev Denies NATO to Establish Facilities in Kyrgyzstan," FBIS, *CEur*, February 25, 1994, pp. 34–35, from Interfax (Moscow), February 22, 1994; "Askar Akayev: Russians Do Have a Future in Kyrgyzstan," FBIS, *CEur*, March 1, 1994, p. 1, from *Pravda*, February 24, 1994.

33. "Concept of Foreign Policy of the Russian Federation," FBIS, *Report: CEur*, March 25, 1993, p. 6.

Conclusion

Alvin Z. Rubinstein and
Oles M. Smolansky

Eurasia is in flux, and the region's "Great Game" involving Russia, Turkey, and Iran as the main protagonists (with China looming in the future as an important player in Central Asia) has begun anew. The collapse of the Soviet empire brought about major political upheavals in the area; first and foremost, the emergence of the new nation states in Transcaucasia and Central Asia. The ethnolinguistic particularism of these and other diverse peoples survived the prolonged period of czarist and Communist rule and provides an essential unifying geographic, psychosocial, and cultural core of beliefs and remembered history—a common heritage. Though weak and vulnerable, Armenia, Azerbaijan, Georgia, Kazakhstan, Kyrgyzstan, Tajikistan, Turkmenistan, and Uzbekistan find their independence, their very ability to survive as nation-states, enhanced by virtue of international recognition and membership in the United Nations. This status requires the regional powers (Russia, Turkey, and Iran) to proceed cautiously and pursue a differentiated policy toward these states—a tactic that in turn affords additional flexibility to the newly independent republics of the former USSR. Nevertheless, ethnic diversity and military power give Russia opportunities in the region that are not available to its rivals.

Transcaucasia and Central Asia constitute a vast borderland over which the Russian, Ottoman, Persian, and Chinese empires vied for position and dominance from the fifteenth to the nineteenth centuries. Ultimately, it was Russian military superiority that prevailed, so that Russia's advances in the nineteenth century established the contours of the czarist and then the successor Soviet regime until the collapse of the Soviet Union at the end of 1991. This Russian expansion, it should be emphasized, was not a unilateral process; rather, it was "the result of a major international power struggle over the legacy of the declining steppe empires."[1] Russia was the big winner because of superior organization, technology, and power. One need not, therefore, look far ahead or far afield for clues to the region's future. History would seem to suggest that this will be fashioned in the twenty-first century as it was in the seventeenth and eighteenth centuries by the complex interplay of developments within the borderlands, by the relations between and among the peoples of the region, by their interaction with the contiguous powers, and by the outcome of the new multipolar competition on both the regional and the wider international scene.

For the new nation-states of Transcaucasia and Central Asia, history has harsh and compelling lessons: either develop strong internal polities and economies or risk conquest by expansionist powers; either cooperate with similarly vulnerable neighbors or fall prey to undue foreign penetration; neglect internal transformation to pursue marginal gains of dubious durability and the consequence will be irreversible decline. Certainly, a combination of economic stagnation and endless mini-wars weakened the steppe peoples and hastened their absorption by stronger powers.

As the essays in this collection suggest, neither Russia nor Turkey nor Iran is able to dominate all of Transcaucasia and Central Asia as the Soviet Union, and imperial Russia before it, once did. The general advantage in the current competition among these three, however, rests with Russia. The weight of its past political, military, and economic rule is everywhere in evidence. From railroads to agricultural and industrial equipment, from textbooks to technocrats, from markets to spare parts, the imprimatur is predominantly Russian, not local, and not international. Decades will be needed to surmount these vestiges of colonialism. In addition, the factors that enabled Russia to establish its hegemony over the region's peoples continue to exist, albeit in modified form:

> Economic dependence on Russia will not disappear soon. Russia will continue to be a major, if not only, market for Central Asian agricultural products, and will continue to control banking, railways, and airlines. Higher education will remain largely in Russian hands, and many members of the native elites will continue to be educated in Russia and to be influenced by Russian culture. Russian political traditions, blending with local practices, will continue to exercise influence even if some republics pro forma adopt constitutions modeled on that of the United States. Russian minorities in each of the republics will exercise strong influence because of their numbers, education, organization, and technical competence.[2]

Notwithstanding Moscow's edge in defining relationships with the new Eurasian republics, none of the former Soviet possessions can be taken for granted. The strategic environment within which Russia now operates has changed dramatically. As it looks ahead, the Russian government sees a growing gap between its desire to be treated as a great power and its actual capabilities. Indeed, Russia faces greater threats to its very survival as a coherent society than at any time since the early seventeenth century. Its economy and overall productivity continue to decline, the limited progress toward privatization and the creation of some market-oriented sectors notwithstanding. All of Russia's institutions, values, and relationships hover on the brink of uncertainty. Separatist impulses threaten its internal cohesiveness in Chechnya and in numerous other parts of the Russian Federation. In such an environment, where domestic problems demand most of the nation's available resources and external enemies do not appear to threaten national security, Russia's ability to undertake aid programs for the former Soviet republics is severely limited. Russia's difficult domestic situation mandates a low-cost strategy abroad and a policy of accommodation, clear priorities, and carefully tempered activism in Transcaucasia and Central Asia. For the time being, it simply lacks the capabilities that made possible its imperial advances in earlier centuries.

Other factors, too, circumscribe Russia's ability to pursue forcefully its interests in southern Eurasia. For one thing, there is the growing nationalism in many of the newly independent states, including those that are governed by the former Communist functionaries. Partly related to this is the depth of intra- and interethnic hostility (as in Nagorno-Karabakh and Tajikistan, respectively). To be sure, such conflicts provide Russia with opportunities to insert itself into the regional picture. However, such intrusions are usually double-edged swords because the antagonists are in no mood to compromise or to listen to (Russian) reason. Finally, the reawakened interest in southern Eurasia not only on the part of Turkey and Iran but also the Western powers provides the leaders of the independent republics with unaccustomed flexibility to pursue their respective interests even if they happen to run against Moscow's wishes.

In any event, the Yeltsin government has been more purposefully active in the Caucasus than in Central Asia, in part because circumstances led local contestants for power to request Russia's help rather than face more immediate threats to their political survival, in part because the interventions were low-cost with quick payoffs, and in part because of the belief that Russia has vital strategic interests there which must be upheld. In the Caucasus, these Russian moves have clearly demonstrated that Moscow holds stronger cards in the region than either Ankara or Tehran.

In the period immediately after the collapse of the Soviet Union, both Turkey and Iran had heady expectations about establishing major influence in parts of Transcaucasia and Central Asia. They apparently believed that ethnic, linguistic, religious, and cultural affinities would pave the way for close ties and a major presence. In this, they egregiously underestimated the functional and operational ties that bind the newly independent states to Moscow. The Turks, in particular, exulted too soon and assumed too much by thinking, for example, that the establishment of a radio station beaming broadcasts to Central Asia would result in immediate outpourings of pro-Turkish sentiments in the region. They were equally mistaken in thinking that they would be welcome to play the role of big brother to the region's Turkic-speaking peoples. Some talk of Turkey's special leadership role was fostered by U.S. officials, but the excitement arose primarily from the Turkish government's sense that Turkey's "isolation" in the Middle East and in Europe was over and that it could once again play a leading role in a region that had known Ottoman rule for 500 years. As Patricia Carley depicts the mood in Ankara, the Turks felt that "after decades of the humiliation of running after others, pleading for acceptance, here was a region where they were welcomed as kin, as brothers, by people who looked up to them. Central Asia was a region so obviously meant for them to lead."[3] Very early on, however, Turkey's Turkic-speaking compatriots in Central Asia—the Uzbeks, Kyrgyz, Turkmens, and Kazakhs—made clear that they had their own political agendas to promote, and that pan-Turkism was very low on their list of priorities.

The situation was exacerbated by the fact that Turkey promised more than it could deliver: its economic assistance has been but a small percentage of the extravagant aid and investment packages that Ankara said it would provide. Iran has found itself in a comparable position. As a result, both countries have learned that limited capabilities mean limited influence. Beset by their own troublesome domestic problems, Turkey and Iran are discovering that influence building is a more costly and complex process than they originally expected. In situations of unfolding regional rivalry among big powers, targeted client states have alternatives, and as usual, political realities are in command. Individual leaders in the Caucasus and Central Asia looking to their own survival and security find the familiar and established Russian connection sturdier and more immediately beneficial than mere courtships from Turkey and Iran. As mentioned earlier, deep residual economic and military interdependence connects the newly independent states to Russia in ways that transcend the expanded but as yet fairly minor relations with Turkey and Iran. In the ongoing competition in Transcaucasia and Central Asia, Russia's combination of persuasion and pressure, as noted, appears to have a qualified edge for now and for the foreseeable future.

Beyond the bilateral skirmishing and maneuvering for presence and influence, we are witnessing a return to a multipolar competition for advantage in Transcaucasia and Central Asia reminiscent of that which took place in the seventeenth and eighteenth centuries. Russia, Turkey, and Iran constitute the immediate strategic triad. However, unlike their past rivalry, today's is cooperative as well as competitive. Witness the shared interest in trade and in configuring natural gas and oil pipelines to boost hard currency revenues for which purpose both the Turkish-founded Black Sea Economic Cooperation Organization and the Iranian-founded Caspian Sea Cooperation Organization have been promoted. Other convergent interests can also be enumerated. High on this list is the prevention and mediation of regional conflicts, which are seen as inherently destabilizing. Concern about regional instability helps to explain the seeming acceptance by all three parties of existing political units and territorial boundaries. All three would also like to encourage foreign investment and the development of a regional infrastructure of railroads and communications in the hope of stimulating technological modernization. Finally, all appear to understand the importance of dampening the nationalism of assertive ethnic minorities, whether they be Azeris, Kurds, or Turkmens.

This guarded inclination toward cooperation exists in the shadow of past conflicts and rivalry, for the traditional adversaries remain deeply suspicious of each other. Each power proceeds cautiously out of the well-founded fear of triggering reactions by either or both of the other two competitors that would jeopardize the fragile tension-reducing accommodation of the post–Cold War period and greatly inflate the costs of playing the regional "Great Game." This crisscrossing of interests makes for tentative alignments. Turkey and Iran pursue their wary accommodation with Russia, uneasy over Moscow's growing assertiveness in Transcaucasia and its network of treaties with the Central Asian republics. But both Turkey and Iran are conscious of the lack of friends on their own borders and, hence, are committed for the time being to policies that would reinforce Moscow's willingness to permit the strategic buffer zone between Russia and them to continue to exist. There are sufficient motives for cooperation between any two of the regional powers when necessary to offset any advantage by the third. Thus, Russia and Turkey both seek to counter Iran's Islamist appeal; Turkey and Iran both oppose any resurgent Russian imperialism; and Iran and Russia both fear Turkic nationalism.

In addition to Russia, Turkey, and Iran—the main historical protagonists—a relative newcomer on the southern Eurasian scene has now become a significant player. The reference here is to the United States and, to a lesser extent, its Western allies. They have been most prominently visible in the realm of economics and, more specifically, in the matter of fuel extraction. Large proven reservoirs of petroleum and natural gas are located in southern Eurasia, particularly in and around the Caspian Sea basin. They include the offshore resources of Azerbaijan and Kazakhstan, as well as the oil and gas deposits on the Caspian's eastern shore in Kazakhstan, Uzbekistan, and Turkmenistan. Since the dissolution of the USSR, the United States has shown great interest in helping to exploit these resources. Five American companies form the backbone of an international consortium, which, in September 1994, signed a major deal with the government of Azerbaijan that provides for the extraction of oil from three major offshore fields. Other U.S. petroleum companies are at work in Kazakhstan developing both offshore and land-based deposits.

Not surprisingly, these economic interests have contributed to the rise of Western political interests in Transcaucasia and Central Asia in the post-Soviet era. Thus, the OSCE and the Clinton administration have inserted themselves into the Nagorno-Karabakh conflict—the first such instance of direct Western involvement in a dispute on former Soviet territory—very much against the express wishes of the Russian government. While the latter is determined to preserve Russia's influence in the former Soviet territories, the United States and its Western allies seem equally bent on securing the survival and autonomy of the newly independent states that have emerged as a result of the collapse of the Soviet empire.

While part of this assertion of Western interests rests on the economic considerations explained above, another more important though usually unstated motive is the strategic objective of establishing a buffer zone of economically, politically, and eventually militarily viable independent states that would separate Russia from the Middle East proper. The driving logic behind this policy is the assumption that the present weakness of Russia is but a temporary condition. While most Western policymakers *hope* that Russia will emerge from its current state with a political system and an economy rebuilt on the model of the Western democracies, and that its leaders will be devoted to peaceful cooperation with other nations and the improvement in the standard of living of its citizenry, prudence requires that this not be taken for granted. Indeed, Western attempts to thwart the reemergence of Russian imperialism are inevitable, given the oft-stated determination, even from prodemocracy politicians in Russia today, to reestablish Moscow's influence in the territories of the former czarist and Soviet empires.

Thus, here the interests of the Western powers coincide not only with those of the new Transcaucasian and Central Asian states but also with those of Turkey and Iran. However, there is also a coincidence of interest between Russia, Turkey, and the West, as well as the governments of the newly independent Eurasian nations, that sets them at odds with Iran: all are determined to prevent the spread of Islamic fundamentalism among the Muslim populations of the former USSR. However, the U.S. determination to isolate Iran in the Middle East and the adjacent regions has found little support in Russia or Turkey or in the Transcaucasian and Central Asian republics. The reason is simple: Iran is far too important on the regional scene to be confronted and alienated, especially insofar as it constitutes an important counterweight in these republics' need to fend off excessive influence from Moscow.

All of this boils down to a situation of uncertainty and flux in which relatively less important regional considerations will be subordinated to the continuing rivalry among the major players for influence in southern Eurasia. In this competition, relations between Russia and its rivals are likely to become more strained, especially if a more assertive and more nationalist regime gains ascendancy in the Kremlin.

Notes

1. Alfred J. Rieber, "Struggle over the Borderlands," in S. Frederick Starr, ed., *The Legacy of History in Russia and the New States of Eurasia* (Armonk, NY: M.E. Sharpe, 1994), p. 65.
2. Firuz Kazemzadeh, "Central Asia's Foreign Relations: A Historical Survey," in ibid., p. 214.
3. See the essay in this volume by Patricia M. Carley.

Index